# BOULDER RUNNING JOURNAL
## 2015

BoulderRunning.com
@2015 Boulder Running & Bäuu Publishers

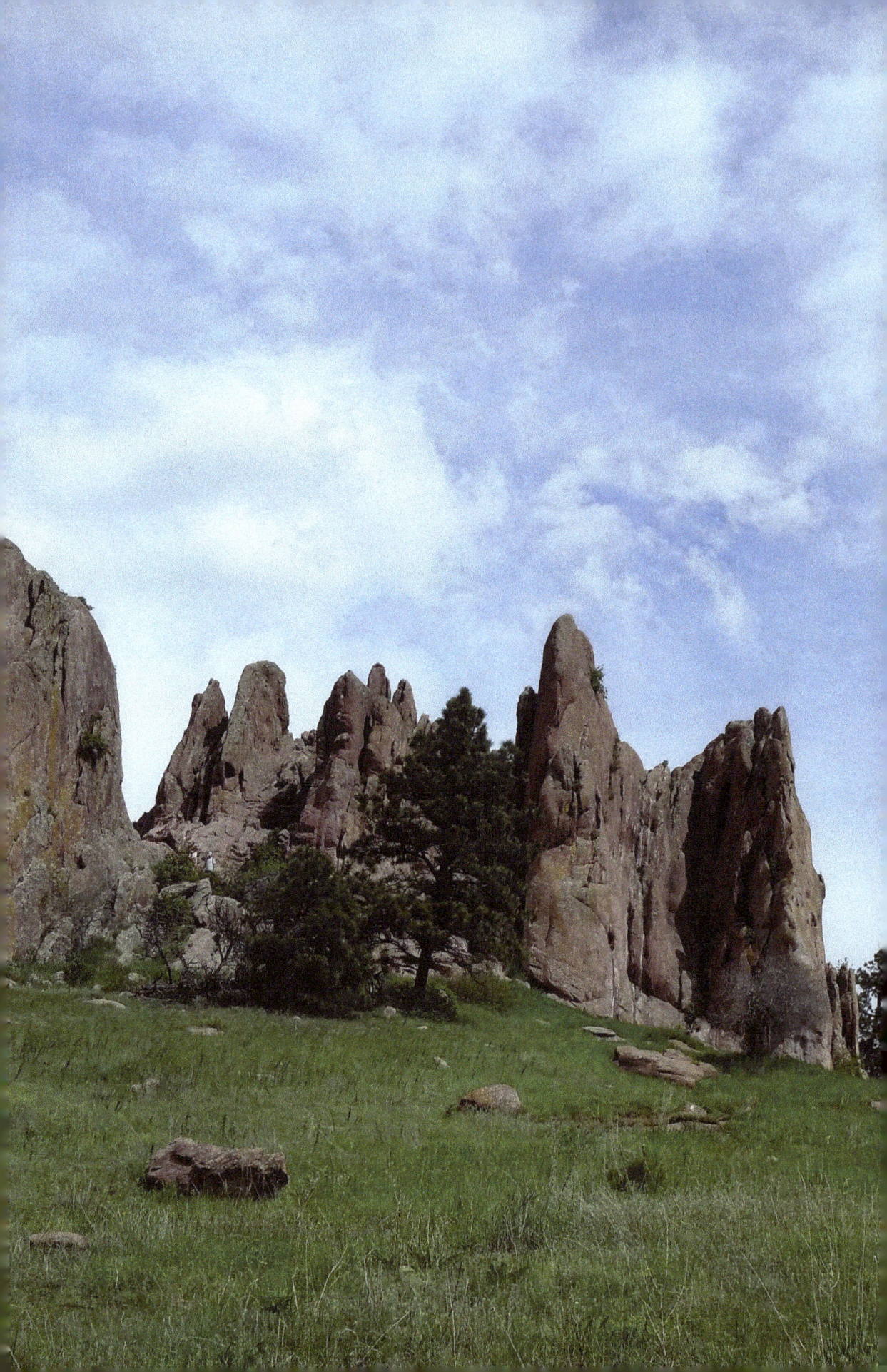

# INSPIRE

As we recently controlled the on-screen presentation behind the scenes at the Fourth Annual Boulder Sports Hall of Fame Induction Ceremony we admired the depth and breadth of talented individuals who were highlighted on the bright front-lit screen. Standing on stage were athletes who had attained the pinnacle of achievement in their individual sports; climbing, triathlon, cycling and running. These and numerous other elite athletes have made Boulder their home and as this year's inductee for running Benji Durden quipped, back in Atlanta he was "the news," but here in Boulder, he was "just one of the crowd".

From its earliest beginnings, Boulder has inspired. Beginning with the Native Americans who would hold running and horse races each summer to the Chautauquan women who carved out the earliest of trails following the wildlife paths, Boulder has inspired people to get outside and push themselves. Gaining momentum in 1971 when Frank Shorter moved here to train, this athletic inspiration is steeped in the geography, the silt, the DNA of the land. There is a running history along virtually every dirt road, trail, track, and grass field. Tap into that history, the collective footsteps of those who have blazed the trail before you, and find what inspires you.

Athletes of all abilities and from around the globe come to Boulder to train, to live, and to build community along the way. Inspiring one another, and in turn inspiring the rest of us. We are all inspired in this place, with the landscapes, the people, and the stories we tell.

From the track to the trail, the road to the mountaintop, the mile to the ultra and all that is in between, we are connected in that we love to run, to challenge ourselves and each other.

We are a connected community sharing stories, adventures, personal emotions, races and more through social media, film, and blogs. The Boulder Running Journal is just another outlet for us to share these stories. A collective. A year in review. We aim to inspire through personal stories, photographs, race results - anything that touches on the human spirit.

Do the most with what you have, whether you are a budding semi-elite athlete aiming for a PR or just hoping to be more active and complete your first 5K. We each aim to push ourselves and to venture into the unknown, beyond our boundaries.

Continue to be inspired by those around you, and in turn inspire others to continue on their quest. Everyday we are inspired by the people around us. The smiles, the hard efforts, the personal stories. In order to grow, we need to define new limits, venture into the unknown, find comfort in discomfort, pushing beyond our boundaries to new levels. For us, this journal is a manifestation in that.
We have been inspired over the years by everyone that has been part of the Boulder community, and we hope that this journal inspires you.

Share your story with us. **BoulderRunning.com/Journal**

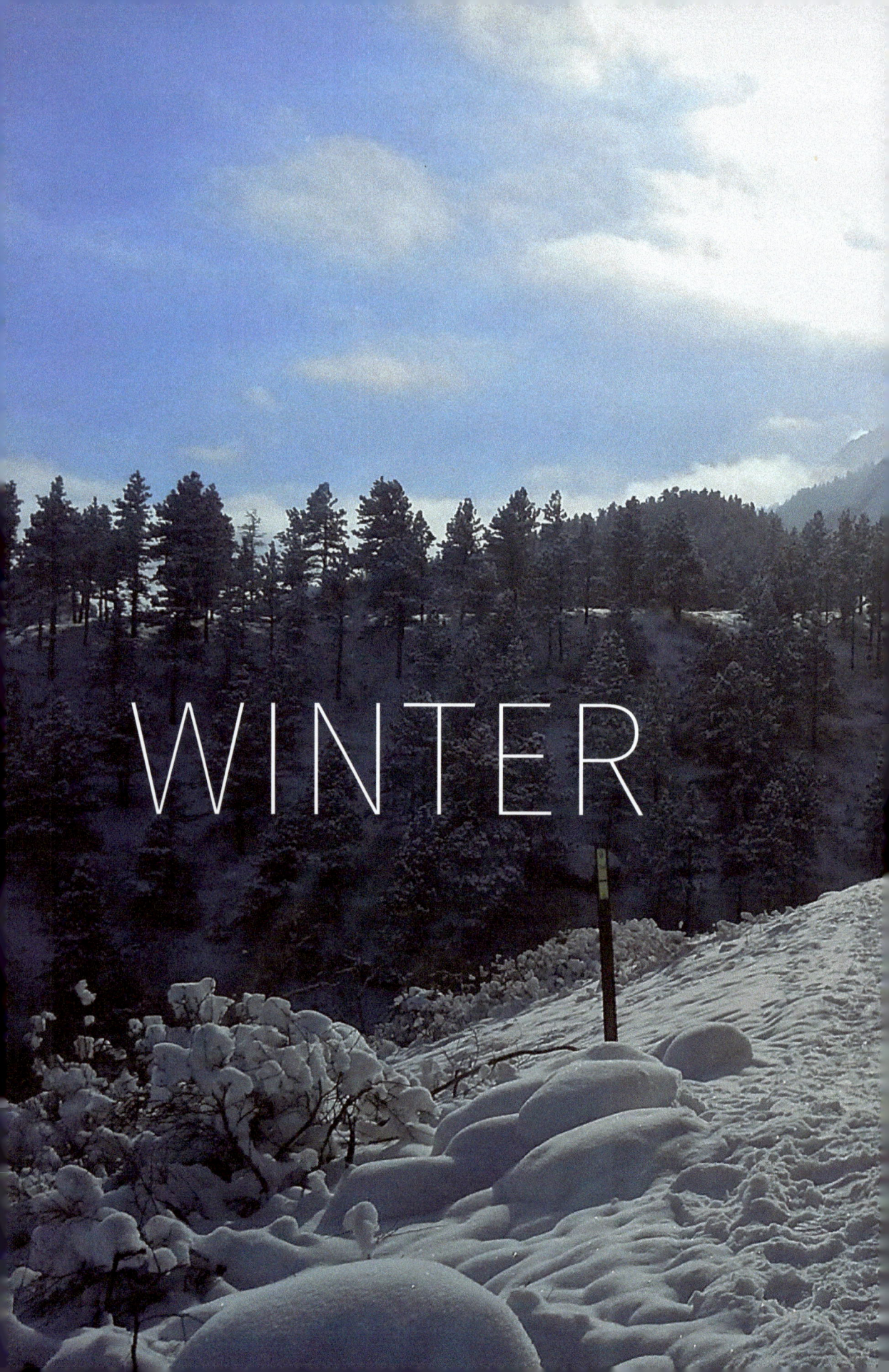

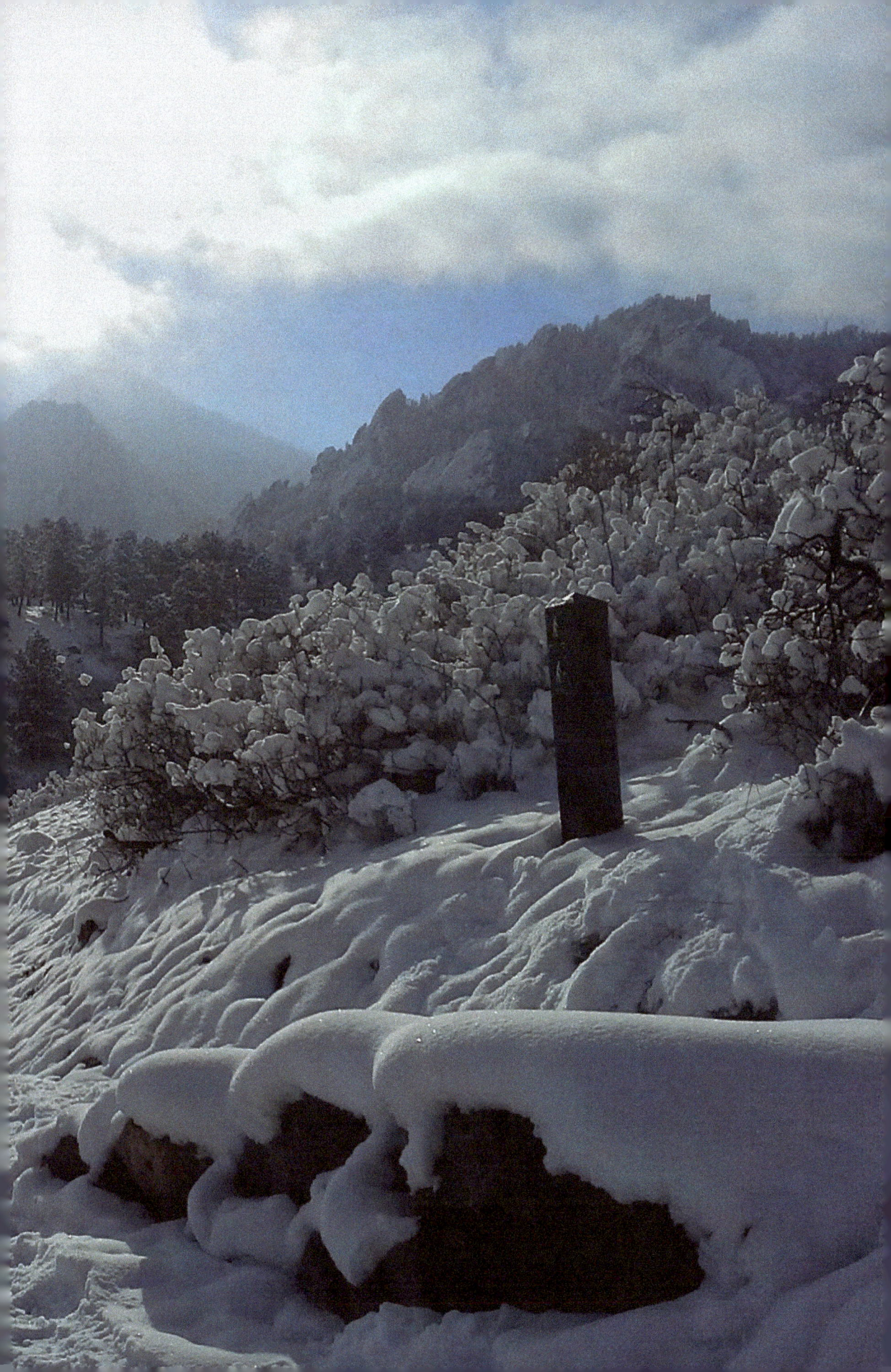

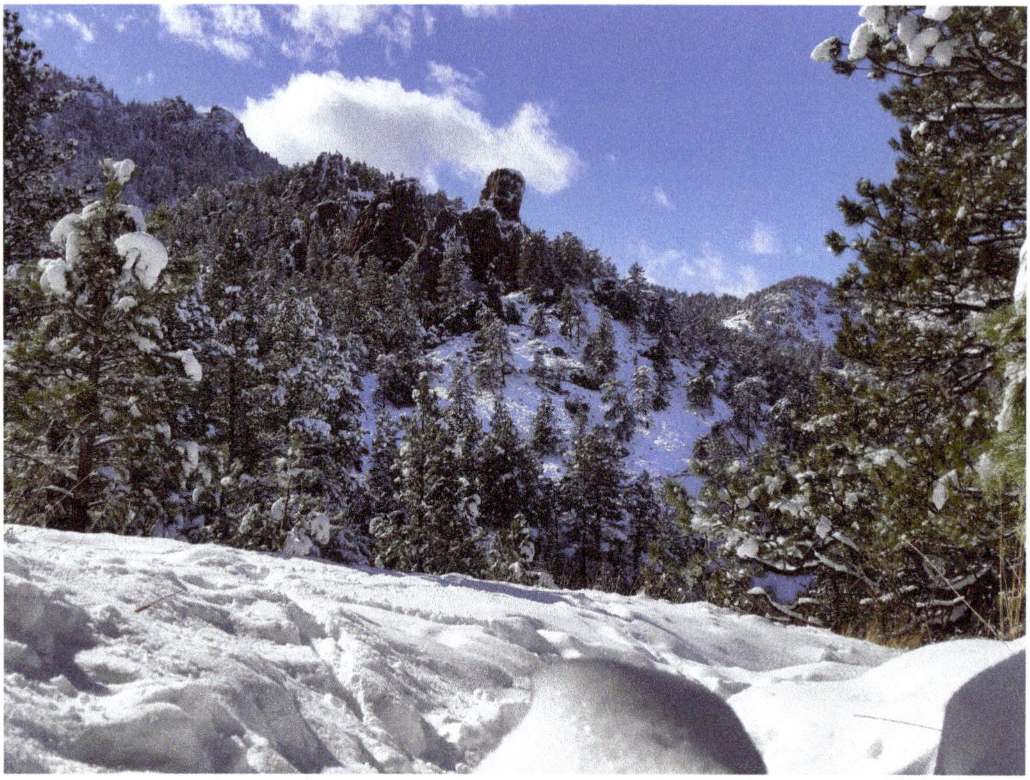

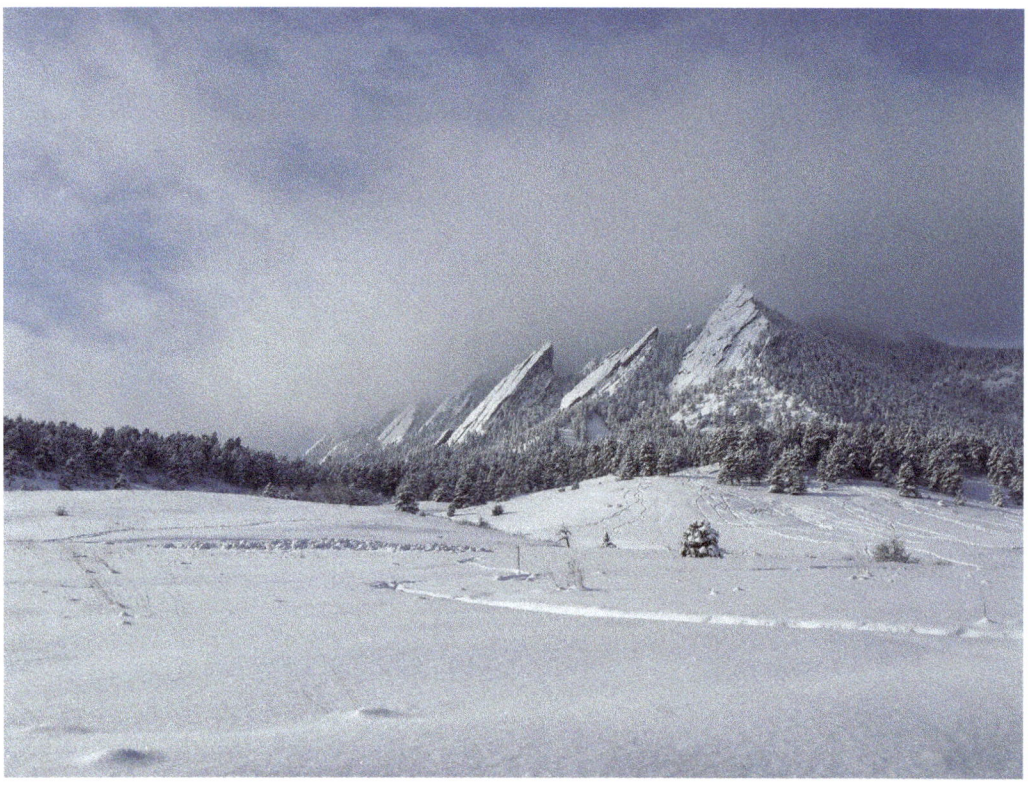

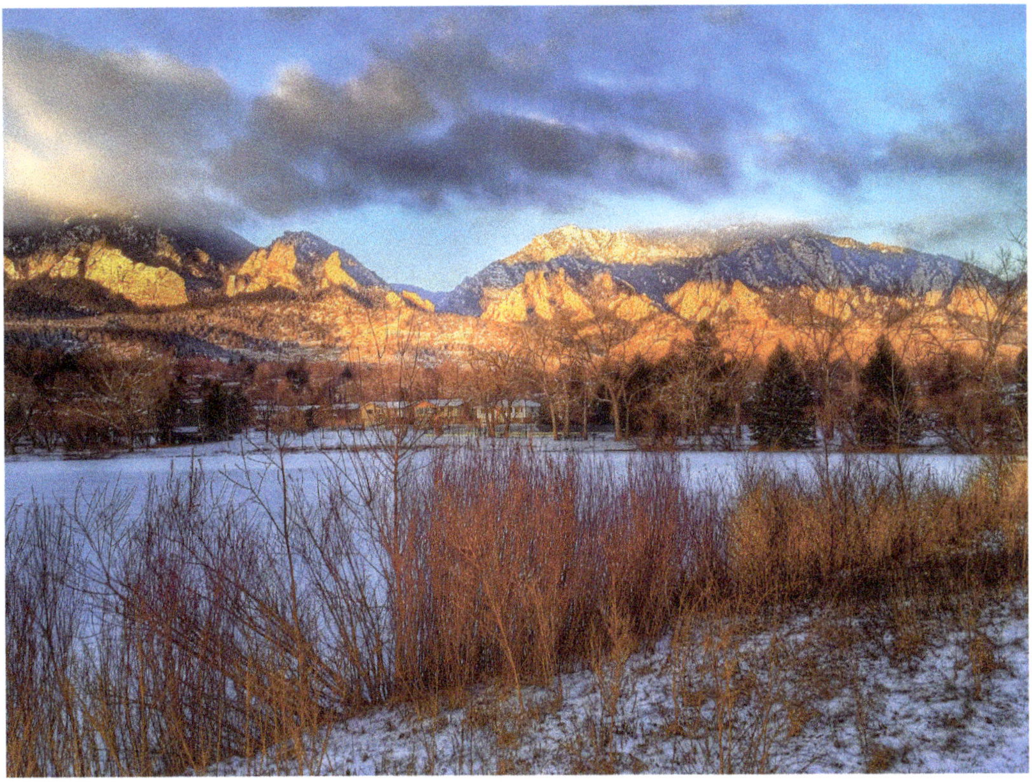

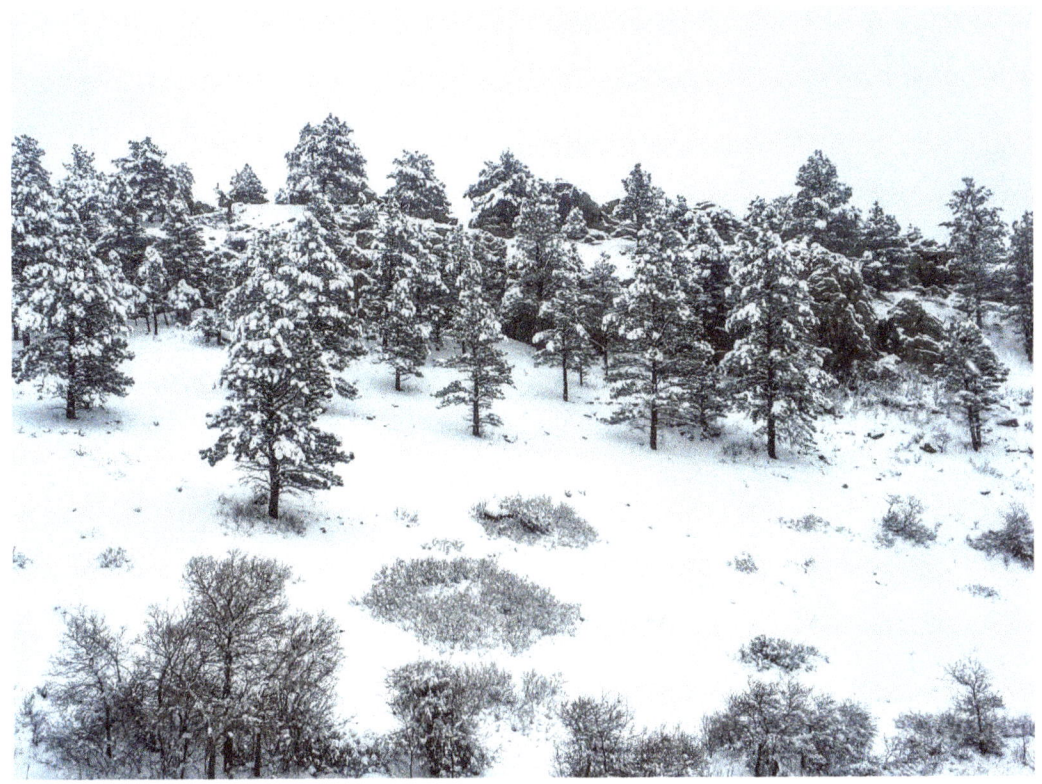

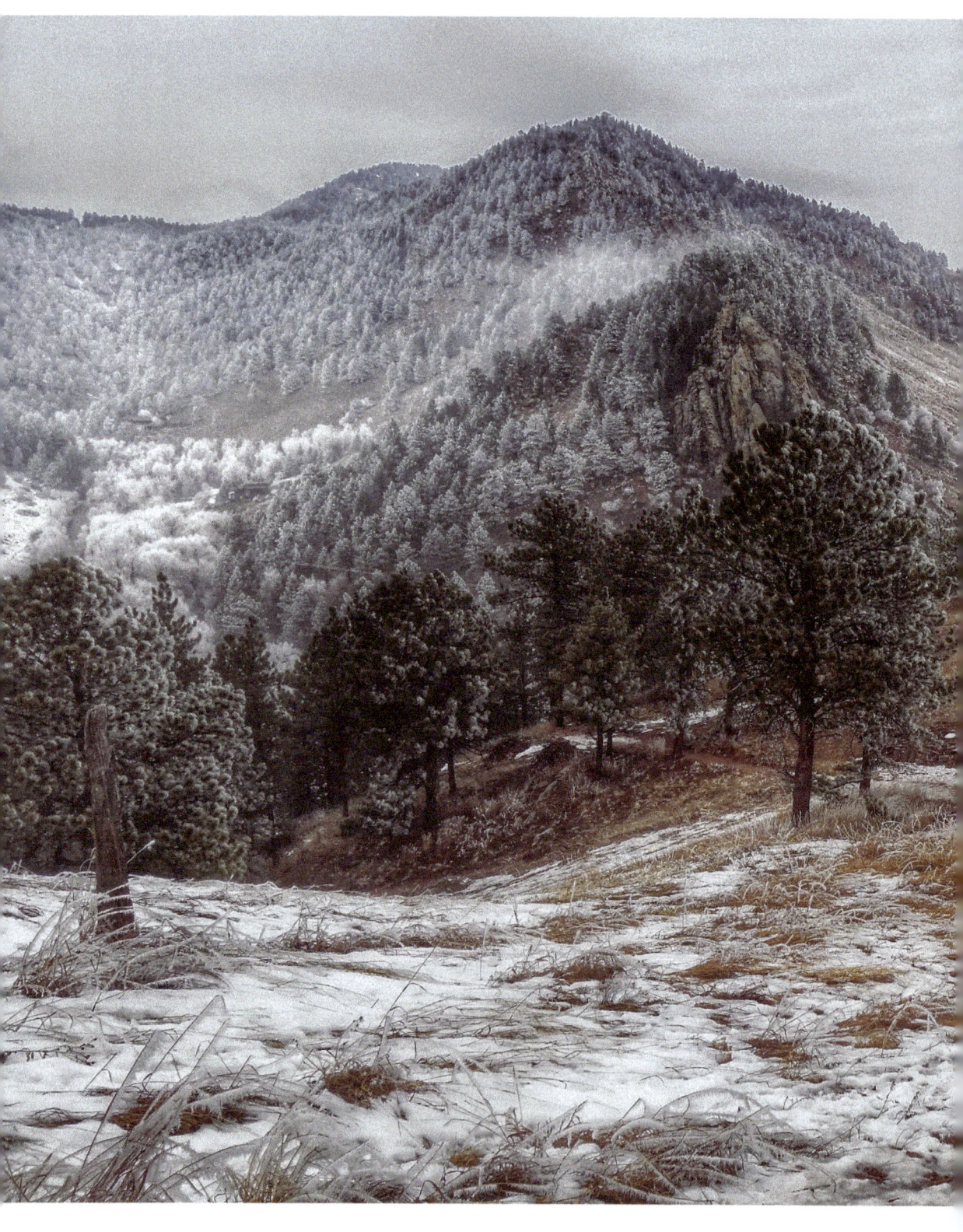

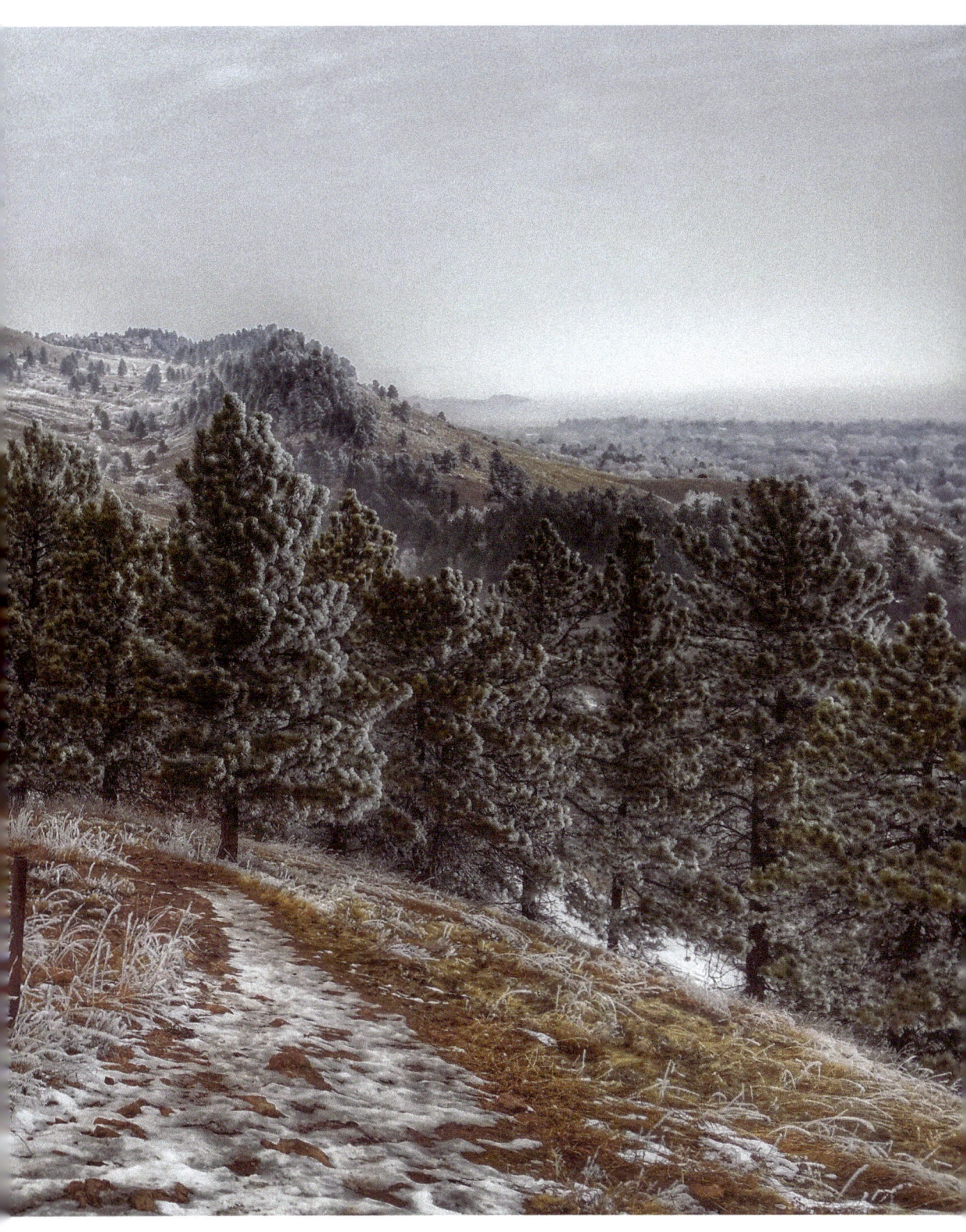

January 1

Not only is it a new day but a new year! Whomever you wish to be, take small steps to start becoming that person today. Believe in you.

Kara Goucher @karagoucher

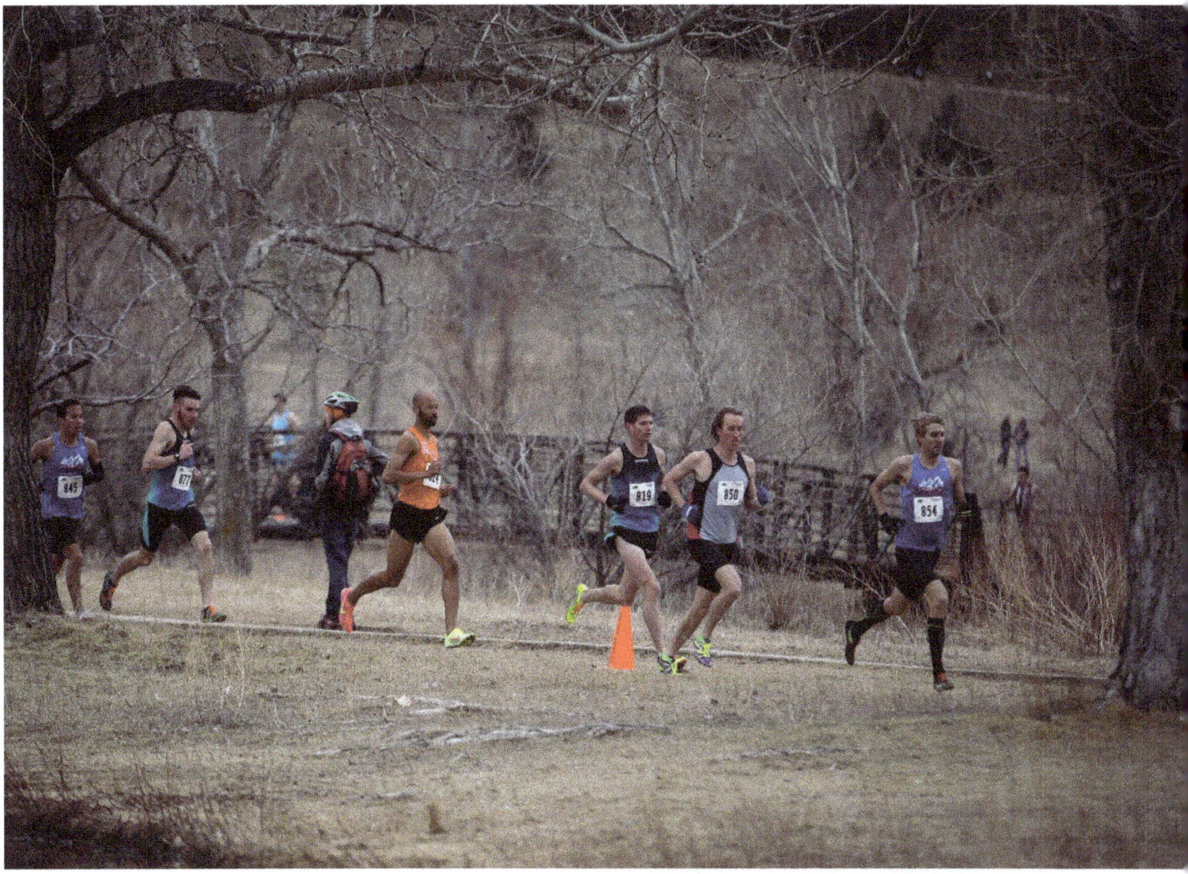

# WINTER CLASSIC 4 MILE

Racing season kicked off with the Winter Classic 4 Mile put on by Flatirons Running Events. The race is a great way to kick off the year for young and old.

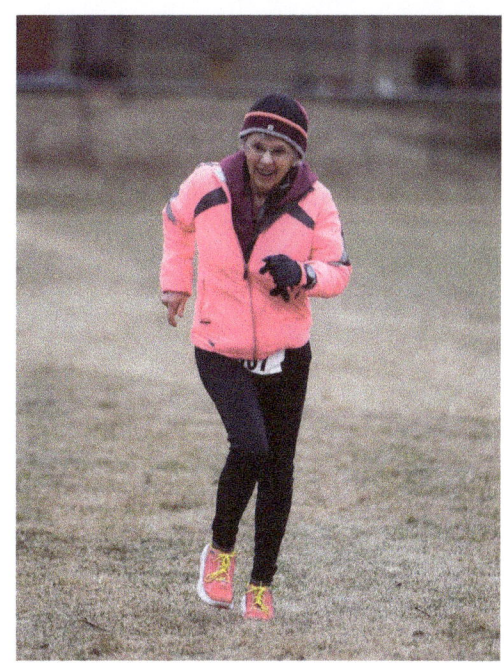

Photos by Glen Delman

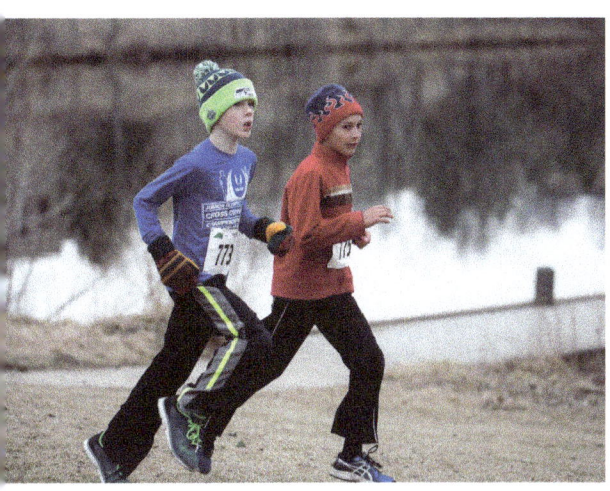

# 9:18.35

## Jenny Simpson opens the season with new 2-mile American Record

By Chris Lotsbom

Heading into 2015, Jenny Simpson was atop the 1,500 meter track world. The 28-year-old from Boulder kicked off her 2015 season in Boston at the New Balance Indoor Games, where she was looking for an American record in the indoor 2-mile.

She just missed the record in 2014, when she miscounted laps and started her kick a lap early.

"I'm in great shape, I'm as fit and as healthy as I've ever been this time of year, so I'm really excited about that," said Simpson at a Boston press conference, flanked by New Balance teammates Brenda Martinez and Emma Coburn.

In 2014, Simpson won the IAAF Diamond League title for 1500m, clocked a personal best of 3:57.22 (coming within 1/10th of a second of Mary Slaney's American record), and won the U.S. outdoor national title in the discipline. In addition, she ran 8:29.58 for 3000m, and repeated as NYRR Fifth Avenue Mile Champion.

To build off her 2014 success, Simpson was not necessarily going to do more in training. Rather, she and coaches Mark Wetmore and Heather Burroughs devised a plan to keep workouts similar while focusing on building confidence and staying healthy.

© 2015 Race Results Weekly, all rights reserved. Used with permission.

"I think it's so tempting after you have a successful stretch of races, or a season, I think it's really tempting to think 'how much more can I get if I add this or add that.' I think the more reasonable, smarter, wiser thing to do is to keep doing what you're doing," said Simpson. In essence, Simpson isn't going to mess with a training philosophy that isn't broken.

Training at altitude in Boulder, Simpson weathered a cold, snowy winter. Yet the two-time Olympian said her fitness is on par to where it was twelve months ago. Last year at the New Balance meet, Simpson committed one of the biggest blunders of her career, mis-counting how many laps remained in the two mile. Had she not kicked a lap early and stopped momentarily, Simpson likely would have broken Regina Jacobs' American record of 9:23.38; instead she finished second in 9:26.19.

> "Last year, yes, I famously made the mistake that you think you're never ever going to make. So many times I've replayed that in my mind and thought I'd never be the person to make such an amateur mistake," Simpson told the media, a smile growing across her face. "I've very much learned from that."

Chuckling, Simpson later added, "I'm really anxious to get 16 full laps in this time," putting emphasis on the word 'full.'

Simpson credits a lot of her successful racing career to Wetmore and Burroughs, who also coached her at the University of Colorado. She has full faith in the pair, giving her comfort going into every race.
"My coaches are the best at that, recognizing where I am in training relative to last year and building on what I've done. I think the biggest thing that I've gained from last year was confidence and experience, and building year on top of year. That doesn't change," she said.

Looking ahead, Simpson admitted she is in a very lucky and unique position. By winning the IAAF Diamond League title in 2014, Simpson automatically qualified for the 2015 IAAF World Championships in Beijing. With her spot on the start line guaranteed, Simpson did not need to worry about chasing qualifying standards or finishing in the top three at the USA Championships. With that in mind, Simpson, Wetmore, and Burroughs etched out a season-long plan beginning at the World Championships and working backwards.

"Coming into this year, it's going to be a very similar formula with similar goals in mind and hopefully 2015 will wrap up in a similar way," she said. "[The year] 2015 is all about putting a star on the World Championships and working back from there. That's where I'm going to be most fit this season."

At the New Balance meet, Simpson faced off against top Ethiopians Sentayehu Ejigu, Gotytom Gebreslase, and Buze Diriba, as well as Americans Stephanie Garcia and Heather Wilson. While she was not be in peak track form just yet, Simpson said she was ready to race up front.

And she was, counting the laps correctly and clocking 9:18.35, to set the new American indoor 2-mile mark.

"I'm January-level fit," she admitted, trying to put her fitness in perspective. "I've had some really great training... I feel good, I feel fit, but I'm not as good as I'll be in August."

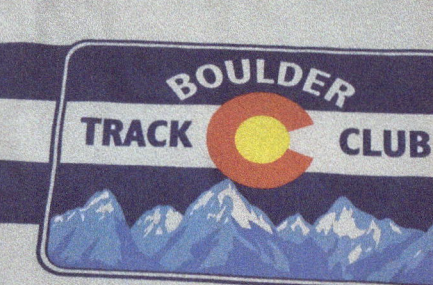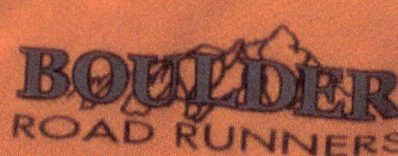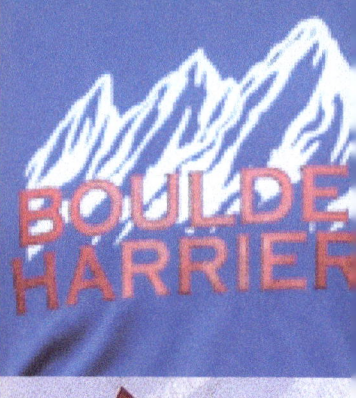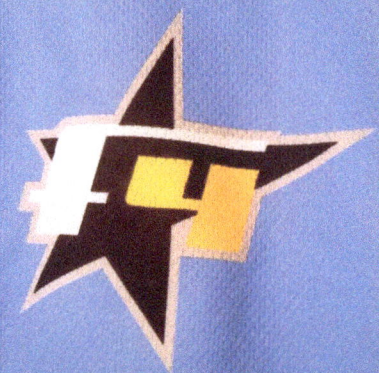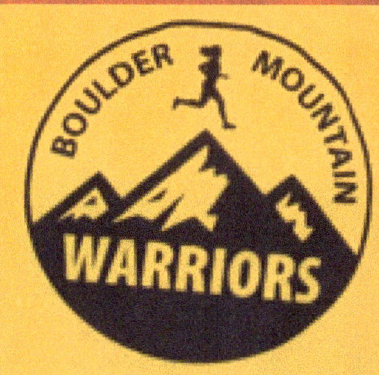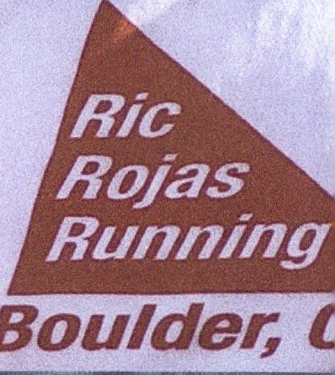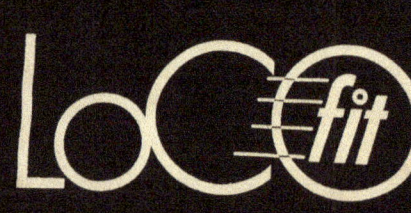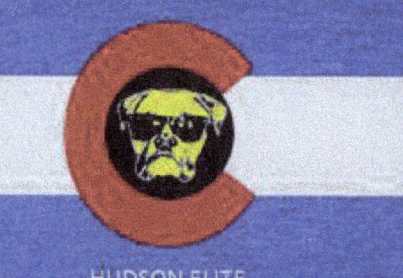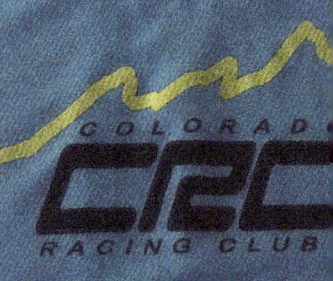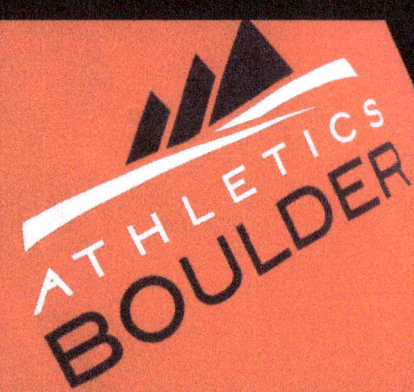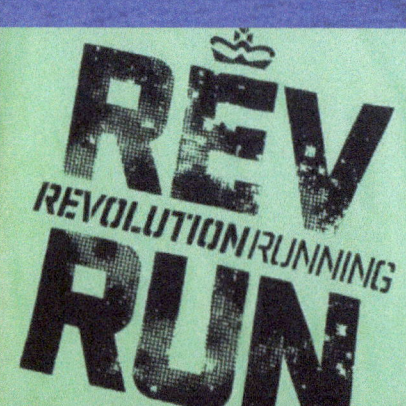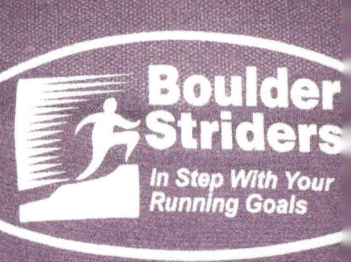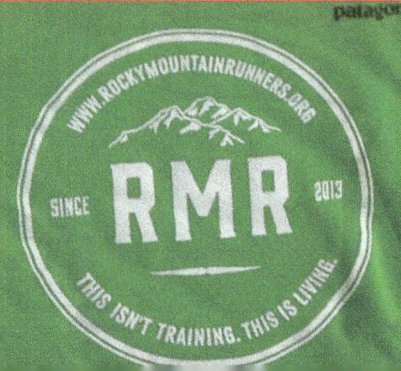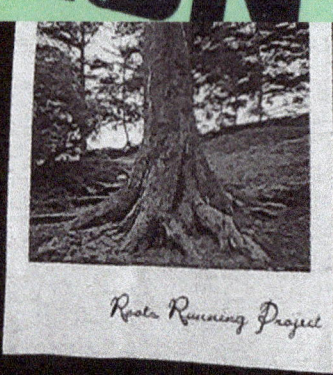

It's a rough, bumpy road back to fitness, but there's nothing like teammates to help smooth out the journey.

Alex Wolf-Root @WolfmanHorsecow

# GROUP DYNAMIC

Long miles; slushy winter slogs; hours up in the mountains; circles on the track: all of these go better with a group of crazy running friends. Conversation and the sharing of the load almost always makes the run or workout more fun and more productive. Over the last few years the number of running groups in the area has increased dramatically; there is no shortage of people to run with. And that doesn't even include the fun runs, the Meet-Ups, the ad-hoc groups or the beer-run groups. If you are looking for training partners, often with common goals, you can find a coach and group that match your needs. Then you can watch your running — and your running friendships — really take off.

**BoulderRunning.com/RunningGroups**

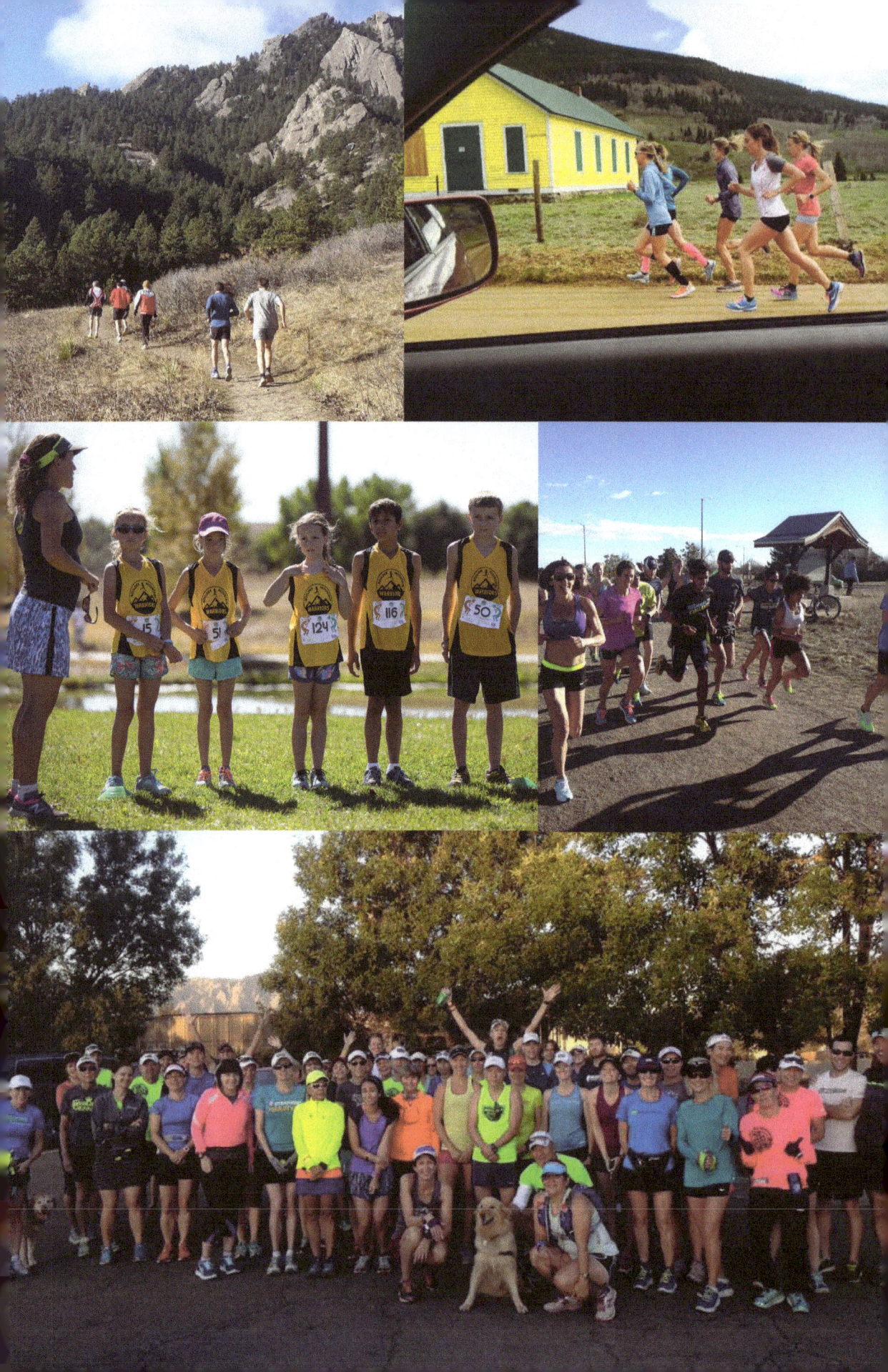

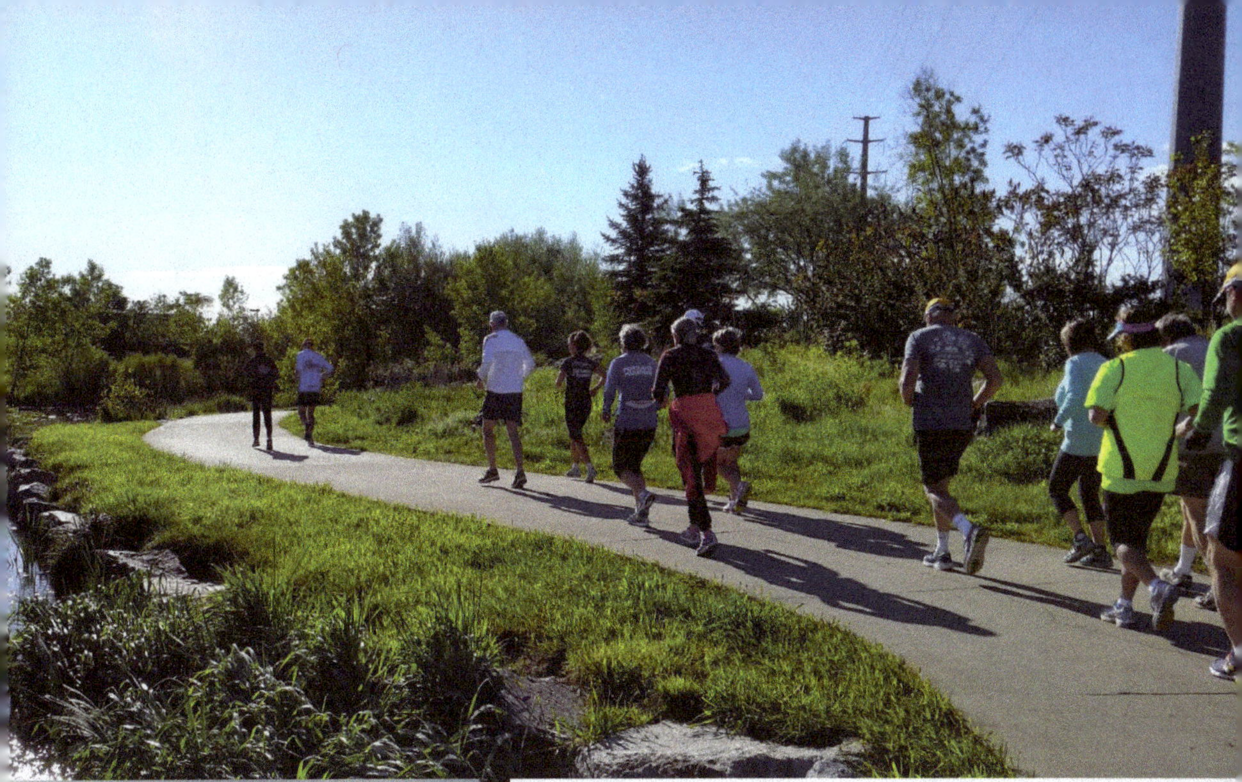

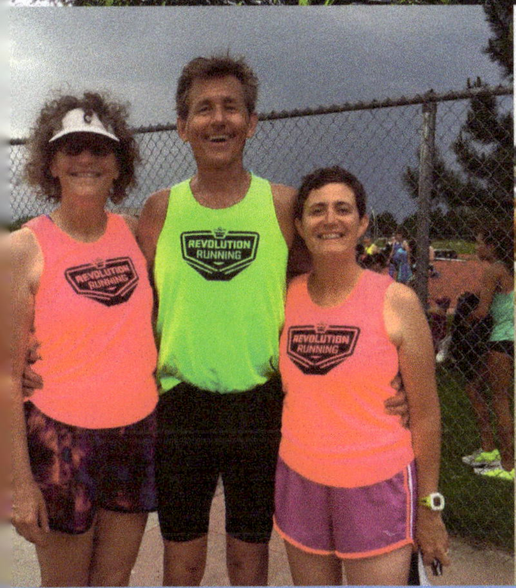

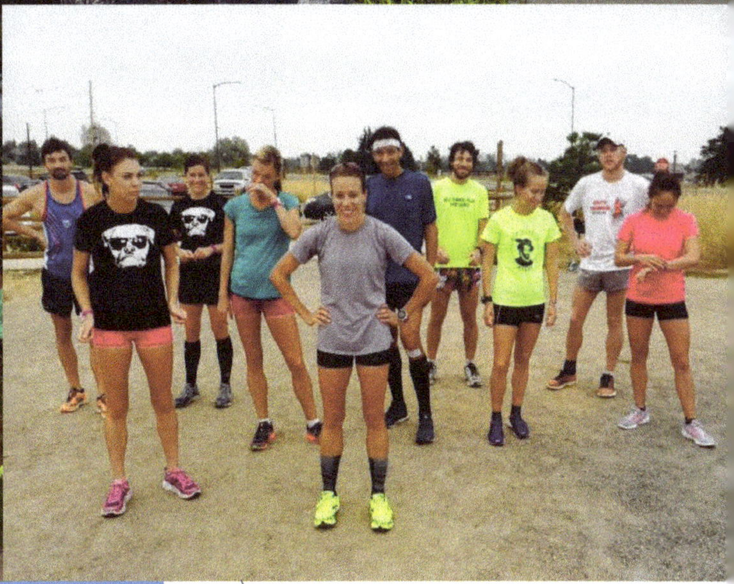

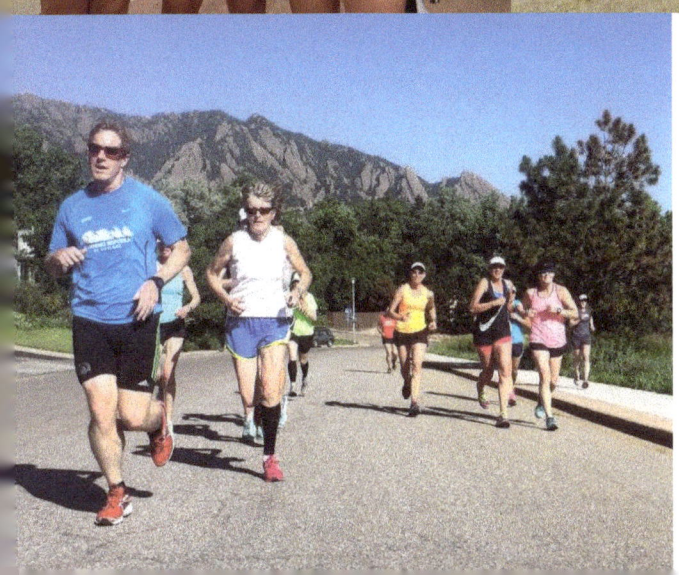

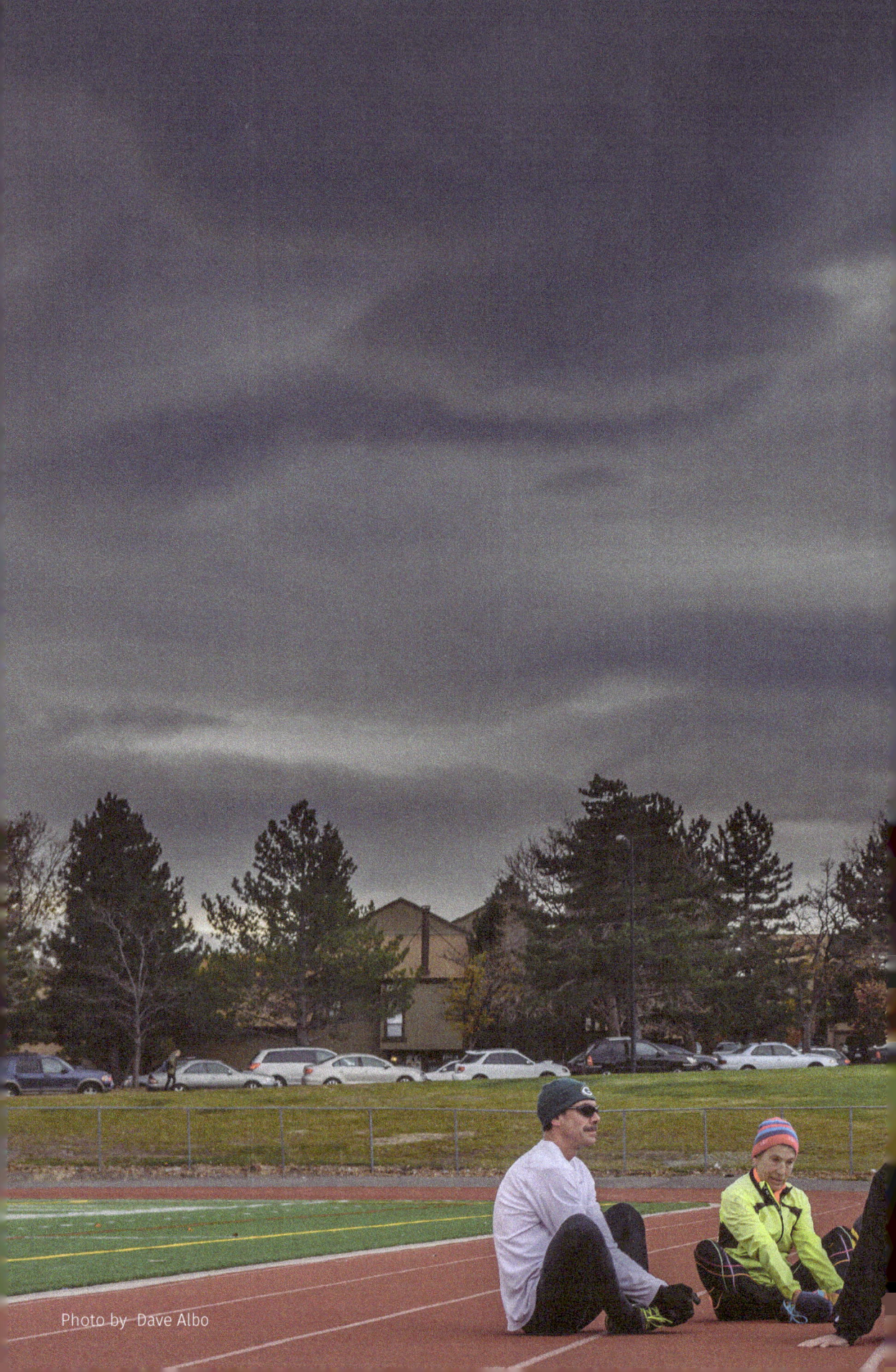

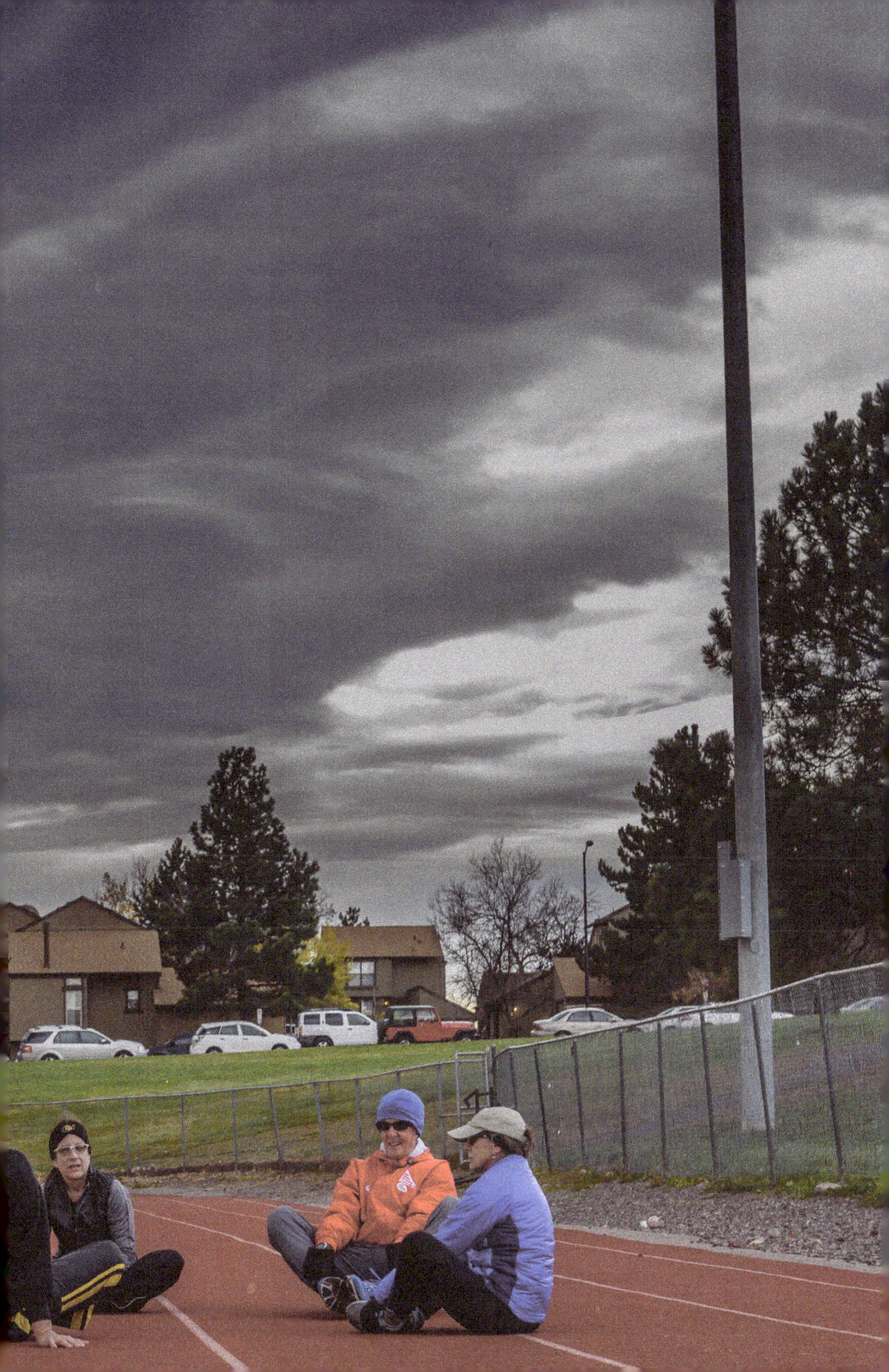

# USA XC

For the second year in a row, Boulder hosted the USA Cross Country Championships. The event was held at the Flatirons Golf Course February 5. The top five athletes from the men's, womens and high school races were selected to race at the Worlds Cross Country Championships in China in April.

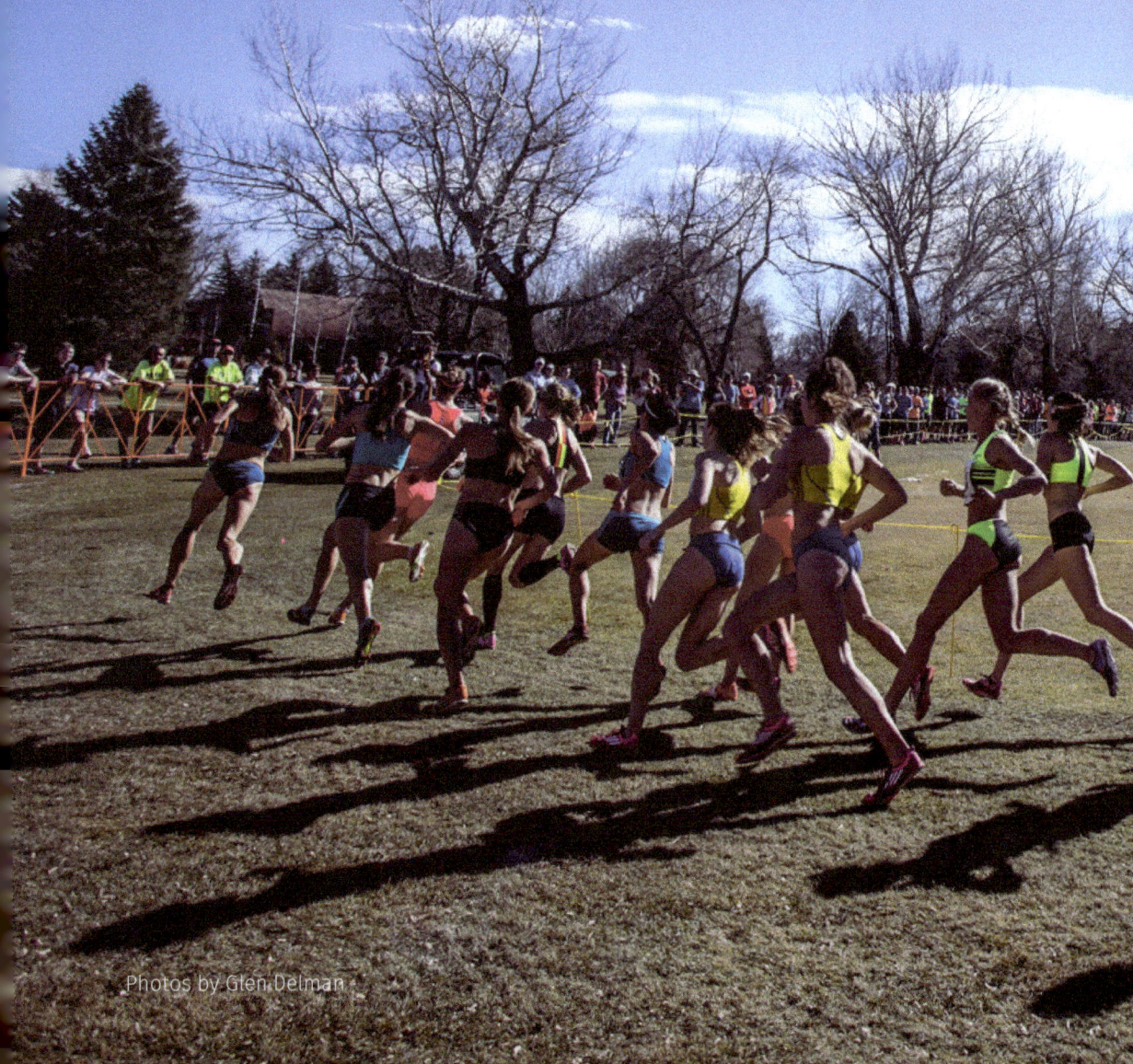

Photos by Glen Delman

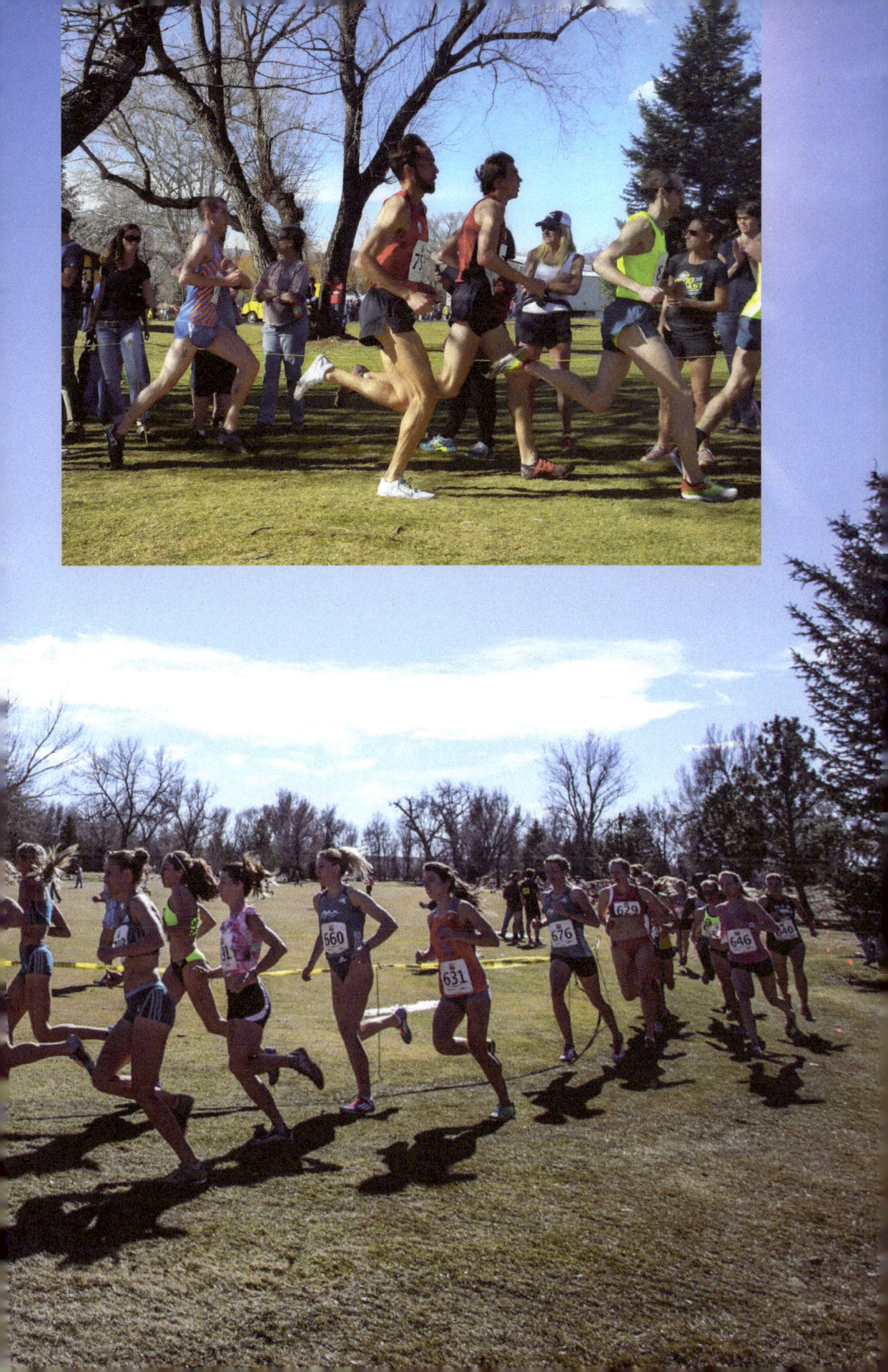

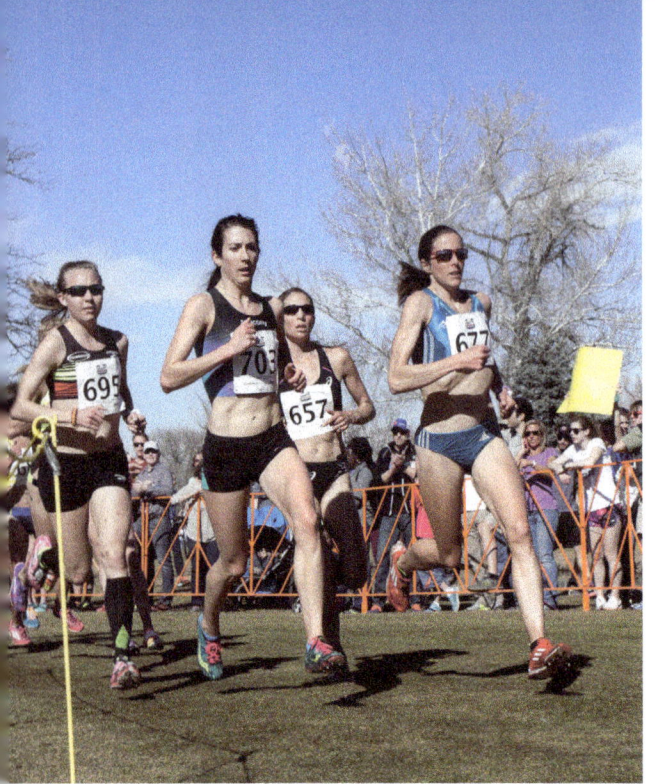

## THWEATT DOMINATES USA CROSS COUNTRY CHAMPIONSHIPS

By David Monti, @d9monti

On a summery day where the temperature hit 75F (24C), Chris Derrick and Laura Thweatt completely dominated the open men's and open women's races at the 2015 USA Cross Country Championships at the Flatirons Golf Course here. Derrick got his third consecutive victory at these championships, while Thweatt --who lives here in Boulder-- got her first. Both athletes led strong American teams for the 2015 IAAF World Cross Country Championships in Guiyang, China, on March 28.

HOMETOWN ADVANTAGE FOR THWEATT

Thweatt had a tougher race on her hands than Derrick. Cheered on by local fans --many wearing T-shirts and some in shorts-- Thweatt ran near the front of the field on the first of four laps, joined by key rivals Sara Hall, Brianne Nelson, Neely Spence, Mattie Suver, Katie Mackey and 40 year-old Jen Rhines. In the fifth kilometer, Thweatt and Hall moved away from the field, and by the 6-K checkpoint they were the only women in contention for the win. Thweatt began to see it was going to be her day.

**"I just felt really relaxed," Thweatt told Race Results Weekly. "That was the goal, to feel smooth the first two (laps) and then to open it up and run for dear life."**

Hall --who joked before the race that the last time she raced at altitude it nearly killed her—began to struggle. Behind her, Suver—who lives at high altitude in Colorado Springs—began to move up and took over second place. Rhines, who had made six previous USA Cross Country teams, moved into third. Spence pulled off the course just before the 6-K mark looking dizzy. After resting, she re-started the race, but was unable to finish.

Thweatt widened her lead in the final two kilometers and, like Derrick, had the finish straight to herself. She finished the 8-K course in 27:42, beating the second place Suver by 31 seconds. She was overjoyed about winning at home, something that Alan Culpepper had done here in 2007.

© 2015 Race Results Weekly, all rights reserved. Used with permission.

"It's something you want, but when it's actually happening you're like, shit, it's actually happening. It was an incredible field, and I knew I was going to have to run as hard as I've ever run before to do it."

- Laura Thweatt

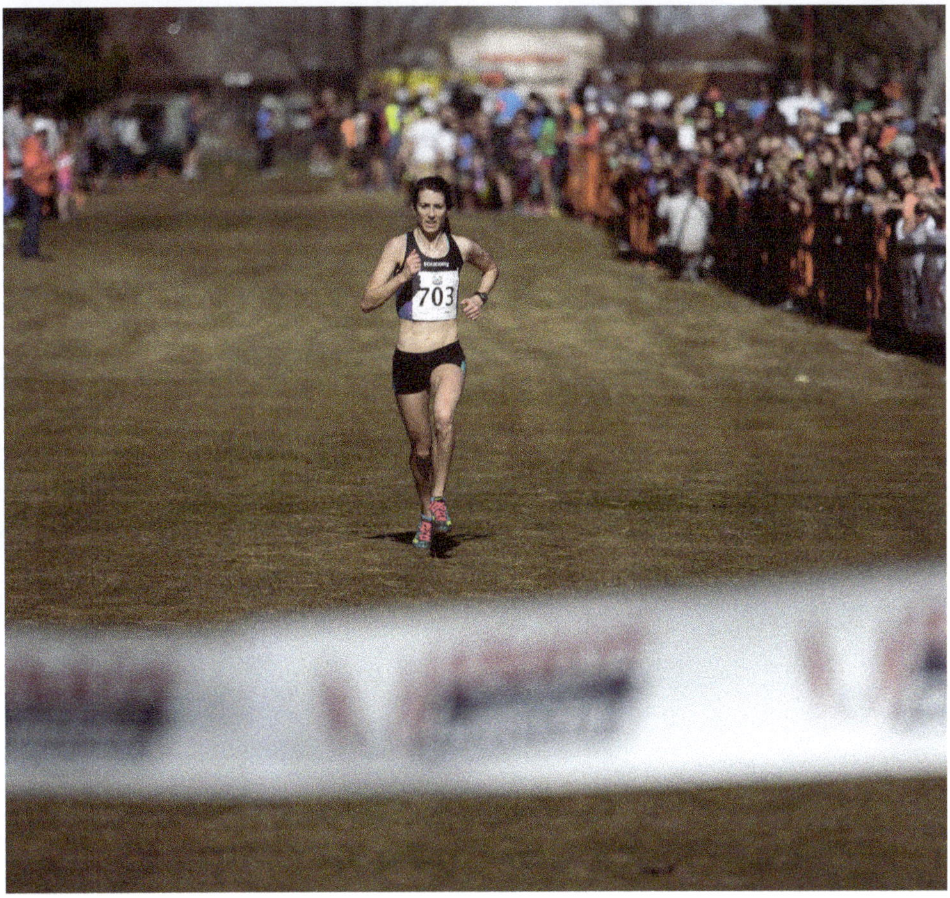

THANK YOU to everyone who came out to cheer @BoulderUSAXC. Wouldn't have been nearly as special w/o you all. @Saucony Racing @runtroopy #BTC

Laura Thweatt @thweatt11

---

To win a national title is hard but to win one in your home town is a lot of pressure but @thweatt11 delivered. #proud

Lee Troop @runtroopy

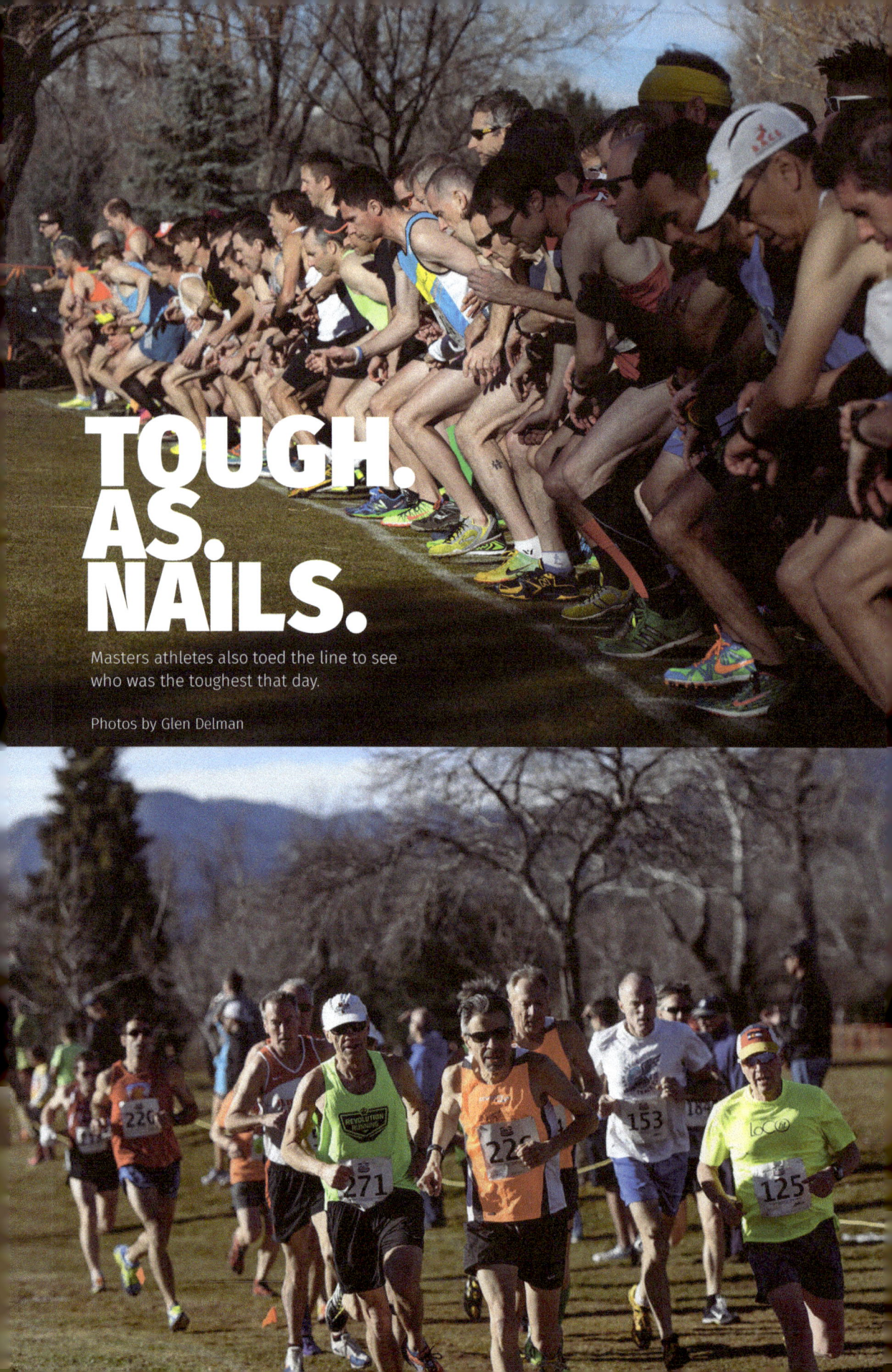

# TOUGH. AS. NAILS.

Masters athletes also toed the line to see who was the toughest that day.

Photos by Glen Delman

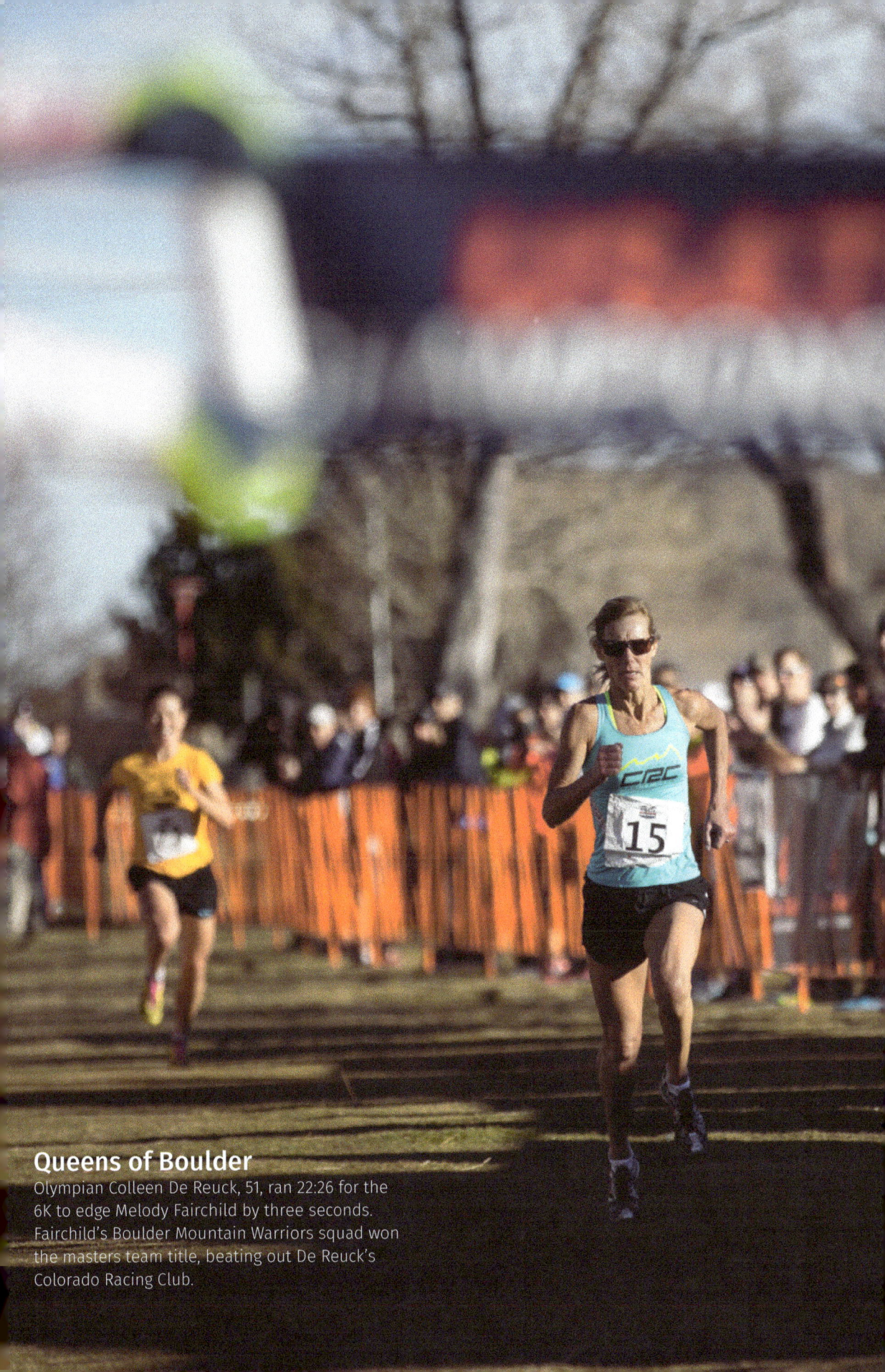

## Queens of Boulder
Olympian Colleen De Reuck, 51, ran 22:26 for the 6K to edge Melody Fairchild by three seconds. Fairchild's Boulder Mountain Warriors squad won the masters team title, beating out De Reuck's Colorado Racing Club.

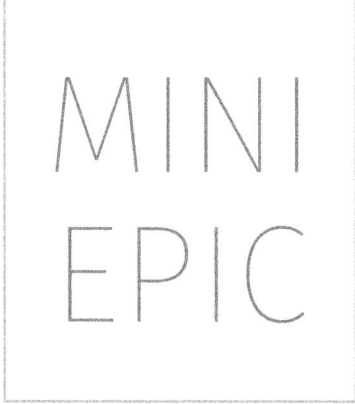

# MINI EPIC

By Todd Straka

Typically my run is squeezed between the over scheduled commitments of family, work and life's other obligations. Fortunately we live is such a place that no matter how much time we have we can manage to see some incredible views and take in the scenery. These are what I call the Mini Epic.

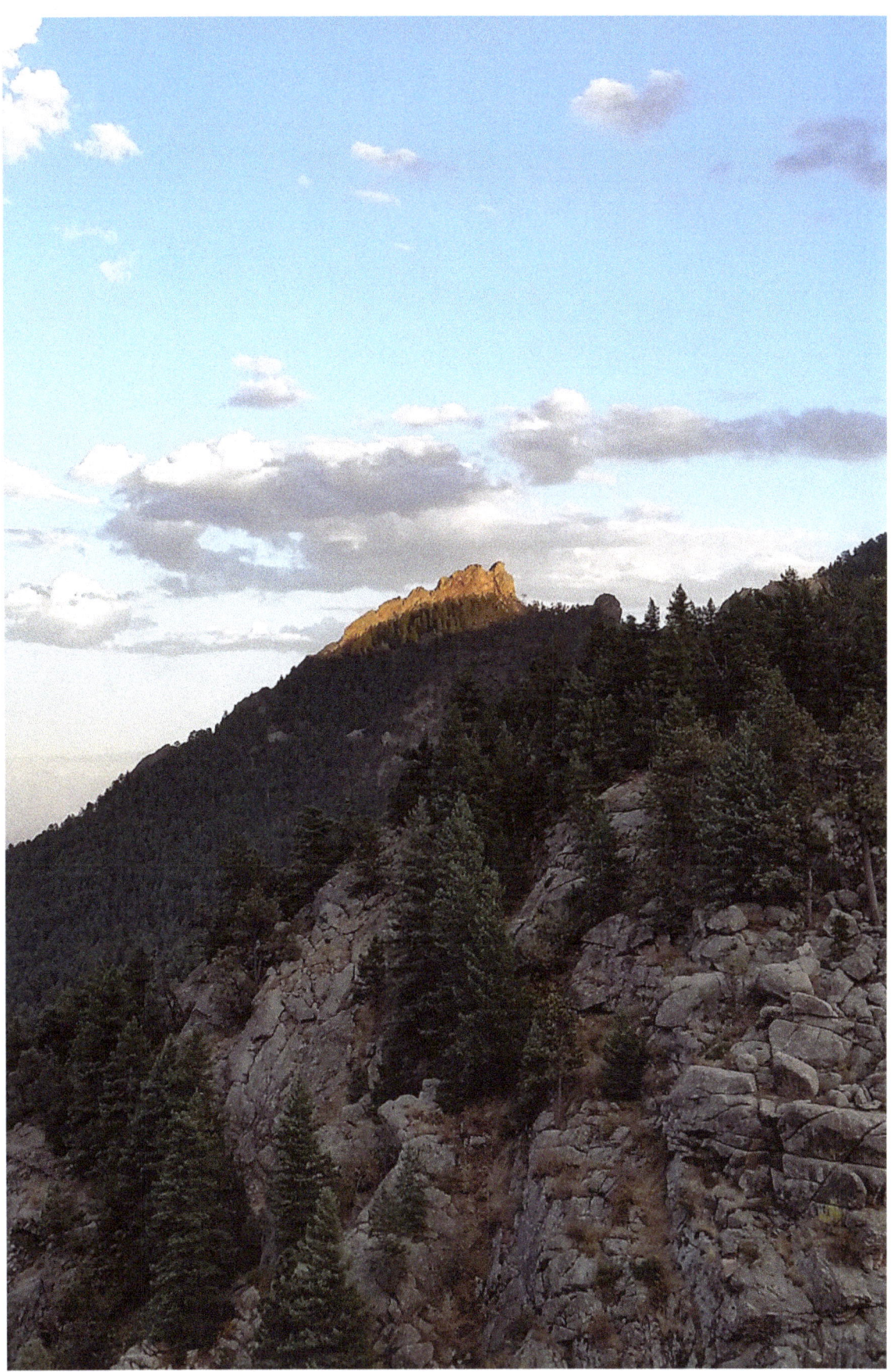

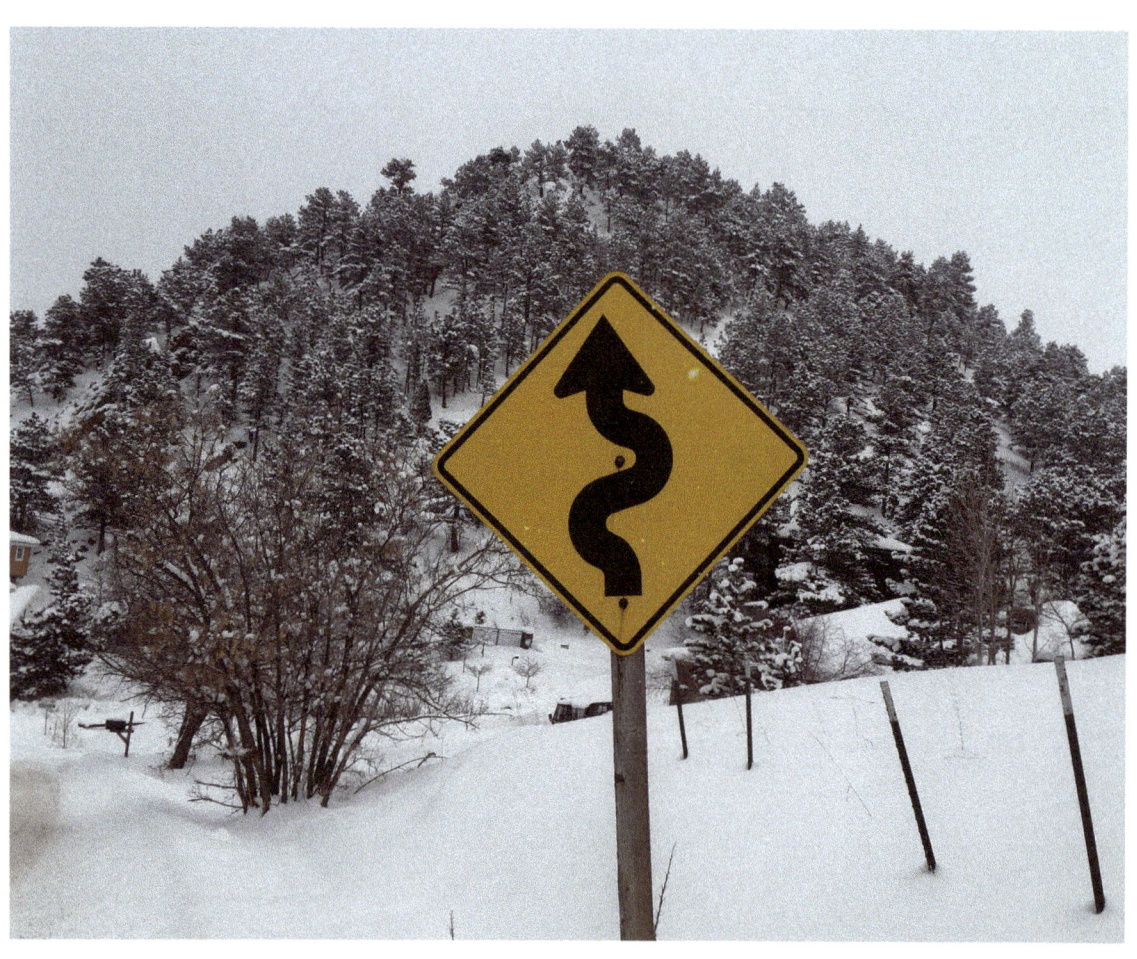

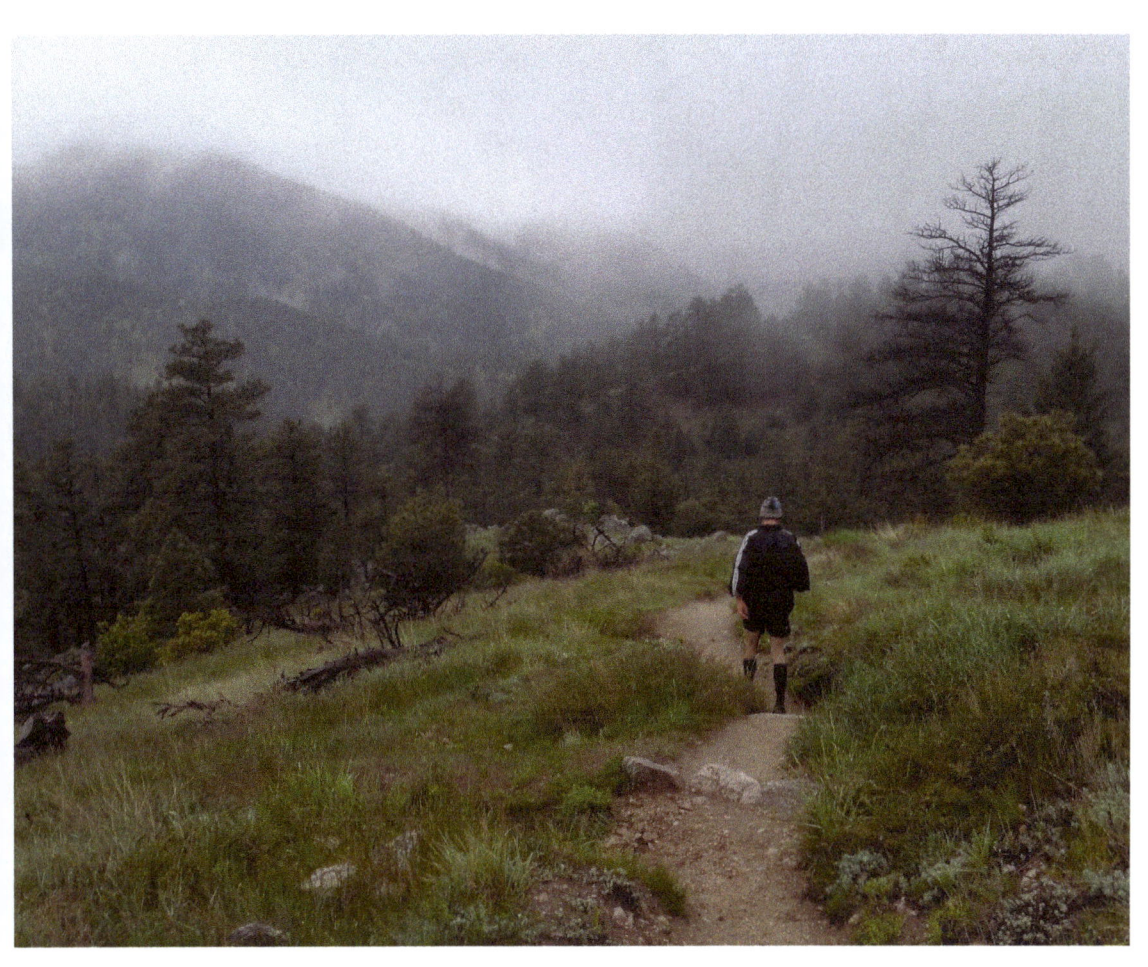

# ONE WORLD RUNNING

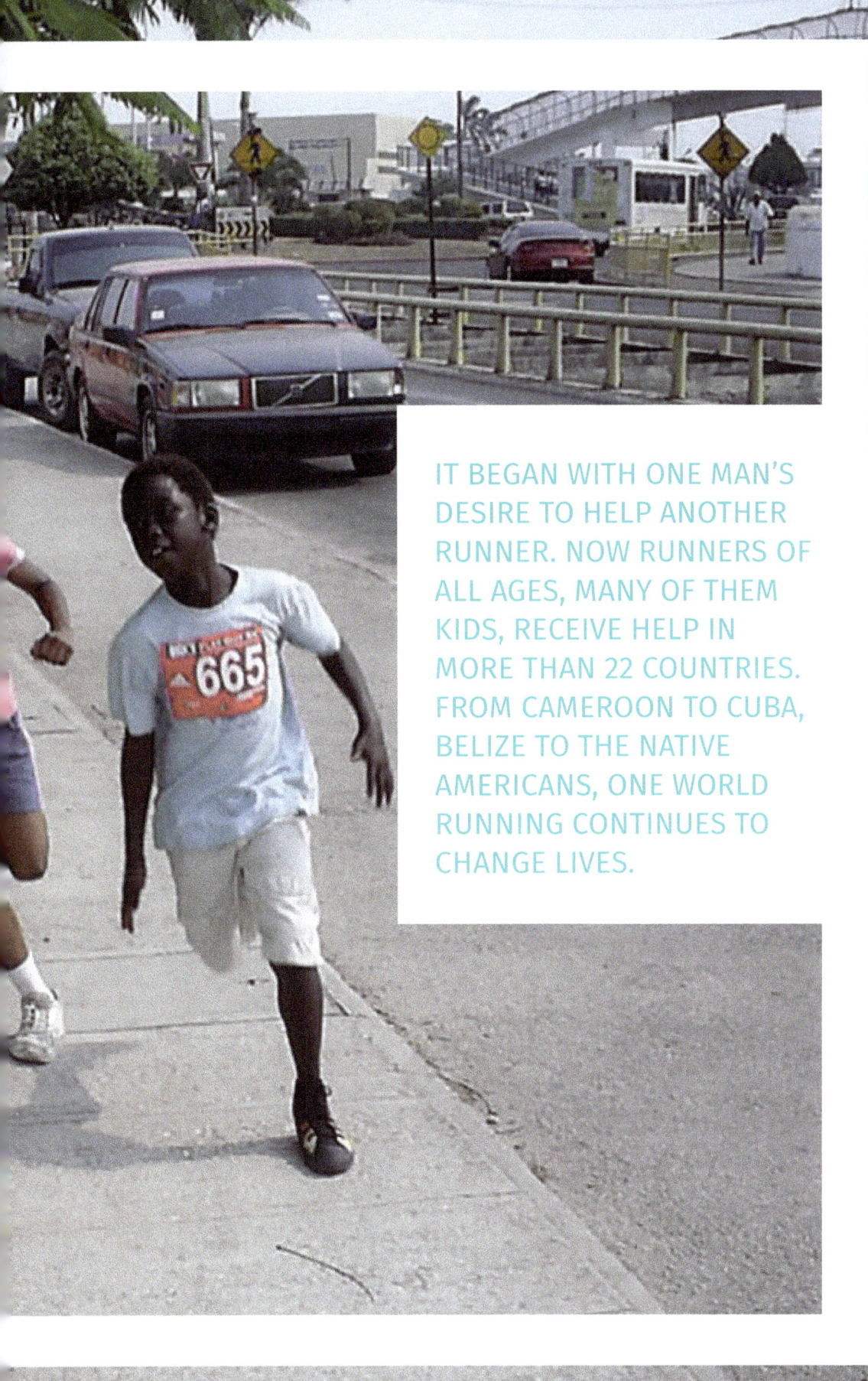

IT BEGAN WITH ONE MAN'S DESIRE TO HELP ANOTHER RUNNER. NOW RUNNERS OF ALL AGES, MANY OF THEM KIDS, RECEIVE HELP IN MORE THAN 22 COUNTRIES. FROM CAMEROON TO CUBA, BELIZE TO THE NATIVE AMERICANS, ONE WORLD RUNNING CONTINUES TO CHANGE LIVES.

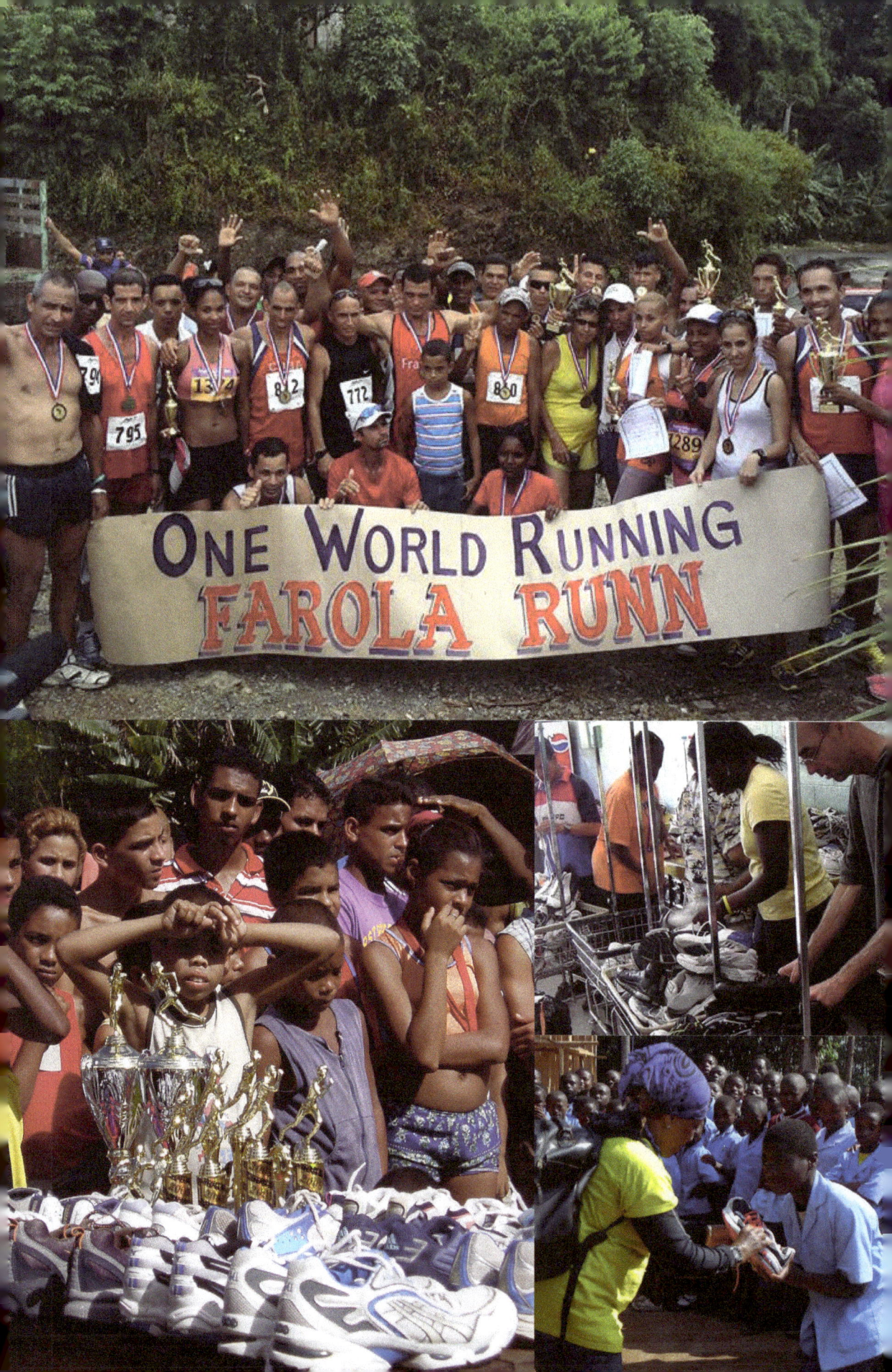

SINCE ITS **FOUNDING IN 1986** BY MIKE SANDROCK, ONE WORLD RUNNING HAS DISTRIBUTED OVER **500,000 PAIRS OF SHOES** IN **22 COUNTRIES.** THE ORGANIZATION SUCCEEDS WITH **100% VOLUNTEER** WORKERS WHO EVEN PAY THEIR OWN TRAVEL EXPENSES. **100% OF $ DONATED** GOES TO THE EXPENSES OF CLEANING, STORING AND SHIPPING SHOES. **UP TO 2,000 RUNNERS PARTICIPATE IN RACES** IN EACH COUNTRY AND EACH PARTICIPANT RECEIVES A PAIR OF SHOES IN THE PROPER SIZE!

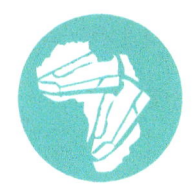

10% OF THIS MAGAZINE'S PROCEEDS WILL GO TO
ONEWORLDRUNNING.COM

# Top Results
## January - March

On January 18th at the Tri-City Medical Center Carlsbad Marathon **Mario Macias** of Boulder came in second with a time of 2:23:02.

**Tyler McCandless** of Boulder ran a 1:03:14 race at the Naples Daily News Half-Marathon on January 28th, fast enough for a solid third place. This was a personal best for McCandless as he began to ramp up for the upcoming season.

At the Miami Half-Marathon on January 25th, **Mario Macias** of Boulder ran a fast race, clocking a time of 1:07:07, which was good enough for third place overall.

On the same day over in New Orleans, **Matt Peharda** of Boulder put in a hard effort at the Rock 'n' Roll Mardi Gras Marathon, resulting in a third place finish with a time of 2:42:06.

Over the January 22-24th weekend, Boulder runners had a strong showing at the Air Force Invitational, which was held at the Air Force Academy in Colorado Springs. **Blake Theroux** ran a time of 1:53.83 in the 800m, which resulted in a third place finish, while **Sara Sutherland** took home third place in the women's race with a time of 2:16.29. **Ben Saarel** of the University of Colorado won the mile race in a time of 4:12.30 for the men, while **Morgan Pearson** came in third with a time of 4:13.90. In the women's mile race **Alicia Nelson** of BRC/adidas won in a time of 5:00.56, while **Maddie Alm** of the University of Colorado came in second with a time of 5:05.55 and **Erin Clark** also of CU, came in third with a time of 5:06.46, also of the University of Colorado. University of Colorado runners also swept the 3000m race, with **Pierce Murphy** taking home the win with a time of 8:38.92, while **Ryan Forsyth** came in second with a time of 8:42.51 and **Paul Miller** came in third with a time of 8:42.79. Boulder runners also swept the women's 3000m race with **Alicia Nelson** of BRC/adidas taking home the win with a time of 10:04.98, while **Kaitlyn Benner** of the University of Colorado came in second in a time of 10:05.23 and **Brittni Hutton** of BRC/adidas came in third with a time of 10:17.95.

At the Pensacola Double Bridge Run held on February 7th, **Tyler McCandless** ran to a comfortable win in the 15 km race with a time of 45:18.

Across the continent, in California, **Ryan Smith** of Boulder won the Sean O'Brien 100k in California on February 7 in a time of 8:42. **Silke Koester**, wife of men's winner Smith, was third in 11:11. At the Sean O'Brien 50 Mile race held on the same day **Britt Nic Dick** came in second with a time of 9:41:53.

Meanwhile, the USA Cross Country Championships were held in Boulder on February 7th, bringing out a large crowd to cheer on the runners. The highlight of the championships came when hometown favorite **Laura Thweatt** of the Boulder Track Club took home the win in a time of 27:42. In the Junior Women's race, University of Colorado runners took home first and second place, with **Kaitlyn Benner** running a time of 21:48 for the win and **Valerie Constien** coming in second in a time of 21:54.

**Dave Mackey** of Boulder was second at the Black Canyon 100K in Arizona on February 14th in a time of 8:33:27. **Gina Lucrezi** of Boulder was 3rd place Female in a time of 11:51:21.

On February 15th the Austin Marathon and Half-Marathon was held on a fast loop course with little elevation change, resulting in fast times for both races. Although no one from Boulder had outstanding races in the marathon, **Michael Kettler** of Louisville ran an excellent time in the half-marathon, coming in third with a time of 1:09:38.

The Alex Wilson Invitational, held in South Bend, Indiana on February 21st always attracts a stout field of track athletes ready to race. Boulder's **Brittni Hutton** competed in the 3000m, racing to a second place finish with a time of 9:25.94.

At the Mercedes Marathon on February 22nd in Birmingham, Alabama, Boulder's **Mario Macias** ran a strong and fast race, crossing the finish line in 2:22:05 for fourth place, missing the podium by only 12 seconds.

On March 1st at the Fort Worth Cowtown Half-Marathon, **Tyler McCandless** came away with second place in a time of 1:06:19 and a very large black cowboy hat.

**Eric Lee** returned to the Mississippi 50 Mile Trail Run on March 7 for the third year in a row, hoping to reclaim his crown. Everything aligned, and he won in a time of 7:03, followed closely by fellow Boulder runner **Jack Daly** in a time of 7:16.

At the Gate River Run 15K held in Jacksonville, Florida, on March 15th **Neely Spence Gracey** finished third in a time of 50:50. The race was the U.S. 15K Championships and had a strong field.

In Denver at the Runnin' of the Green 7K, also held on March 15th, **Benjamin Zywicki** of Louisville came home with the win in a time of 22:22. **Nicole Camp** of Longmont was the winner for the women in a time of 26:20.

Over the March 20th-21st weekend, Boulder hosted the Colorado University Jerry Quiller Classic. In the 1500M Boulder Track Club's **Sean Quigley** came away with the win in a time of 3:54.67. He also won the 3000M race in a time of 8:35.79. In the women's races, **Lucy May** came in second in the 800M with a time of 2:15.19, while in the 1500M it was **Sara Sutherland** who took second in a time of 4:30.07 followed by **Maddie Alm** for third in a time of 4:33.28. **Kaitlyn Benner** won the 3000M with a time of 9:48.74, followed closely by **Maor Tiyouri** in a time of 10:10.92 for second and **Val Constien** for third in 10:17.30.

**Cassie Scallon** of Boulder battled Catrin Jones at the Chuckanut 50K in Washington on March 21. The two raced neck and neck at the finish, with Cassie finishing just four minutes back in a time of 4:29 for 3rd place. This race marked Scallon's return to racing from long-term injury.

Starting at 11:00am on March 25th, **Nick Pedatella** of Boulder and Scott Jaime of Highlands Ranch ran 142 miles in 30 hours, 21 minutes and 58 seconds to set a new supported FKT (Fastest Known Time) on the Kokopelli Trail.

**Tyler McCandless** once again proved that he has some speedy legs at the Ukrop's Monument Avenue 10K held on March 28th in Richmond, Virginia. The race was the Collegiate Running Association 10K Championships and Tyler outran a strong field, winning the race in a time of 29:38.

At the Behind the Rocks 50 mile race in Moab, Utah on March 28th, **Alberto Rossi** took third in a time of 8:36:35. **Silke Koester** took home the win for the women in a time of 9:22. In the 50K race, **Yves-Marie Hervault** ran a strong race for third place in a time of 5:13:19.

**Michele Yates** of Littleton won the Gorge Waterfalls 100K in Oregon with a time of 11:03:05 on March 30. Michele set a new course record, even after being temporarily lost as part of the course was vandalized.

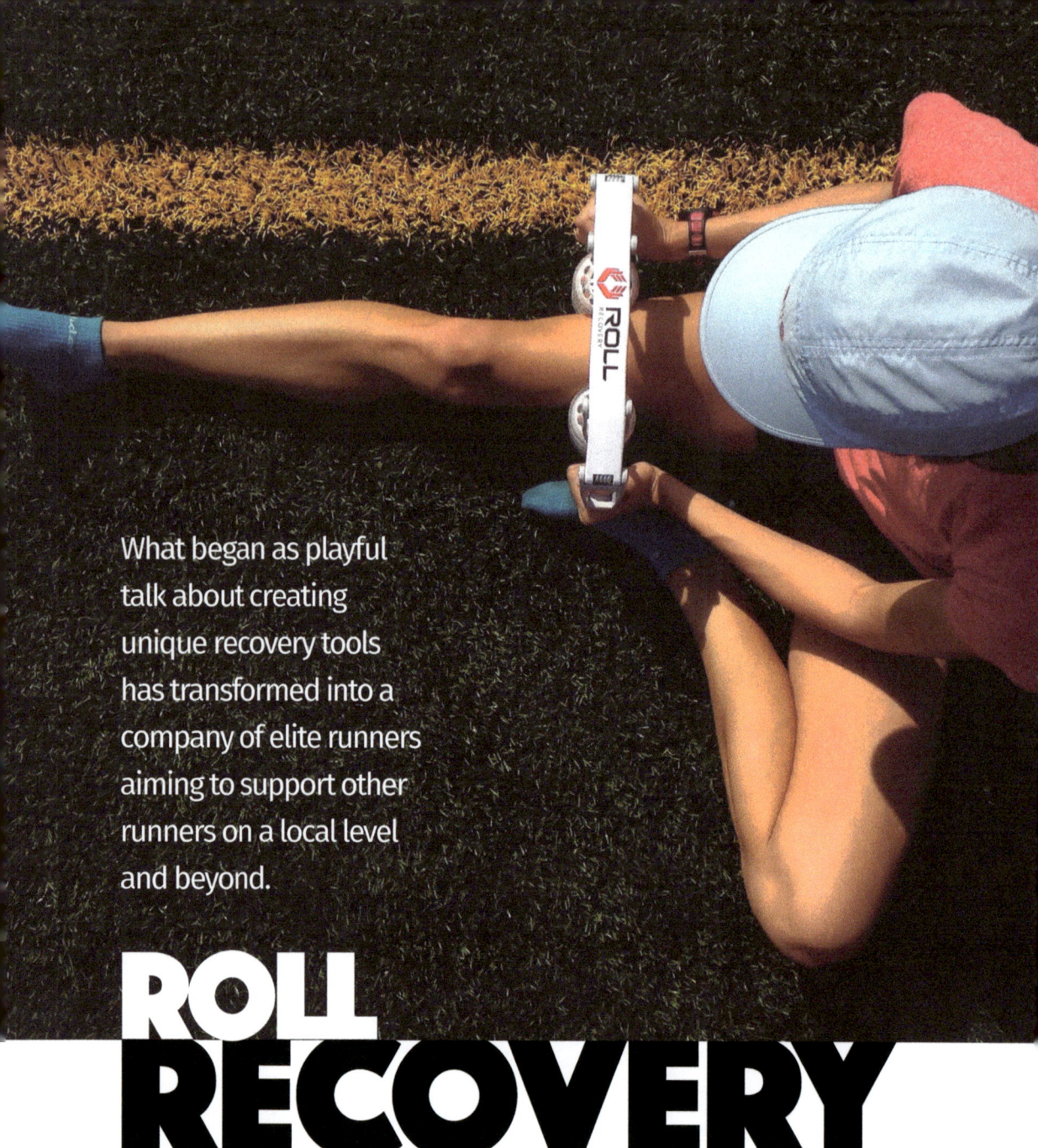

What began as playful talk about creating unique recovery tools has transformed into a company of elite runners aiming to support other runners on a local level and beyond.

# ROLL RECOVERY

Words by Jenny DeSouchet
Photos courtesy of @jesssbarnard and @RollRecovery

# RECOVER

ROLL Recovery has developed an established role in the running community over the last few years with the help of the dedicated, vivacious, and supportive Boulder running community.

The company truly began in the garage of runners Jeremy and Adriana Nelson in 2011, where Jeremy began building a recovery tool to support their endurance training— Jeremy preparing for half and full marathons, and Adriana maintaining high mileage as a professional marathoner. The two feel that the support for start-ups in Boulder made possible the transition from a couple with a new invention—the R8— into a successful community-based company. As far as they're concerned, Boulder is the Silicon Valley of the outdoor world, making it a perfect place to start a company of their own.

Jeremy and Adriana, and now a staff of six others, have set out to foster an atmosphere of community for runners from the inside out. Each employee pursues elite running to some degree. On staff are multiple Olympians, the 1996 New York City female marathon champion, Chicago Marathon runner-ups (two of them), elite trail runners, and a couple of runners who just love to kick butt on Strava (OK, that's just Jeremy). These passionate runners create what Jeremy calls a "breeding ground for innovation" when it comes to creating new recovery products because they know exactly what runners need to feel good. ROLL Recovery specifically employs local elite runners to support them financially and offer a flexible, runner-friendly environment.

Support for elite runners does not stop in Boulder, though. With an expansive ambassador program, ROLL Recovery supports elite athletes across the world by providing R8's and constant well wishes in training and races. They are well aware of the financial needs of professional runners, and want to contribute what they can to help the sport prosper. The company simply hopes to see athletes everywhere performing their best, and aids in this by providing exceptionally designed tools in addition to a community-driven support system for runners. Such a mission has mutually benefited and contributed to the Boulder running community, thriving off the amazing energy that radiates here.

ROLL Recovery founders Jeremy and Adriana Nelson

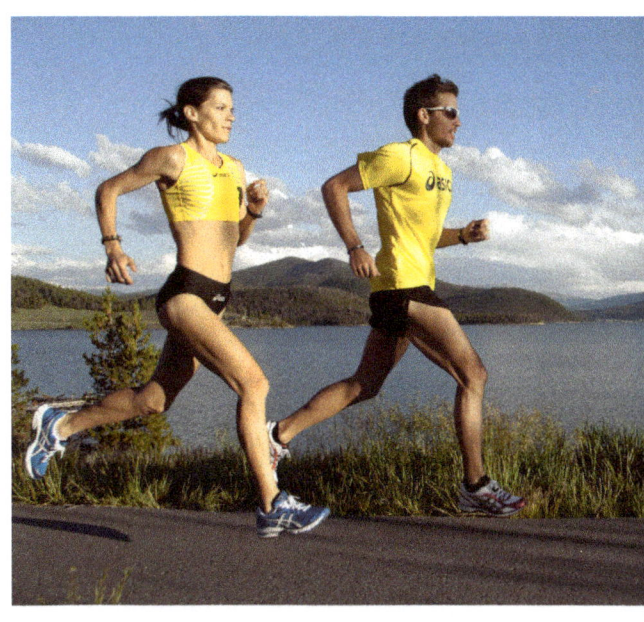

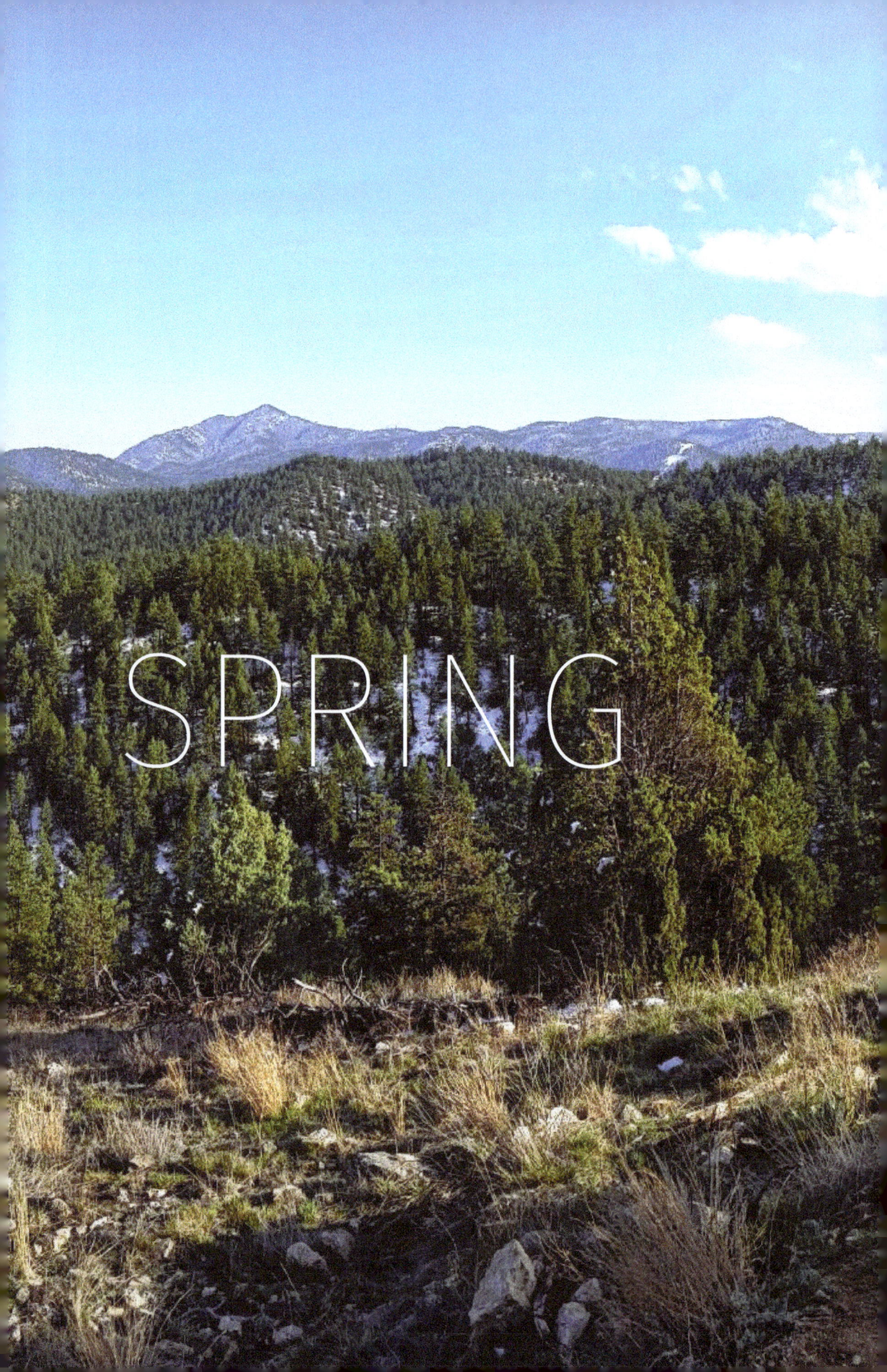

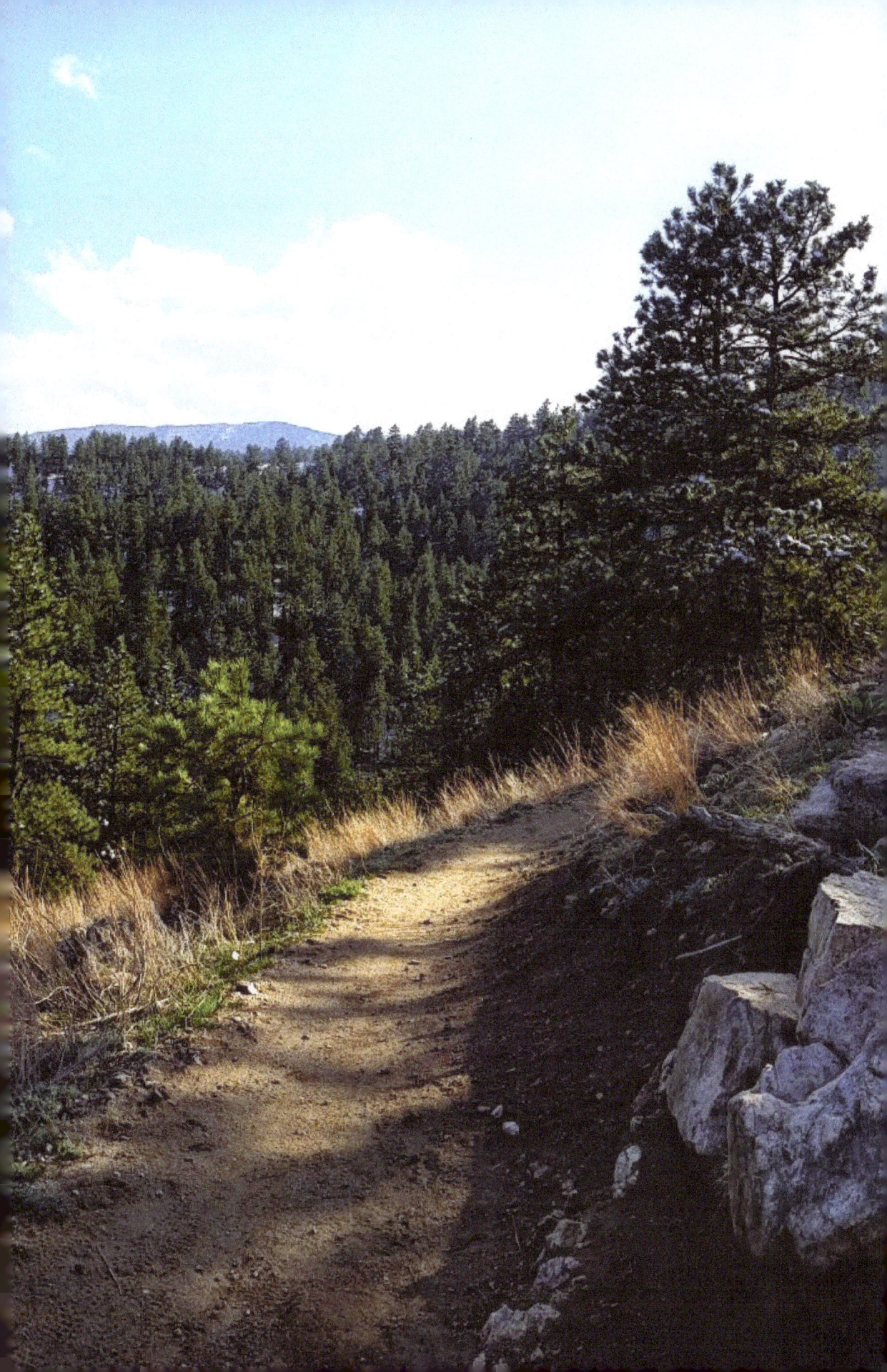

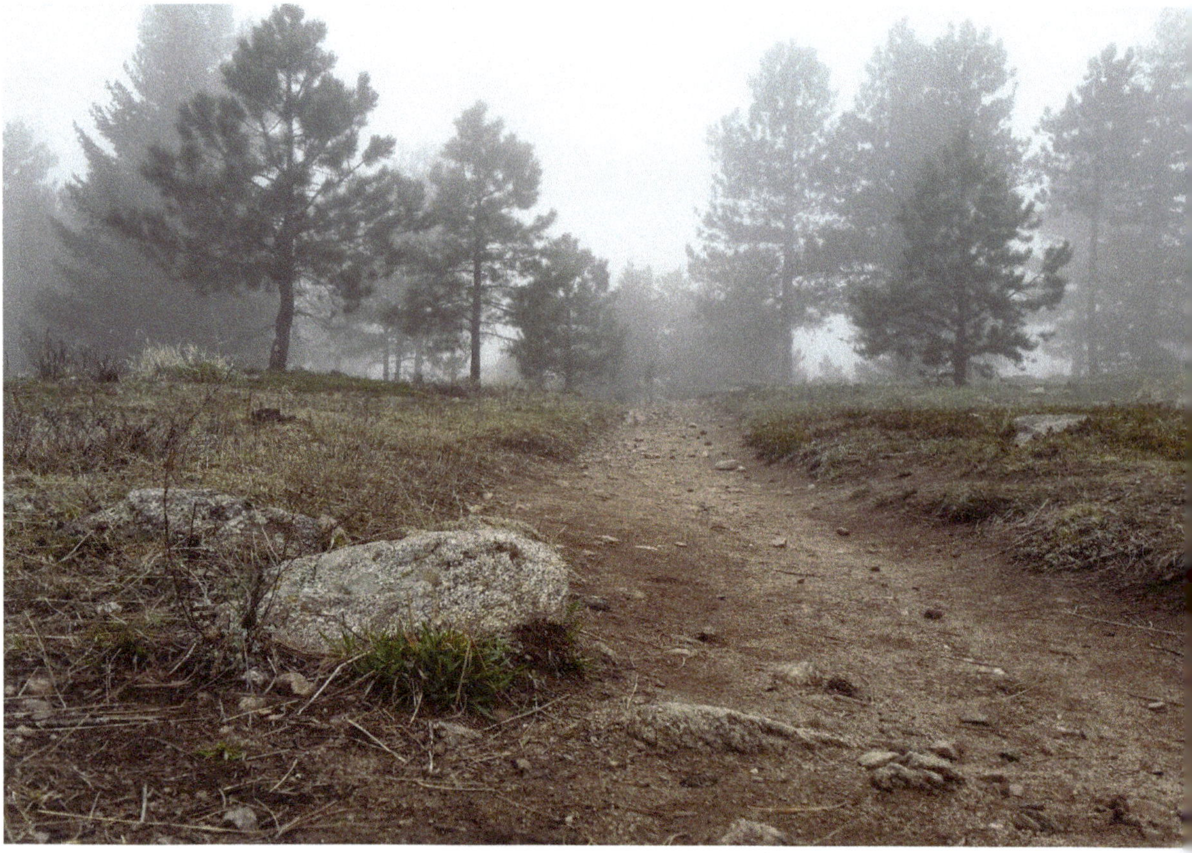

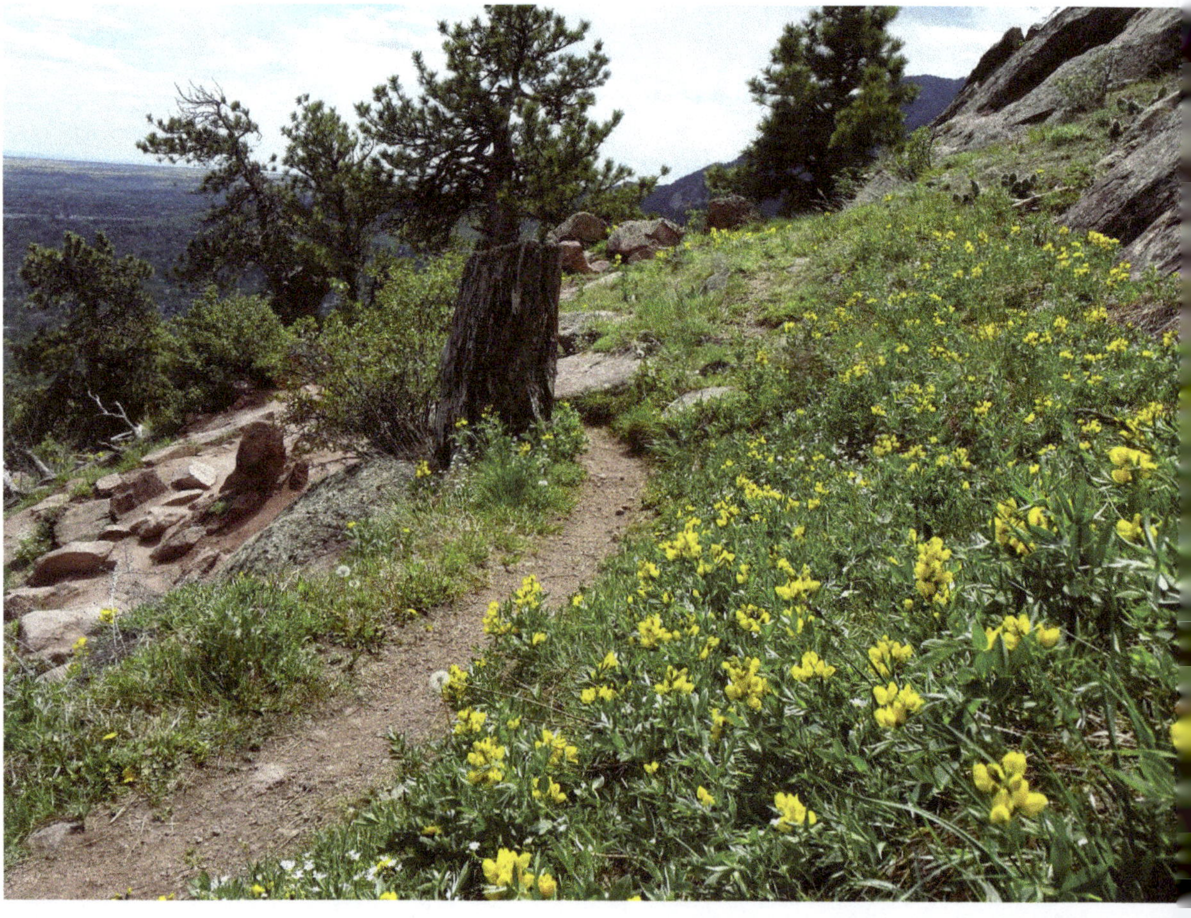

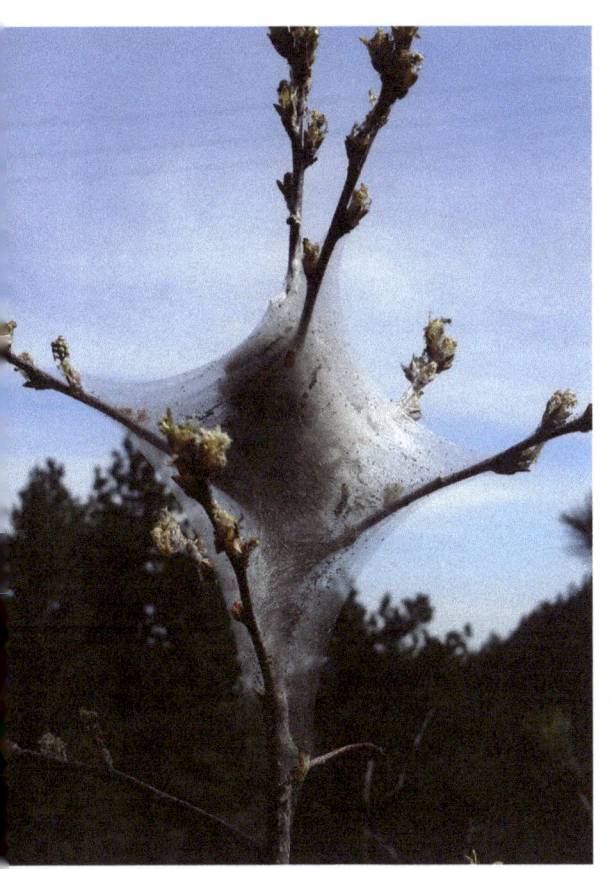
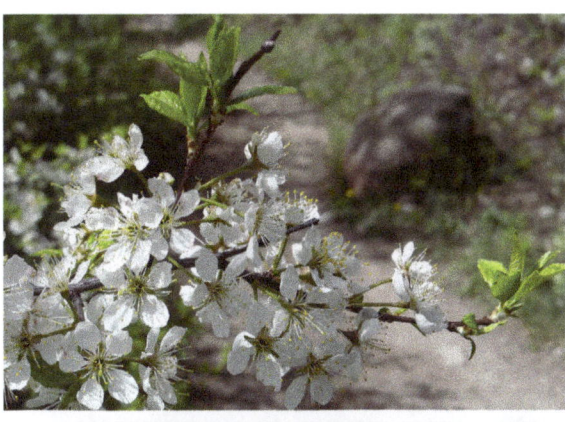
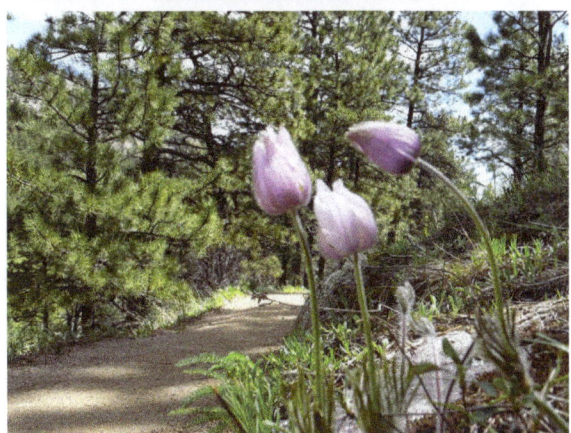

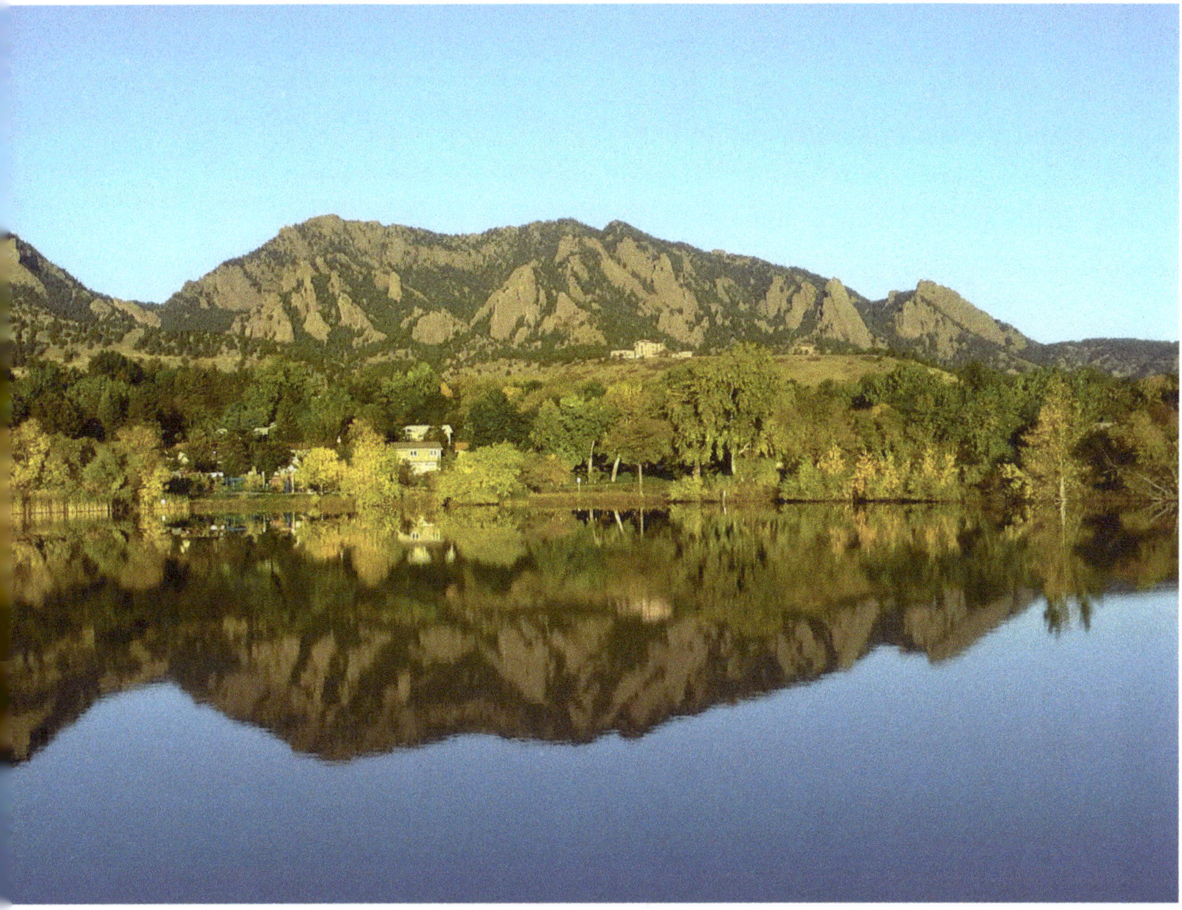

# Imposter, Poser, or A Real Runner?

Words by Amanda McCracken @writermccracken

Here in Boulder we work with and train alongside world class athletes. We have humble friends who have Olympic silver medals tucked away in drawers. We swim in the lane next to the triathlete who just won the Ironman championship. On the climbing wall, we look up at experts who just returned from conquering the Dolomites. When you live with and train among la crème de la crème, it's awfully hard not to develop imposter syndrome — feeling like you don't belong or deserve to call yourself a real runner.

Looks are deceiving here in Boulder. We live in a town where a 45 year old looks like a 35 year old and beats a 21 year old collegiate runner (all while pushing a stroller in a skirt). That 21 year old might feel like an imposter after being beaten by a masters runner until she realizes that runner was a four-time All-American track star.

And at some point this All-American, now middle-of-the-pack, runner begins to question her own legitimacy. How she used to define a real runner (a top ten finish, a sub-3 hour marathon, a sponsorship), something she identified with, no longer applies to her.

The "retired" athlete identity crisis is a very real diagnosis in our community. "Do I just fade away or fall into another category?" a runner recently asked me after claiming that her performance is now on par with participating not competing. Another friend questioned his legitimacy to continue competing. At 47 he worried his 4:50 mile wasn't fast enough. If you once were able to run a sub-18 minute 5k, can you still say you are a "sub-18 minute 5k" runner just as a world record holder can still say they are "world record holder" after it's broken?

My running coach and dear friend Steve Jones set the marathon world record (2:08:05) in Chicago in 1984. A self-proclaimed "journeyman runner", Jones came to the sport with an iron will and very little money in his pockets. His accomplishments in many ways paved the way for the popularity of the sport. However, his comments were recently the target of an on-line debate over what it means to be a real marathoner. In an interview with **Competitor Magazine** editor Brian Metzler, Jones said, *"I don't believe that starting and finishing a marathon makes you a marathoner. I don't believe that. If you're racing it to go as fast as you can, that's completely different than being part of an event and just wanting to get from point A to point B."*

I understood why people were enraged. But I also roughly understood where he was coming from. I say "roughly" because, unlike my coach, I will never come close to setting any world record. Having been both a runner simply happy to complete a marathon and a runner driven to break three hours (which I've yet to do), I too believe there's a difference between racing and participating. And yet, it's not the talent that distinguishes you, but the grit you use to become the best possible XYZ you can be.

**Whether or not someone is enjoying running also defines someone who is a real runner. A boy whose parents forced him to join the cross country team and a girl whose volleyball coach made her run a mile as punishment for being late will never call themselves real runners. There was no delight in the action. There is a great deal of difference between doing and being. Just because I walk doesn't make me a walker nor does eating food make me a foodie.**

It's not about how fast you are, what new records you set (because you've created a new category), how long you can last before your kidneys fail you, or whether or not you wear the newest compression socks and talk about fartleks at breakfast. Do you love the identity because of how it "looks" on you when you wear it? Or do you love the identity because of how its real experiences feel in your body? The tattered Velveteen Rabbit was very real because the little boy loved him based on the experiences they'd shared together.

A writer friend, new to trail running, now frequently posts pictures to twitter of his recent running adventures he's writing about for big magazines. I often curse out loud when I see these posts, "Who does he think he is calling himself a trail runner, when I've been doing it since I was 14?! Where are his knee scars from countless falls?" And then I step off my mountain peak and remind myself nobody really owns the patent on what makes a real trail runner. My judge-bug takes over when I feel his impostrous claim, without much investment, seems unearned. It cheapens my uniqueness, or as my coach says, "It devalues (my identity as a runner)."

We are equally as guilty of feeling the effects of imposter syndrome as spreading the disease. When you complain about having run a 3:30 marathon when your goal was sub three hours or having only run 15 miles instead of the planned 20, don't forget to consider your company—perhaps runners who run 20 miles a week. Our words make them feel like imposters—unworthy of calling themselves runners.

In the end only we are the ones responsible for feeling like our accomplishments are less than what they were because others are now doing the same (just differently). I cast off the inner voice of inadequacy with the help of Eleanor Roosevelt's voice:

## "Nobody can make you inferior without your consent."

When I begin to feel the effects of the imposter-bug (self-doubt, unrealistic expectations, lack of celebration), I remind myself what it might feel like to be running anywhere else in the world where you don't routinely bump into an Olympian in the grocery aisle. I imagine all the people in the world who ask me how long is my marathon, who tell me they only run when chased, and who think the trails I run are for animals. Gaining perspective grants us the grace to validate and respect ourselves and others in our Boulder community for the athletic identities we claim as real.

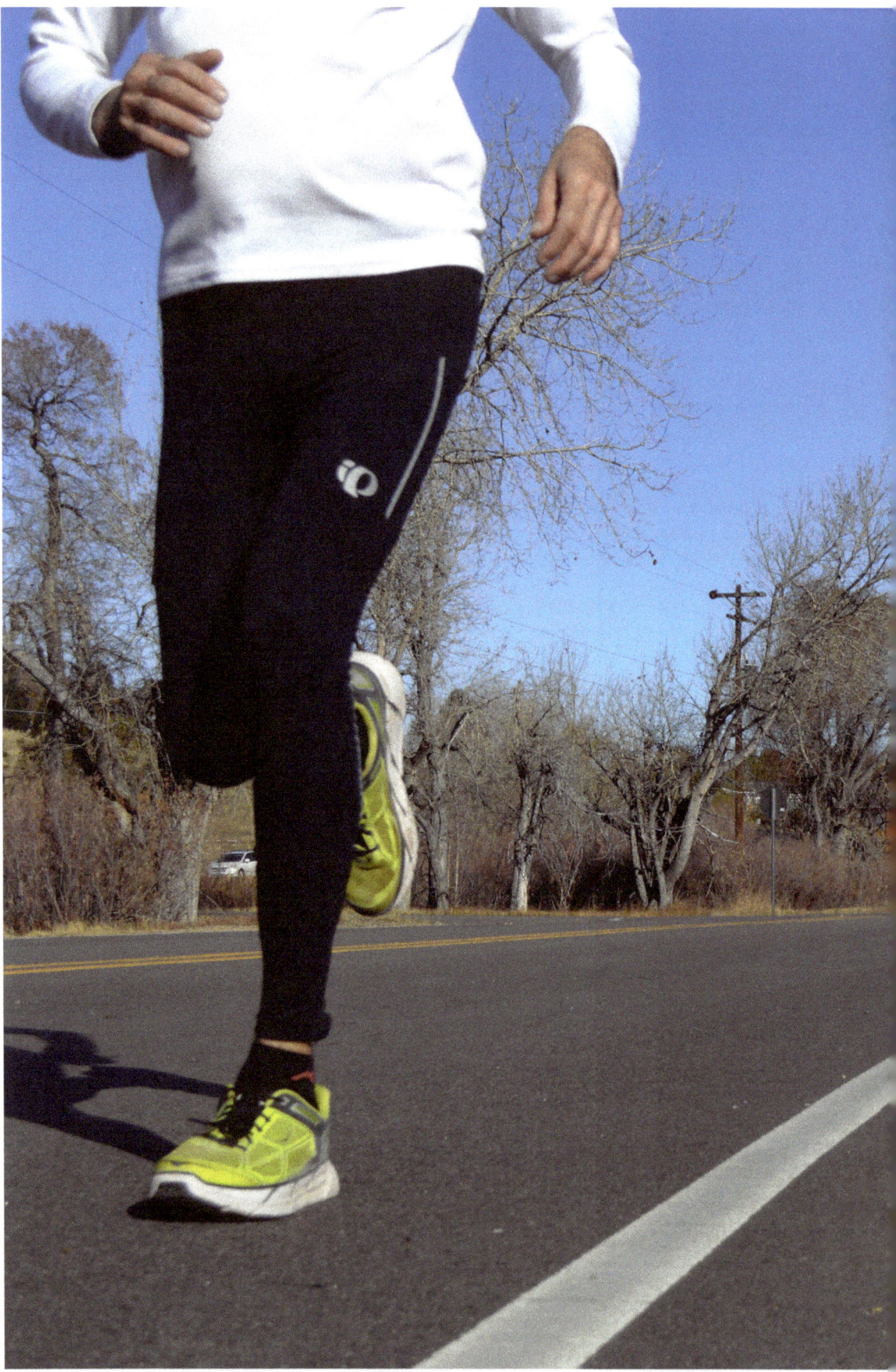

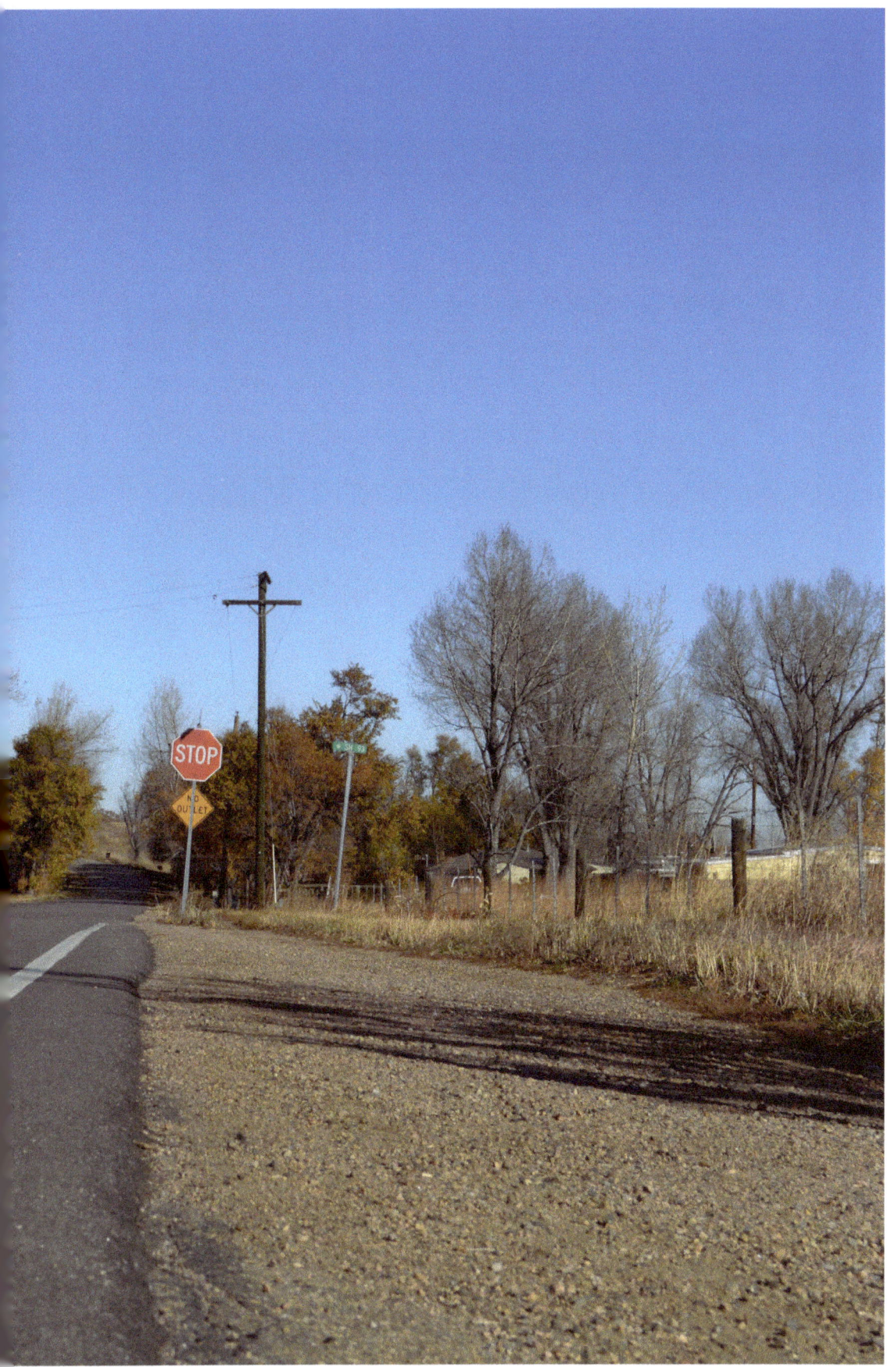

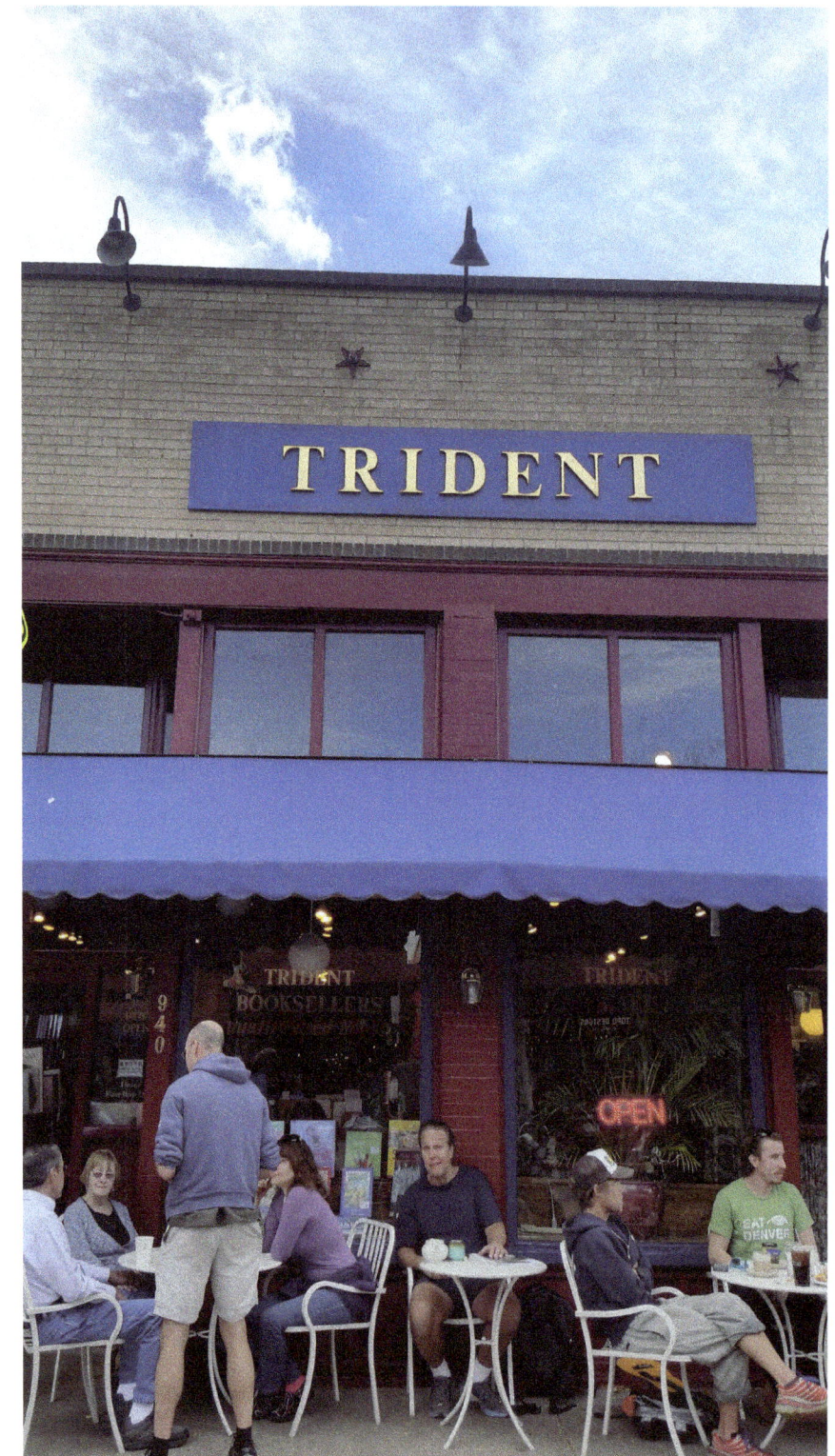

"The Trident is home to a plethora of brilliant minds overdone on caffeine. For the past 35 years I have always found it an ideal place for a good brew and someone guaranteed to provide one party to an offbeat conversation."

—

**Lorraine Moller**

1992 Olympic Marathon bronze medalist; winner of the Boston and Osaka Marathons among her 16 marathon victories; author, "On the Wings of Mercury."

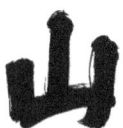

Runners and books go together.
Find them both at the Trident Booksellers and Café.

"Micah has a message of hope; a message of peace; a message of community, of following where your spirit takes you, whatever dream you might have,"

Maria Walton, True's girlfriend and "Run Free" producer

# RUN FREE DEBUTS IN BOULDER

"Run Free – The True Story of Caballo Blanco" is a feature length documentary about Micah True, the ultra runner who called Boulder home and who lived and ran with the Tarahumara Indians of the Copper Canyons in Northern Mexico.

He created a unique 50-mile foot race to help the Tarahumara Indians preserve their running culture and was the inspiration for the best-selling book "Born to Run – A Hidden Tribe, Super Athletes and the Greatest Race the World has Never Seen" by Christopher McDougall.

Filmed over the course of five years, the movie tells the story of this amazing race through the eyes of its founder Micah True and the participants in the race (Mas Loco). Because Micah True died shortly after the race featured in this film, this is the only footage of it's kind in the world, where Micah True tells his own story in his own words. There are other stories from Barefoot Ted, Scott Jurek, Luis Escobar, dozens of Mas Locos and several of Caballo's friends in Boulder, CO.

On hand to tell stories in person were, from left to right, Mike Sandrock, Maria Walton (La Mariposa), Barefoot Ted, the filmmaker - Sterling Noren, and Buzz Burrell who moderated the questions.

Long live the spirit of Caballo Blanco, Boulder remembers and loves you.

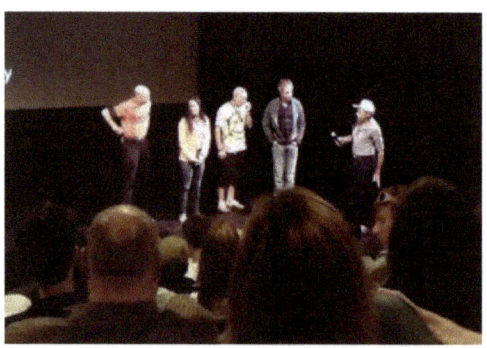

"The film made me feel how loving and caring he was,"

Timmy Olson, Western States 100 Champion.

"As the film shows, Micah was an outstanding human being,"

Anton Krupicka, a two-time Leadville 100 winner who used to see True at the public library in Leadville when both were up there training.

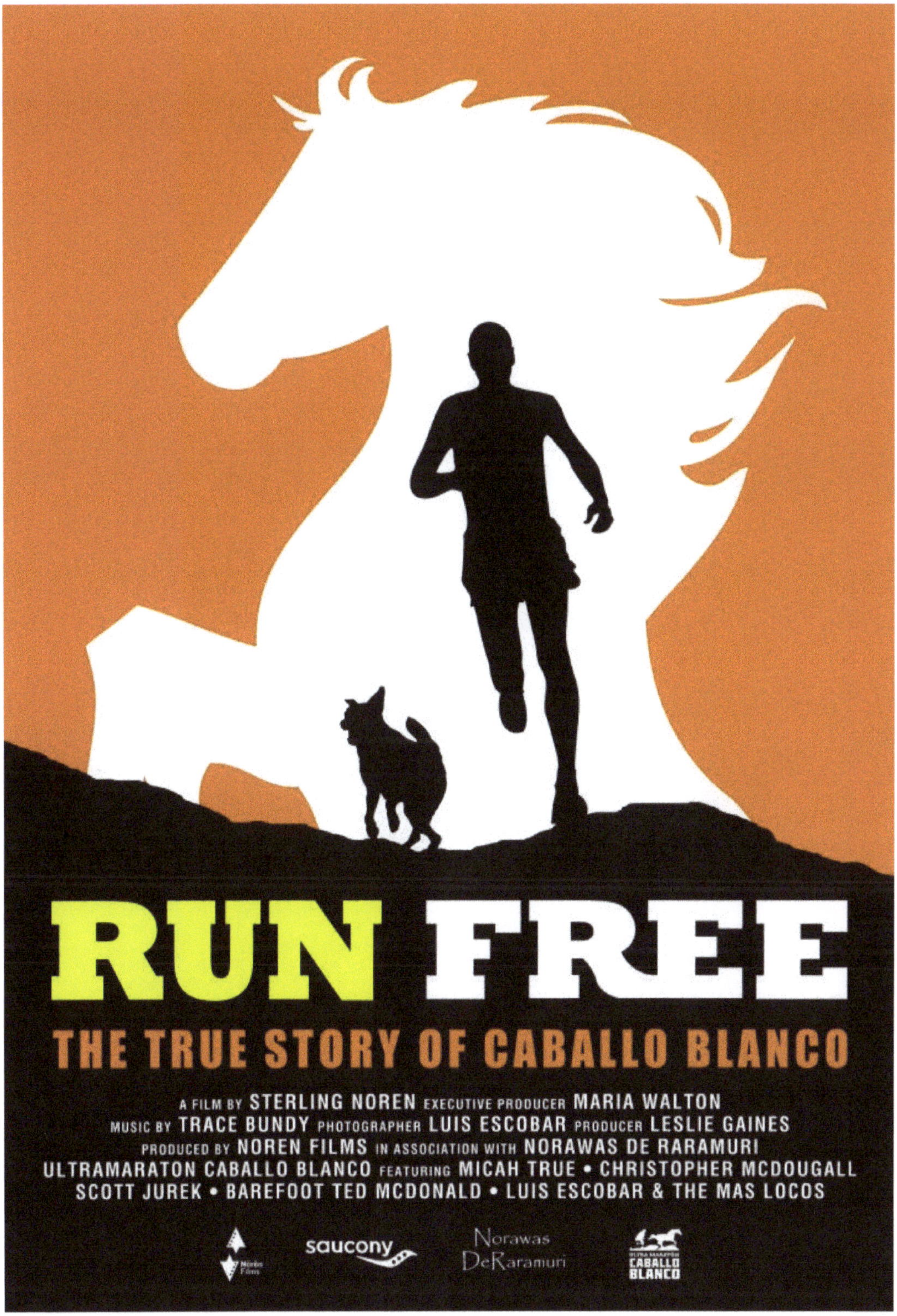

# RUN FREE
## THE TRUE STORY OF CABALLO BLANCO

A FILM BY STERLING NOREN  EXECUTIVE PRODUCER MARIA WALTON
MUSIC BY TRACE BUNDY  PHOTOGRAPHER LUIS ESCOBAR  PRODUCER LESLIE GAINES
PRODUCED BY NOREN FILMS IN ASSOCIATION WITH NORAWAS DE RARAMURI
ULTRAMARATON CABALLO BLANCO FEATURING MICAH TRUE • CHRISTOPHER MCDOUGALL
SCOTT JUREK • BAREFOOT TED MCDONALD • LUIS ESCOBAR & THE MAS LOCOS

 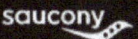 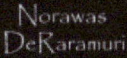

# DUZER DOES COPPER CANYON

Words and photos by Ryan Van Duzer

### A badge of honor

Colorful Caballo Blanco posters proudly adorn the walls and doors of just about every business in Urique and surrounding towns in the Copper Canyon. Ultra Maratón Caballo Blanco is a huge deal for the local economy and equally important for the Tarahumaran runners, who all receive corn vouchers for participating.

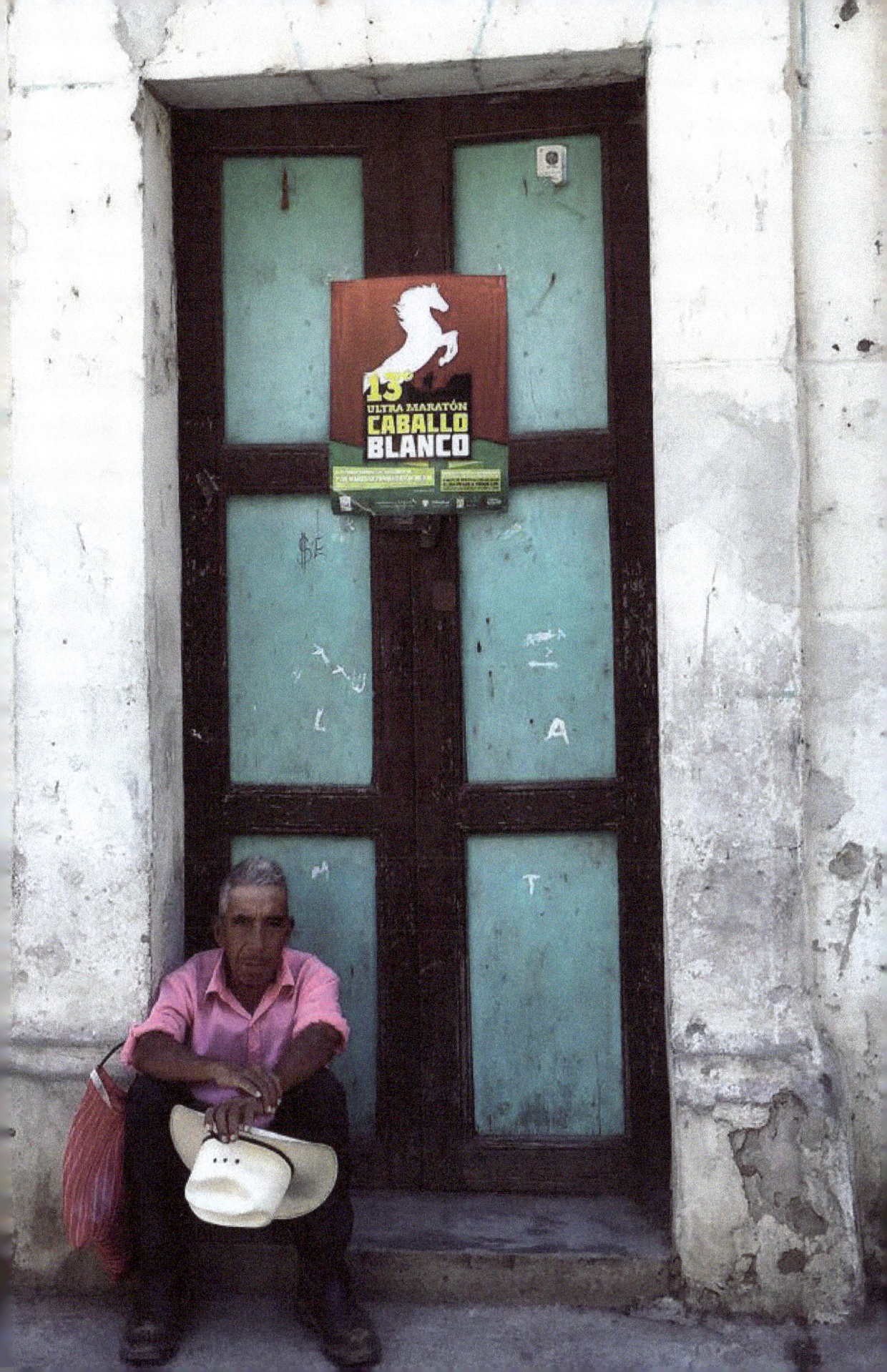

I read the book
"Born to Run"
and was inspired
to travel down to Mexico
and give this race a shot.
I love a good adventure
and the hidden canyons
in Northern Mexico really
spoke to me.

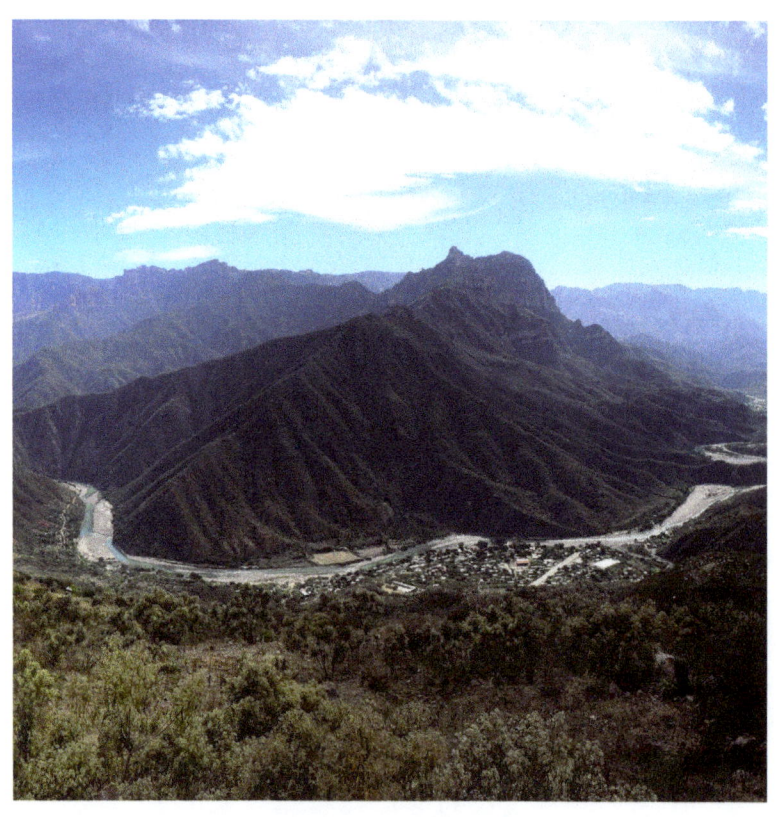

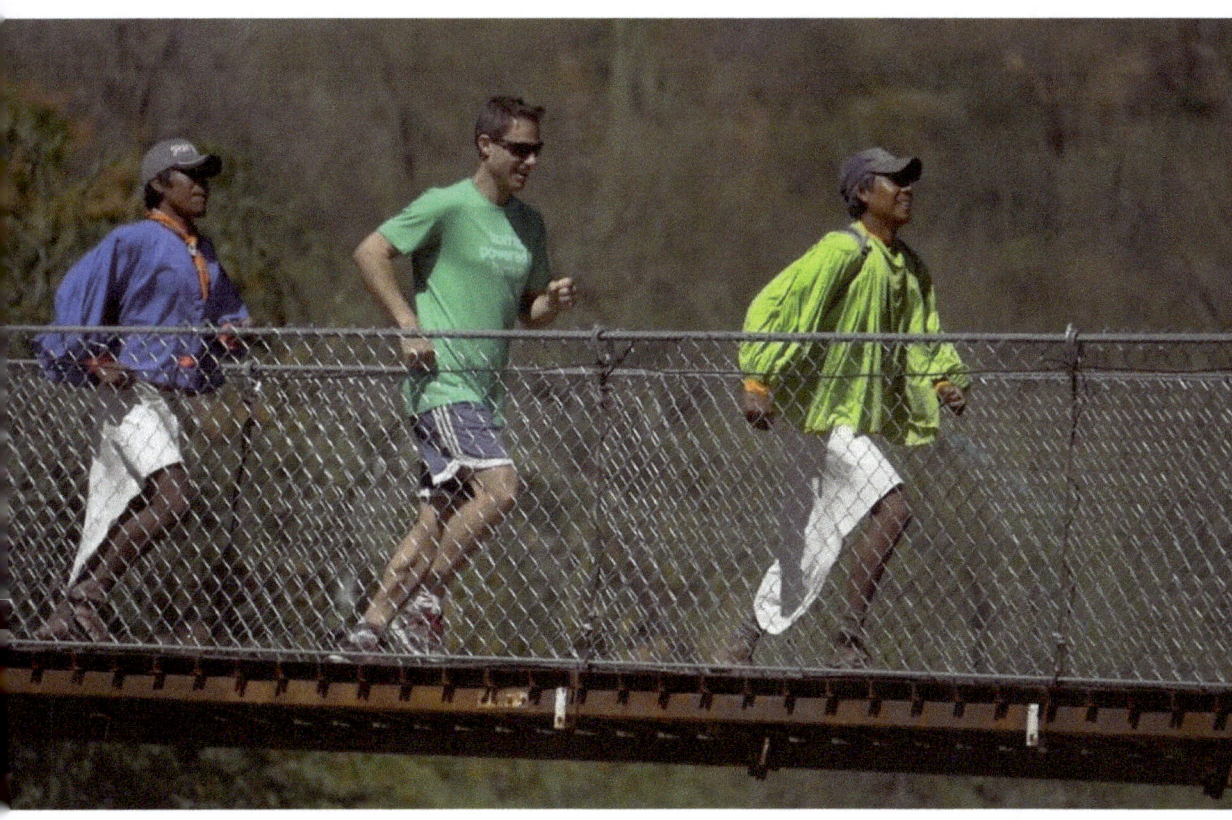

I thought it would be fun to take buses all the way there, making it more of a journey. I started right outside my doorstep on the SKIP and with my friends Larkin, Sarai and my brother Ethan, we made it all the way down to Urique,

48 hours later.

The canyons were just as beautiful as the book described, rugged and awe inspiring! We met people from all over the world who had also read the book and been inspired to run. It was such a fun community of people. The days leading up to the race were filled with practice runs and social time. Urique seemed like such a peaceful place.

Things changed the evening before the race. The organizers called everyone together to the town square and told us that the race was canceled, that narcos had come into town, kidnapped two police officers and murdered one. They said that there were gun battles in small villages along the course and it was not safe.

We were all heartbroken, but understood. Caballo wanted this race to be a beacon of light, of hope and of peace. The circumstances this year simply weren't in line with his vision, so Maria, his girlfriend, called it off. I respected their decision but was very sad, mostly because these people live with this violence all the time.

We gringos simply got on a bus and left town.

—

Editor's Note: *Currently it remains uncertain whether the race will be run again or not. Narcos continue using the Copper Canyon area for drug running. Until it is safe again, the race will not occur.*

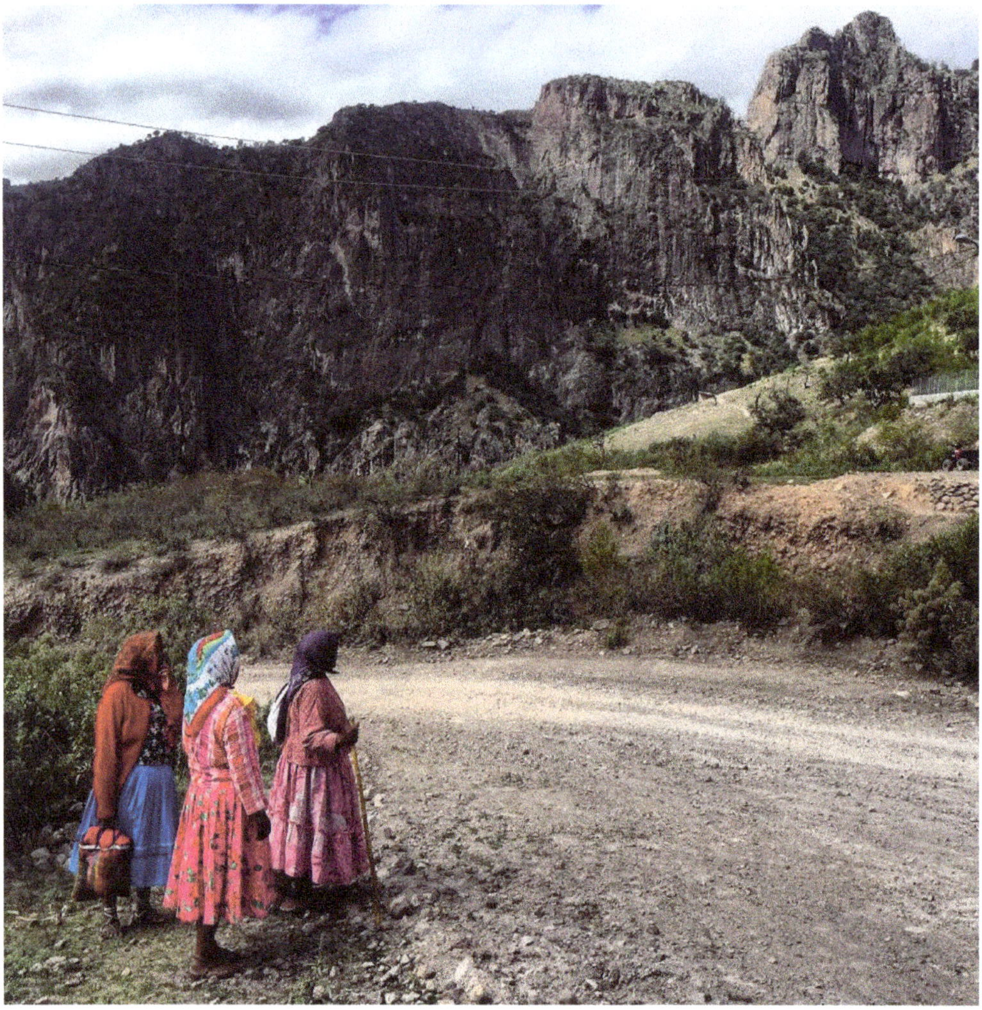

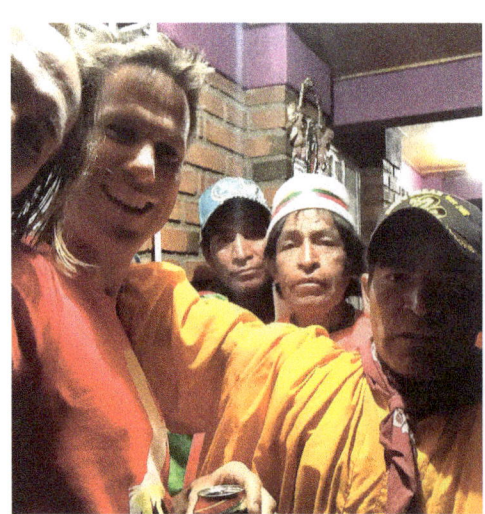
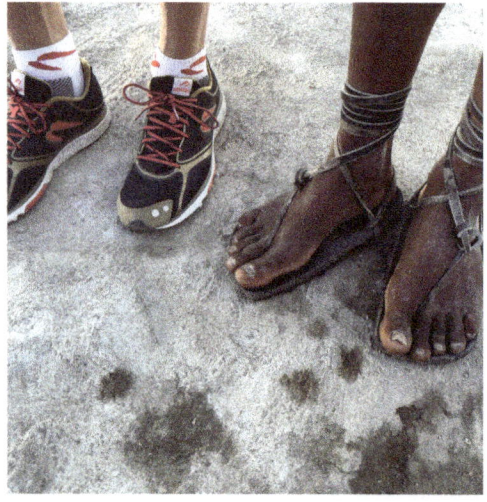

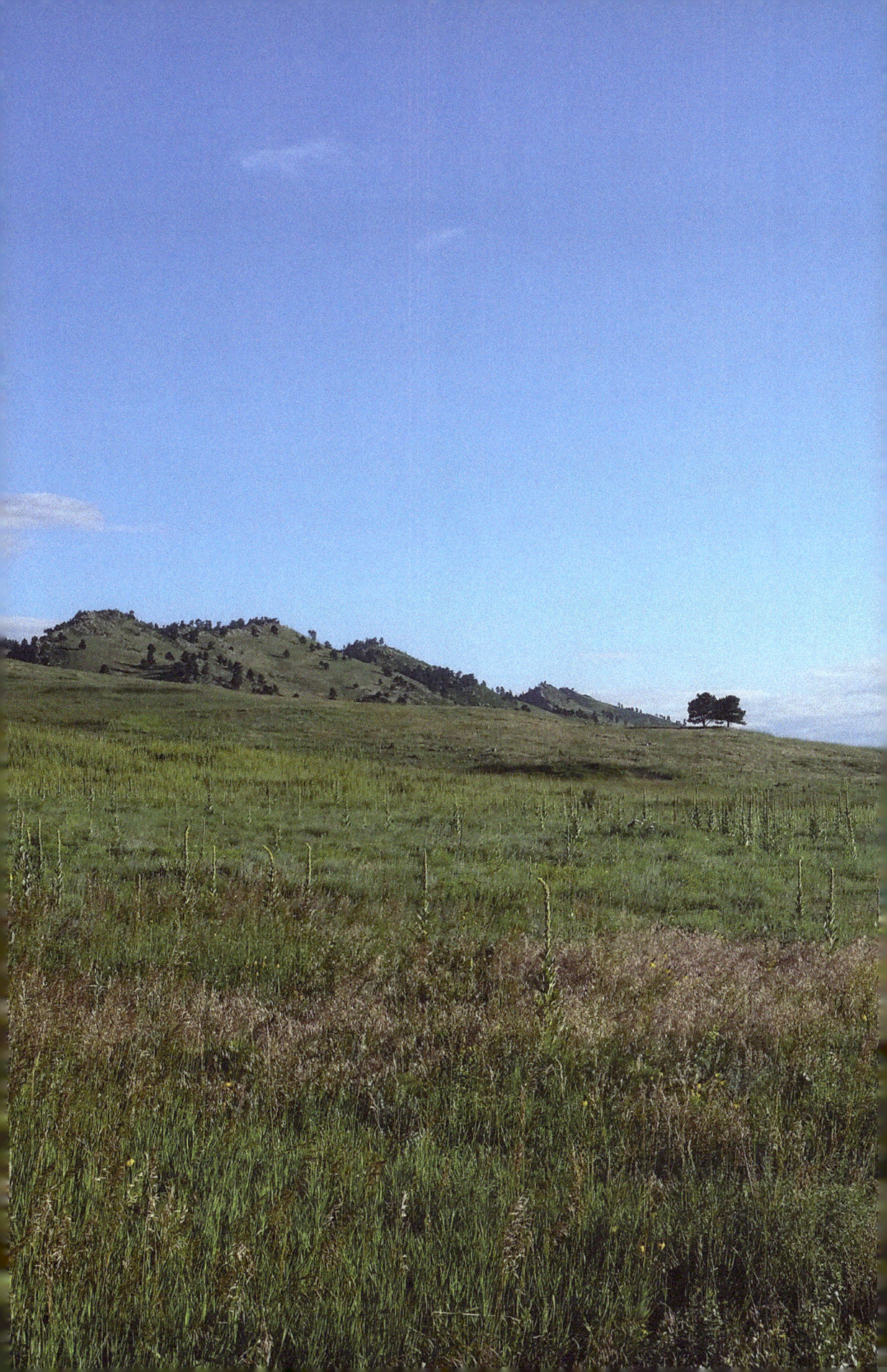

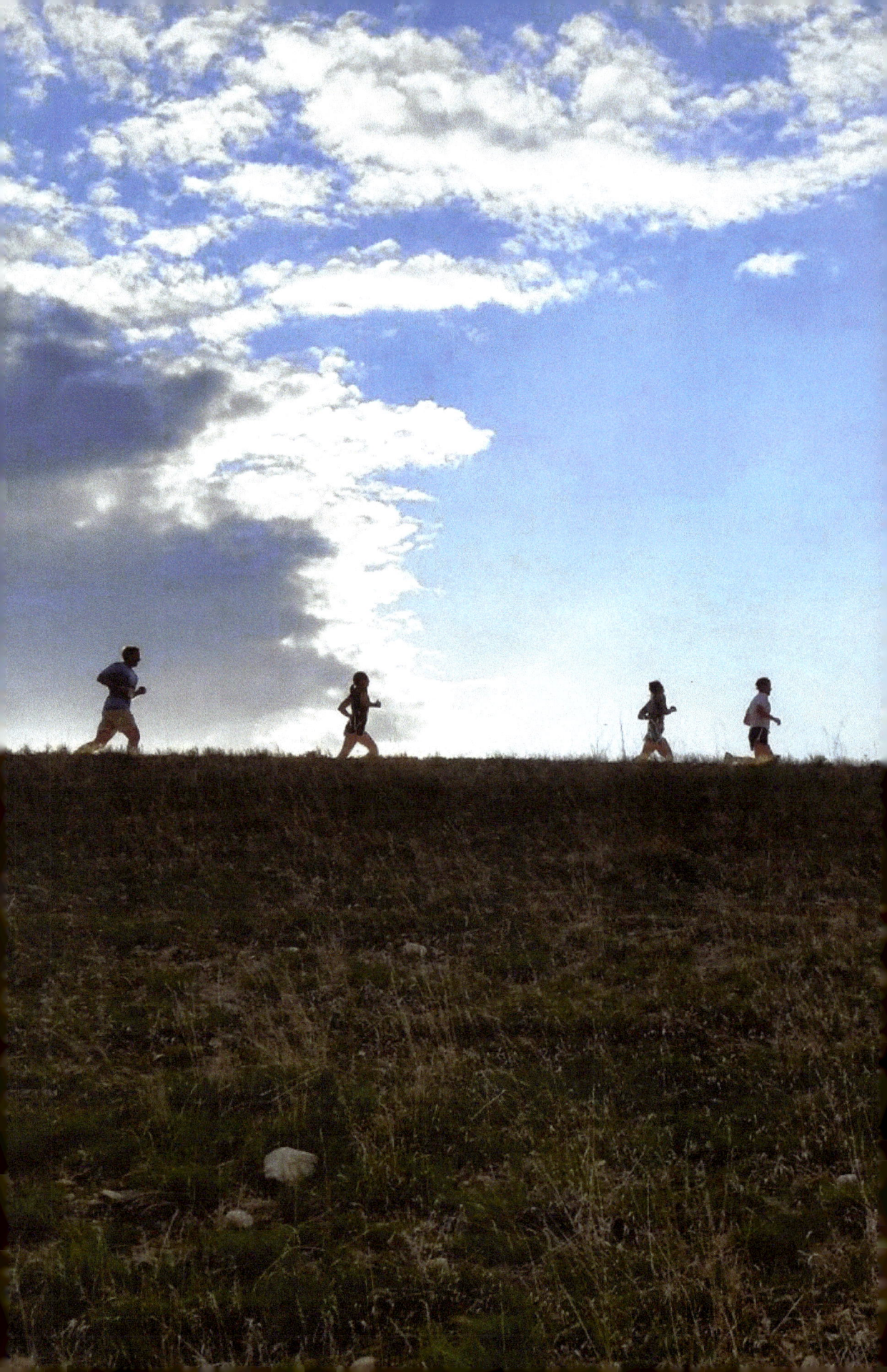

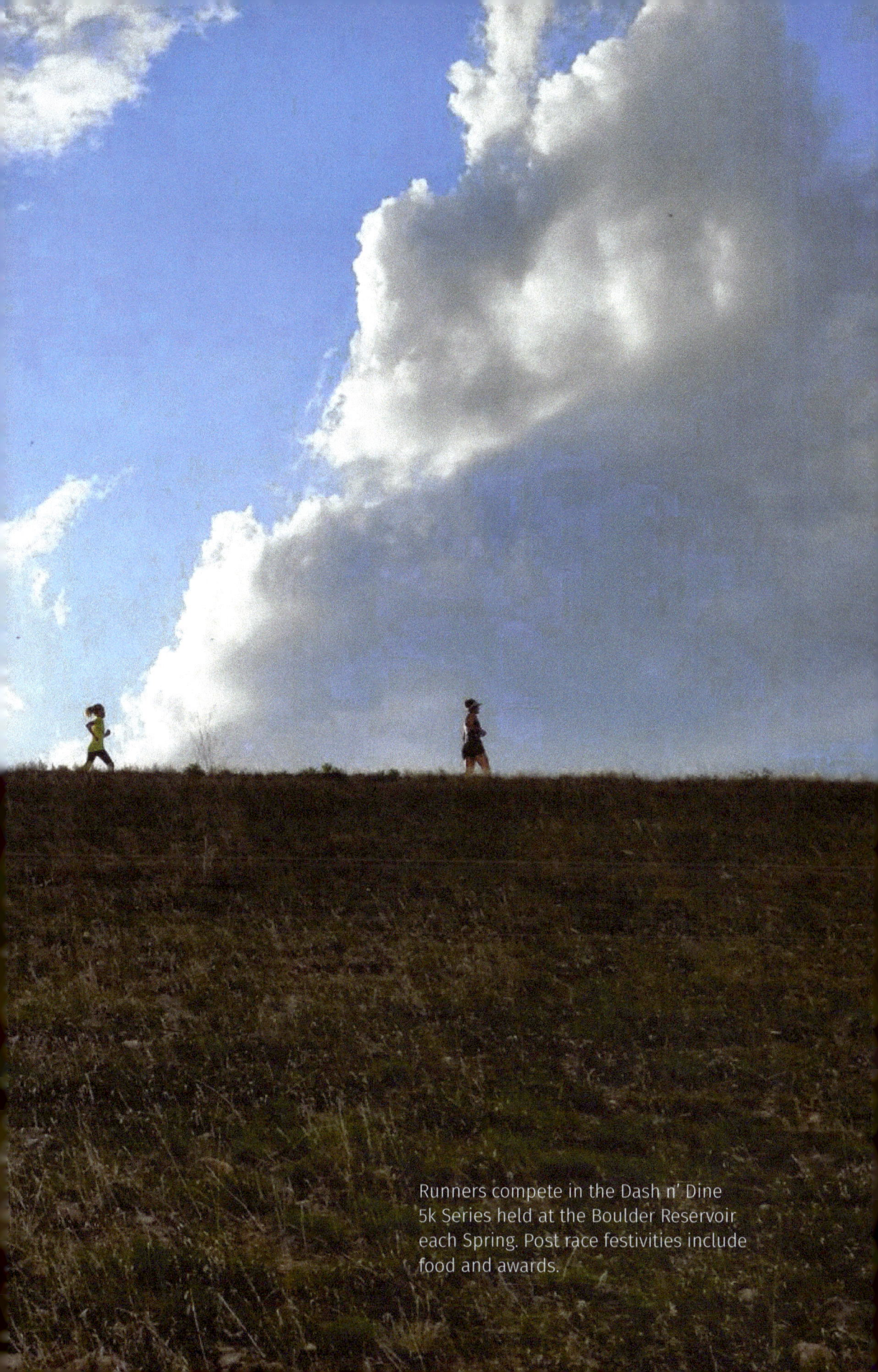

Runners compete in the Dash n' Dine 5k Series held at the Boulder Reservoir each Spring. Post race festivities include food and awards.

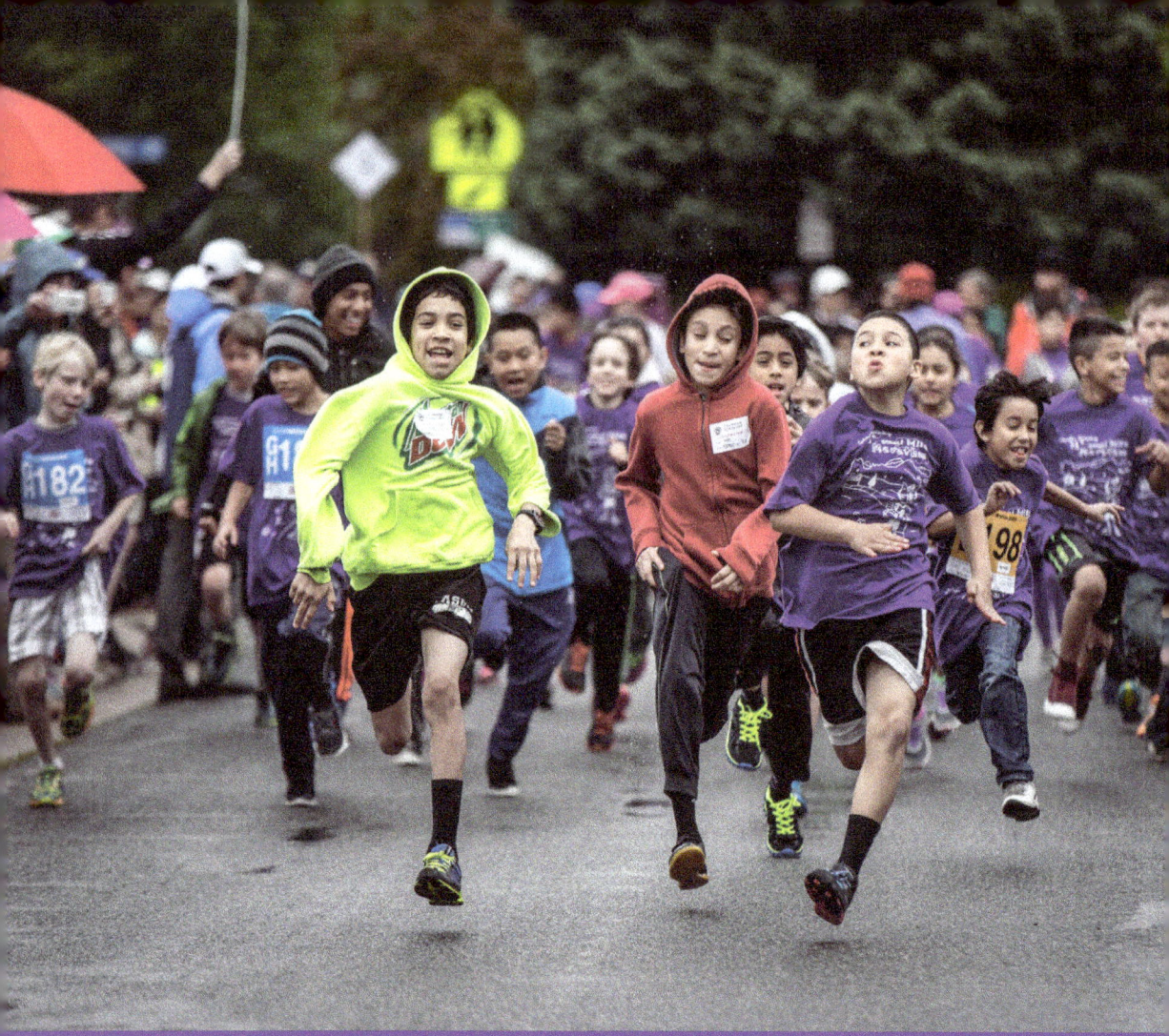

# THE COLUMBINE MILE MARATHON

Photos by Glen Delman

In its 30th year, the Columbine Mile Marathon is a tradition for grade schoolers to get ready for the Bolder Boulder. Despite damp weather, the kids were out to have fun. Supported by local recognizable runners from age groupers to Olympians, they truly felt the spirit of the sport.

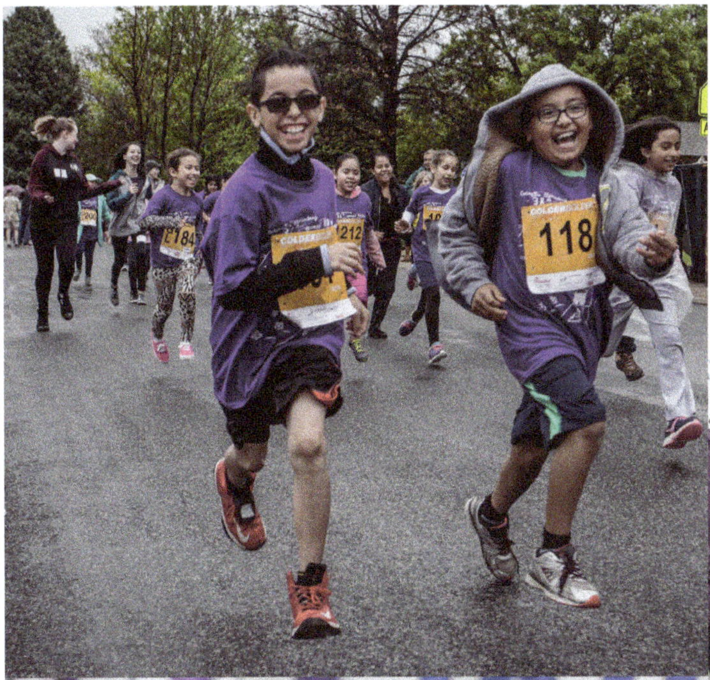

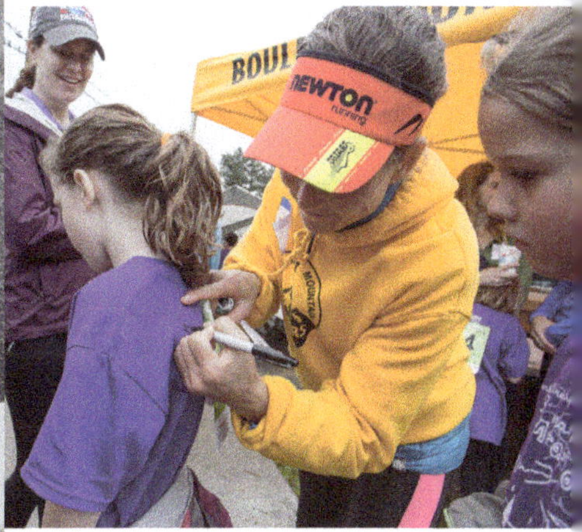

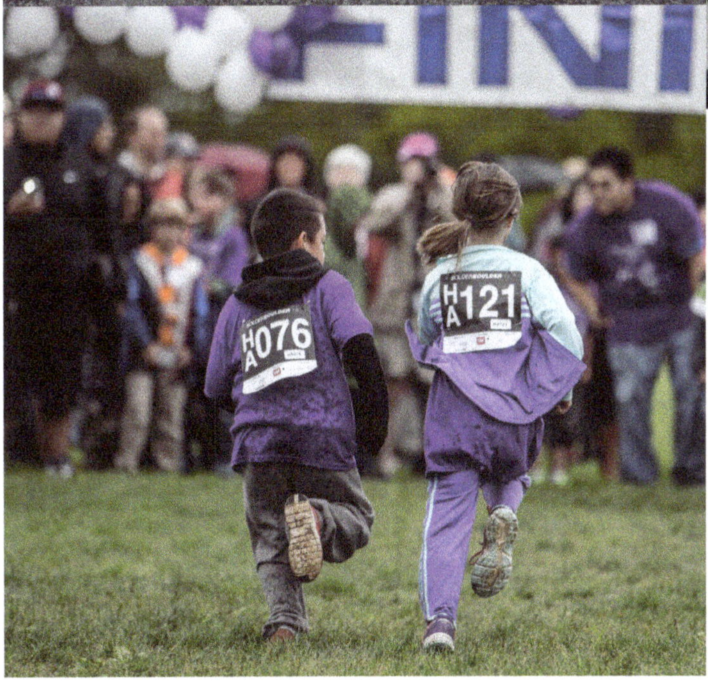

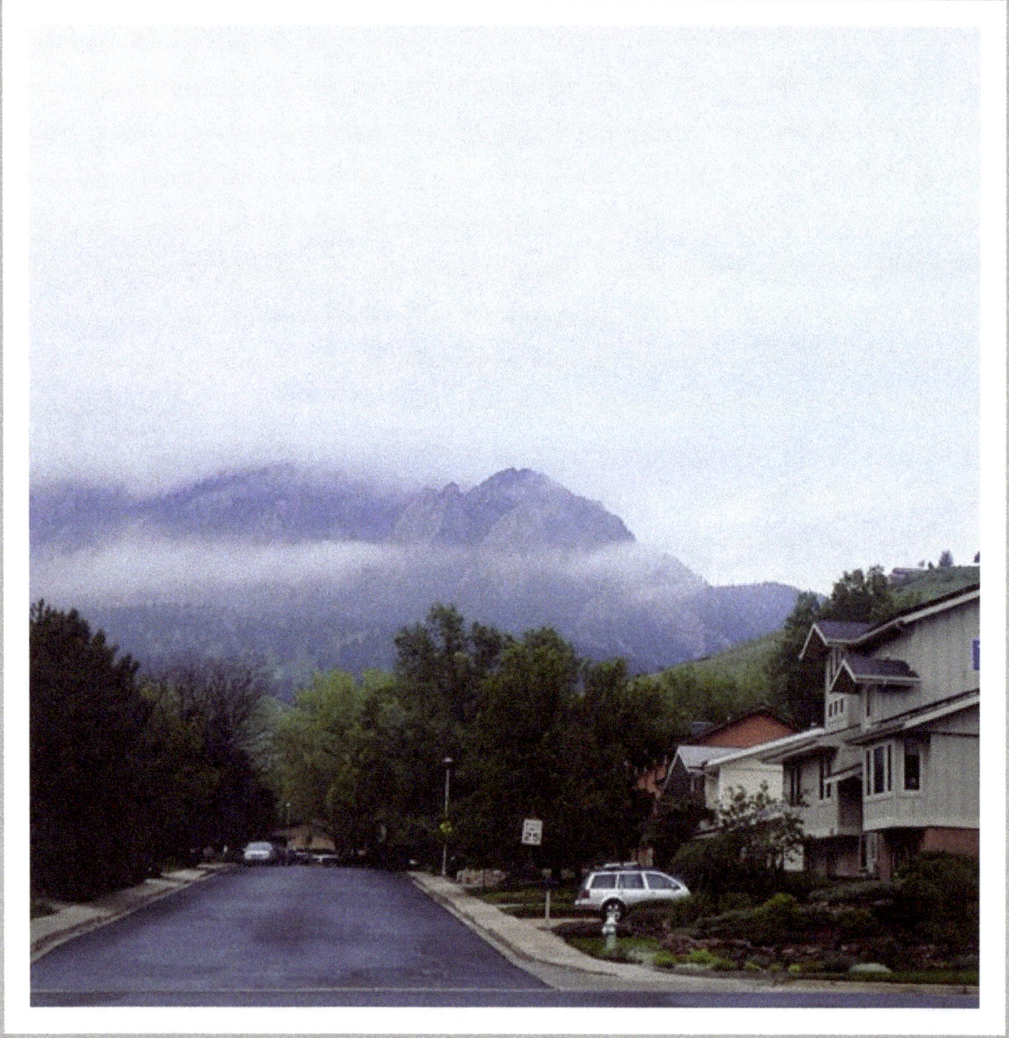

**May 23** @davemackd
Sigh. Heading to the 8500' office. 7 days a week. Tough job. Someone's gotta do it.

On an unusually misty May morning, highly accomplished trail runner Dave Mackey set out to run up Bear Peak from his home as he had done over a thousand times before.

What happened on that run — massive leg injuries and a dramatic rescue after a rock gave way under his feet near the summit of Bear Peak — made it anything but routine.

Dave spent 3 weeks in the hospital, endured 12 surgeries, and bone grafting. Now, six months later the light at the end of the once dismal tunnel is growing stronger. As he talked about in a recent slide show about his experience at the Marathon de Sables at Flatirons Running, he is now riding his bike, swimming and occasionally going on hikes with friends and family on his crutches. Jokingly he mentioned that he may have to go after some "low hanging fruit" in regards to FKTs on crutches. His spirits remain as high as his outlook on life.

*"If I ever get to run again it will be even that much more special."*

The thing about Dave is how he carries himself. He's one of the best all-around athletes in Boulder—and has been for years—but he doesn't make it a point to glorify his own greatness or draw attention to himself. His humility and understatedness are as much a part of who he is as his trail running, rock climbing and mountain biking abilities. His priority in life seems to be being a good guy first—a good husband, father and friend—and being a gnarly mountain endurance athlete a distant second. - Brian Metzler

# MACKEY STRONG

**June 7** @davemackd

This photo now takes on completely different meaning to me than when I took it May 23rd. Felt so good then going out for the morning run, to the place that had much power and magic to me, right out the door. Don't know how many times I've been up there, every time fantastic. Ran across my favorite shortcut trail to Mesa, over and up to Shadow canyon, South Boulder to Bear Peak. Then I misstepped, and my world has completely suddenly changed. I really shouldn't be intact or even alive perhaps.

Thank you so much for words of encouragement, visits, jokes and the good gallows humor over this: if you saw where I am right now it really is quite Medieval and laughable in this ICU room. What I am going through though is nothing compared to millions of people's lives every day. Some friends have told me of their struggles and accidents which helps immensely. Thank you again to Ellen, close friends and my kids for pulling me through. Don't take for granted what you have, value it.

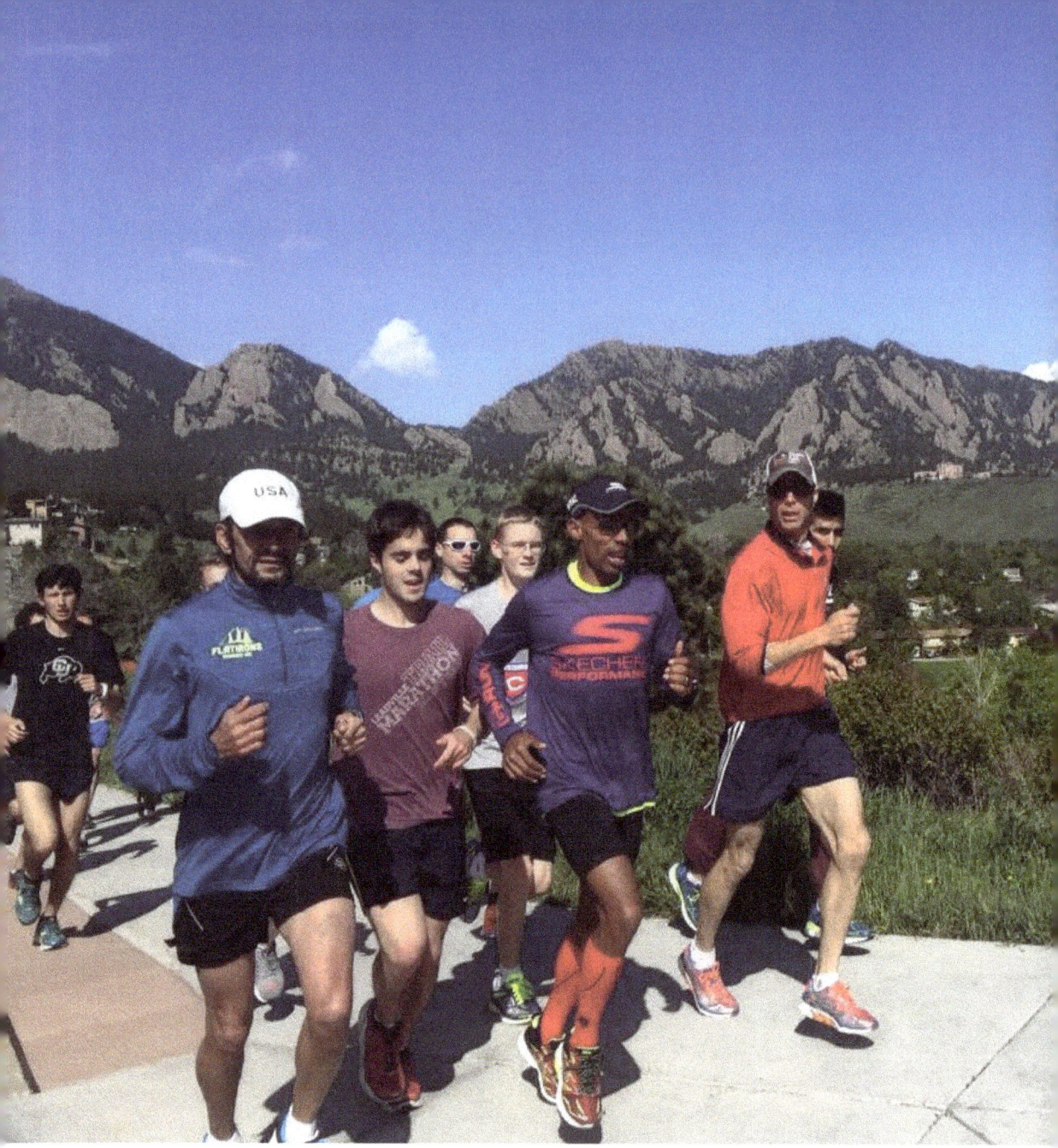

Bolder Boulder shake out run with Olympian Meb Keflezighi.

Photo courtesy of Flatirons Running

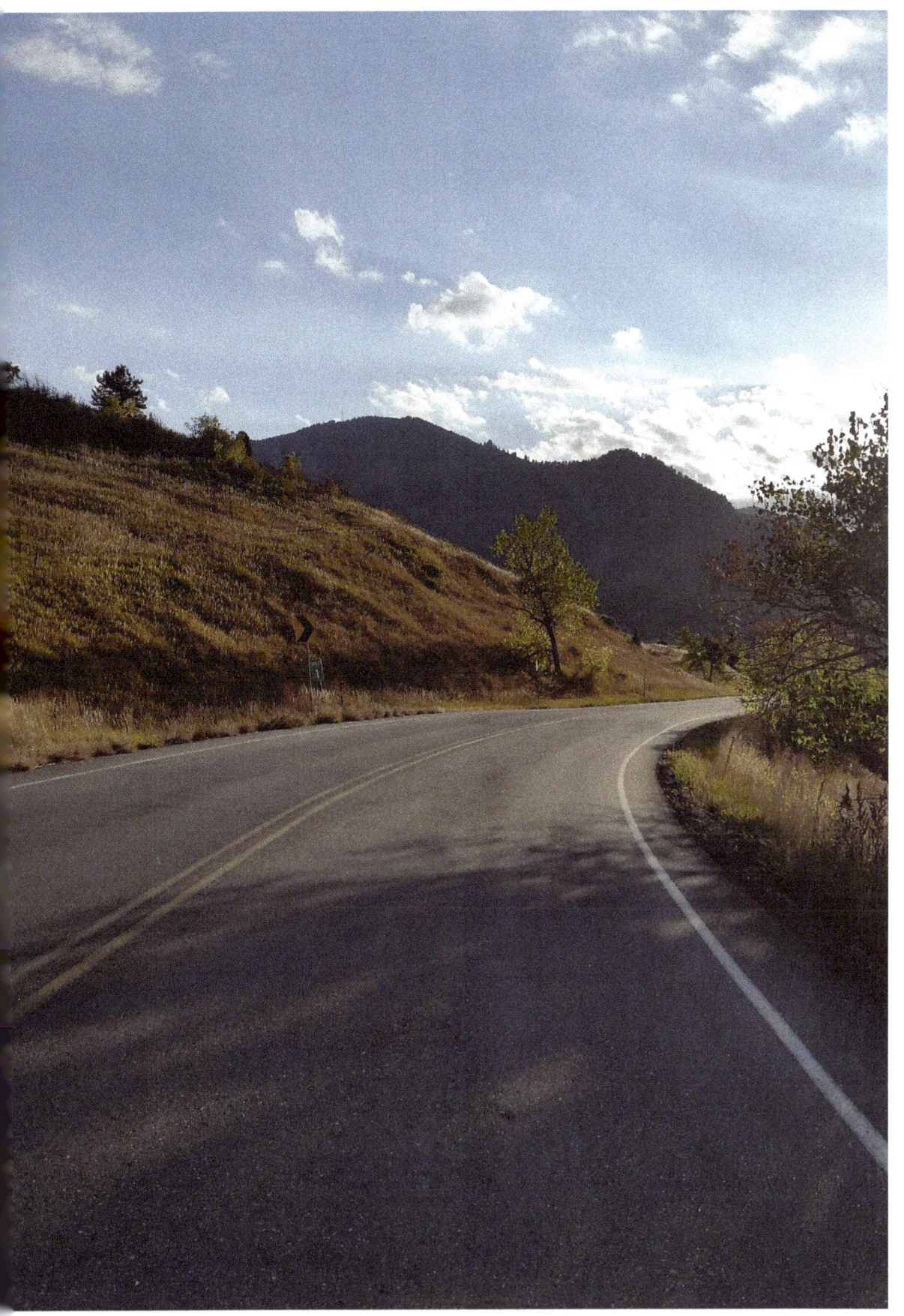

# BE BOLD

We believe running with 50,000 of your closest friends, may be the best way celebrate Memorial Day.

Photos by Glen Delman and Dave Albo

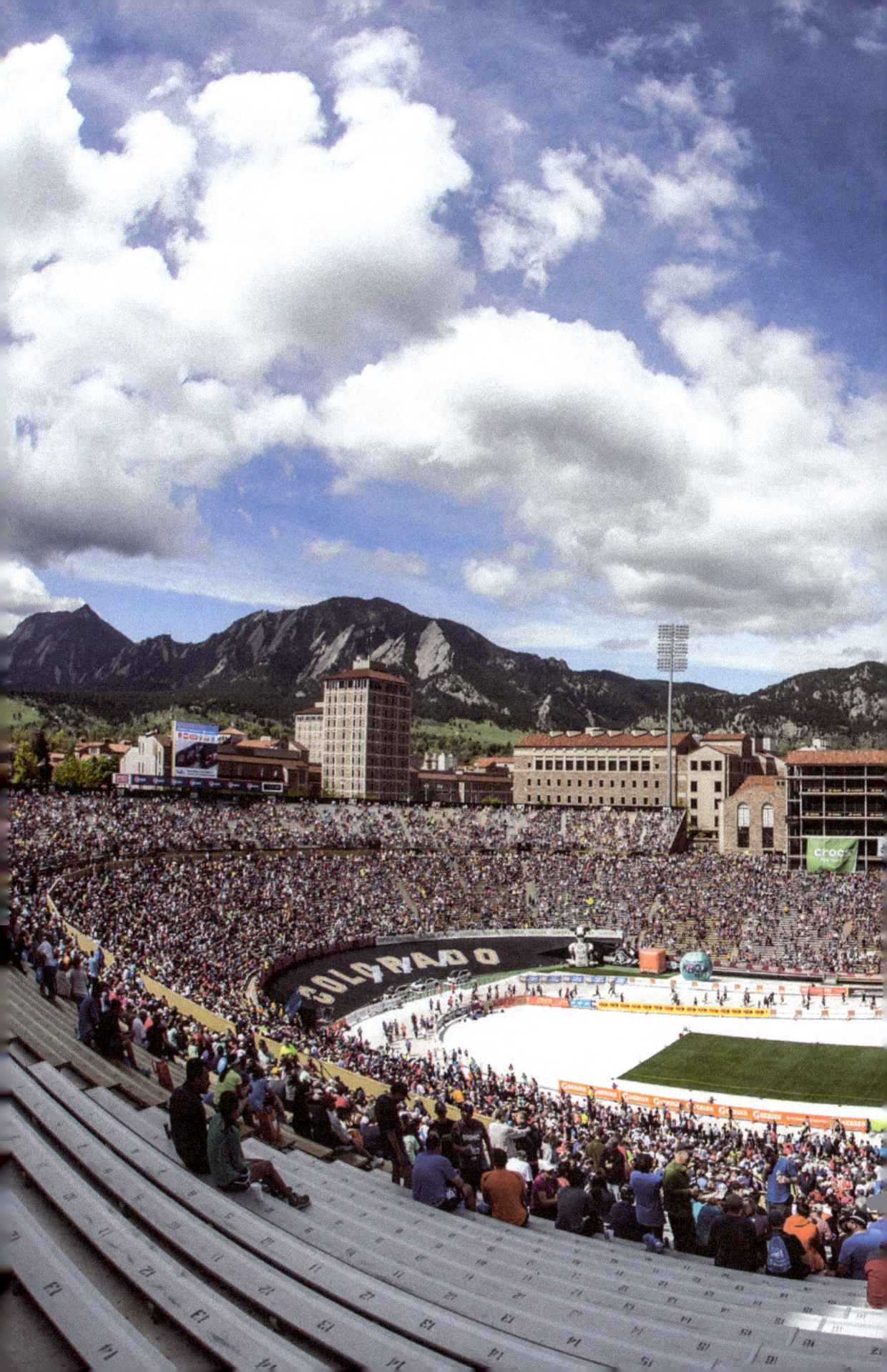

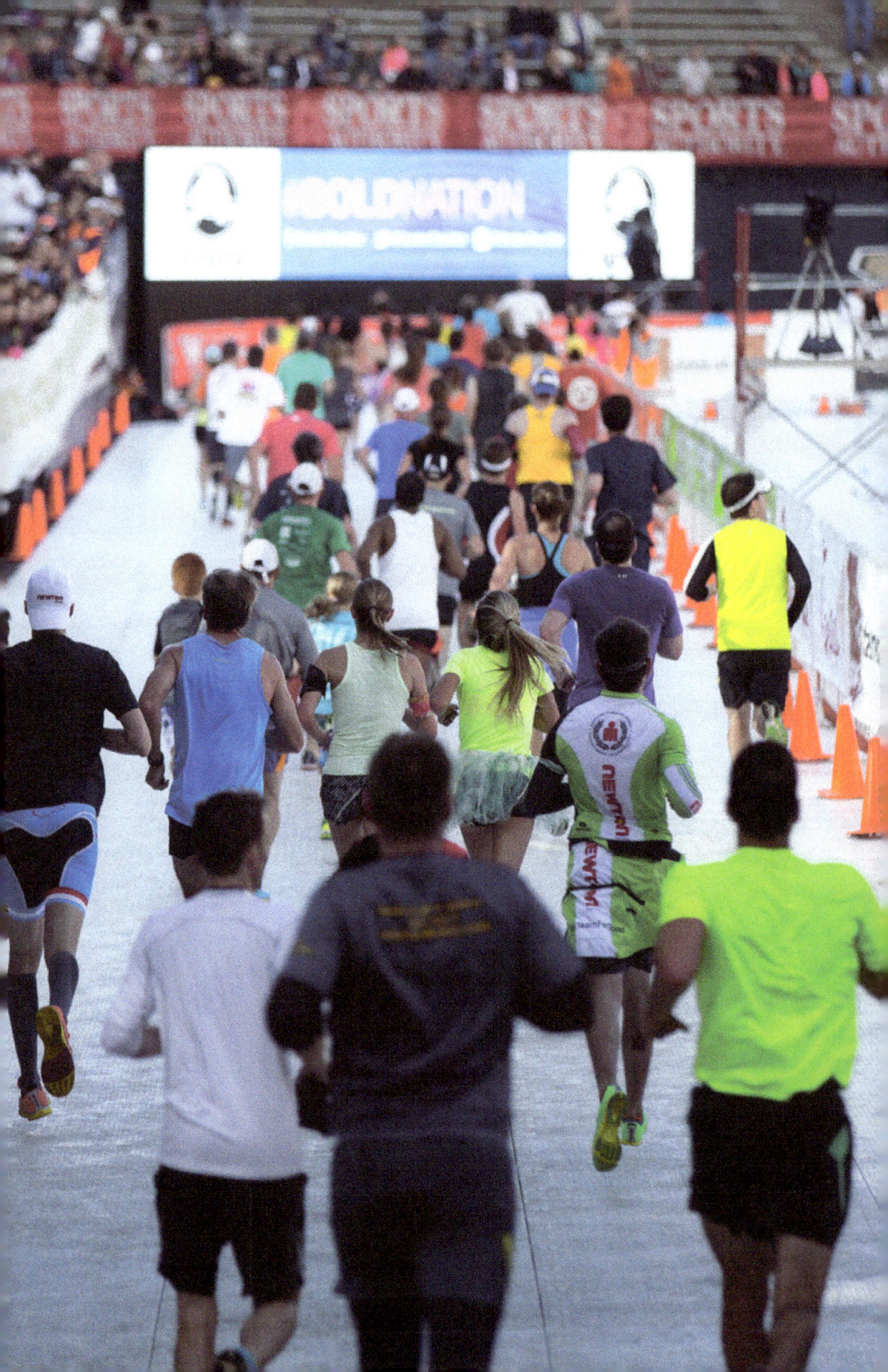

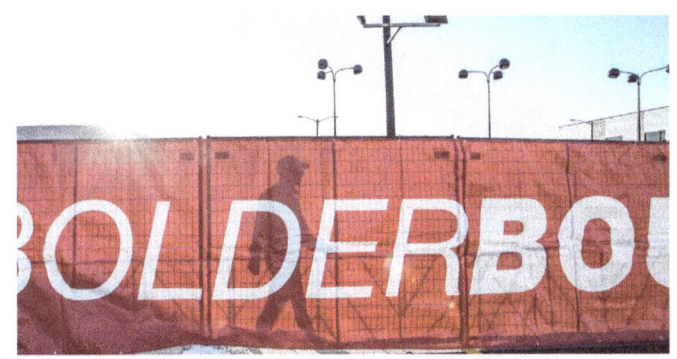

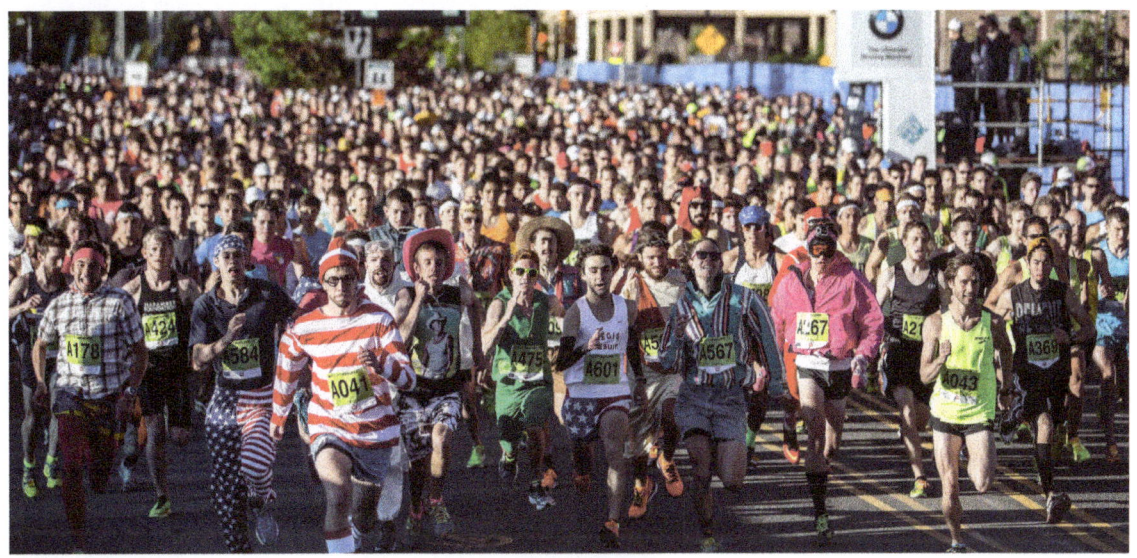

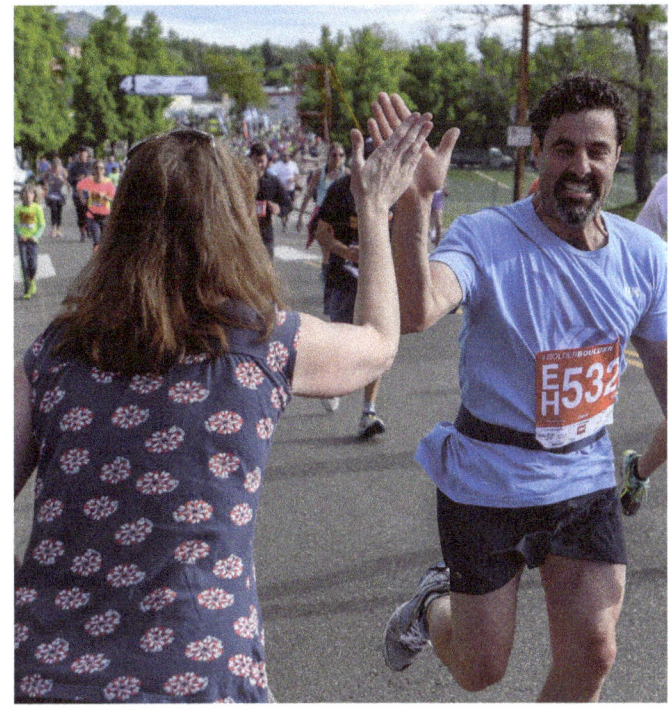

Slip n' Slide,
cupcakes,
a trampoline,
belly dancers,
Elvis, a drum circle.

Sounds like a party.
No, Bolder Boulder.

@saragiboney

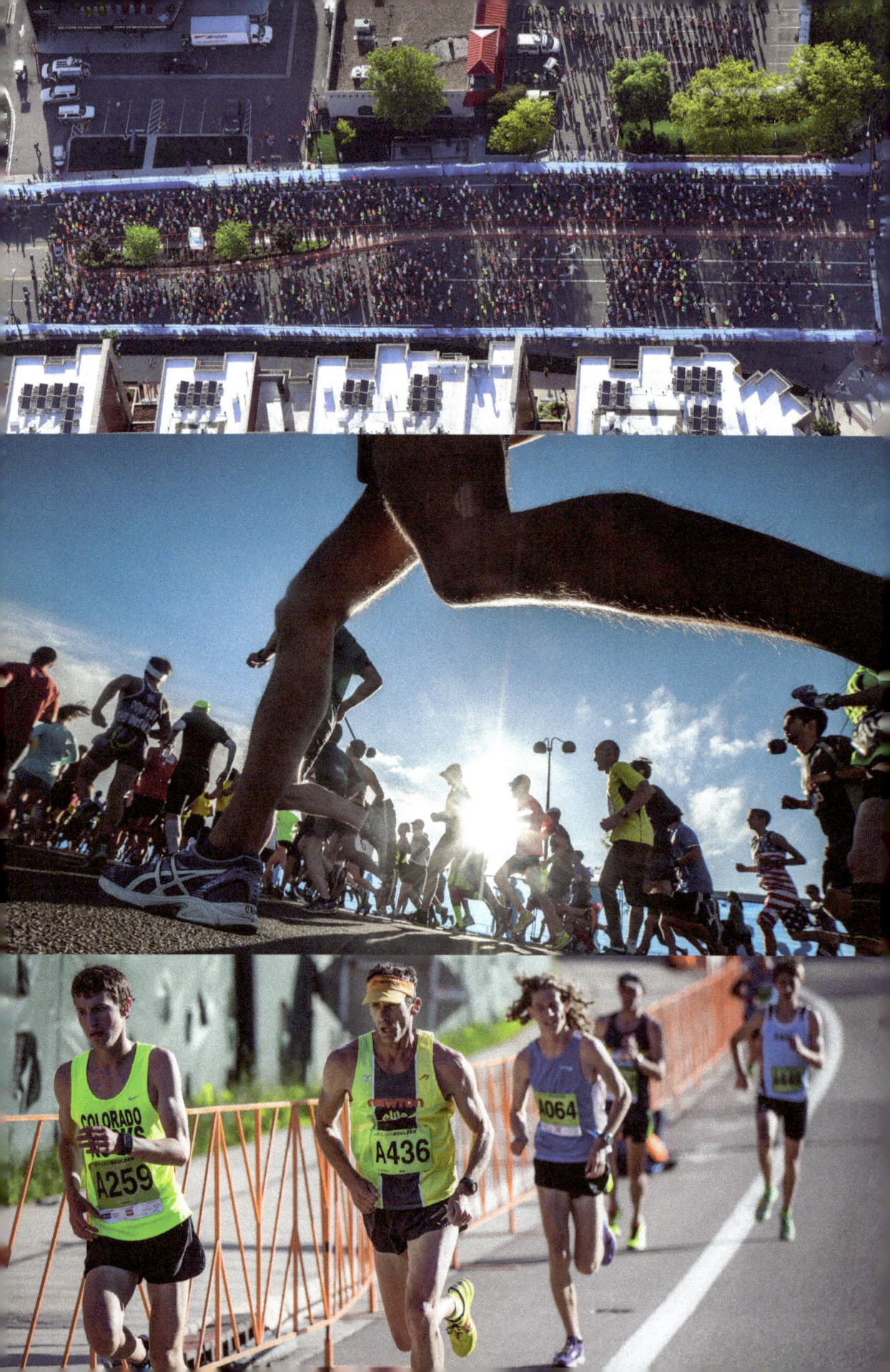

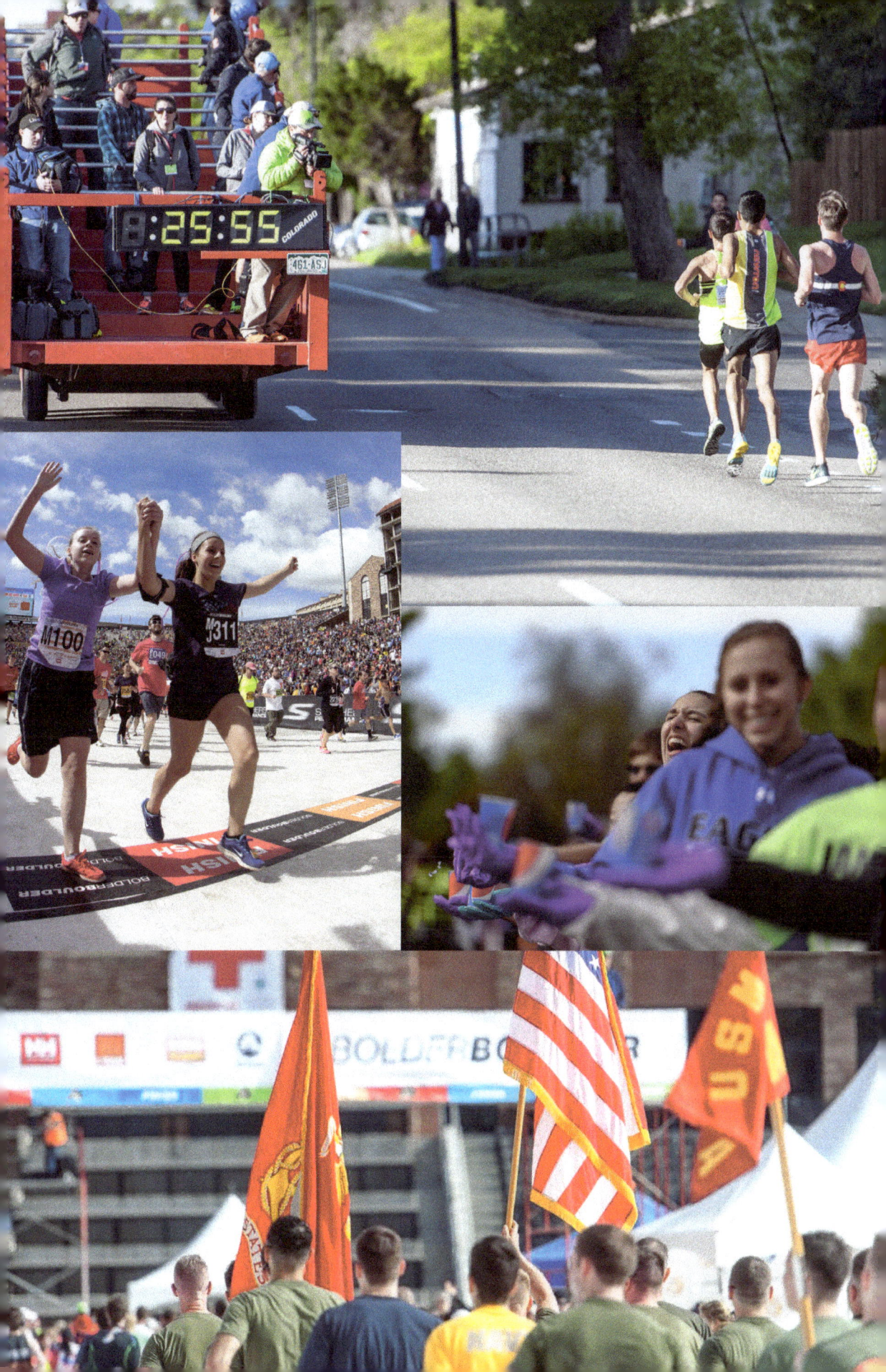

# AGE CHAMPS

Celebrating the everyday athlete, the BolderBoulder is the only race in the nation to recognize the top winners in each age bracket. Not age group, but age. Here are your 2015 Age Champions. Each is awarded a **Leader of the Pack** technical tee.

| Age | Name | Time | Name | Time | Age | Name | Time | Name | Time |
|---|---|---|---|---|---|---|---|---|---|
| 6 | Maxwell Wu | 1:01:44 | MacKenzie McIntosh | 56:34 | 50 | Bob Weiner | 33:59 | Shannon Teslow | 44:39 |
| 7 | Logan Coughlin | 47:25 | Anna Cobb | **50:35 *** | 51 | Peter Tel | 37:18 | Colleen De Reuck | **37:56 *** |
| 8 | Keegan Geldean | 44:35 | Teah Roberts | 55:45 | 52 | Andy Ames | 35:47 | Mary Alico | 41:25 |
| 9 | Evan Armstrong | 43:34 | Madison Shults | 51:30 | 53 | Thomas Kehoe | 38:21 | Terri Cassel | 43:42 |
| 10 | Bradley Troyer | 42:02 | Bryanna Hoffman | **41:14 *** | 54 | David Litoff | 36:03 | Laura Bruess | 42:45 |
| 11 | Dylan McIntosh | 43:39 | Alayna Szuch | **39:00 *** | 55 | Dan King | 36:37 | Nina Caron | **41:32 *** |
| 12 | Michael Dudzic | 39:00 | Sydney Thorvaldson | 41:22 | 56 | Jay Survil | 39:06 | Delcia Litt | **40:57 *** |
| 13 | James Gregory | 35:14 | Riley Geldean | 39:47 | 57 | Paul Hughes | 39:51 | Patti Galleher | **44:09 *** |
| 14 | Tyler Scholl | 35:58 | Isabella Heart | 41:22 | 58 | Kyle Hubbart | 38:23 | Ann Campbell | 48:29 |
| 15 | Blake Davis | 35:06 | Lauren Gregory | 37:50 | 59 | Dan Spale | 37:45 | Susan Schulte | 48:15 |
| 16 | Cameron Dimas | 34:45 | Jenna McCaffrey | 40:16 | 60 | Martin Lascelles | 41:53 | Martha Staten | 52:25 |
| 17 | Paul Roberts | 32:22 | Erin Thomas | 40:03 | 61 | Rich Sandoval | 43:38 | Mary Ann Moseley | 45:55 |
| 18 | Marcelo Laguera | 33:28 | Isabelle Kennedy | 40:25 | 62 | Heath Hibbard | 41:03 | Mary E Black | 52:20 |
| 19 | Chris Erwin | 33:02 | Hannah Driscoll | 41:49 | 63 | Roger Allen | 47:19 | Carla Pederson | 50:10 |
| 20 | Jason Engel | 33:38 | Anna Long | 42:30 | 64 | Doug Bell | 39:00 | Tina Albert | 50:06 |
| 21 | Daniel Shellhouse | 32:55 | Janelle Lincks | 38:11 | 65 | Bernie Redlinger | 47:38 | Edie Stevenson | 47:15 |
| 22 | Riley Coates | 31:15 | Ellie Salthouse | 38:05 | 66 | Jim Reynolds | 45:51 | Lorraine Allen | 54:03 |
| 23 | Alexander Monroe | 31:04 | Sarah Ingles | 38:41 | 67 | Klaus Weickmann | 49:01 | Laurie Rugenstein | **48:38 *** |
| 24 | Jeremy Drenckhahn | 31:45 | Maor Tiyouri | 35:50 | 68 | Dave Dooley | 44:43 | Cathy Morgan | 55:32 |
| 25 | Tyler Curtis | 32:11 | Brittni Hutton | **34:32*** | 69 | Elliott Henry | 47:04 | Karen Karl | 59:40 |
| 26 | Craig Curley | 31:09 | Maggie Callahan | 36:04 | 70 | Dennis Bird | 49:24 | Lola Ackerman | 56:10 |
| 27 | Alejandro Jimenez | 32:16 | Emma Keenan | 36:20 | 71 | Tom Lemire | 48:37 | Judy Megibow | 1:00:25 |
| 28 | Tyler McCandless | 32:34 | Monica Folts | 38:43 | 72 | Ed Craighead | 46:32 | Dorothy Reid | 1:12:30 |
| 29 | Austin Richmond | 31:30 | Carol Smith | 37:02 | 73 | Byron Melendy | 55:07 | Dianne Fuller | 1:05:52 |
| 30 | Scott Dahlberg | 31:09 | Kara Henry | 37:00 | 74 | Don Larson | 50:27 | Barbara Brockman | 1:05:10 |
| 31 | Crosby Freeman | 33:30 | Melissa Cunningham | 37:20 | 75 | Gene DaGiau | 52:58 | Constance Ahrnsbrak | 57:40 |
| 32 | Steve Chu | 32:10 | Sarah Pizzo | 36:58 | 76 | Bill Obert | 1:03:12 | Ginnie Vaughan | 1:15:11 |
| 33 | Ben Payne | **30:41 *** | Melissa Dock | 36:53 | 77 | Jack Barry | 1:00:07 | Judy Smythe | 1:27:09 |
| 34 | Joshua Eberly | 31:33 | Jessica Parry-Wiliams | 37:43 | 78 | Paul Turley | 1:03:42 | Libby James | **53:37 *** |
| 35 | Paul Petersen | 33:20 | Amy Robillard | 39:07 | 79 | Richard Quigley | 57:56 | Jean Wilson | 1:33:32 |
| 36 | Ian Huang | 36:07 | Megan Greene | 39:25 | 80 | Chuck Merry | 1:02:05 | Barbara Gurtler | 1:23:34 |
| 37 | Brian Livingston | 35:06 | Brandy Erholtz | 38:54 | 81 | Rodney Link | 1:12:54 | Anita Gershten | 1:32:13 |
| 38 | Chaiwat Engtrakul | 35:38 | Claudia Becque | 38:54 | 82 | Richard Nagler | 1:13:29 | Mary Kay Rachwalski | 1:24: |
| 39 | Andy Rinne | 34:57 | Brooke Kish | 37:14 | 83 | Mike Fenerty | **1:05:04*** | Nona Chamberlin | 1:26:30 |
| 40 | Greg Nash | 36:37 | Sarah Rebick | 41:03 | 84 | Jesse Aweida | 1:06:51 | Marjorie Eddiy | 2:13:02 |
| 41 | Clifton Railsback | 36:20 | Bean Wrenn | 38:24 | 85 | Rod Smythe | 1:28:41 | Beatrice Hill | 1:45:59 |
| 42 | Chris Grauch | 34:31 | Dana James | 41:42 | 86 | Kenneth Green | **1:24:02*** | Audrey MacDonald | **1:28:48** |
| 43 | Chris Dawes | 36:35 | Corey Hooten | 43:31 | 87 | George Downing | **1:20:02*** | Margaret Lamitie | 2:17:45 |
| 44 | Marty Wacker | 36:37 | Nuta Olaru | 37:02 | 88 | Ray Schramm | **1:22:55*** | -- | |
| 45 | Kevin Konczak | 35:32 | Constantina Dita | 41:54 | 89 | -- | | Janet Grenda | **1:47:32*** |
| 46 | Sven Haug | 36:46 | Sabine Preisinger | 43:05 | | | | | |
| 47 | Steve Fossel | 38:57 | Christine Adamowski | 41:06 | | | | | |
| 48 | Todd Straka | 36:25 | Susan Nuzum | 41:14 | | | | | |
| 49 | Robert Gilbert | 38:48 | Leslie Hoffmann | 42:30 | | **\* New BB Age Record!** | | | |

# WE'VE RUN THIS TOWN SINCE 1979

## BOLDER**BOULDER**

WE NEVER THOUGHT OUR LITTLE ROAD RACE WOULD TURN INTO AMERICA'S ALL TIME BEST 10K, BUT WE ARE SURE PROUD THAT IT HAS. JOIN US ON MEMORIAL DAY.

- THE PRAIRIE RUNNER
- CHASE AND HOBBS — THE ULTIMATE GUIDE TO TRAIL RUNNING
- THE BEST FRONT RANGE TRAIL RUNS — JONES
- TRAILHEAD — LISA JHUNG
- RUN LIKE A CHAMPION — CULPEPPER
- HAL KOERNER'S FIELD GUIDE TO ULTRARUNNING — KOERNER
- TALES FROM ANOTHER MOTHER RUNNER — McDowell and Shea

# Local Authorities

Local authors released seven new books this year. Topics ranged from trail running to running your best in any race.

### The Best Front Range Trail Runs
Peter N. Jones

### Trailhead
Lisa Jhung

### Hal Koerner's Field Guide to Ultrarunning
with Adam Chase

### Run Like a Champion
Alan Culpepper

### Top Secret Black Book of Training
Brad Hudson

### Tales from Another Mother Runner
Contributions by Terzah Becker, Rachel Walker and Michelle Theall.

### Out There: A Story of Ultra Recovery
David Clark - 2015 eBook release

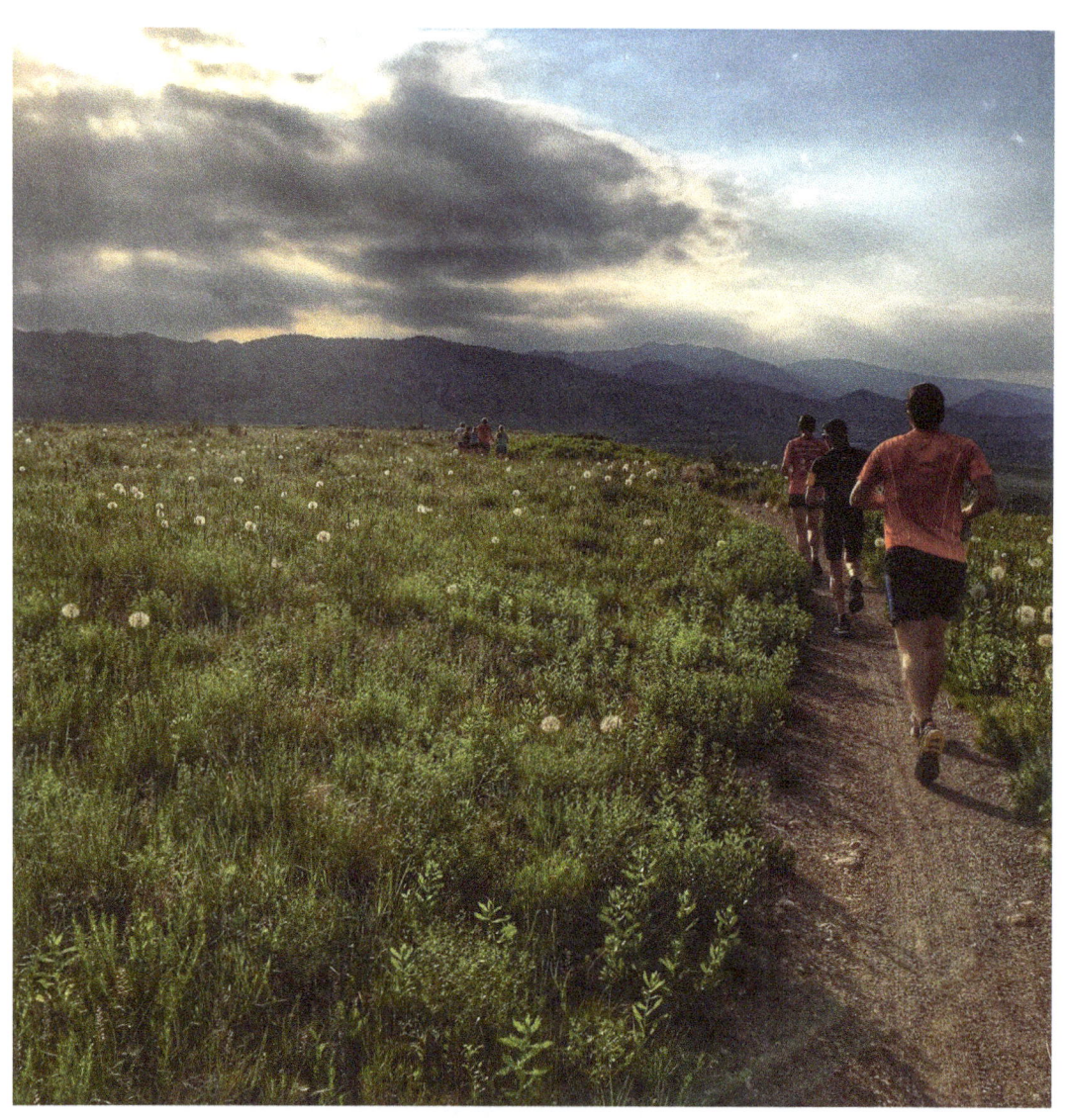

Photo courtesy of Flatirons Running

# Top Results
## May-June

The 37th Annual Bolder Boulder 10K was held on May 26th, bringing once again an international cohort of athletes to the Boulder area to race one of the largest and most competitive 10Ks in the country. Although no Boulder area athletes ran well in the International Team Challenge several Boulder runners had extremely good races in the Open event. For the men, Lyons' **Alexander Monroe** ran an exceptional race, crossing the finish line in 31:06 for a solid third place overall. In the women's race, Boulder runners dominated, with **Maor Tiyouri** coming in second in a time of 35:54, while **Maggie Callahan** came in third with a time of 36:11.

Between May 21th and May 30th, **Greg Salvesen** completed and won the Infinitus 888K in Vermont in just under 9 days. That is 551 miles!

At the Dam to Dam Half Marathon in Des Moines, IA on May 30th, Longmont's **Nicole Camp** had a solid race, running a time of 1:17:16 for second place.

On May 30, the Quest for the Crest 50K was held in Burnsville, North Carolina. As part of the U.S. Skyrunner Series, the event boasted 11,000 feet of elevation gain. **Josh Arthur** of Boulder ran to a solid third place in 6:13.

Also on May 30, the ever popular Ultimate Direction Dirty Thirty 50K was held just outside of Black Hawk, Colorado. Drawing a stout field from the local Front Range, local **Kerrie Bruxvoort** ran to the top spot on the podium with a time of 5:46, while Anita Ortiz of Avon came in second with a time of 5:50 and **Silke Koester** of Boulder ran 5:54 for third place.

The Music City Distance Carnival in Nashville, TN is a highlight for track runners in June, attracting a competitive field from around the country. Boulder sent a competitive field to the event, consisting mostly of Boulder Track Club athletes. In the 800M, **Jordan Jennings** ran a good race, finishing fourth with a time of 1:51.20. **Alex Monroe** came in second in the 5000M event with a time of 14:10.23; **Maor Tiyouri** also place second in the 5000M women's race with a time of 16:30.45 while **Alexa Rogers** finished sixth in a time of 17:04.27 and **Sarah Hutchings** finished eighth in a time of 17:28.99.

The Garden of the Gods 10 Mile Run on June 14th once again delivered a fast race despite the altitude and rugged course. **Amanda Lee** came in third for the women with a time of 1:06:51.

On June 20th at the Steamboat Classic 4 Mile, Boulder runners took two spots on the podium. **Sean Quigley** finished second with a time of 18:29 while **Jeffrey Eggleston** finished third in a time of 18:32.

Also held on June 20th, the Sunrise Stampede 10K in Longmont had a good showing of Boulder athletes, with **Mario Macias** winning the event in a time of 31:05, while **Justin Young** of Louisville came in second in a time of 32:27 and **Guy Alton** of Boulder rounded out the podium for third in a time of 33:41. For the women, **Dani Wanner** of Longmont came in second with a time of 44:10.

Finally, out in New Hampshire the 55th running of the Mt. Washington Road Race was held on June 20th. Coloradans took the top three spots, with Boulder's **Andy Wacker** running up to the summit in the second fastest time of the day in 1:00:59.

On June 21st Boulder runner **Silke Koester** ran the Bighorn 100 Mile race in 24:1:29, coming in 2nd place. At the 50 Mile race, **Brad Poppele** came in third with a time of 8:45:33 while **Darcy Piceu** of Boulder ran a fast time of 8:49:19, coming in 1st for the women and 4th overall.

Back in Colorado, at the North Fork 50K/50 Mile run on Saturday, June 27th with **Cindy Stonesmith** of Louisville come in second in the 50K race in a time of 5:37:43.

At the San Juan Solstice 50 Mile Run in Lake City, Colorado on June 27th, **Luke Jay** of Littleton was second in a time of 9:28:35.

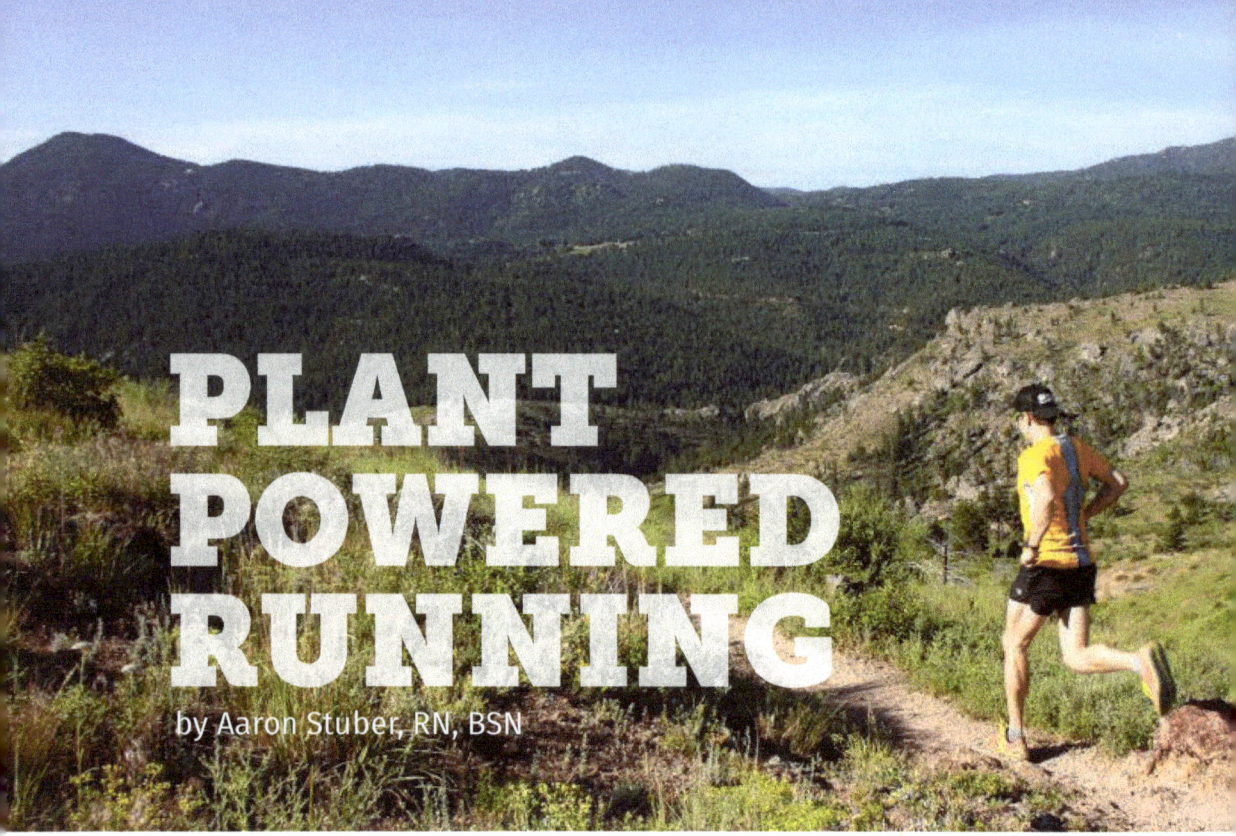

# PLANT POWERED RUNNING

by Aaron Stuber, RN, BSN

Photo by Lindsay Hiatt Photography (lindsayhiattphotography.com)

For the past 4 years, I have been running and racing on trails at progressively longer distances, improving my speed, endurance and proficiency on steep, technical terrain. Now well-acquainted with ultra-long distance running at altitude, I believe the importance of accelerated recovery is paramount.

Athletes, particularly those inclined to endurance sports, can enjoy significant performance and recovery benefits by centering their diets around whole, plant foods.

Recent published studies have shown that the oxidative stress caused by prolonged, intense exercise can be significantly reduced with certain antioxidant rich plant foods (not pills), improving recovery time and performance.
Healthy Skoop has created a line of organic, plant-based products that make it easier for athletes and non-athletes alike to make this important shift in their nutrition. Products like Super Skoop, a new formulation that includes pea, rice and hemp protein plus dozens of other greens, berries and pre-biotic fibers make for a super convenient and efficient way to take advantage of nature's pharmacy.

I supplement my plant-based diet with Skoop's entire arsenal, including A-Game, B-Lovely and Ignite, the exciting new beet-based endurance blend. Ignite is especially useful for endurance athletes because it combines D-Ribose with nitrate-rich beets, which studies have shown to boost endurance by increasing cardiovascular efficiency. As a registered nurse and health coach/nutrition consultant, I often have my patients and clients take advantage of these amazing products to improve their health and support them in transitioning to a whole food, plant-based diet and lifestyle.

Aaron Stuber is an ultra endurance athlete, cardiovascular nurse and founder of The Plant-Based RN, a health coaching/nutrition consulting service. He lives in Boulder, CO with his wife and daughter. You can find Aaron at theplantbasedrn.com.

# healthy Skoop

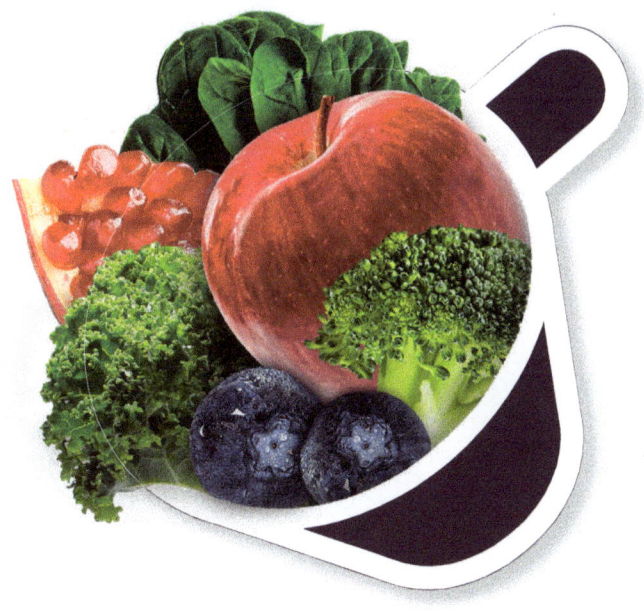

## PLANT-BASED NUTRITION
### Boulder, Colorado

Get your super on with our plant-based protein and superfood blends!

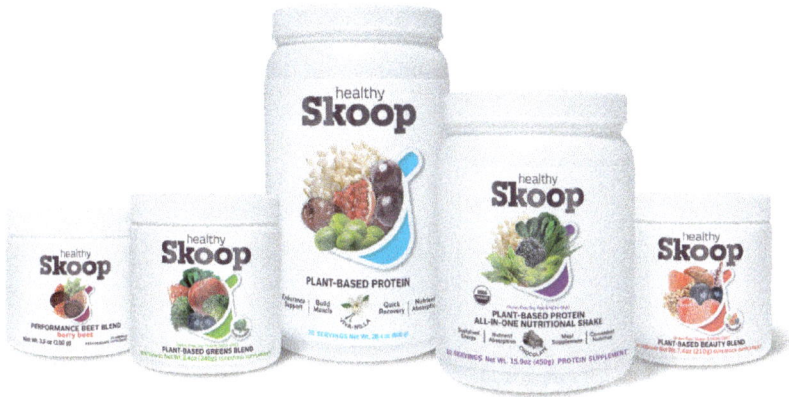

**HealthySkoop.com**     Follow us  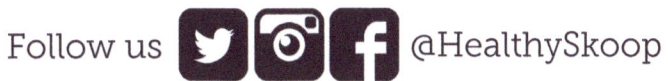  @HealthySkoop

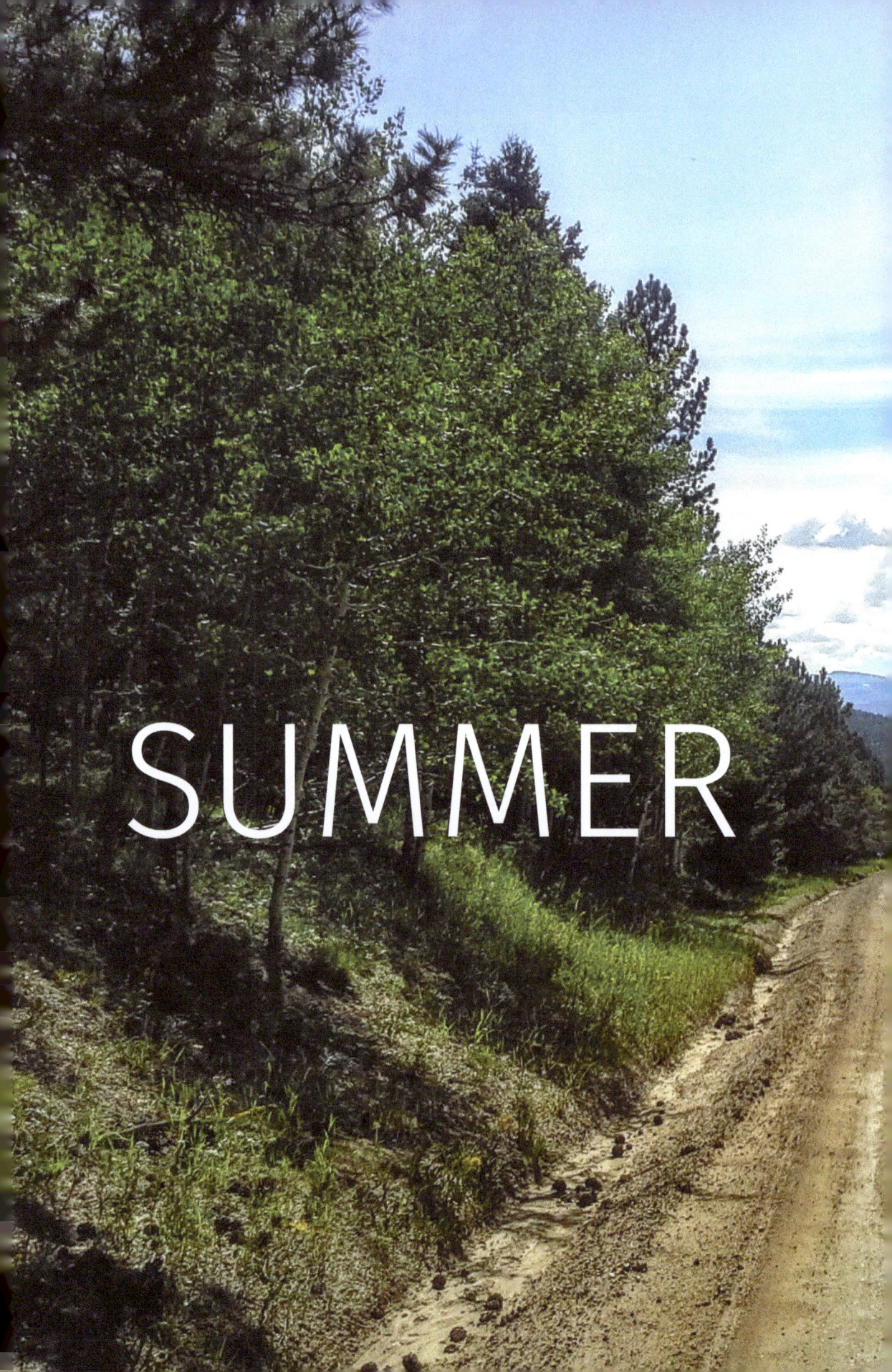
# SUMMER

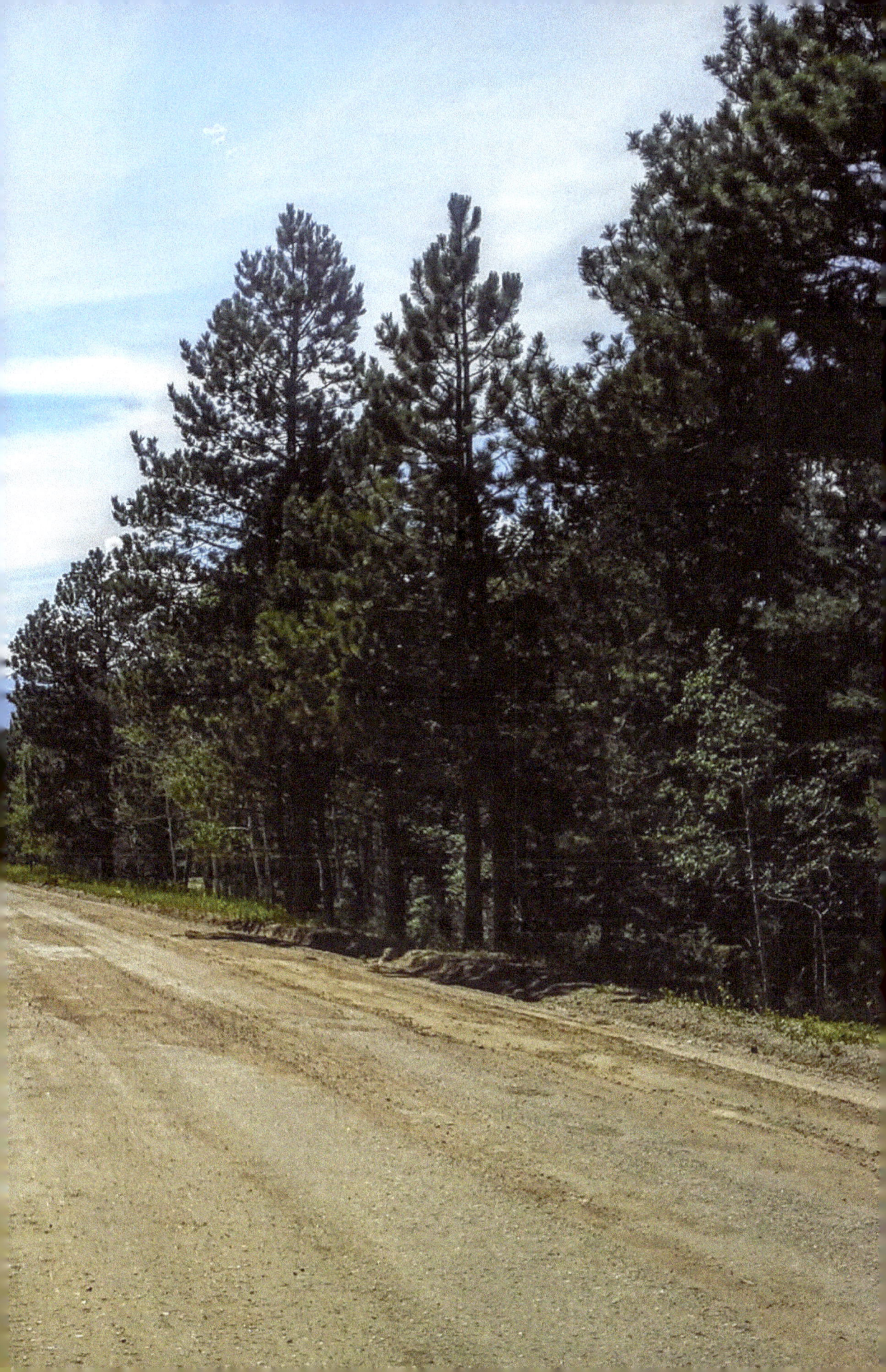

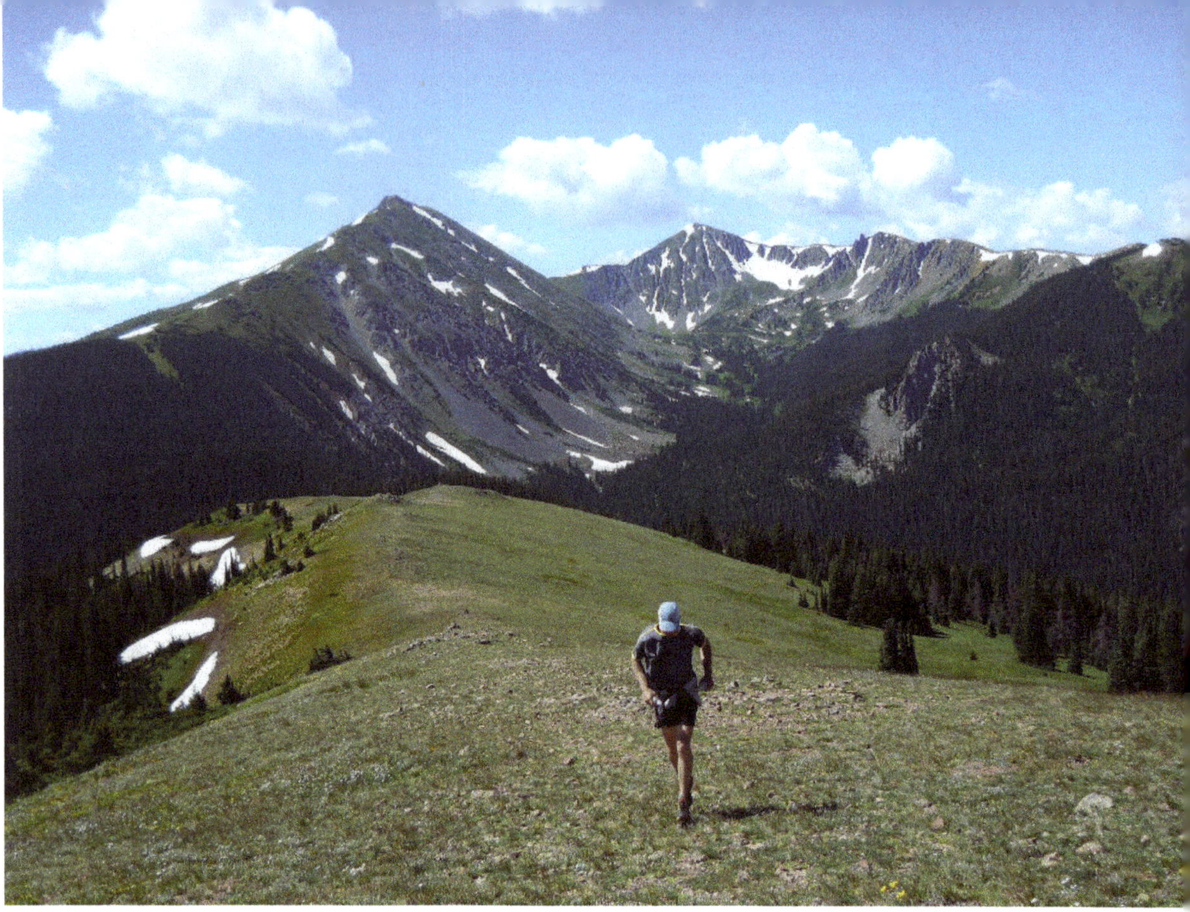

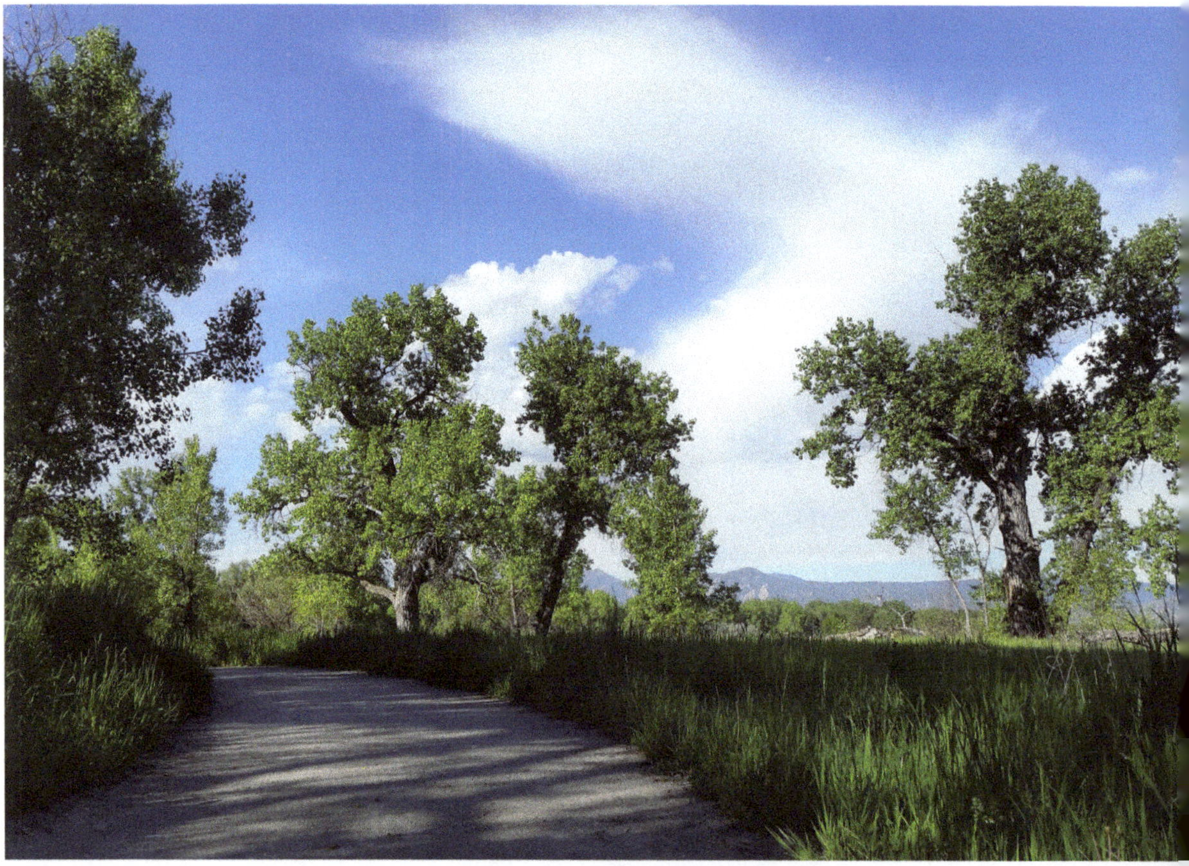

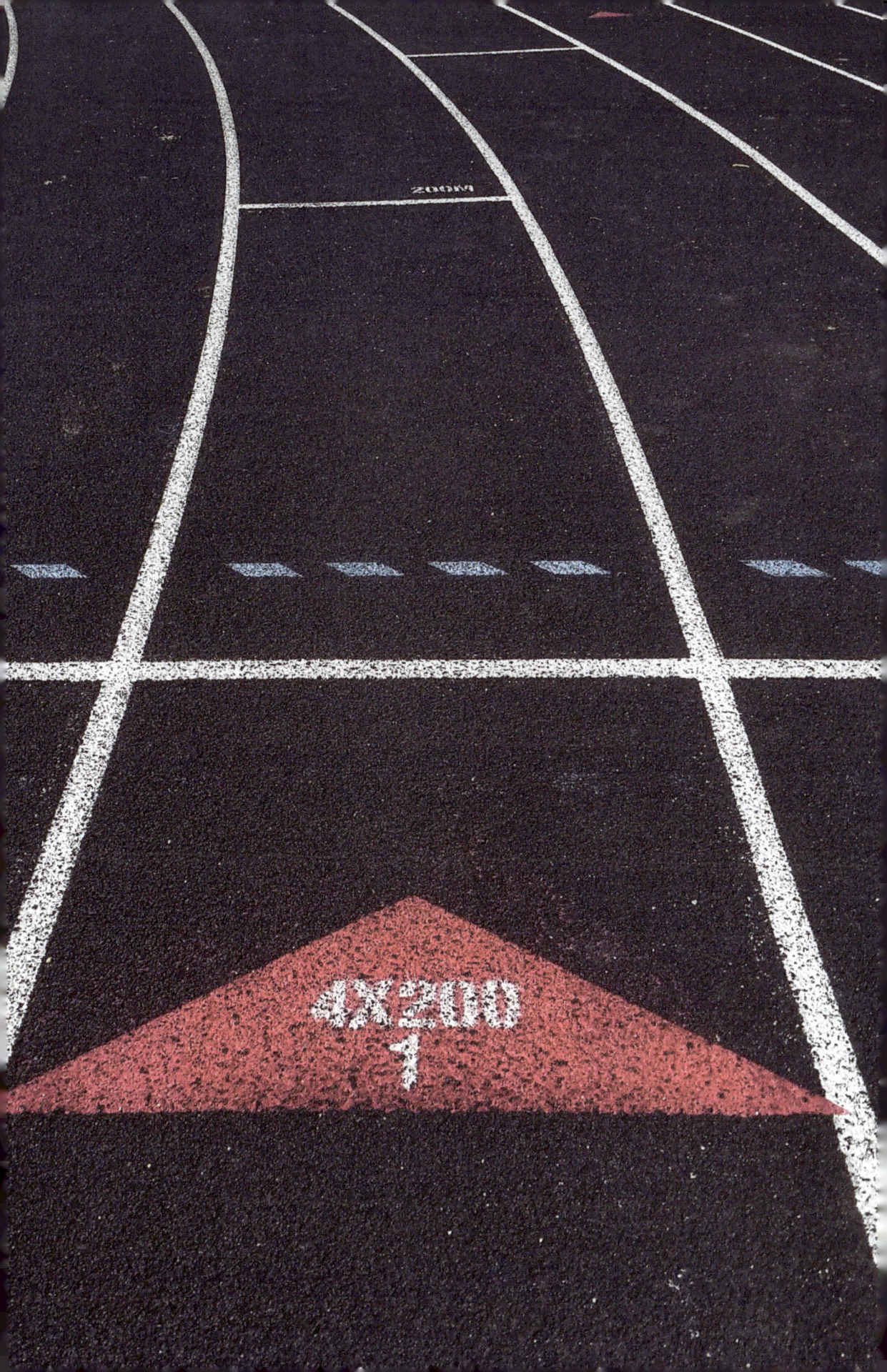

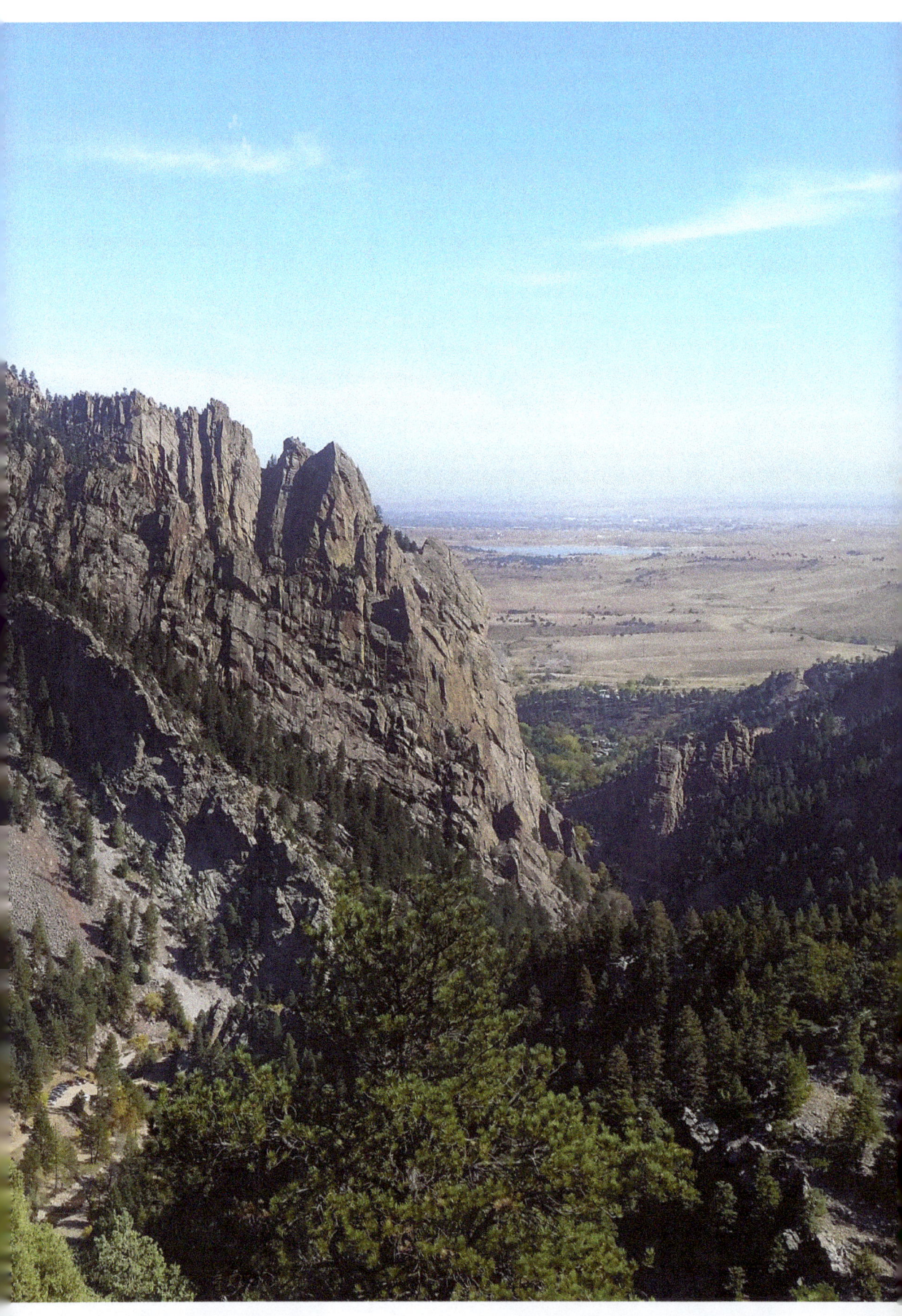

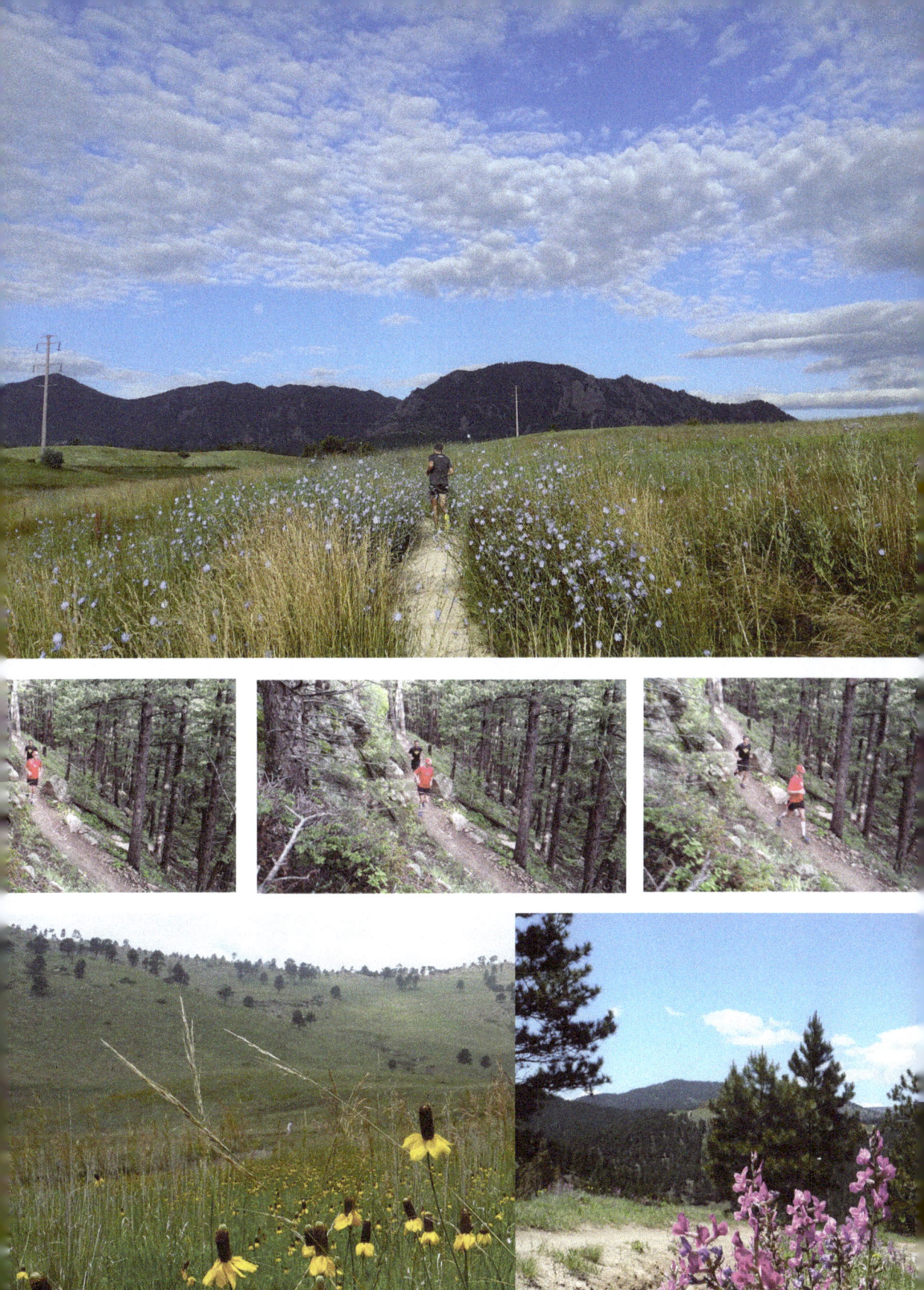

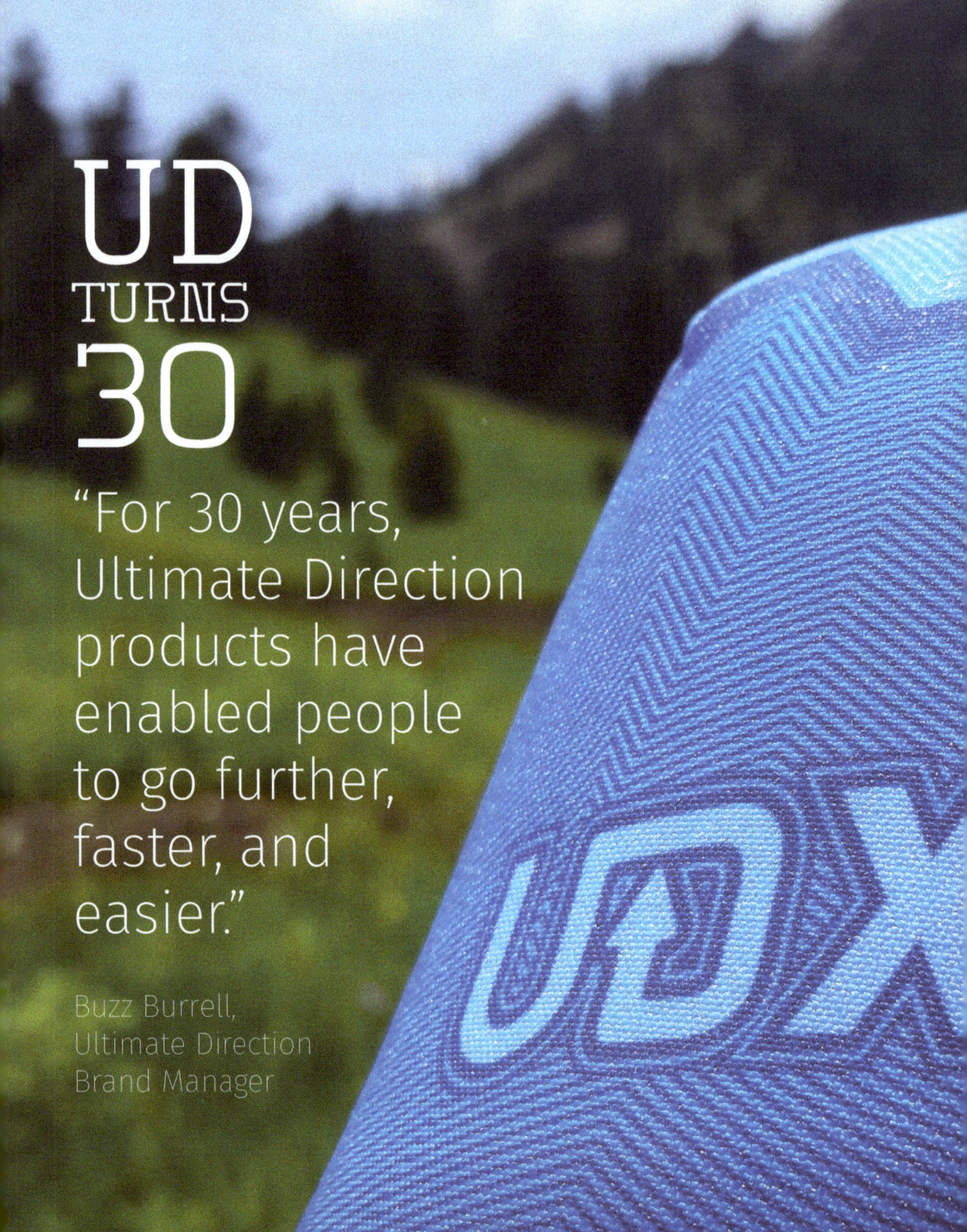

# UD TURNS 30

"For 30 years, Ultimate Direction products have enabled people to go further, faster, and easier."

Buzz Burrell,
Ultimate Direction
Brand Manager

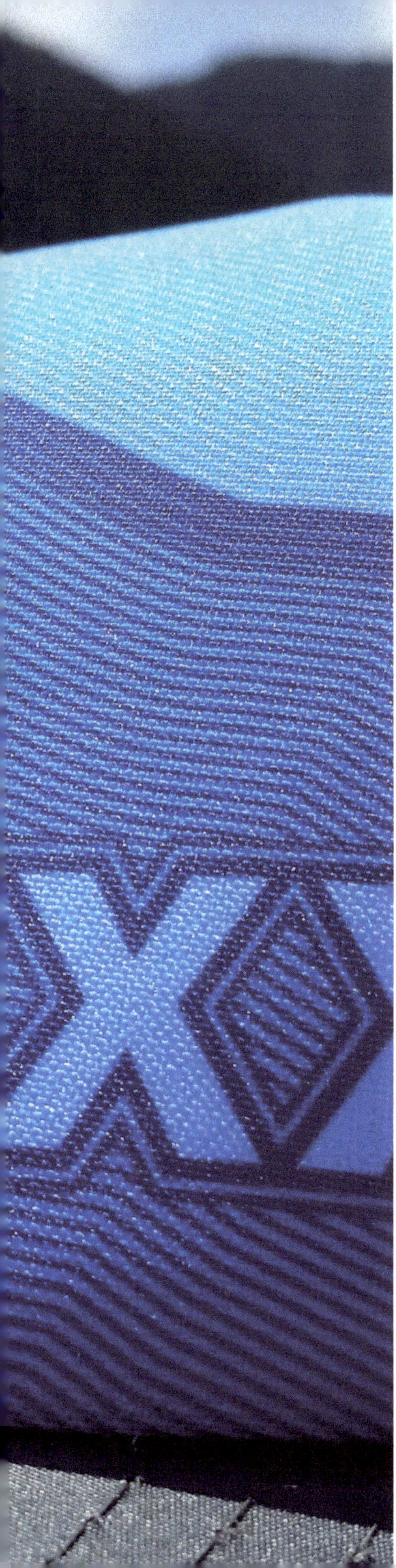

When Trail Running luminary Buzz Burrell joined UD as their Brand Manager he quickly developed a top notch athlete "advisory board" consisting of Scott Jurek, Anton Krupicka and Peter Bakwin. As a team, they created the category-defining Signature Series vests, the Scott Jurek Essentials collection and the first-ever line crafted specifically for women, the Jenny Collection. UD continues to innovate new specialty running products, and we are hoping the next 30 years prove to be just as exciting. Thanks for being part of the Boulder Running Community.

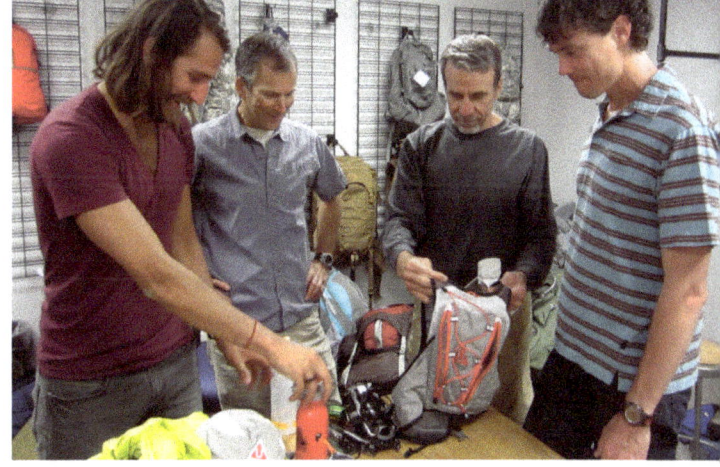

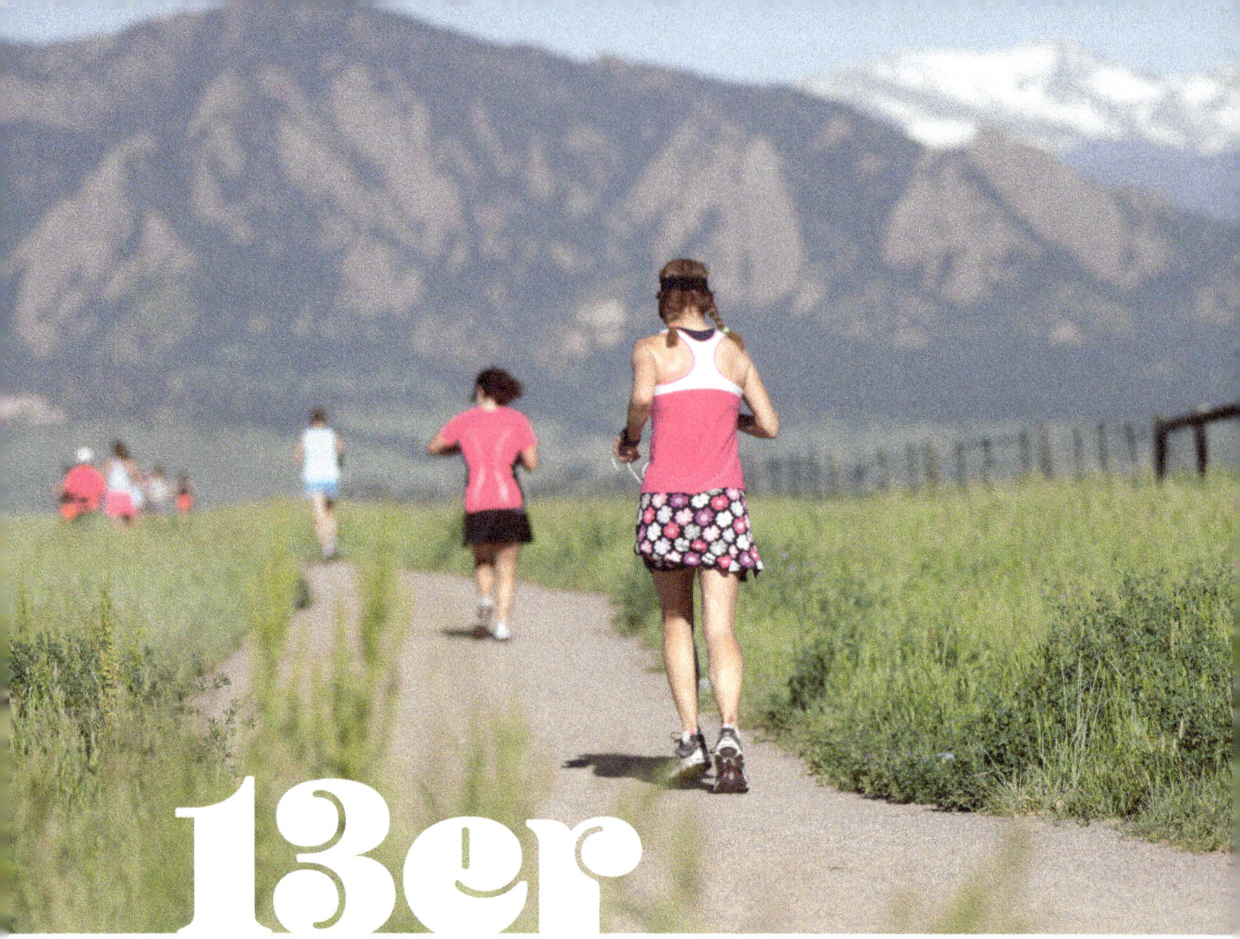

# 13er

The thing I like best about this race is the fun, casual vibe, it's very unique. While there is the expected 'competitive energy,' you'll also find a relaxed, fun, 'let's run, then hang-out-and-shop vibe!'

It creates a very social atmosphere. Now, If they would just add bottomless Mimosas to the event, I'd never leave!

- Lisa Wilson

The Skirt Sports 13er is a 13.1 mile women's race with the motto "it's not half of anything." This year's beautiful but tough, hilly course is unique to the area. It boasts grand views of the Front Range from Davidson Mesa and a hill aptly named "The Bad Relationship" because you don't know how bad it is until you're over it!

With more than 500 women participating, it has been Competitor Magazine's "Best Women's Event" three years running. All finishers get Kim & Jake's Cakes, finisher's skirts and gift certificates.

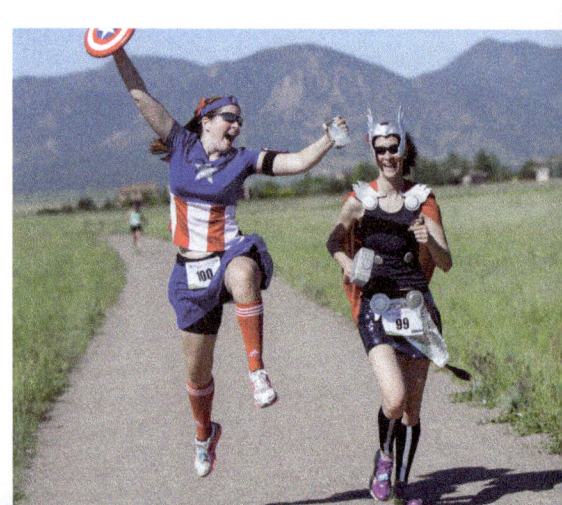

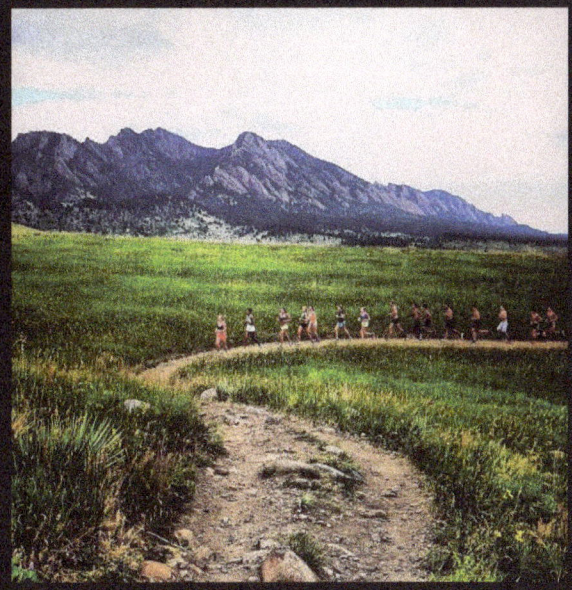
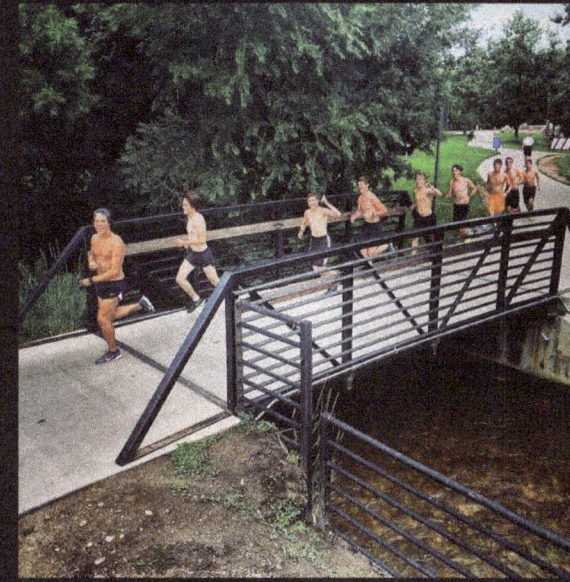
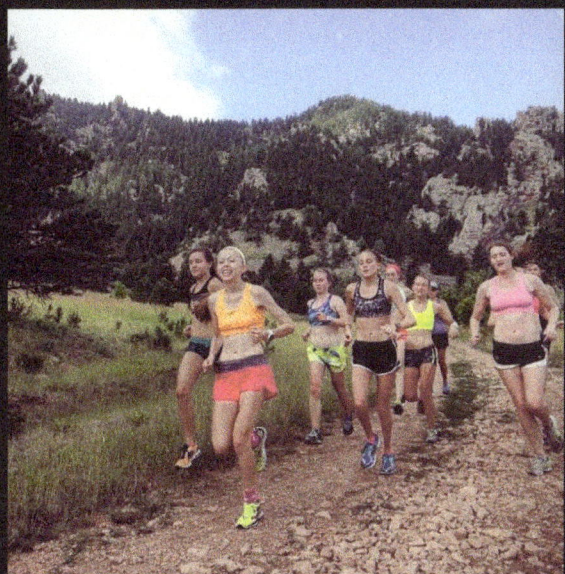
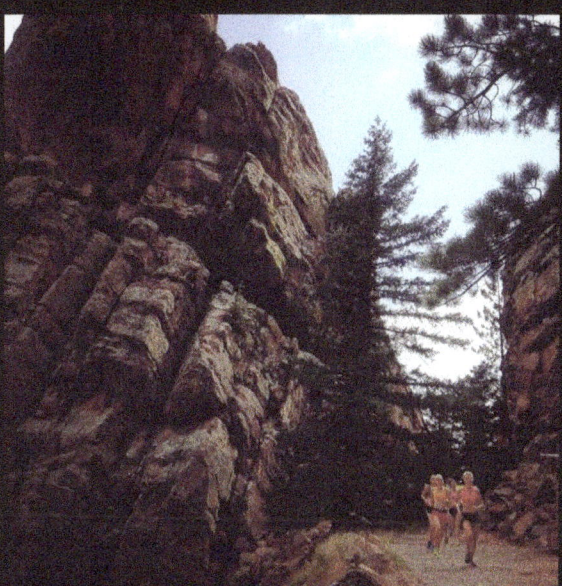
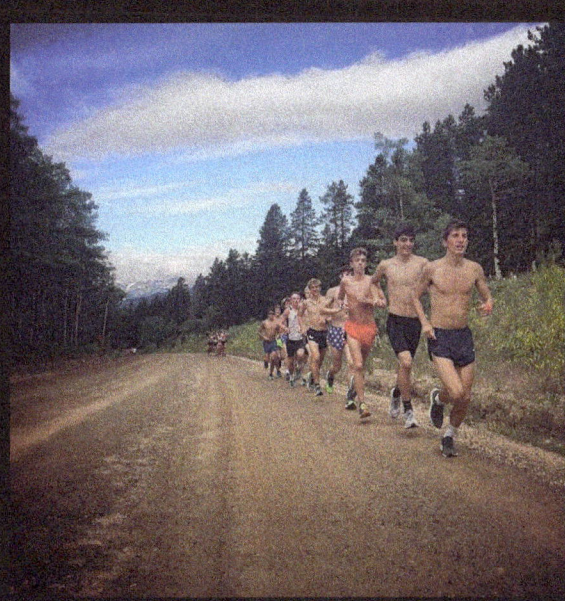

# BOULDER RUNNING CAMPS

The Boulder Running Camps are the nation's premier running camps for prep students, offering a unique blend of challenging running opportunities and valuable learning experiences.

boulderrunningcamps.com

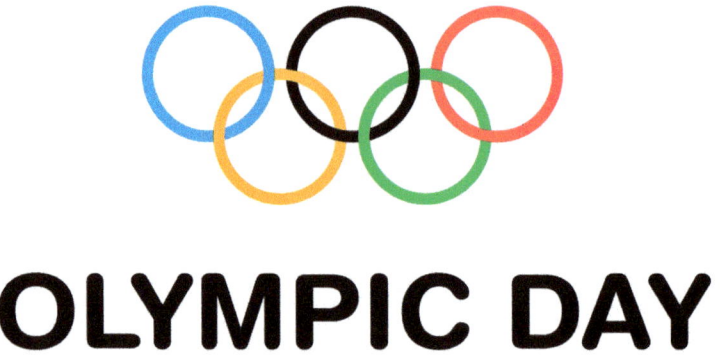

# OLYMPIC DAY

**June 27, 2015 - Boulder, CO - Potts Field**

Local Olympians were recognized at the official Olympic Day celebration held in conjunction with the Boulder Road Runners summer track meet on June 27th. Olympians from multiple sports attended, including runners Nuta Olaru, Gold Medalist Constintina Dita, Kathy Butler, Bronze Medalist Lorraine Moller, Lee Troop and Silver Medalist Frank Shorter. Athletes of all ages were able to meet, hear stories from their heroes and catch a glimpse of the Olympic Relay torch. The evening concluded after a few track events, before the typical summer lightning storm rolled in.

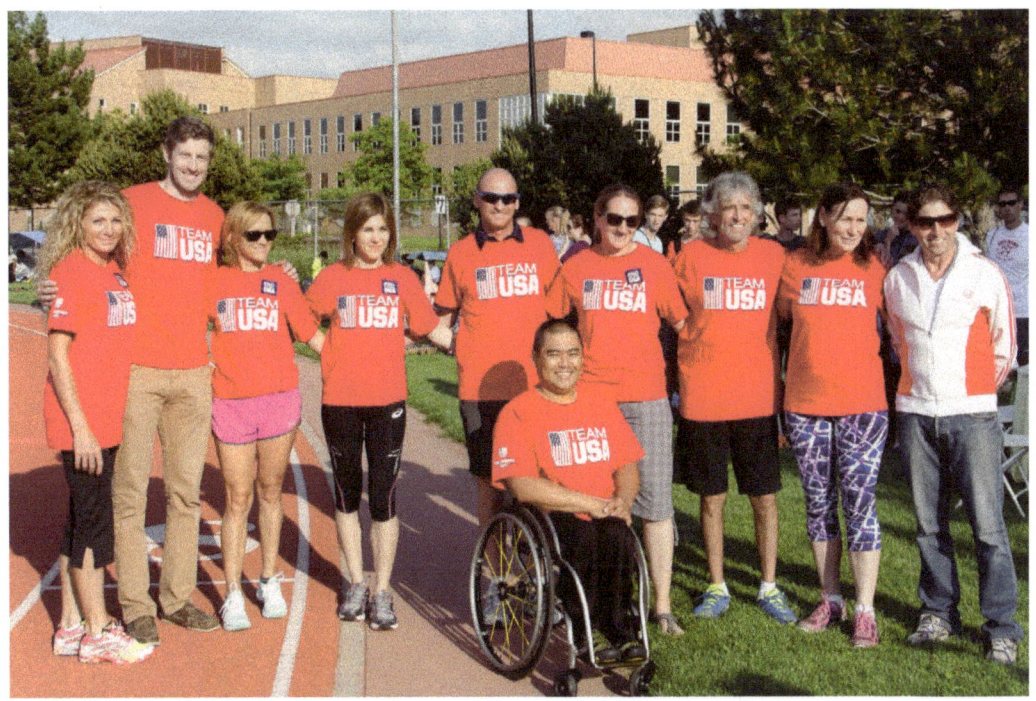
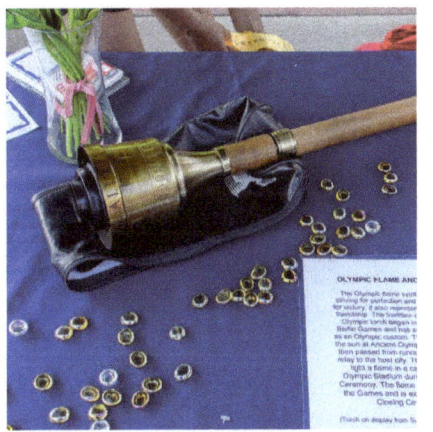
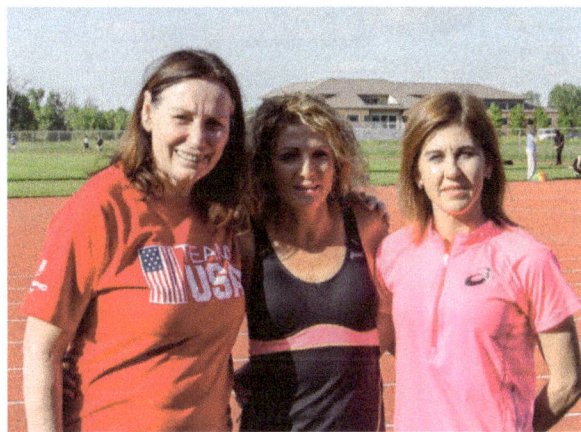
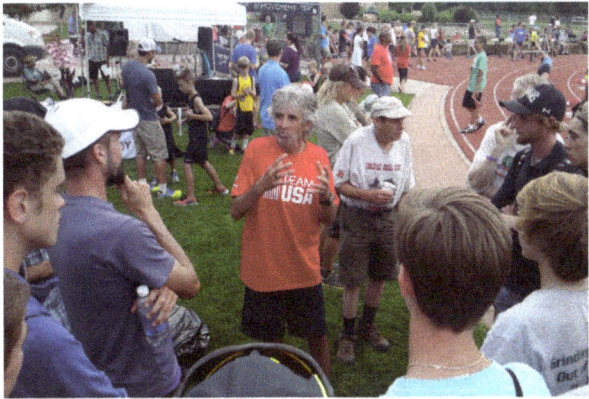
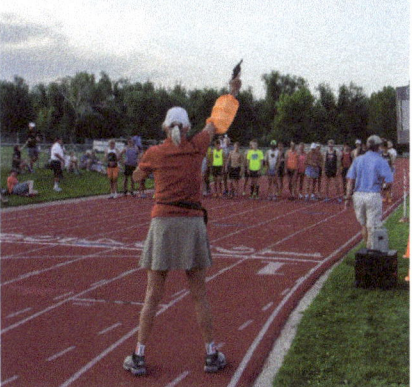

Olympians of all sports stand up to be recognized - The Olympic Torch - Marathoners Lorraine Moller, Gold Medalist Constantina Diță and Nuța Olaru - Gold Medalist Frank Shorter talks to young runners and Lorraine Greene starts the meet. Photos by Tevis Morrow.

Boulder has long been known as a running community and I have been fortunate to be a direct recipient of that positive attribute. The residents truly appreciate why athletes pursue endurance sports at the highest level and understand what it takes to achieve such a level. Boulder is a special place in many ways and included in that profile is the proliferation of the runner mindset. **That mindset is about the continued process of challenging yourself to reach goals while also enjoying the process along the way."**

- Alan Culpepper

# 2015 USATF Outdoor Track and Field Championships

Eugene Oregon

Running has given me a place where I belong and freedom to imagine great possibilities. Racing is one expression of my gratefulness #raceday

Jenny Simpson @trackjenny

Simpson defended her 1,500m title, running 4:14:86 and earning a spot in Beijing.

Being a track fan is so much more stressful than being a track athlete... sweating so much more as a spectator.

Emma Coburn @emmajcoburn

Coburn ran 9:15.59 to win her 4th U.S. title in the 3,000m steeplechase.

Sometimes you get knocked down, but don't worry, I'm not out.

Kara Goucher @karagoucher

Goucher finished 18th in the 5K in 16:05 after just a few months back from surgery.

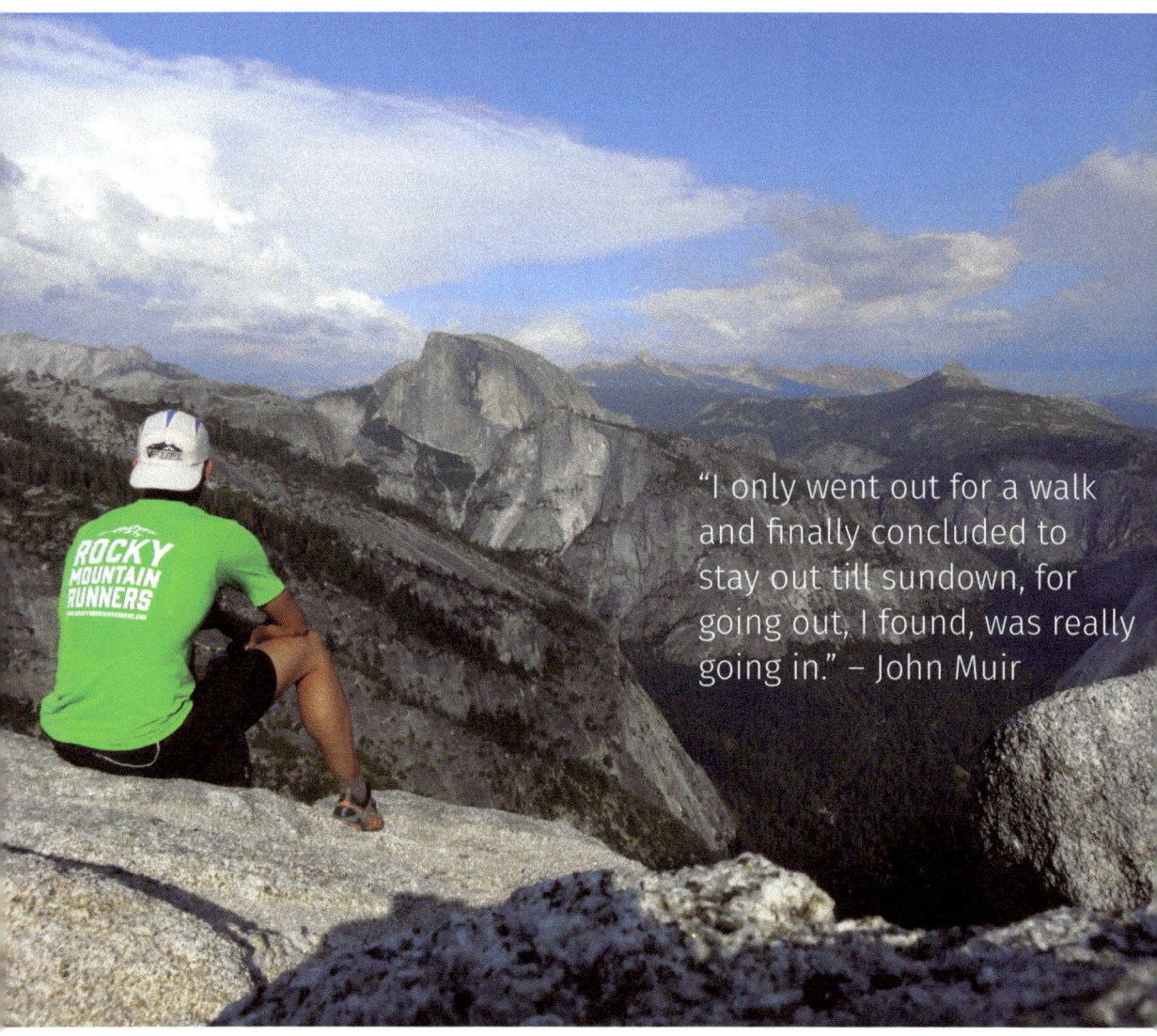

"I only went out for a walk and finally concluded to stay out till sundown, for going out, I found, was really going in." – John Muir

Words and photos by Eric J. Lee

As I sat atop El Capitan watching the sunset over the Yosemite Valley, the immensity of the day was finally settling in. I was going to run 65 miles with 16,000' of vertical gain/loss, unsupported, around one of America's most iconic sights on a loop that had never been done before, let alone in a single push. The idea arose when I was poring over maps and searching for some mountain inspiration for the summer of 2016 and noticed a series of trails that ringed the Yosemite Valley high along the rim. My searches brought up zero hits; had this really never been done before? That got me even more excited; not only did it promise surreal scenery but also the novelty of setting an 'Only Known Time.'

While one can reach all the viewpoints and waterfalls of the Yosemite Valley via short day hikes, something about linking them all together and taking in all the different views of Yosemite's iconic granite monoliths in one day made it that much more special. Stunning view points, lonely single track through forest meadows, rocky granite mountain tops, gushing waterfalls and a testing bushwhack to the finish proved to be an amazing 17 hour journey. Races may offer you competition, but only by putting yourself out there in the unknown can you find adventure and better understand the healing properties of Nature that John Muir often spoke of.

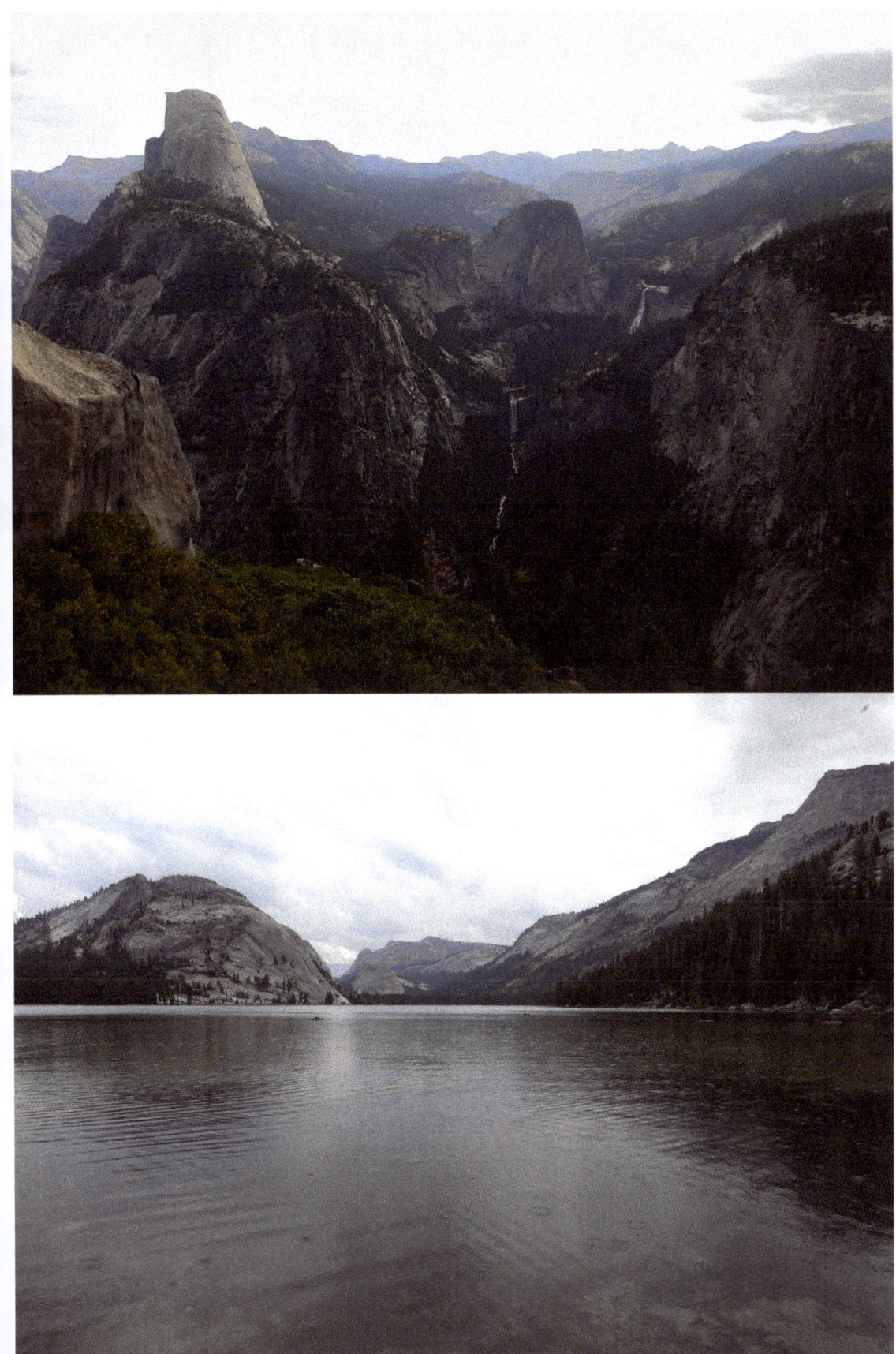

**Specialty Running** saw quite a bit of change this year. Between new store openings, buy outs, and changes of ownership, runners now have even more options in Boulder to find the right fit in shoes and community.

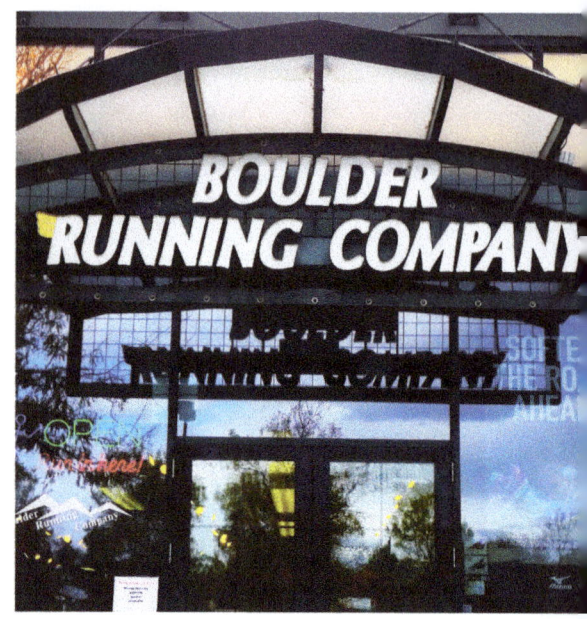

# RETAIL THERAPY

**Boulder Running Company** continues the legacy started by Mark Plaatjes and Johnny Halberstadt with co-managers Suzanne Connor and Ryan Lassing.

**Flatirons Running** partnered with New Balance and Strava to open its one of a kind Run Hub experience.

Three-time Australian Olympian Lee Troop bought **Fleet Feet Sports** from Lilly Johnson, who continues working at the store.

**Newton Running** opened its flagship store downtown on the Pearl Street Mall.

Former elite Tony DeBoom opened the **Endurance Conspiracy** with apparel celebrating the culture of endurance athletes on East Pearl Street.

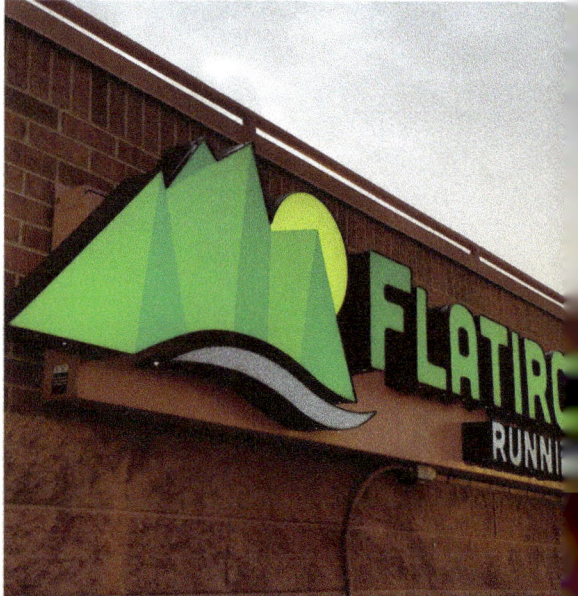

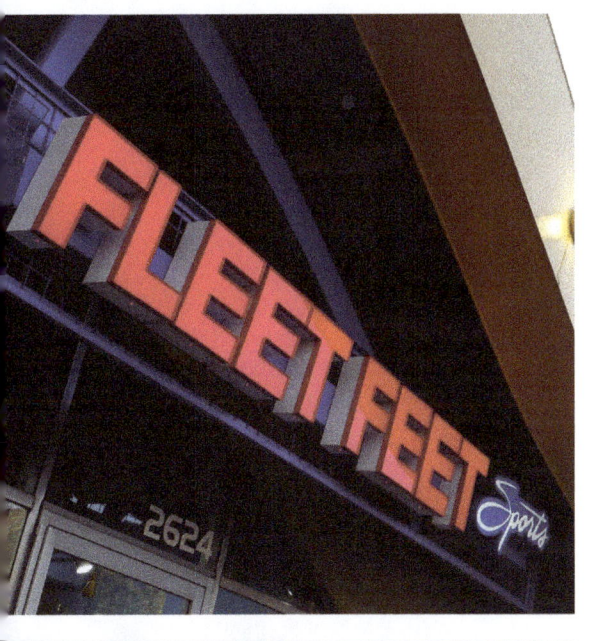
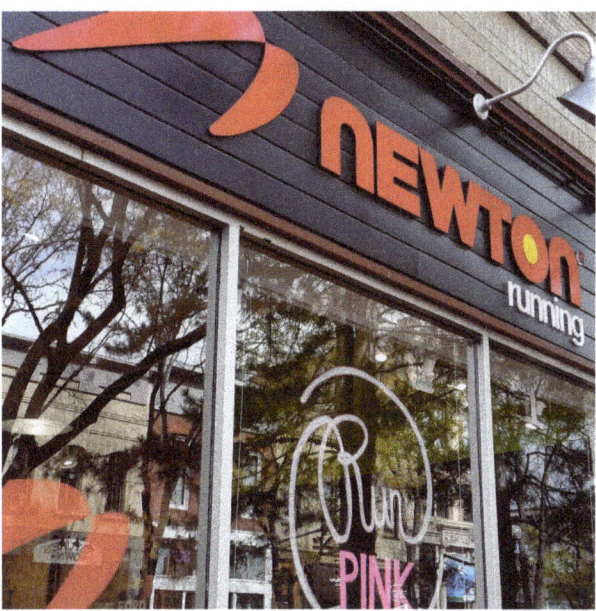
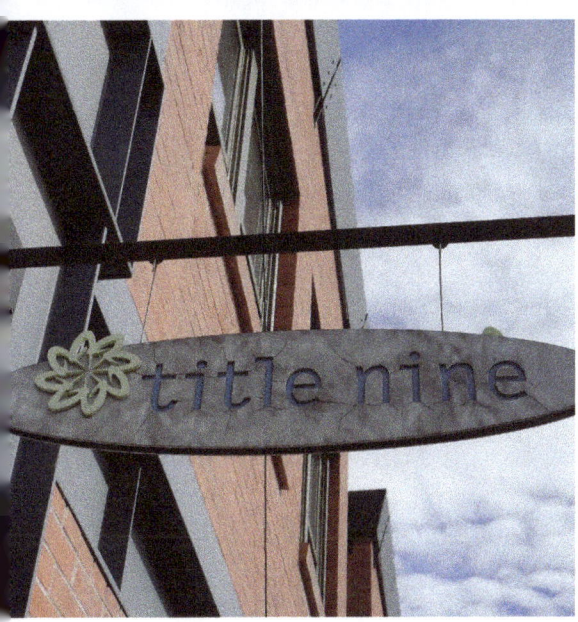
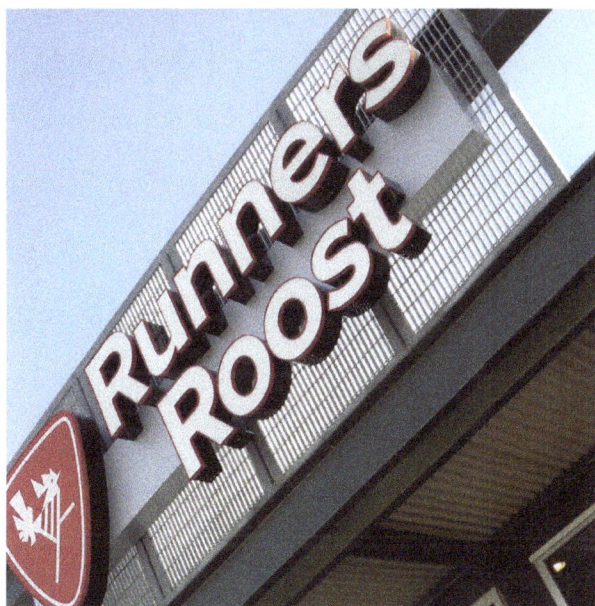
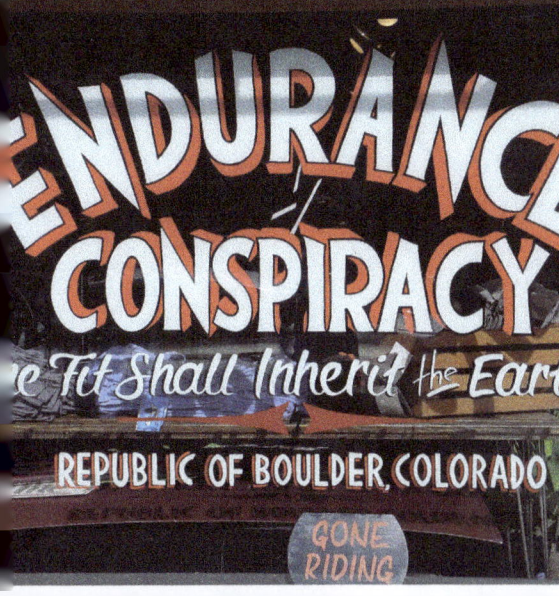
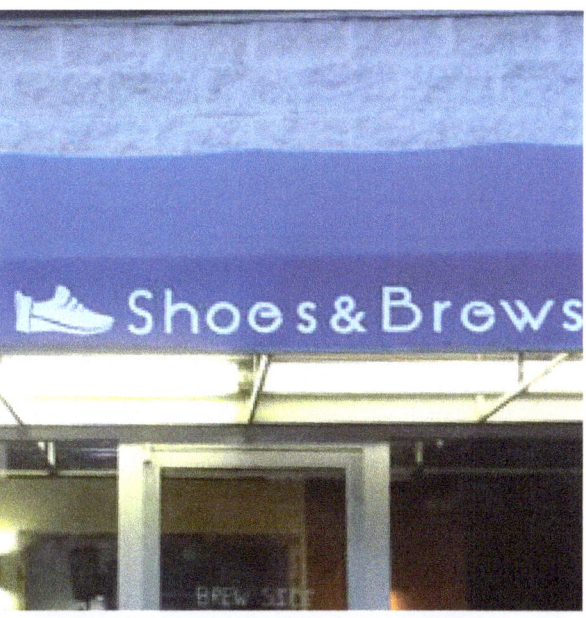

Words by Peter N. Jones

# Scott Jurek:
# THE HARDEST RUN I'VE EVER DONE

On July 12th, Boulder's Scott Jurek completed a journey of epic proportions, successfully running the entire length of the Appalachian Trail

## 2,185 miles
## 46 days
## 8 hours
## 7 minutes

His time broke the previous **Fastest Known Time** by 3 hours and 13 minutes, set in 2011 by Jennifer Pharr Davis.

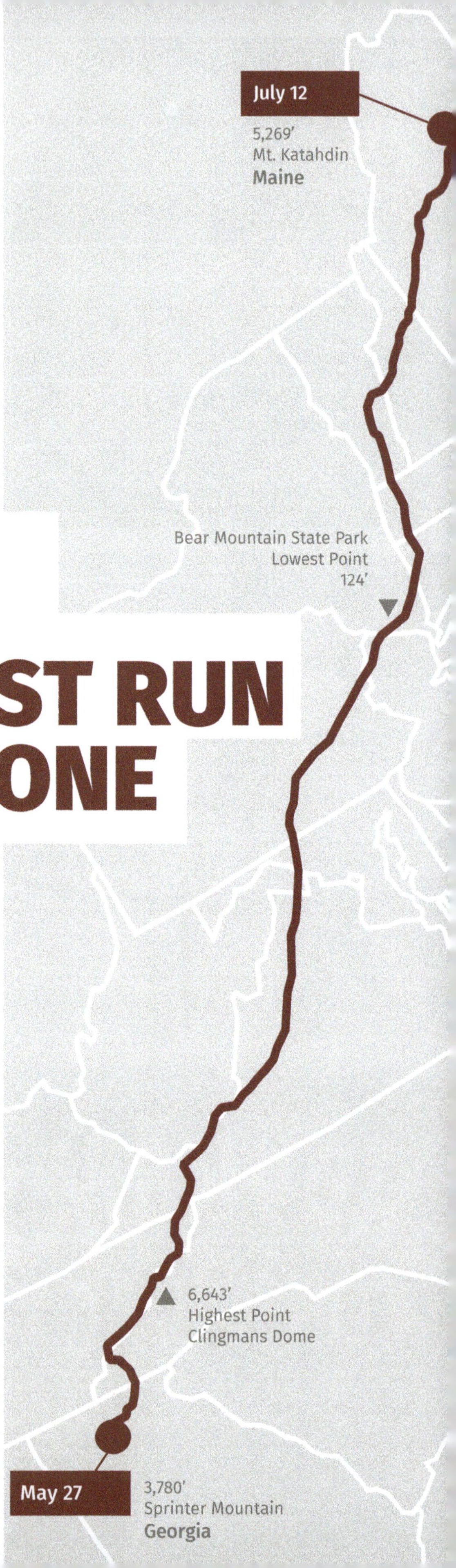

**July 12**
5,269'
Mt. Katahdin
**Maine**

Bear Mountain State Park
Lowest Point
124'

6,643'
Highest Point
Clingmans Dome

**May 27**
3,780'
Sprinter Mountain
**Georgia**

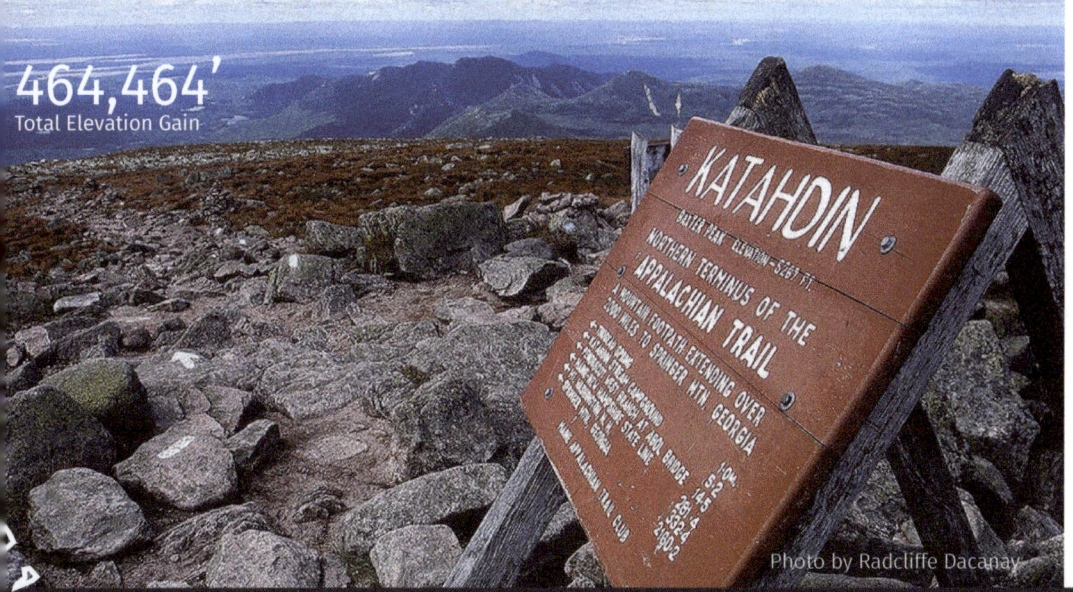

**464,464'**
Total Elevation Gain

Photo by Radcliffe Dacanay

*"Nothing, at least in my career, has ever come close to that. Just the amount of physical, mental, and even beyond what it required in some ways didn't surprise me because I knew what an endeavor it was, but it also just... yeah, nothing else compares. It was amazing."*

- Jurek told iRunfar in an interview after the achievement.

Over the course of Jurek's run, he lost 20 pounds, dealt with an injured right knee and left quadricep, survived downpours and other extreme weather. Starting at Springer Mountain in Georgia on May 27, Jurek averaged 47 miles a day over the 2,185 mile trail, arriving atop Mount Katahdin in Maine on July 12th.

"For the past month and a half I dreamed of getting to the top of Katahdin. After 46 days, 8 hours and 7 minutes it was a reality and the feeling was unlike anything I've experienced. The path takes us places we never imagine," Jurek stated on his Facebook page. Reflecting on his achievement, Jurek noted on his website: "Completing the Appalachian Trail was one of the toughest and most rewarding journeys of my entire life. The lessons that Jenny and I learned on the trail we will never ever forget. I hope to have inspired at least one more person to get outside, enjoy and protect the wilderness... My goal is to inspire others and I look forward to cheering them on as they experience their own version of adventure."

# Running Shorts

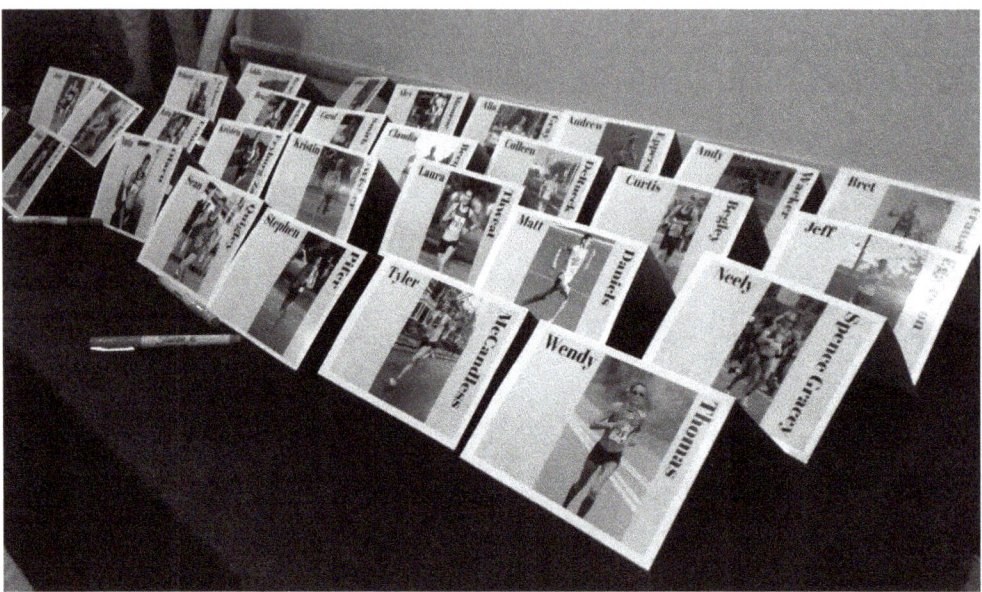

Congratulations to all of the Olympic Marathon Trials qualifiers. There are over **40 runners from Colorado** so far with more than 30 of them in the Boulder area. At the First Annual Boulder Running Gala held by **Hudson Elite** in November, there were cards for each of the athletes that people could sign and wish them well. The Trials will be held in Los Angeles this February.

**Dave Dooley**, long time Boulder Road Runner member and engineer at Ball Aerospace, just logged his 100,000 mile at age 68! That's almost 4 times around the world in 40 years of running and he can still do a 44 minute 10K. In the BolderBoulder he placed in the top twenty all-time of his age, 29 times between 1985 and 2015 (including six all-time bests).

**Delcia Litt** made the Colorado's Fastest Runners list by Colorado Runner Magazine for women 55-9 with her 10 K PR of 39:43.

**Chris Grauch** of Boulder was named Master's Mountain Runner and Sub-ultra Trail Runner of the Year by the USATF. To be considered for the award, an athlete must show top results in U.S. mountain and trail competitions from October 23, 2014 through November 10, 2015. Chris had a strong season, finishing second overall at the Leadville Heavy Half and winning the Master's race at the USATF Half Marathon Trail Championships held in Bellingham, Washington.

The **BRR 60+ Men** took the national title in their division at the USATF 5 Kilometer Master's Road Race Championship in Syracuse, NY on October 4th. The BRR team of John Victoria, Doug Bell, Devin Croft and Jan Frisby bested a field of eight other teams to earn the club's second national title in 2015.

Edie Stevens set a new Masters Record at the US National 12k in the W65-69 age group in a time of 53:50.

**Emma Coburn** earned a berth to the World Championships after her 4th U.S. Championship in the Steeplechase in June.

**Jenny Simpson** capped off her race season with her 4th win in a row at the 5th Avenue Mile in NYC.

> Jenny Simpson @trackjenny · 22h
> Perfect way to finish the season. A win on US soil. #5thAveMile #NYRR #teamNB #NYC @NBRunning

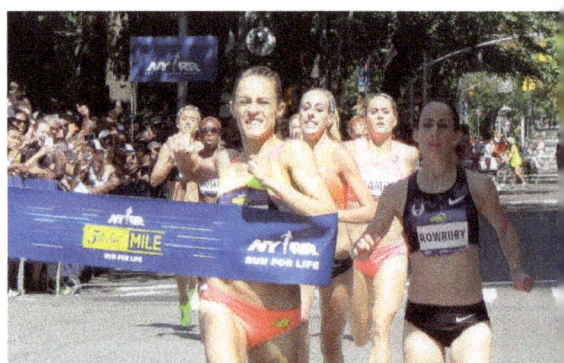

Andy Wacker **of Boulder**, took home the silver medal at the World Mountain Running Distance Championships on July 4th in Zermatt, Switzerland in a time of 3:03.51. Team USA took home the Bronze.

Sprinter **Cathy Nicolletti** ran All-American standards this summer in the 60m, 100m, 200m, 400m, & 800m races.

"The 800 was actually quite a reach for me since I'm a sprinter but I made it w 12 seconds to spare. I was going to try for the mile but that was just too much for my little sprinter legs"

Photo: Dave Albo

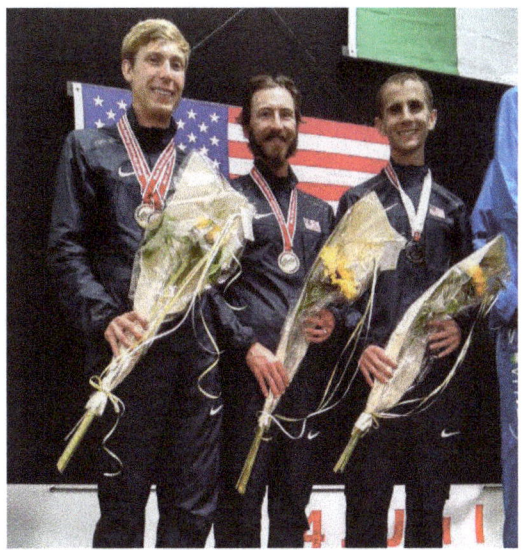

TEAM USA - Photo: @AtraTrailRunner

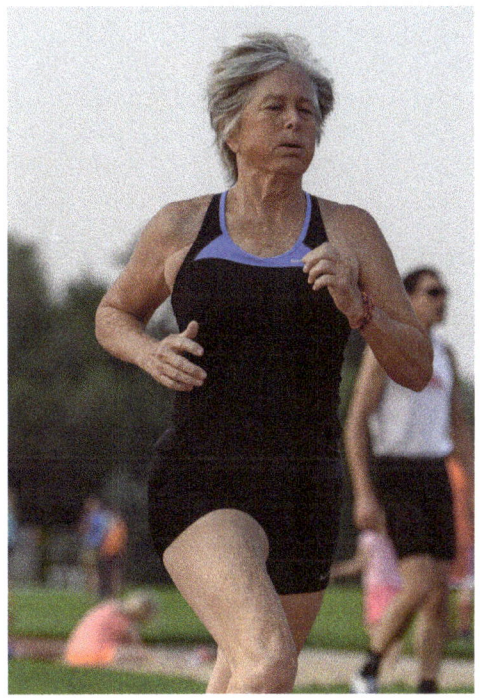

## SO LONG SAFETY PINS

What's worse than coming to the start line of a race to find out your shoelaces are undone? Perhaps it's that crooked bib you can't quite get straight. **Racxers** is a new alternative to pinning your race number on, and looking good for race day.

The pins are made up of strong rare-earth magnetics to clamp your race number to your race kit saving the dreaded snagging or holes in your high performance clothing. And now you can make sure that bib is placed just right. Racxers was founded this year in Boulder, by avid athletes Robert Ferris, Torin Koos, and Nick Kadlec.

Offered in packs of 4 and 8, ever set of Racxers pins come in a compact tin carrying case for easy storage in between races. As a great gift for family and friends, it's quickly being added to the essential race-day gear list. racxers.com

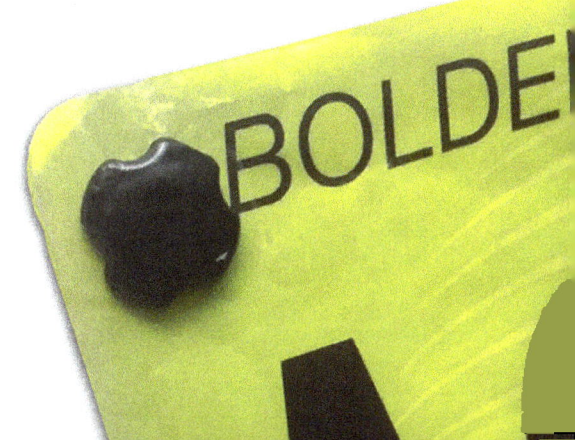

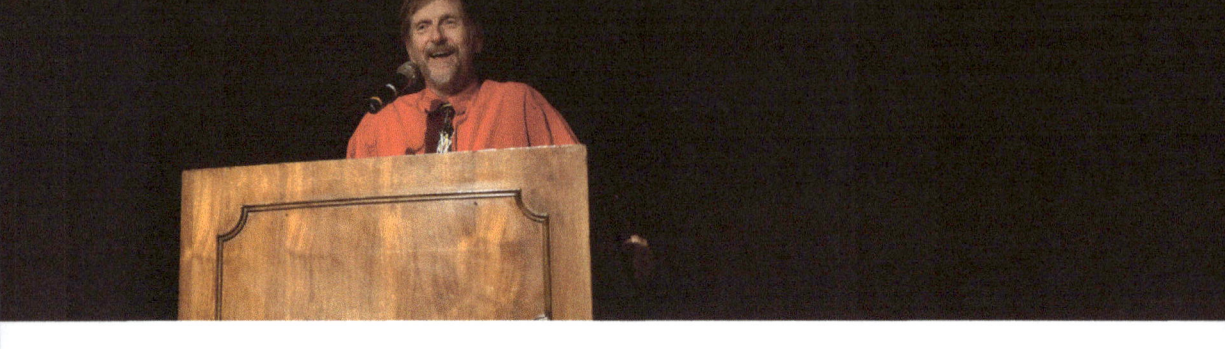

# Durden Inducted Into Boulder's Sports Hall Of Fame

Runner Benji Durden joined three of Boulder's best endurance athletes from the past at the 2015 Boulder Sports Hall of Fame induction ceremony which took place on Sept. 26 at the Avalon Ballroom. Cyclist Dale Stetina, triathlete Tim DeBoom, and climber Lynn Hill rounded out the class of inductees.

This was the 4th annual induction ceremony; past running inductees include Steve Jones, Lorraine Moller and Frank Shorter.

Benji was recognized for his many years of high performance running, but also his commitment to the running community in Boulder as he times a majority of the races in town - you may have seen him behind the scenes. He continues to run and has run over 100 marathons and just completed his 50 marathons in 50 states with his wife Aimee.

He noted that he knew Boulder was the place to be after moving from Atlanta where everything he did was news, like running in the heat in 3 layers of sweats. On one of his first runs after moving to town, he noticed people doing para-gliding, cycling, running, swimming, and was relieved to find he was "just one of the crowd".

---

"The first time I saw Benji run I immediately thought of his form as compact, efficient and quiet He finished first in the race that day and shortly thereafter made the 1980 Olympic Marathon team. Yes, he "was robbed" and the surprise qualifier from Georgia never made it to Moscow but, nonetheless decided to stay in and give back to his sport. He found his calling as a timer of races, a constant presence at events around the area. The elite runner became an elite timer. For years these runners, no matter how fast they go, have known they can count on an accurate time and place quickly provided. Benji's recognition is long overdue!"

- Frank Shorter

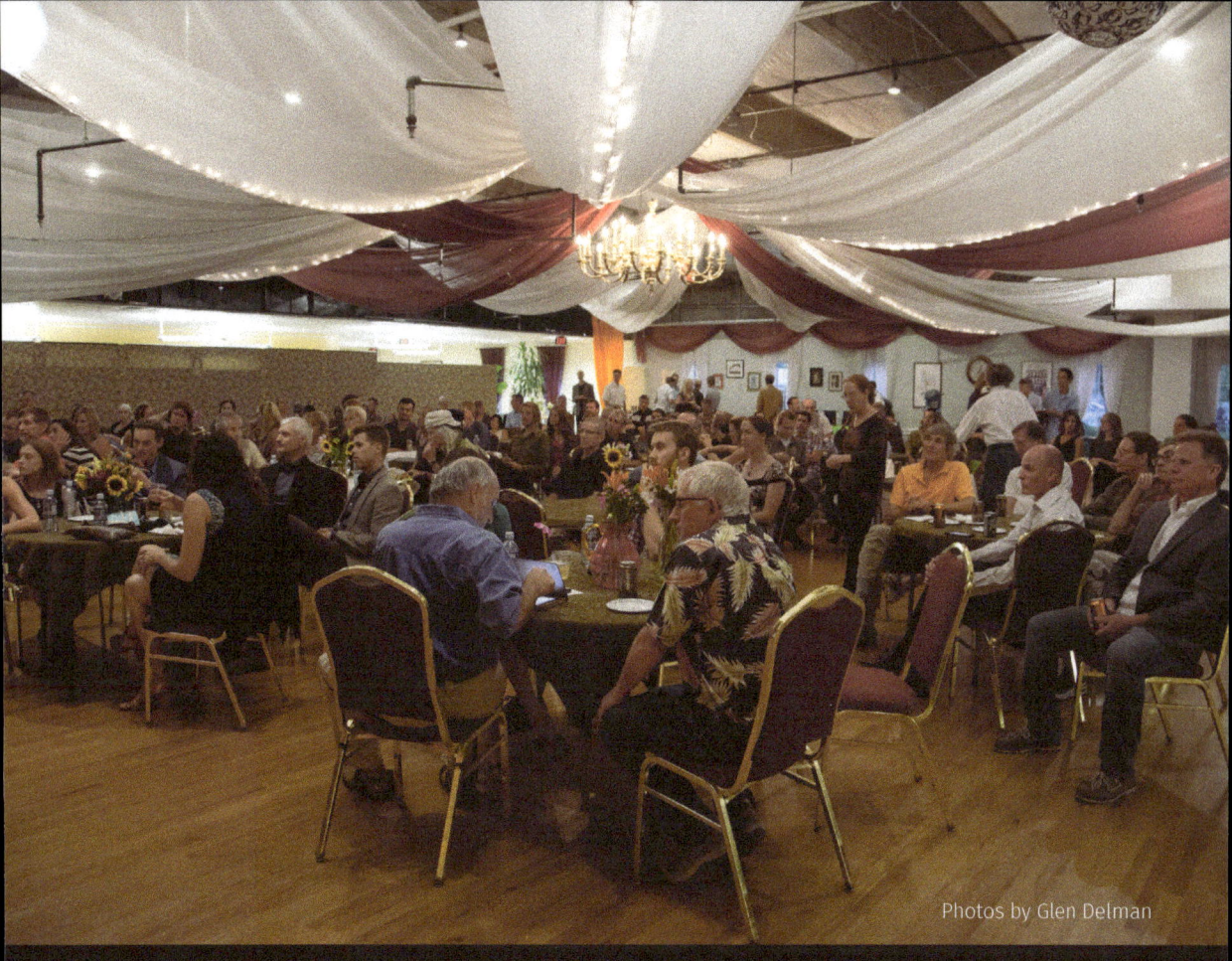

Photos by Glen Delman

"The idea is to honor Boulder's athletic legacy. There are many deserving athletes here that newcomers might not know about. They deserve another moment to shine."

- Organizer Anders Mavis

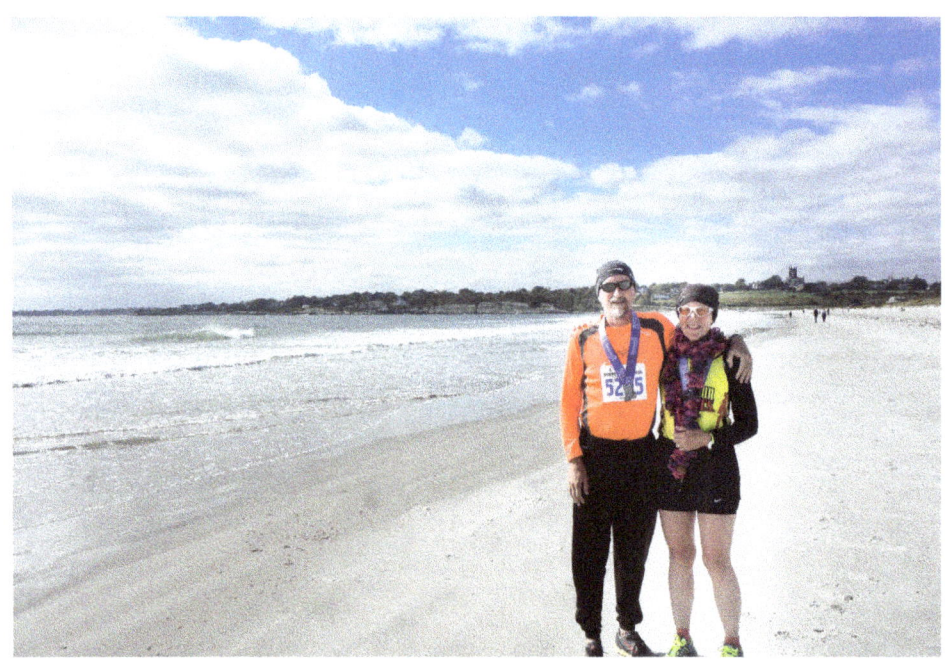

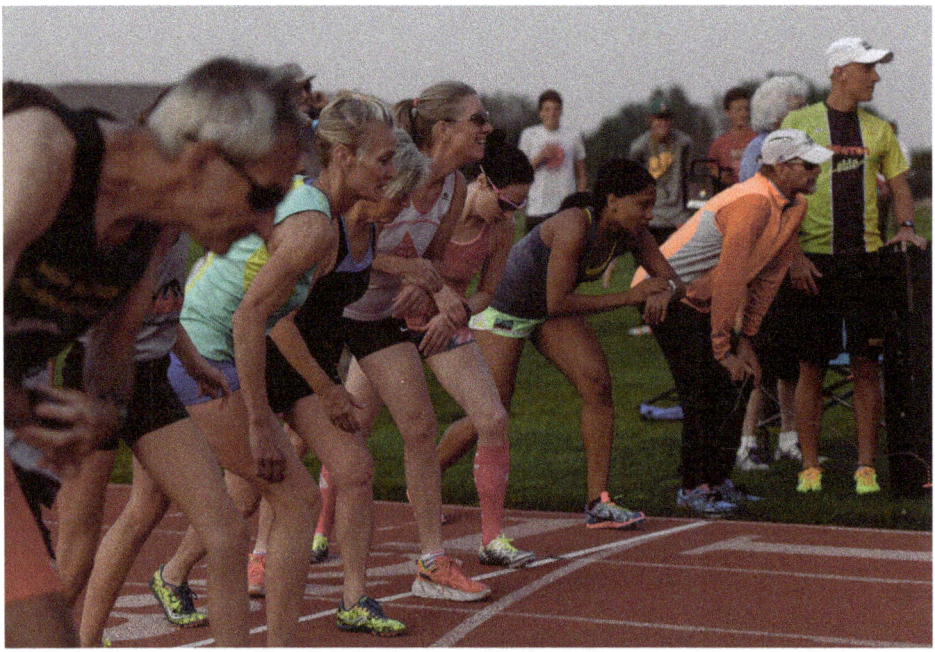

Celebrating Aimee's 50th Marathon in 50 States & Benji in a pre-race timing check.
Images courtesy of Benji & Aimee Durden & Dave Albo

At roughly the halfway mark of the 1982 Houston Marathon, Benji Durden glanced over at Bill Rodgers, America's best marathoner. This was the point in a marathon where four-time Boston winner Rodgers typically took off.

**This time, however, it was Durden who dropped the field, staying up front with Dick Beardsley for five more miles, chatting with media on the press truck, before running in unpressed to finish in 2 hours, 11 minutes, 11 seconds for the win.**

Such was Durden's fitness that he could run 26.2 miles at a 5-minute-mile pace, and feel good at the end.

In the early days of the running boom, he was fast enough to beat — more than once — legends such as Rodgers and 1972 Olympic gold medalist Frank Shorter.

Durden's own chance at Olympic glory looked to be coming in 1980, when he placed second in the Olympic marathon trials. However, like the other U.S. Olympians that year, Durden did not get a chance to compete in Moscow because of the U.S.-led boycott.

"That was the highlight of my career," Durden, whose marathon best of 2:09:57 came at Boston in 1983, said after a recent fun run at Flatirons Running, where he is a regular. Younger runners gathered around as Durden, with winner Tony Sandoval, recounted his race at those 1980 Olympic Trials.

It would have been fun to see how Durden, now 64, would have done in the Olympics, as he often ran his best when it counted. It's likely he would have been in the mix, based on a long career that included numerous wins and battles with other elites during road racing's "golden era."

Words by Mike Sandrock - Courtesy of The Daily Camera
Images courtesy of Benji Durden

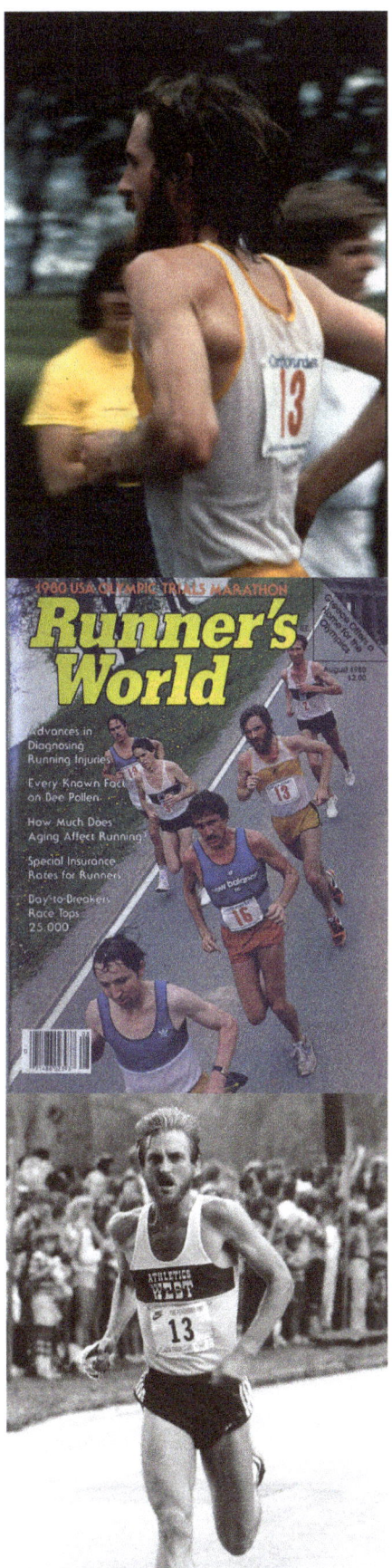

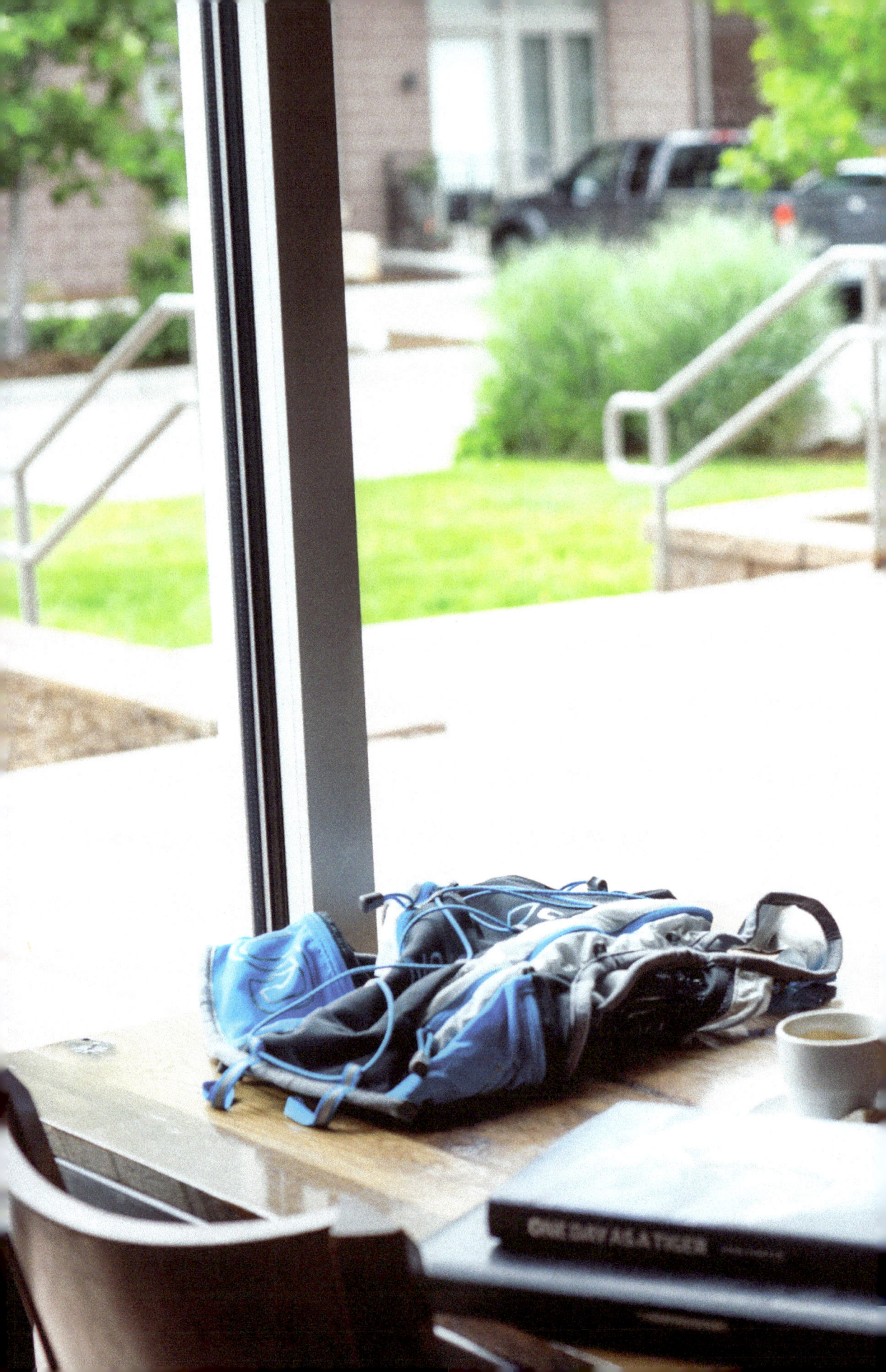

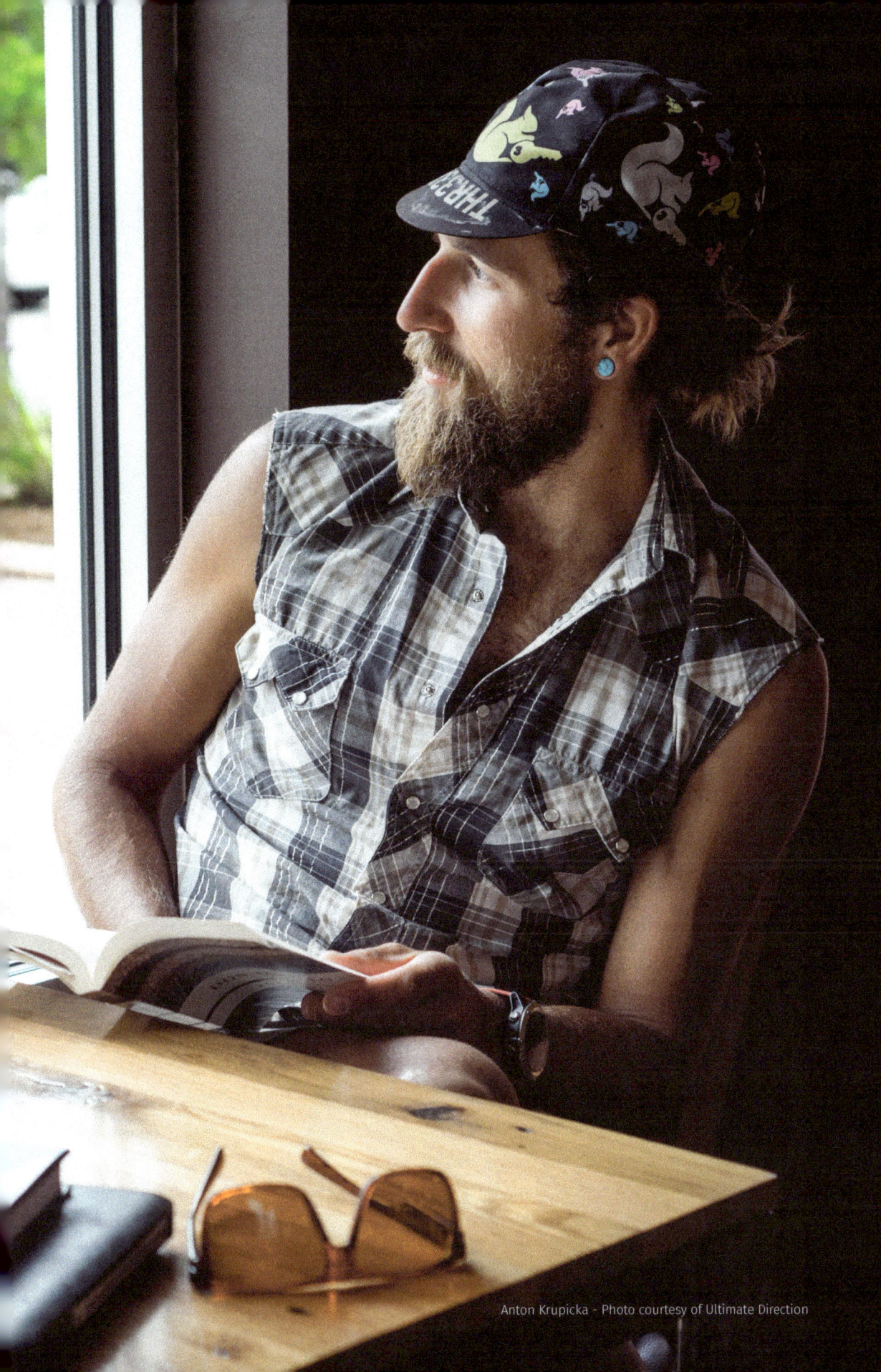

Anton Krupicka - Photo courtesy of Ultimate Direction

Culture of Run

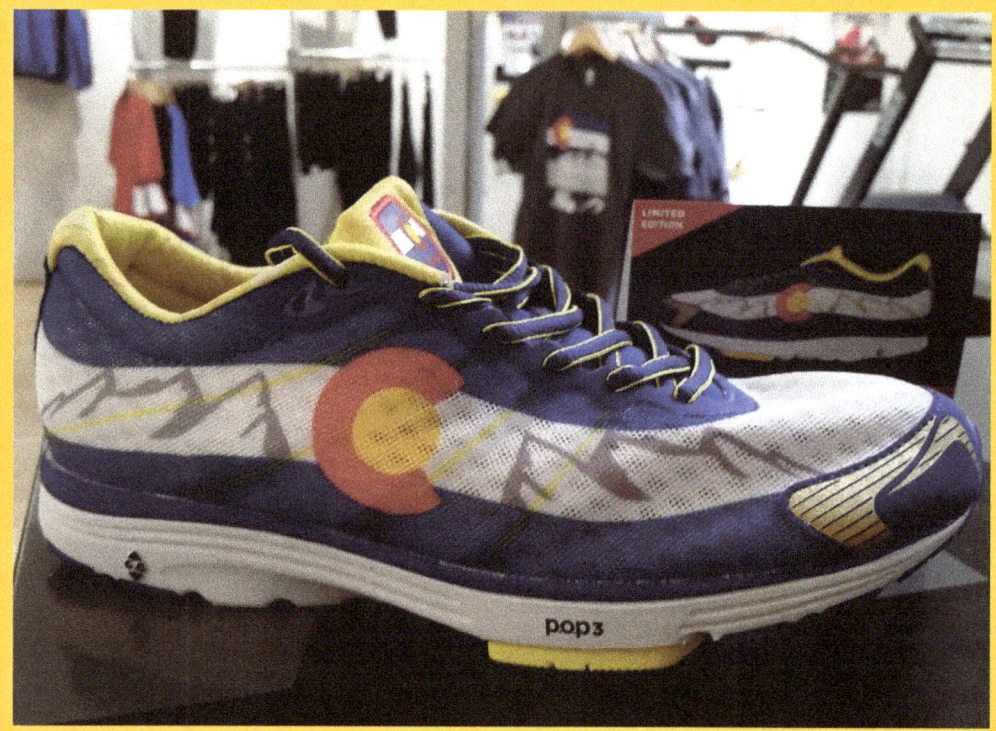

To celebrate its Boulder heritage **Newton Running** released a limited edition "Colorado" shoe that was made available just in time for the IRONMAN® Triathlon held in Boulder over the summer. It is only available at its Flagship store on Pearl Street.

The shoe, based on its Aha platform, has a lightweight and breathable upper featuring a likeness of Boulder's Flatirons and the Colorado flag printed on the upper.

Other details, including the laces and tongue, play off the yellow and blue of the Colorado flag, while the top of the tongue features a prominent Colorado / Newton Running logo. The inside of the shoe features a topo map and the words Born in Boulder on the heel cup.

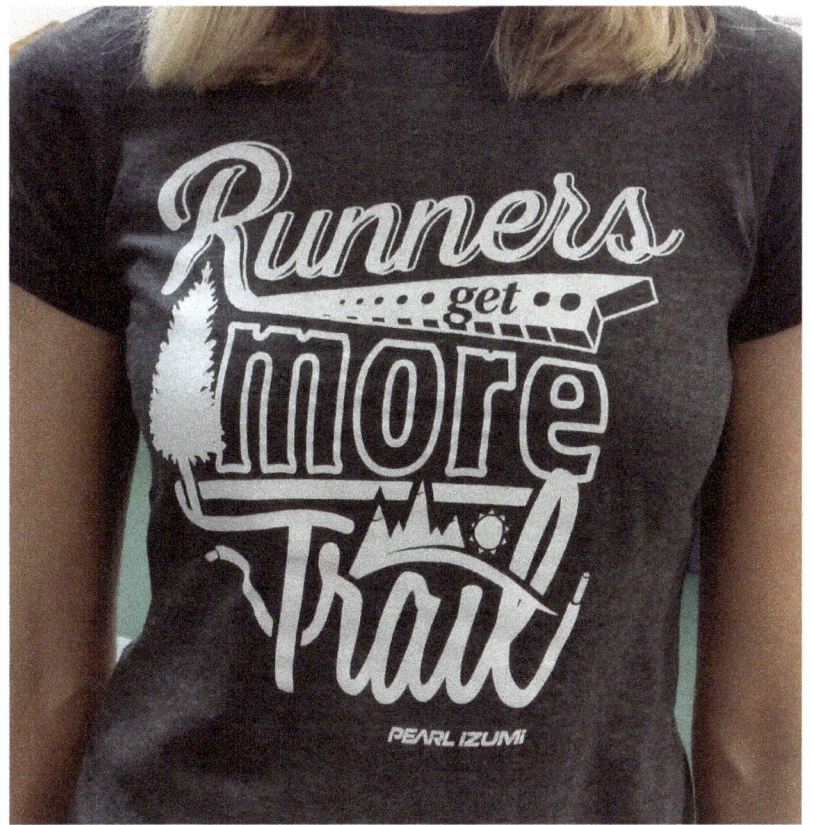

**Pearl Izumi** launched its Run Ambassador program in 2015. The team currently consists of over 250 road and trail-running enthusiasts who represent 36 U.S. States and Puerto Rico.

"The 2015 Pearl Izumi Run ChamPIons are our newest athletes and brand ambassadors. The team consists of the runner who is able to squeeze in a few miles a few times a week, to the ultra runner who is training for the next big endurance race." said Emelie Ortiz, head of global brand marketing at Pearl Izumi Run.
via malakye.com

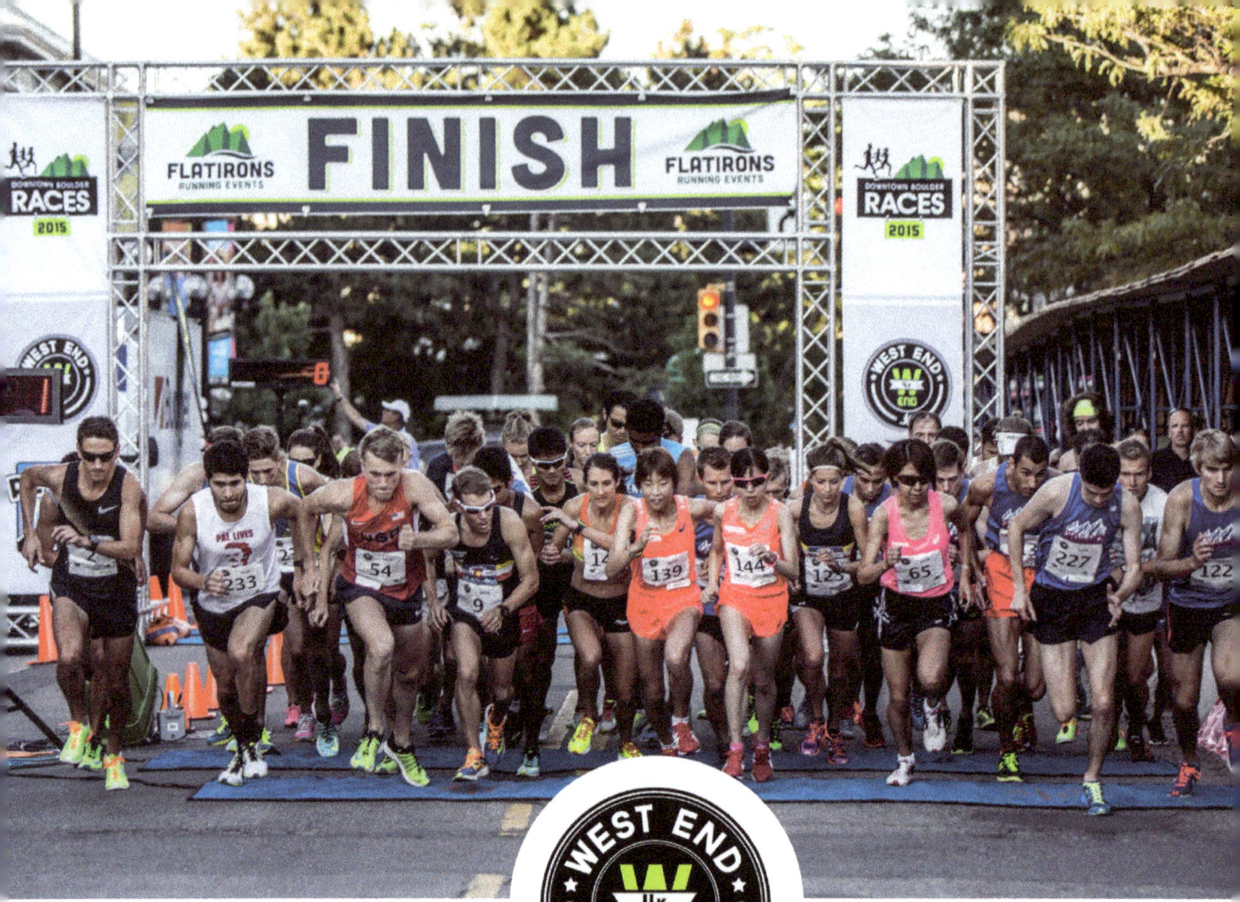

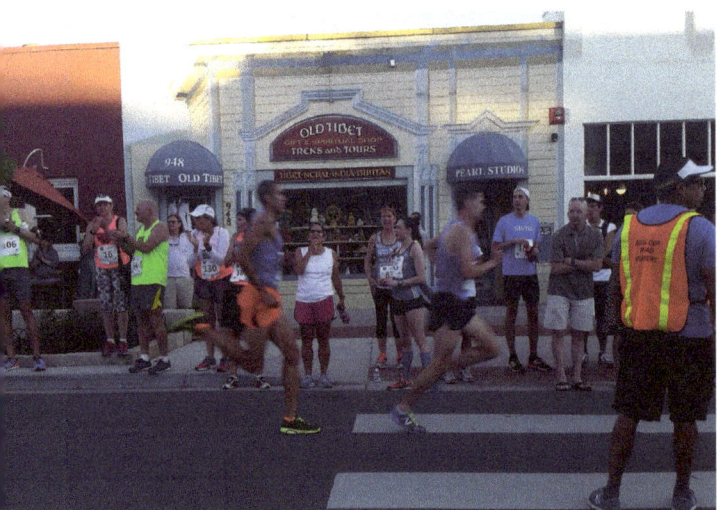

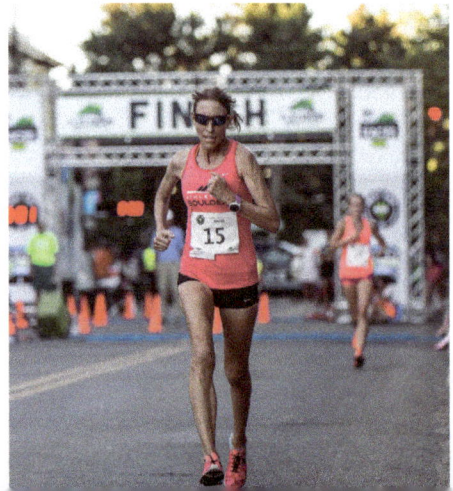

The West End 4K, after a year hiatus due to construction, returned to the West Side of Pearl Street. The spectator friendly 2-lap course was familiar, but an extra kilometer was added to deepen the challenge. Along with its open division, it was host to the area's Corporate Challenge. Another change to the format seeded the elite men and women in the same wave to cap off the exciting evening.

# "You want to be on top of your training, not buried under your training."

- Bob Kennedy, first non-African under 13 minutes for 5k.
  from podcast #3 3/4/2015

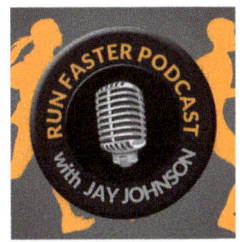

Coach Jay Johnson hosts the Run Faster Podcast, with guests ranging from Olympians like Dathan Ritzenhein, Lee Troop and Bob Kennedy, to running icons like Bart Yasso. Among the most popular podcasts are those with Dr. Richard Hansen, one of the smartest minds in running, and Steve Magness, coach and author of "The Science of Running."

Subscribe on iTunes: **"Run Faster Podcast"**
or visit **www.CoachJayJohnson.com** for the latest episodes.

**Running and racing** have been a part of my life for over three decades. I have enjoyed some markers of personal success and enjoyment over these years: a high school conference win here, toeing the line against Olympians in races (no wins there!), and many miles with friends. Now in my so called "middle years" I even get the great joy of getting to share the occasional run with my teenage children who have taken up cross country.

I run a bit of everything.

Ultramarathoners think I am short distance guy. Milers think I am an ultra guy. Roadies see me as a trail runner and the folks that hit up Green Mountain in Boulder every day might think I am nuts for going around in circles on a track for workouts. However, nearly all of them think one thing I do is really out there.

And that something is

# PACK BURRO RACING

Words by George Zack

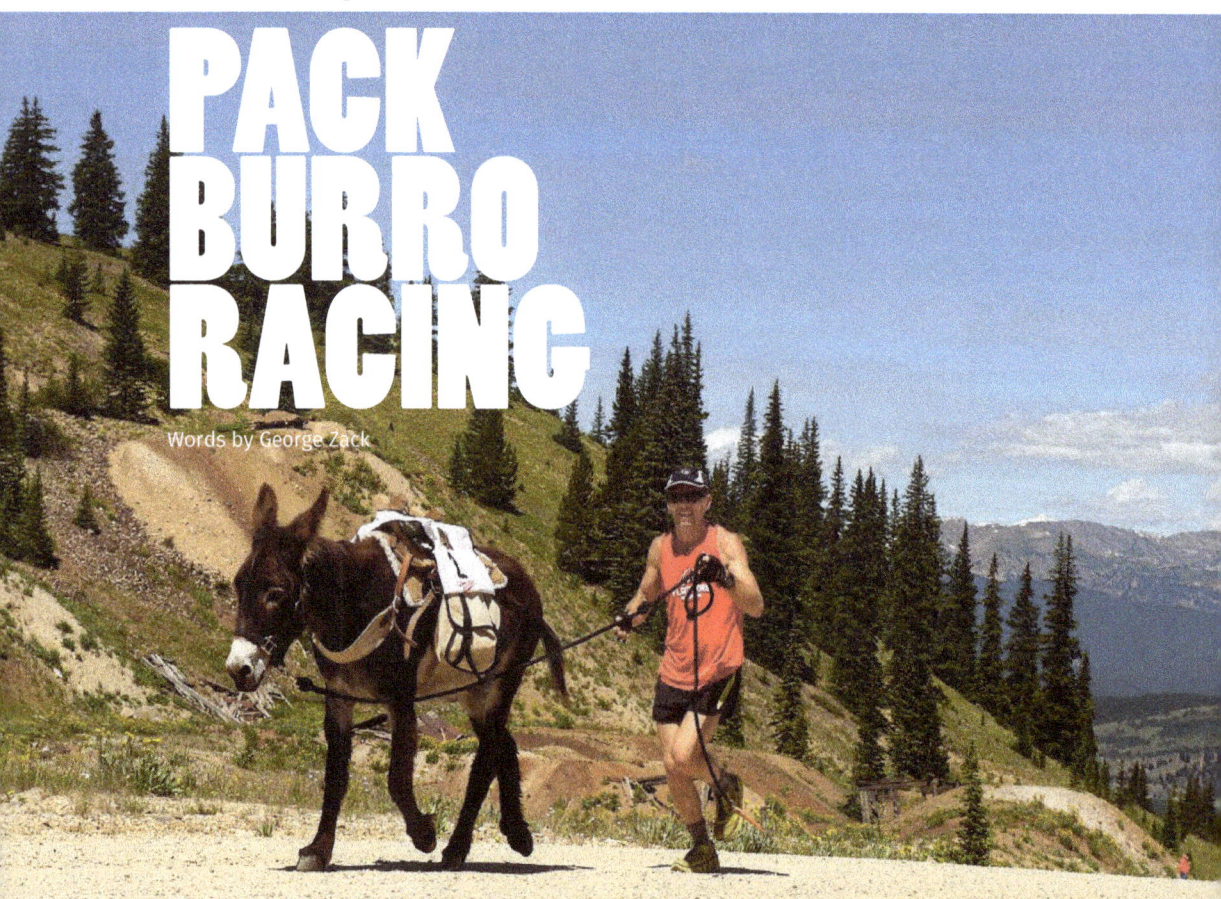

Photo by Joe Zamudio

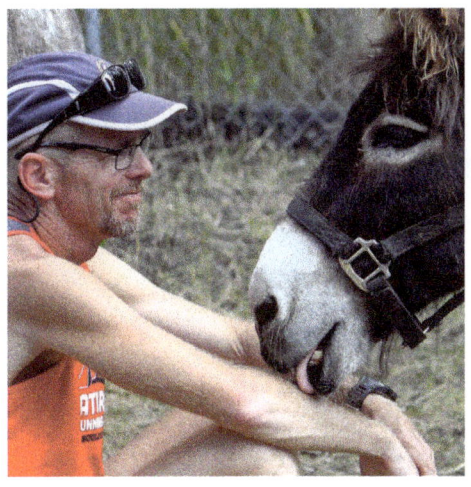

Photo by John Brisenhan

## Triple Crown Winners
George Zack and his ass, "Jack"

Pack Burro Racing is a sport run predominantly in Colorado in mountain towns in the summer to recognize the history of the burro and mining in these locations. A burro is the same as a donkey except we prefer the Spanish word here in Colorado. In these races, the runner runs adjacent to a burro, connected by a lead rope no longer than fifteen feet. The burro carries at least thirty three and a half pounds in a pack saddle. This saddle must carry a gold pan, a pick axe and a shovel (remember, it is about mining).

After hearing about it for years, I took up Colorado's Official Heritage Sport in 2010. My foray into this game was in Fairplay, Colorado.

Fairplay is like many mountain towns. It was a hub of activity at the base of fourteen thousand foot mountains a century ago when miners tried to change their fortune by seeking out gold and other precious ores. The miner's companion was often a burro who'd haul gear in and loot out.

The legend of Pack Burro Racing is that two miners came to the same claim at the same time with their burros fully laden with gear. The miners then both raced back to the town's assayer office to see who could stake the claim first. The other legend is a couple of old timers in a bar came up with the idea as a way to attract people into town to spend a few bucks in the area that had otherwise started to dry up.

The Fairplay race, or Burro Days, also serves as a town fair and has been going on for more than 65 years. Racing teams of runner and burro climb up out of town at 10,000 feet in elevation to Mosquito Pass at over 13,000 feet. And then they make their way back down to complete the 29 mile effort in what is called "The World Championship of Pack Burro Racing."

Pack Burro Racing, as you would expect, is full of stories. Anytime you put fifty-some four legged animals on the start line that are stronger than the people handling them and with their own intentions, you get a show. The people are colorful stock making for a live personalized TV reality show. Unlike other races where a runner ultimately only can control their effort and performance, Pack Burro Racing is different in that it is a team event.

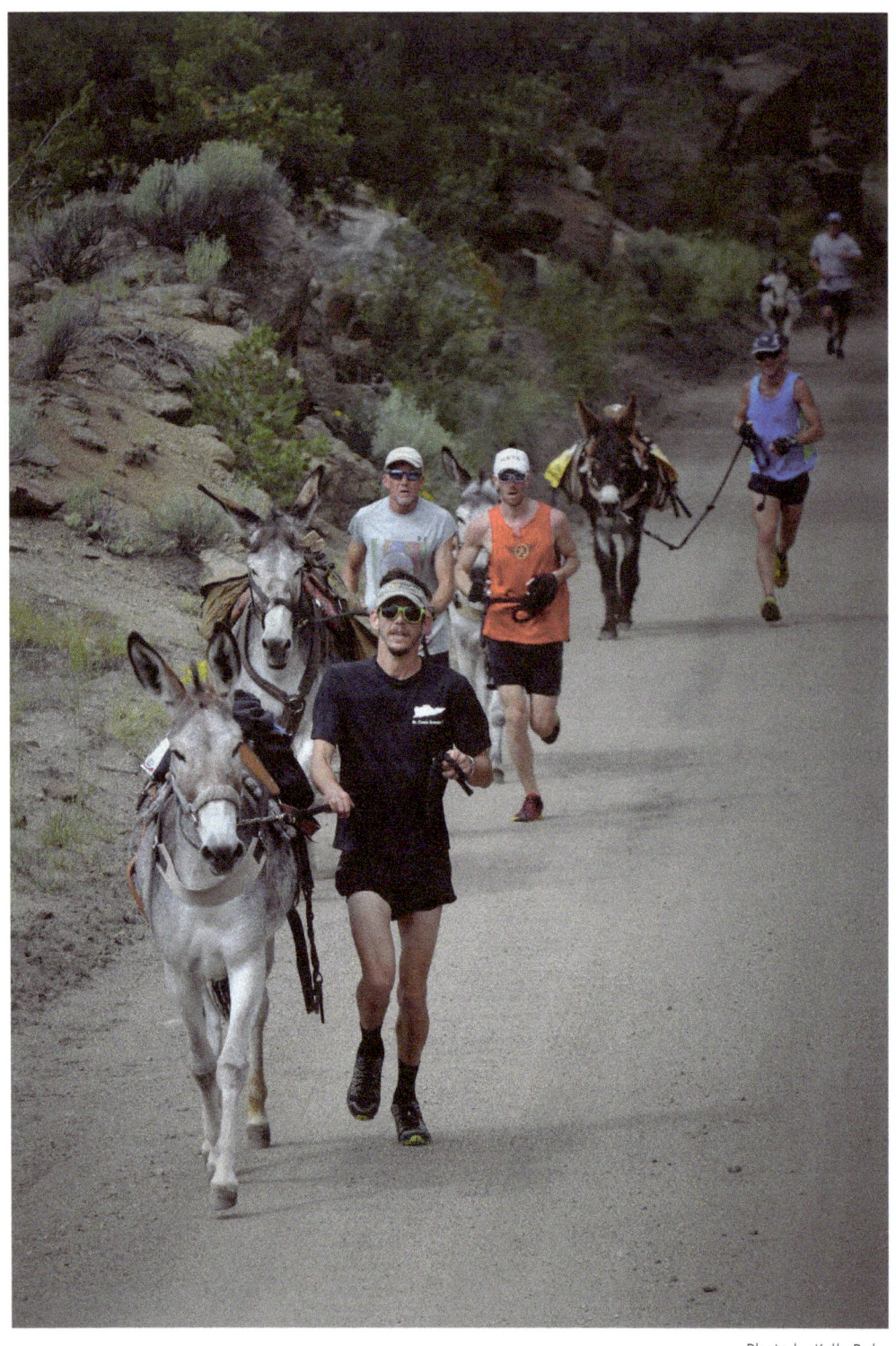

Photo by Kelly Doke

It is the runner and the burro. Many a talented and hardworking runner has shown up to one of these races with intentions of carrying over their individual success into Pack Burro Racing. They often end up back in the pack and disappointed as they learn the burro may have very different perspectives on what is going to be accomplished on race day. Hal Walter, a winner of the Fairplay race seven times, has quipped, "No donkey wakes up in the morning thinking they are going to run as hard as they can to Mosquito Pass and back today."

But we humans do have such expectations and so this sets up for an interesting partnership between man and beast. The most successful racers are those who have "a relationship with their ass." Burros are historically known as being stubborn. The reality is actually they are cautious, self-preservationists who are not interested in engaging in activities they deem as outside their boundaries.

I have raced with a burro named Jack in all my races. In one of my first races Jack and I came to a small mountain stream. The depth of the water was perhaps enough to roll over the top of my shoe at its deepest. I proceed across the stream expecting to lead Jack through via our rope. Jack however decided the stream was something that represented impending doom and refused to cross. Despite my pleas and encouragement, he'd have nothing to do with crossing the stream. After several minutes (which in a race often can feel like hours as you sense competitor teams gaining on you or getting further ahead), I walked Jack a few hundred feet up to another part of the stream where he determined it was okay to cross.

Realizing Pack Burro Racing is an event that requires trust and coordination in this team means one has to also recognize it is best to not set expectations towards a particular result other than just enjoying themselves in the Rocky Mountains for a day with a beautiful animal that is counting on you to do right by them.

## I have "built a relationship with my ass" with running and racing Jack over the years.

We seem to get over creeks okay now most of the time. I think he enjoys running with me. This year some friends brought him out to see me at the 50 mile mark of the Leadville 100 miler. Not expecting this, I was pleasantly surprised to see my racing partner. For the short run on the old washboard mining road up to the ghost town of Winfield, Jack sided next to me. I took the rope as he expected and he then upped his pace happily to his seven minute a mile trot. I had to let him go as such a pace was too much for me at that point in the race.

Coming into this summer of Pack Burro Racing I had to learn to trust Jack as well. I thought as an 18 year old burro, his fastest days were behind him and that we'd have no shot at winning any races. But he proved me wrong and this year we won the "Triple Crown" by winning Burro Days, the 12 mile race in Buena Vista at Gold Rush Days and the 22 mile Boom Days race in Leadville.

I will continue to race roads, trails, and track; hills and flats, short races and long for as long as this body will let me. Hopefully, the number of race days ahead of me is at least equal to those behind me.

Call me what kind of runner you want but I gladly embrace the label of **Pack Burro Racer.**

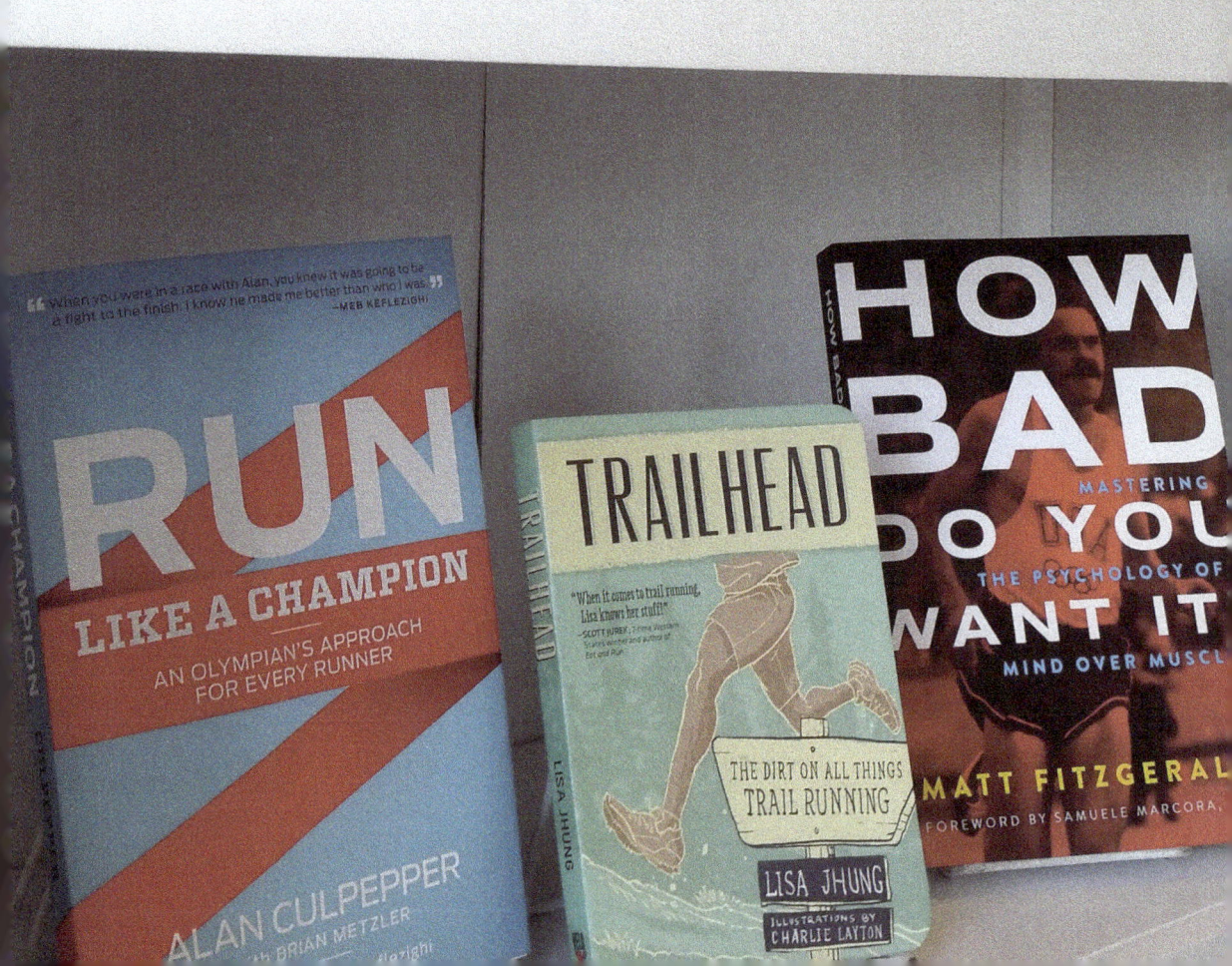

# VeloPress
# A Boulder Original
Words by Peter N. Jones

Boulder is a breeding ground. More top athletes, World Champions, Olympians, and bad ass people have called Boulder home than perhaps any other place in the country. There are at least 20 runners who have already qualified for the Olympics living and training in town. The current record holder for the Fastest Known Time on the Appalachian Trail – Scott Jurek – lives in town. The current USATF Trail 50K Champion – Andy Wacker – calls Boulder home. Laura Thweatt, the USATF Cross Country Champion lives, trains, and works just off Broadway. On a regular basis one can run into a former World Record holder in the Marathon, one of the fastest mountain runners in the country, and a two-time winner of the Ironman World Championships all in the same checkout line at Whole Foods. Boulder simply breeds champions.

But it's not just world class athletes that call Boulder home. Some of the most innovative, popular, and forward thinking companies in the outdoor industry have been born and bred right here. Ultimate Direction, Roll Recovery, Pearl Izumi, Newton Running, and many others started in Boulder and continue to call Boulder home. VeloPress – located in east Boulder just off the creek path – is one of these companies, starting as a side project of a cycling newsletter and becoming the leader of books about endurance sports.

"We started 30 years ago as an off-shoot of VeloNews, gathering their best articles or photos of the year into books. We published some of the first training books in English. Now we are the largest publisher of endurance sports books, and the number two publisher in running books." That is one of the first things Dave Trendler, director of sales and marketing for VeloPress, told me when I went in for an interview. The other thing he wanted to make sure I took away was that:

"Being part of Boulder's community has been essential to our growth and success. From the athletes to the coaches, being based in Boulder has allowed us to tap into the best of the best, and that is reflected in our books and authors."

Two-time Olympian and author of the book *Run Like A Champion* Alan Culpepper agrees with that statement: "The team at VeloPress are athletes and enthusiasts in their own right so they have a unique ability to help shape and mold a book into a product that resonates with the audience. In my book they helped me find my voice as a writer. As someone new to the process of book writing they really walked me through it step by step with encouragement while still challenging me along the way to produce my best work. I can't say enough great things about the group at VeloPress."

To some extent, VeloPress is simply following the path that is so commonly found among Boulder's long list of top athletes and top outdoor companies: adherence to high standards, the use of expert authors, and a deep commitment and love of the sport. Matt Fitzgerald, author of *How Bad Do You Want It* and one of the top selling running authors in the country summed it up like this: "I think the most important ingredient in Velo's success is that they know their market and how to reach it. Other publishers market every book the same way, whether it's about running or something else. Velo targets runners specifically. I've done enough books with enough publishers to know that what Velo is doing makes a difference."

VeloPress was not always number two in the running market. In fact, it has been a concerted effort to climb up the podium and to strive for that number one spot. Supported by the VeloPress team, that effort has been spearheaded by Casey Blaine, acquisitions. Casey, a dedicated runner herself who trains with the local Boulder group Boulder Banditos, has specifically sought out some of the best of the best in the sport and brought them under the VeloPress roster. From coach, foot guru, and author of *Natural Running* Danny Abshire, to ultrarunning legend Kilian Jornet and his *Run or Die* autobiography, Casey has tapped into the running community in Boulder and beyond to produce some of the most sought out books on running.

*Trailhead* by Boulder author Lisa Jhung is the latest book, and the third book published this year by VeloPress involving Boulder authors. "Velo really got behind me as a writer and amateur illustrator, having faith in me and the idea for my book. I'm really happy with how the book came out, and how VeloPress has supported me through the whole process. And with Velo being here in Boulder, I loved being able to have face-to-face meetings along the way. *Trailhead* was my first book, and having a close connection to my publisher in both proximity and in the good people there was valuable for me."

# "We have been in Boulder helping runners get faster and, in turn, Boulder has helped us stay on the pulse of running," said Trendler. "To some extent, VeloPress is a direct outcome of being part of the Boulder running community."

And that symbiotic relationship continues to grow, with over twenty titles dealing with running, from half-marathons to ultrarunning, from strength training to yoga. VeloPress is a Boulder original, and just like the athletes who call this amazing town nestled up against the foothills home, is a reflection of the community as a whole – dedicated, inspiring, committed.

To go for a run among dense trees, to pop out onto a snowy mountain view, to wind back down into town is a treat I never take for granted. I've lived in some great trail towns, but the beauty of Boulder is that you have all this great outdoor activity, and a fun downtown with great restaurants, bookstores, music and more. For me, Boulder is the perfect balance and size.

- Lisa Jhung, Author of *Trailhead*

# RIVALS

### "Hey, Sandrock!"

The voice was a thunderbolt out of the blue, freezing me in my tracks.

I turned and there he was, Dan Skarda, and instantly I was taken back many years to the Illinois high school sectional cross country meet. It was the qualifier for state — very deep and competitive.

I can still vividly recall the first 400 meters. The sectional meet was held at Crystal Lake, on a hilly, wooded course roughly 50 miles west of Chicago. After a start across an open meadow, we had to make a 180-degree turn around a pole.

My team, highly ranked Maine South, got off well, and I was among a large group near the front. I was running on the inside closest to the pole, and as I slowed to go around it, a runner pushed me from behind, his voice ringing out:

"Watch it!"

Before I could react, I was knocked over. Falling, I glanced to my left and saw a skinny, wide-eyed guy in a red and grey Mundelein singlet running right over me. Fueled by adrenaline, I jumped up and rejoined the pack.

Adrenaline, however, does not last long, and I soon fell back, finishing out of the top 10, missing out on qualifying for the state meet. Our other top runners did not have their best days, either, and Maine South finished out of the team qualifying as well.

"Harriers falter at sectionals," read one headline.

Years passed by. Then, a decade or so later, I was racing the Zoo Run in Denver's City Park. Catching up to a runner who looked to have gone out too fast, I looked over and had a shock of recognition: It was unmistakably Skarda, the same runner who had knocked me over that long-ago fall day at Crystal Lake.

"Vindication," I thought. Beating him would not turn back the clock, but it would be sweet. It was not to be, however. Not that day or any of the other roughly 50 times we've raced over the years. Skarda has that knack of racing well to go along with his talent (he was a 4:09 miler and 2:16 marathoner).

Somehow, he always squeezes out a kick at the end, edging me by less than a couple of seconds sometimes. Our rivalry faded in recent years as we both slowed, but every now and then I'd see him on a run and shake my head.

"You racing Pearl Street?" he asked, as we talked.

We have battled at the Downtown Boulder Race Series many times. I was planning only to watch and cheer this year, but impetuously taking up his implied challenge, I said, "Yeah, you?"

"Yup." We eyed each other for a moment, looking each other up and down. He looked fit.

"Training much?" I asked.
"Nah; it's sad how slow I run. You?"
"Not much; mostly jogging."

The following evening, I went to the Boulder Road Runners all-comers meet at Potts Field. I ran the mile and clocked 5 minutes 59 seconds. Faster than expected. It was time to call in the big guns.

First, I asked Jason Simpson, husband of World Championship 1,500-meter gold and silver medalist Jenny Simpson, for one his wife's mile workouts. No go. Simpson is way too smart for that. He suggested I talk to her coach, Mark Wetmore.

Wetmore was helpful, outlining a couple of weekly workouts in the month leading up to Wednesday's race. Not to sandbag, but with the recent hot weather, I did not do any of Wetmore's workouts, content to simply get a short run in.

Last week, I checked in with Alan Culpepper, the local coach, former 3:56 miler and author of "Run Like a Champion." Understanding what a rivalry means (he had many epic battles with fellow Olympian Meb Keflezighi), Culpepper provided a "five-day secret training plan." It included some short intervals "to dial in race pace/effort," but not enough to leave me tired.

Culpepper's plan, sent over by email, ends with this: "Wed: a.m. easy 10 minutes and some stretching; p.m. Take down Dan."

That's what I'll aim to do. And if not, there are plenty more races on the calendar. Neither of us is going to stop running anytime soon.

Editor's Note: Skarda remains undefeated.

Words by Mike Sandrock - Courtesy of the Daily Camera
Photos by Glen Delman and Dave Albo

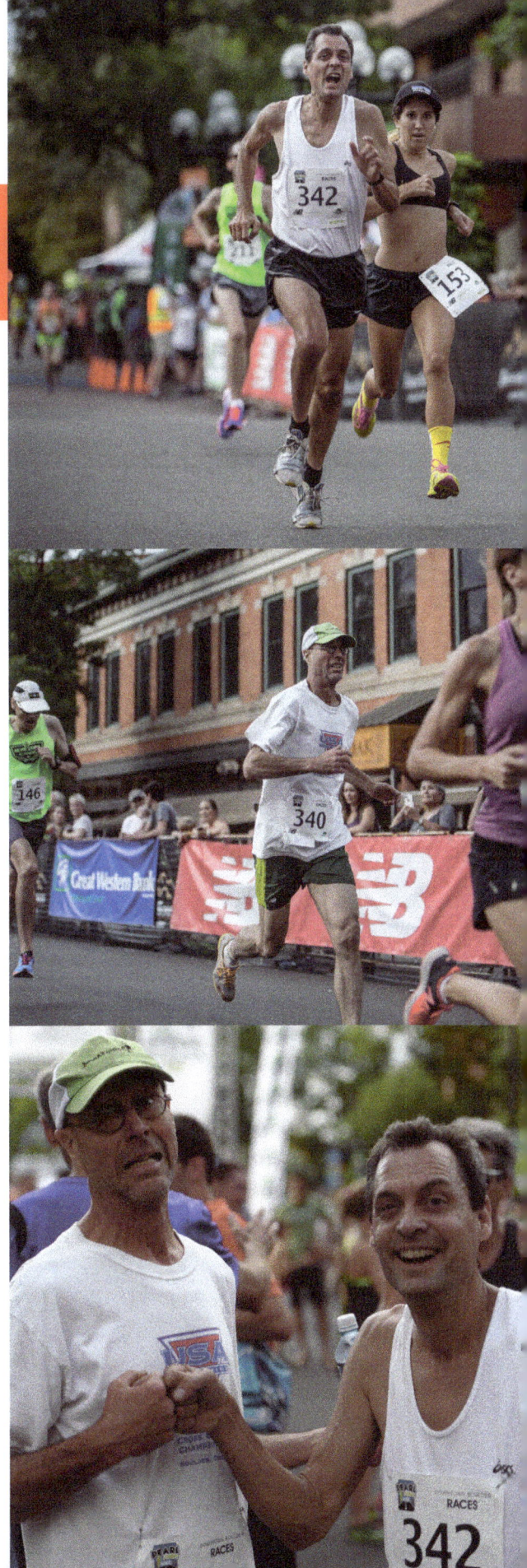

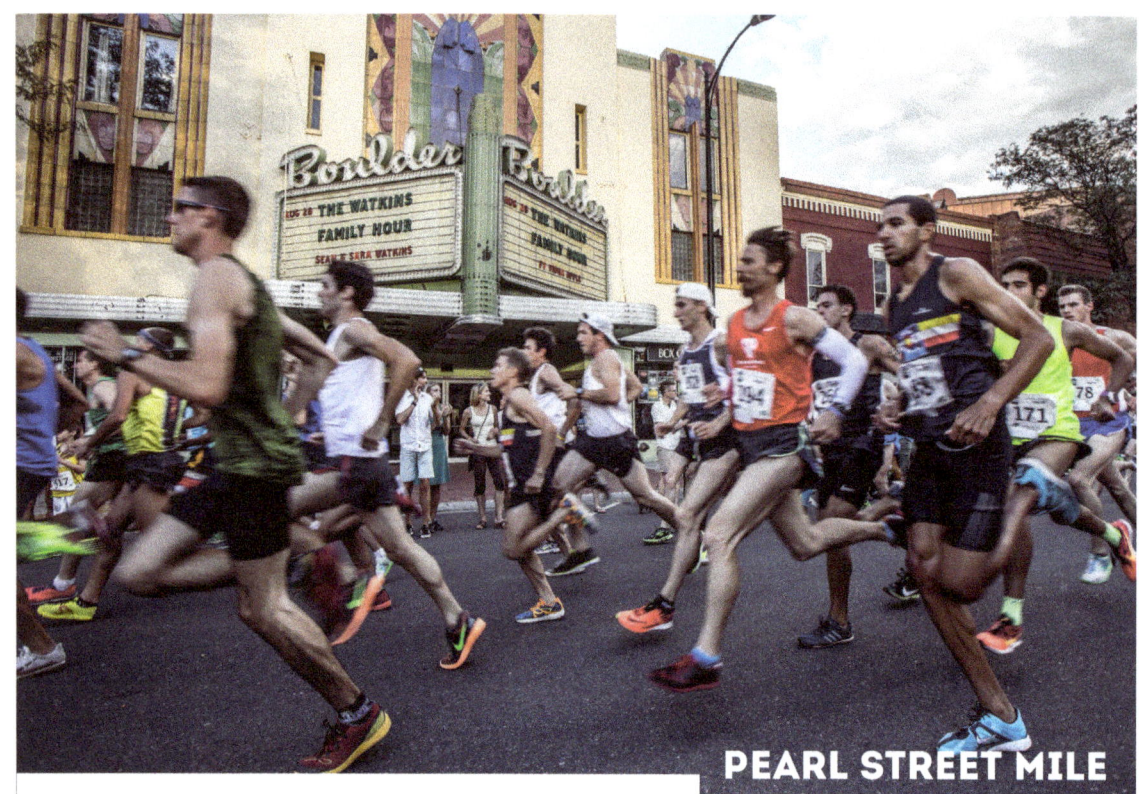

**PEARL STREET MILE**

Coming off the final turn in Wednesday evening's 18th annual Pearl Street Mile, Stephen Pifer was right where he wanted to be, poised on leader Ryan Poland's shoulder. But when Pifer, an ex-University of Colorado star and 3:56 miler, started his finishing kick, Poland matched him stride for stride on his way to edging Pifer by one second, 4 minutes 7 seconds to 4:08.

It was a course record in a venerable race that has seen many local and national elites test themselves over the deceptively tough loop, that starts and finishes on 14th Street on the Pearl Street Mall. The previous record of 4:11 was held by Australian Shaun Creighton.

"Pifer is a great runner, and I knew he would be right there at the end," said Poland, 23, who grew up in Westminster and is a recent University of Portland grad with a personal best mile of 4:01. 'When I took the lead (just after 800 meters, on the turn from Pearl Street onto 19th Street) I wanted to take control. I didn't look back, but I knew he would be coming."

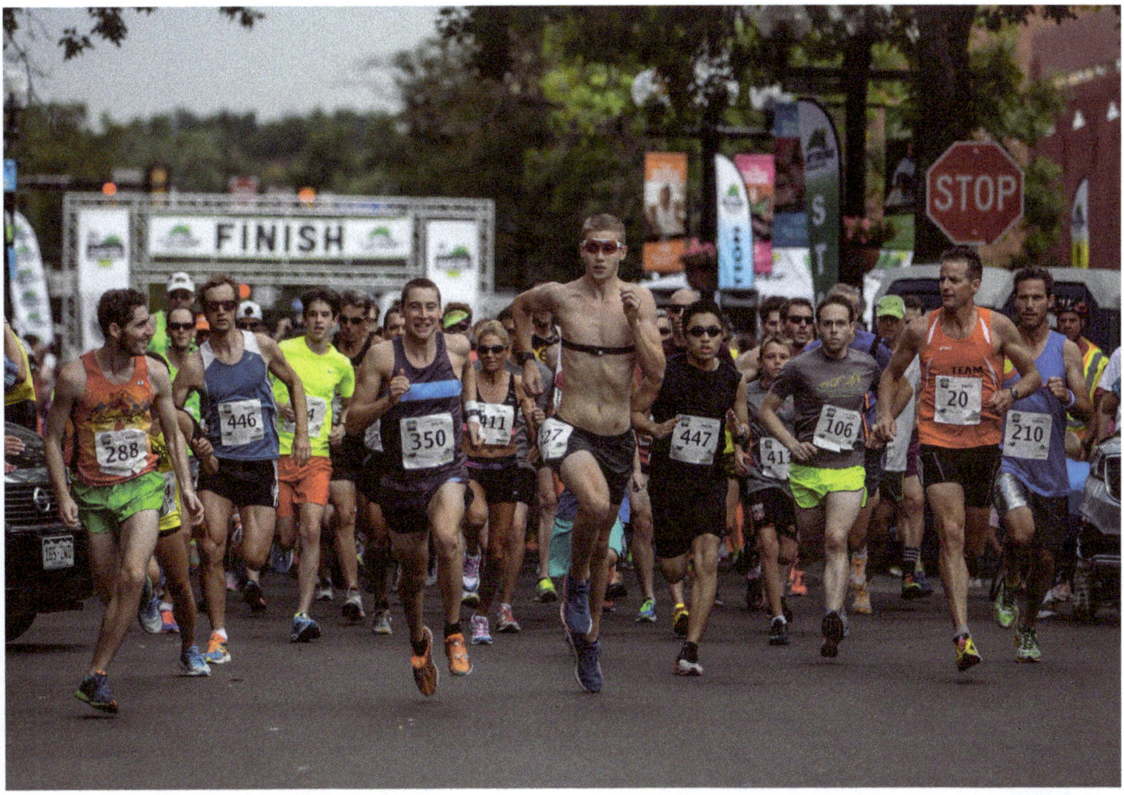

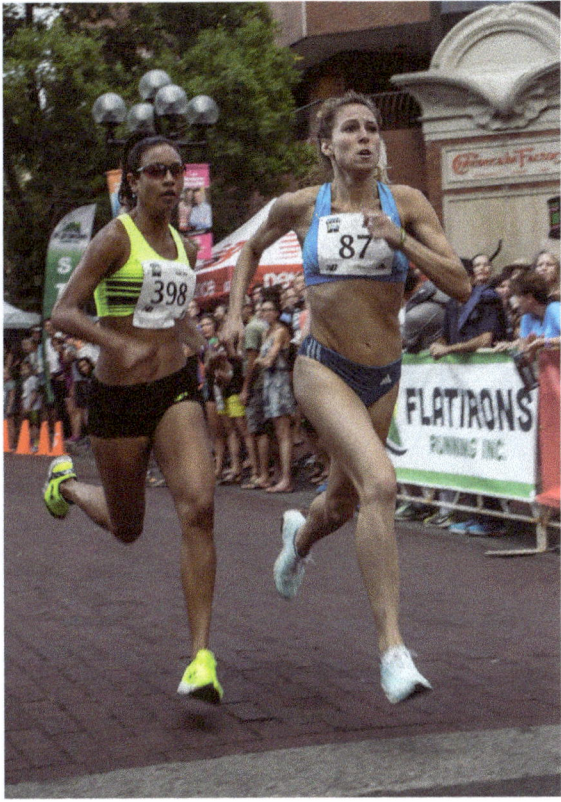
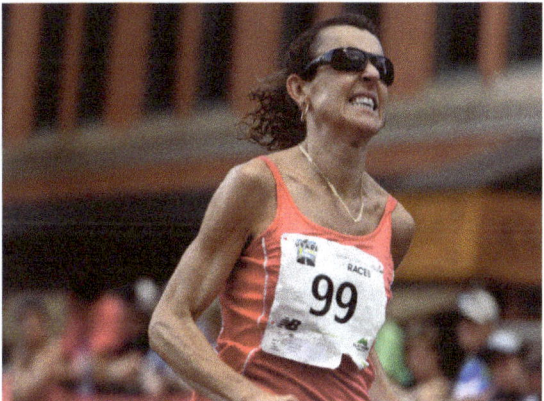

Photos by Glen Delman and Dave Albo

# PEARL STREET MILE

Photos by Glen Delman

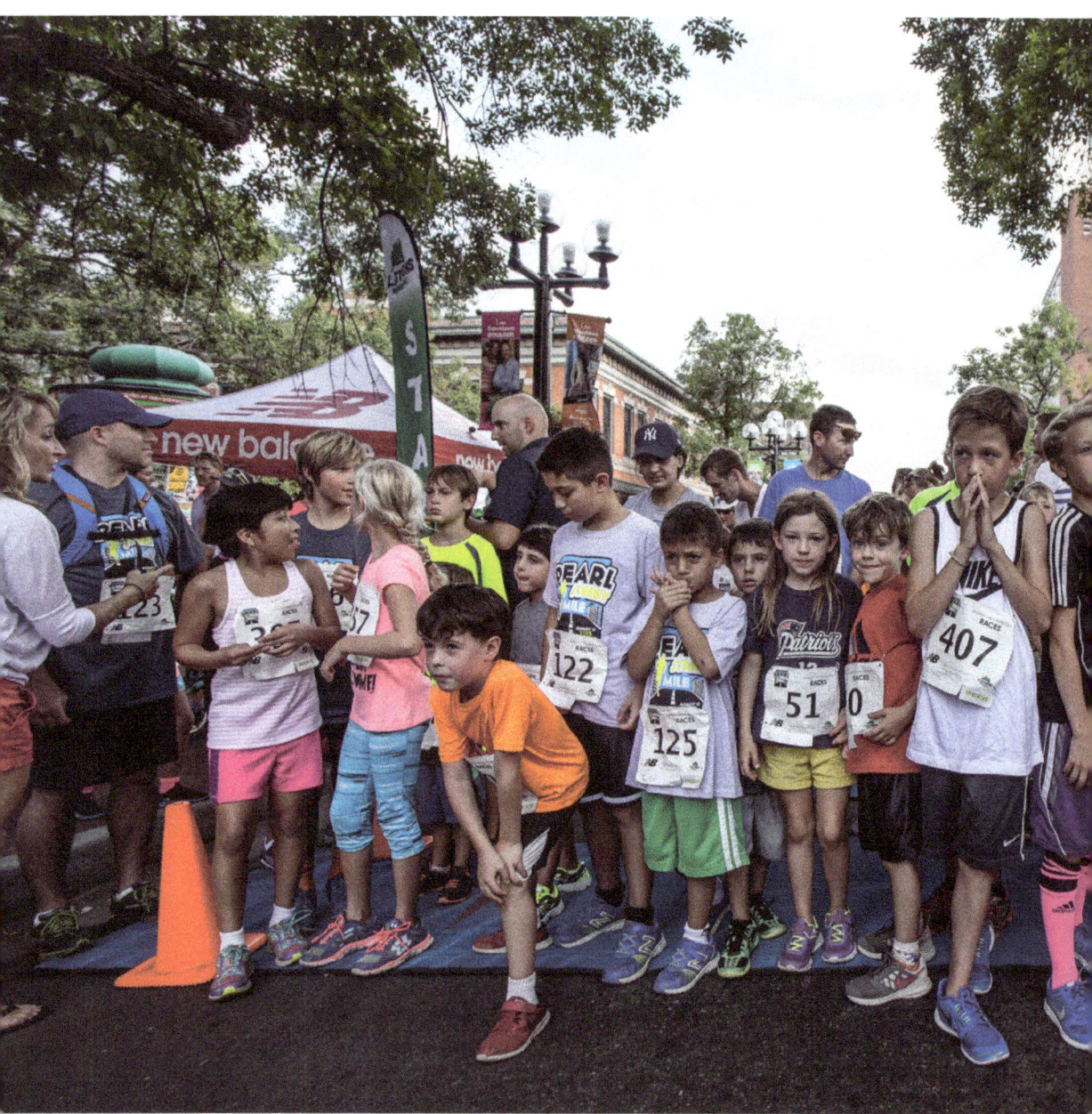

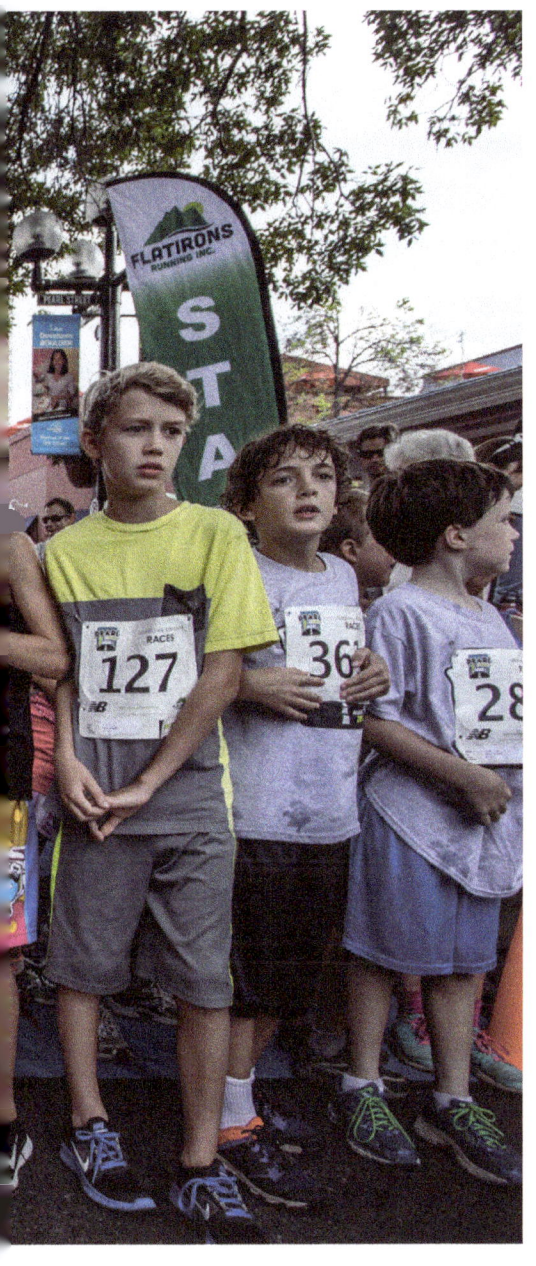
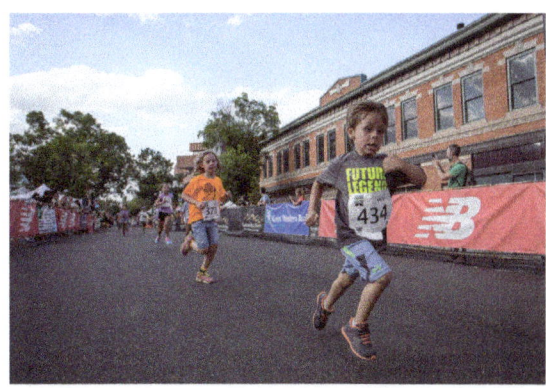
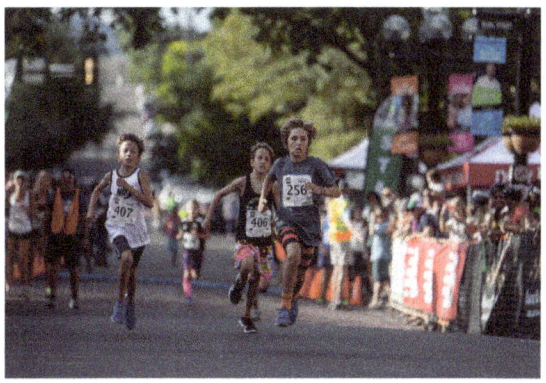
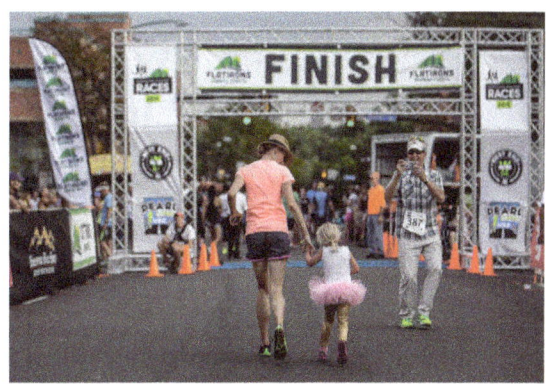

# ADVENTURE RUNNING

Words by Bill Wright

Boulder is blessed with truly unique geology. Nowhere else in the world are there thousand-foot slabs of moderate climbing difficulty that are fifteen minutes from a trailhead that is in a vibrant city. While to some of us it is now obvious, it took awhile before these rocks were fully exploited. While the climbing isn't that difficult, 5.6 or easier, technically rock climbing had always demanded a rope, except for the few crazy soloists.

Soloing 5.6 doesn't get you any attention, so why risk it? For a few early visionaries, it was just plain fun. Gerry Roach, Kevin Cooney, Bill Briggs, and Buzz Burrell found that scrambling up the Flatirons was just a nice detour to their regular trail runs. Much more engaging than just a trail run, scrambling became their routine. Since these early pioneers considered these outings more of an adventure run than a rock climb, it was natural to start recording their times.

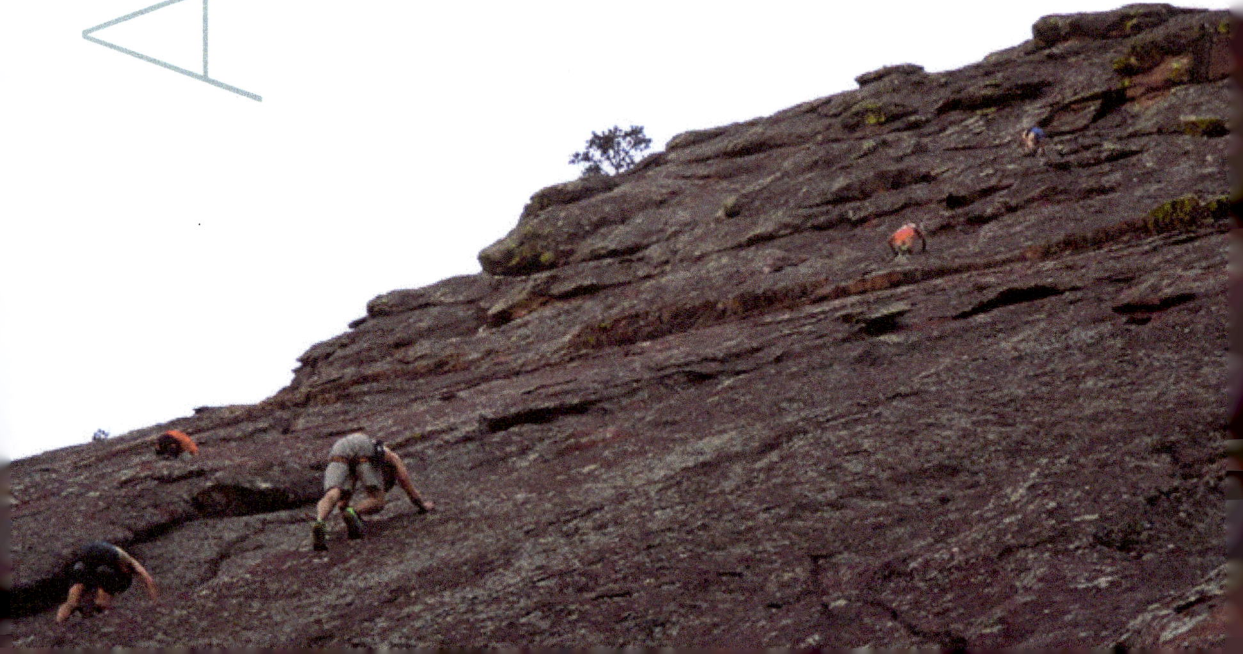

Now once you write down a time, it isn't long before even the least competitive person will try to better that time.

I'd heard about these guys. I remember Gerry claiming less than an hour to climb the Third Flatiron. That seemed impossible to me. How ignorant I was...

**I'd been an avid trail runner since I moved back to Colorado in 1994, competing in the Pikes Peak Ascent and Marathon. When a serious climbing accident prevented me from more athletic climbing, I turned to the Flatirons to rehab. There I discovered a whole new genre of climbing: scrambling. I found tremendous satisfaction on the easy east slabs of the Flatirons.**

My sons were born in 1995 and 1998 and my climbing changed from day-long outings to just a couple of hours. Upping my speed and efficiency, I found I could get in nearly a day of climbing before work and have all evening for my family. In order to do that in the Flatirons it meant combining my trail running with climbing. As my experience grew I became more and more comfortable leaving the rope behind. It was time to see if that one-hour Third Flatiron time was hearsay or real.

I organized some friends to give this a try. One friend set up the rappel ropes and three or four of us gave it a go. To my astonishment, I broke an hour. My buddy Ken Leiden was so intent on breaking an hour that he ran all the way back to the parking lot in his climbing shoes. In these early speed efforts, we still carried our climbing shoes, switching into them for the rock climb and then back to our running shoes.

So, was my 49-minute time the fastest anyone had done this, I wondered. Then I met Bill Briggs. He'd done the Third in just under 37 minutes. I'd met one the founding fathers of Flatiron speed. Buzz Burrell was concentrating on the First Flatiron and had a similar time on that. He'd also linked up the Top Ten climbs from Gerry Roach's Flatiron Classics guidebook. Inspired by these two pioneers, I became hooked on the Flatirons.

With John "Homie" Prater, Mark Oveson, and George Bell we formed the Satan's Minions Scrambling Club. The name was given to me when a friend of a friend read my description of a typical morning outing: we'll run five miles, climb 2500 vertical feet, and solo ten pitches of 5.5, and we'll be back at the car by 8:30 a.m.

My knowledge of the Flatirons grew as I eventually became the first person to climb every single route in Gerry's guidebook. My Third Flatiron time trial became an annual event. Word spread and the Minions grew in numbers. In 2004 I decided that one dash up the Third wasn't enough. It was just too much fun. At the time I was very into the Tour de France, so without much creativity I dubbed my five-event series the Tour de Flatirons.

While Bill Briggs was retired from speed scrambling, Buzz was still going strong and still one of the fastest scramblers. Nevertheless, the Tour probably started a year or two late for him to take the title. The Minions now had some young guns who were expert climbers and very fast runners. Jon Sargent won the first Tour.

**The next year national champion trail runner Dave Mackey joined the Minions and entered the Tour. Another Minion, Stefan Griebel, was quickly gaining fitness and drive. These two would go on to dominate the Tour de Flatirons for the next decade and eventually own every single Flatiron record, including, finally, Briggs' record on the Third Flatiron.**

Today the Tour de Flatirons is bigger than ever. Over thirty different scramblers competed in the 2015 Tour and a new king was crowned: Matthias Messner. Matthias even set the new record on the First Flatiron: 32:18. The energy is high and the camaraderie is higher. The positive energy still inspires me, as I fall down through the ranks.

I hope I'm still out giving my best even when I'm DFL.

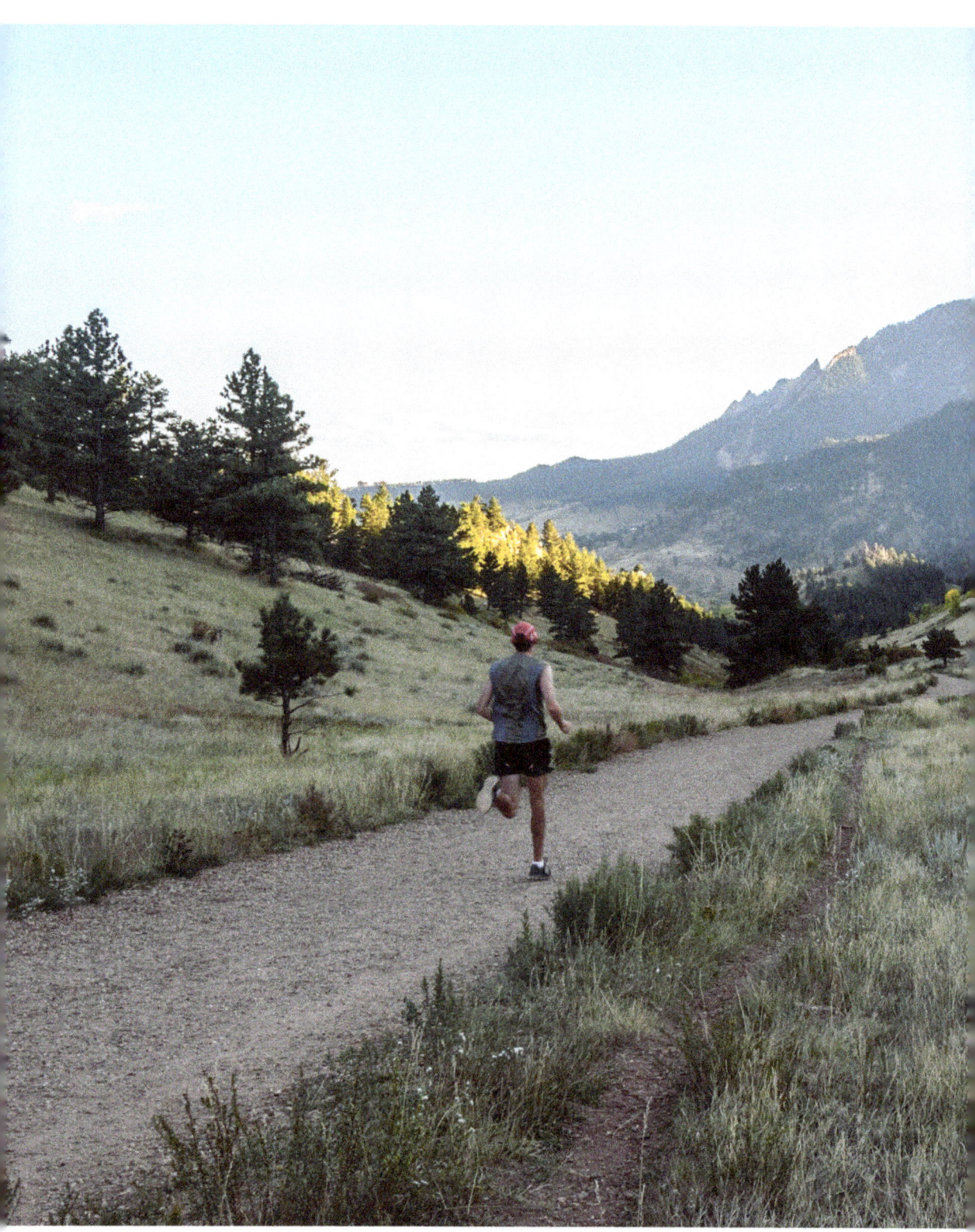
Photo by Ryan Lawrence Photography

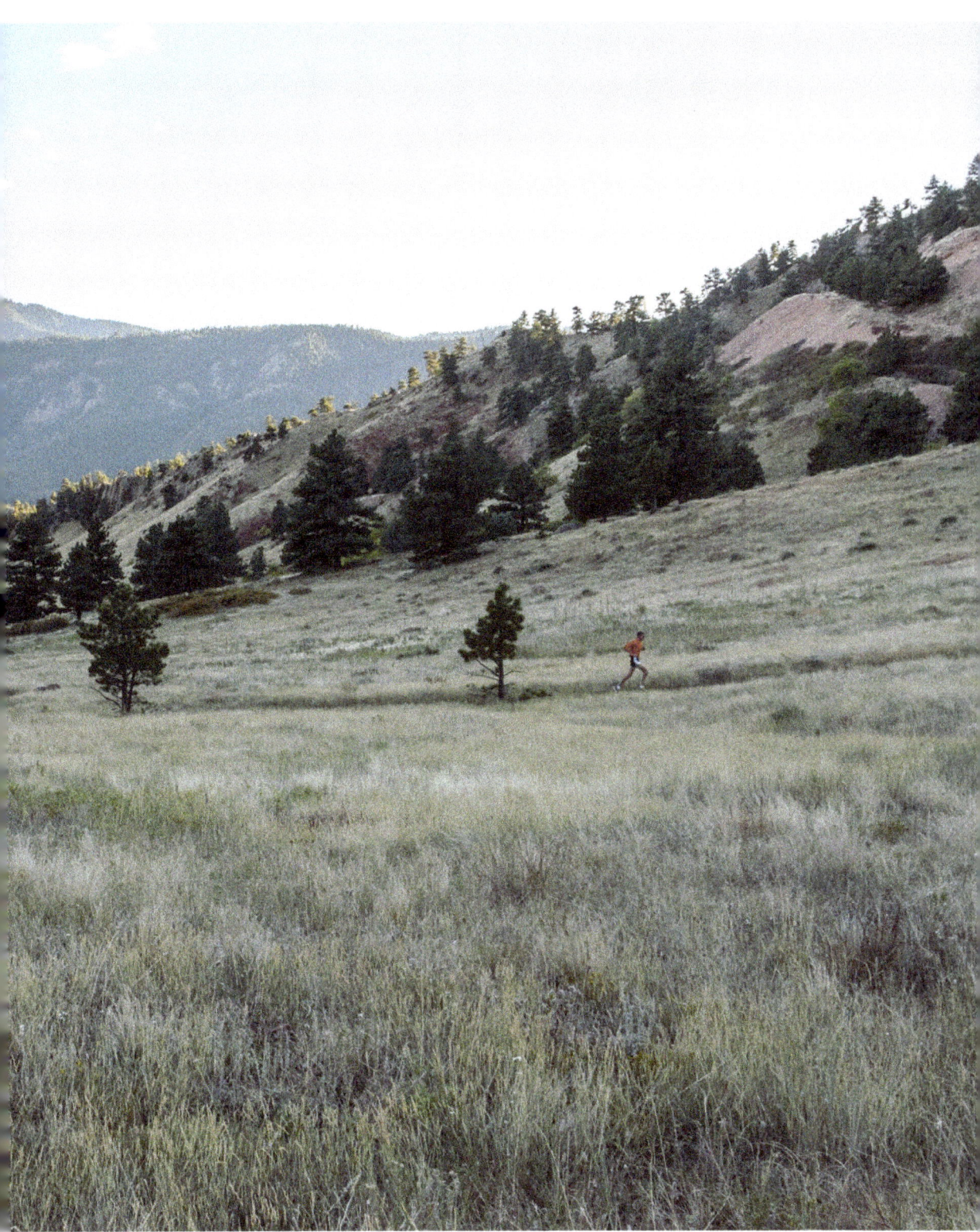

The allure of Mt. Sanitas is its accessibility because it is right there, standing on its own, smirking over Boulder.

"I can do that!" is how most people feel about our backyard peak, but once they've ascended the rocky and somewhat technical trail to the top, they are treated to the thrill of both the view and sense of accomplishment because the effort is substantial and not as easy as it appears.

- Adam Chase

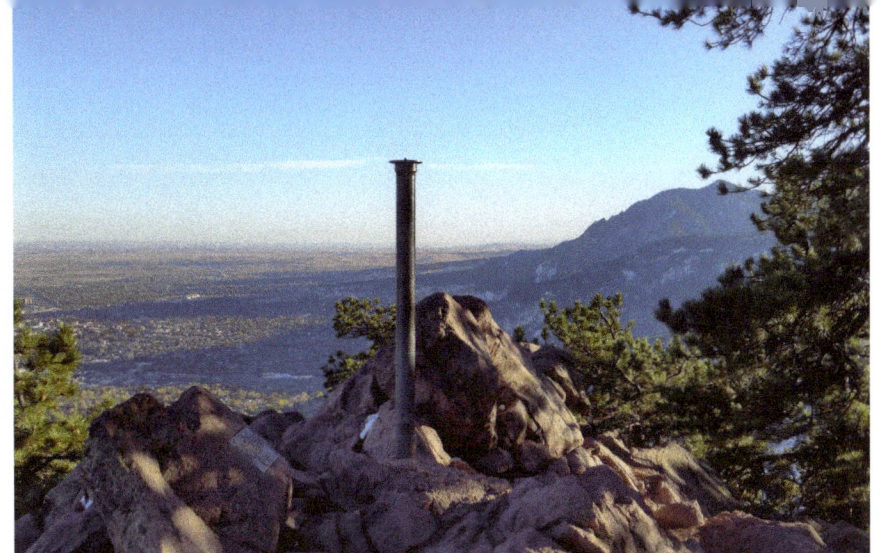

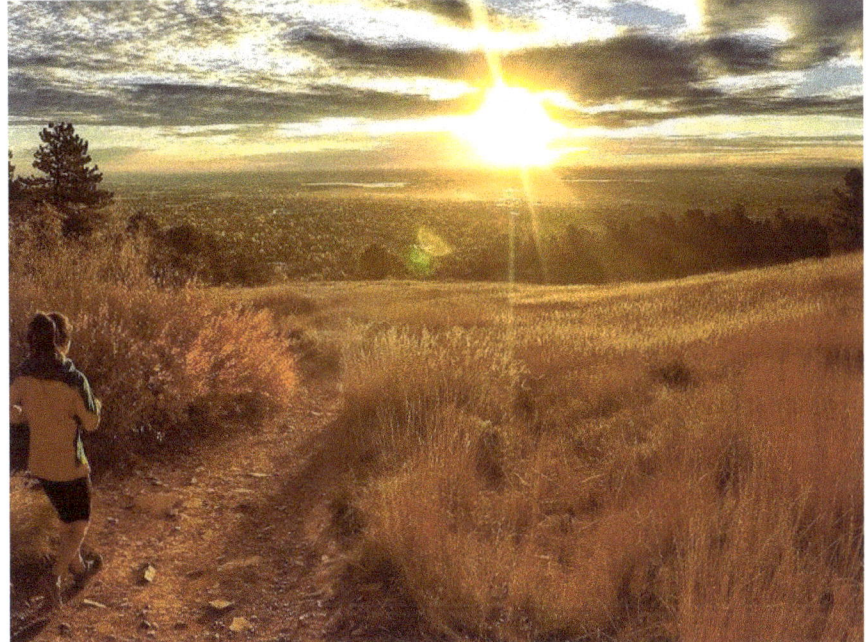

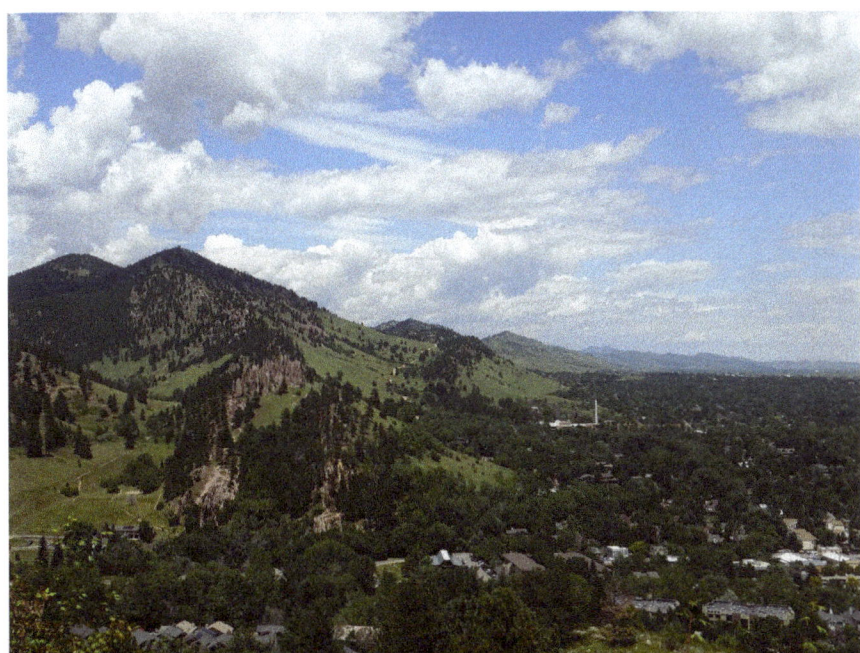

Photos by
Todd Straka
Stefanie Kamm
Todd Straka

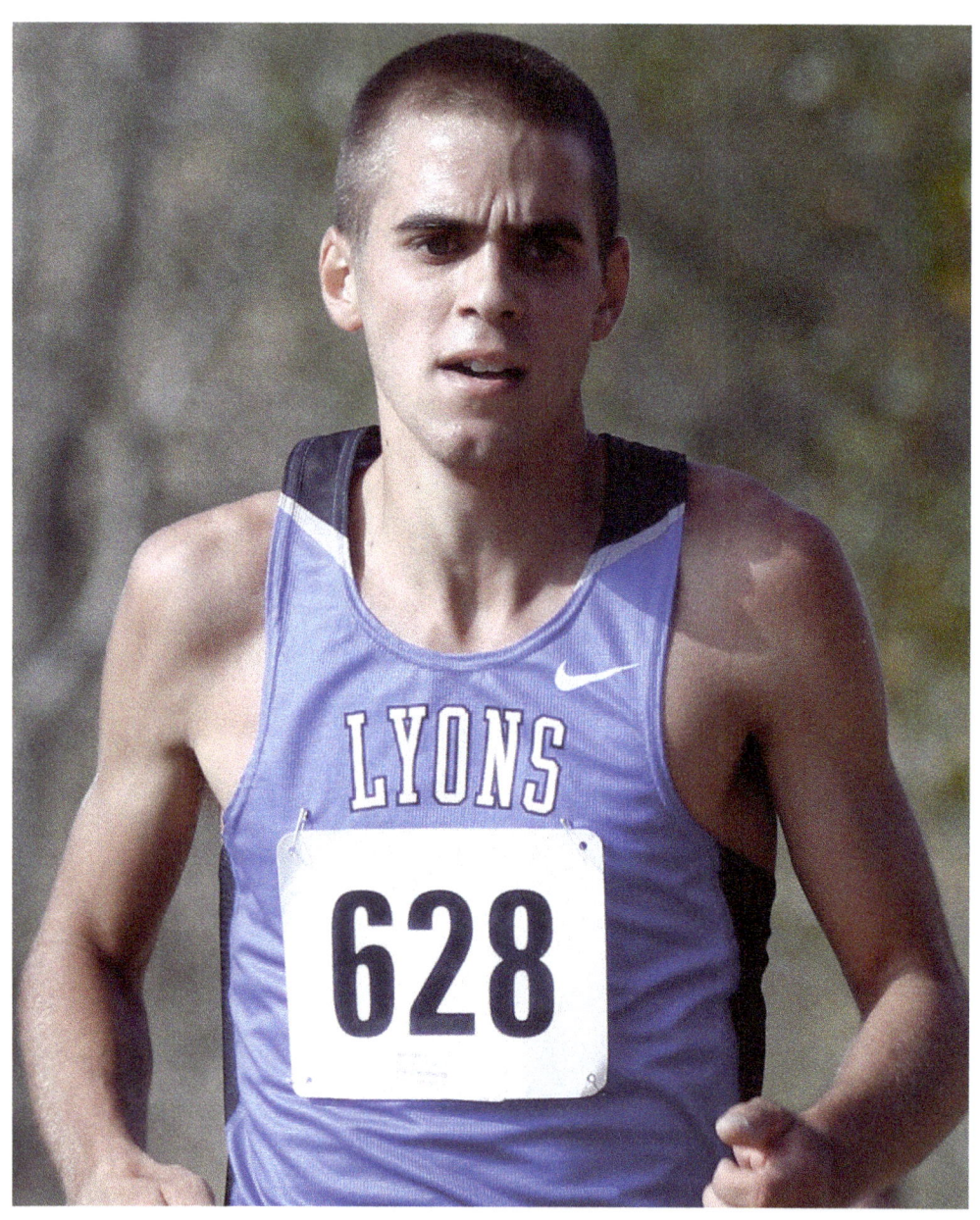

# 4PEAT

Words by Jeffrey Boele
Photos by Renee Haip

Running began early for Paul Roberts. Paul's first years were spent running around with his siblings in their kitchen and living room and then on to parks in Longmont. Twenty minutes here, 30 minutes there, the occasional speed workout around a soccer field; these were the foundational beginnings of one of Boulder's most recent running prodigies.

Born the fourth of ten children, much of Paul's running around was just trying to keep up. After several years away from the sport, Paul's father Mark, decided to get back into running. When some of his older kids showed an interest and some aptitude, running became a daily routine. As a vehicle to develop self-discipline and a work ethic, running was something to replace the chores that Mark had done in his childhood growing up on a farm just outside of Boulder.

When Paul was eight, the Roberts family moved back to that same farm to take over the responsibilities from Mark's mother, Judy. On the 10-acre plot just north of town, Paul had a new home for running. The parks of Longmont were replaced with laps around the property, including a 1/4 mile loop in the back pasture for workouts. Paul's most vivid memory of early racing was against his older sister Melissa. Her tendency was to "sit and kick," with Paul doing all the leading, and then Melissa nipping him at the finish line.

In 2007, at age 9, he decided he had enough. At the Macintosh Lake Mud Hen 5K run, he employed a furious start ensuring some distance between himself and his nemesis. The goal on that day, other than beating Melissa, was to break 20 minutes. Paul crossed the line in 19:16, some 40 seconds clear of his sister. Check and check on the goals.

This result however wasn't the first sign of his running prowess. In 2004, at age six, he entered the Bolder Boulder 10K, a must for any running family in the area. For his efforts, Paul took top honors in his age group. Since then, he has made winning his current age group something of a tradition. His streak is intact at 12 years and counting as of this printing.

Another streak that Paul contributed to was the Roberts reign atop the Bolder Boulder family division. Starting the same year as his first Bolder Boulder, the Roberts' claimed 1st place. This streak would run for six years before the competition was discontinued. It was as if the race directors knew Paul would keep tipping the scales in his family's favor. The following year, 2011, Paul would set the age group record for 13 year olds, running 35:12. He had one previous record in 2007 as a nine-year-old. But he was not done at two age group records. In 2013 as a 15-year-old and 2014 as a 16-year-old, he also netted course best times for those age categories. His age group records - (42:47, 9yrs, 2007), (35:12, 13yrs, 2011), (32:41, 15yrs, 2013), (32:09, 16yrs, 2014).

The last year of the Bolder Boulder family category happened to be Paul's first year with another family, the Lyons Lions middle and high school cross country and track teams. As a 6th grader, Paul began competing in both sports in earnest. During his first cross country season he would finish 2nd at the John Martin Invite in Fort Collins. That would be his only defeat at the middle school level in either cross country or track.

Upon entering high school, Paul's reputation as a potential force in the distance running ranks preceded him. The first fall saw Paul and freshman teammate Joel Such join an already formidable Lyons high school cross country squad. These two stellar freshman proved vital contributors to Lyons first ever team title. Paul would also find himself atop the podium the entire season and the state championship race was no different. On the day, the 2A classification winner would end up with the second fastest mark for the course.

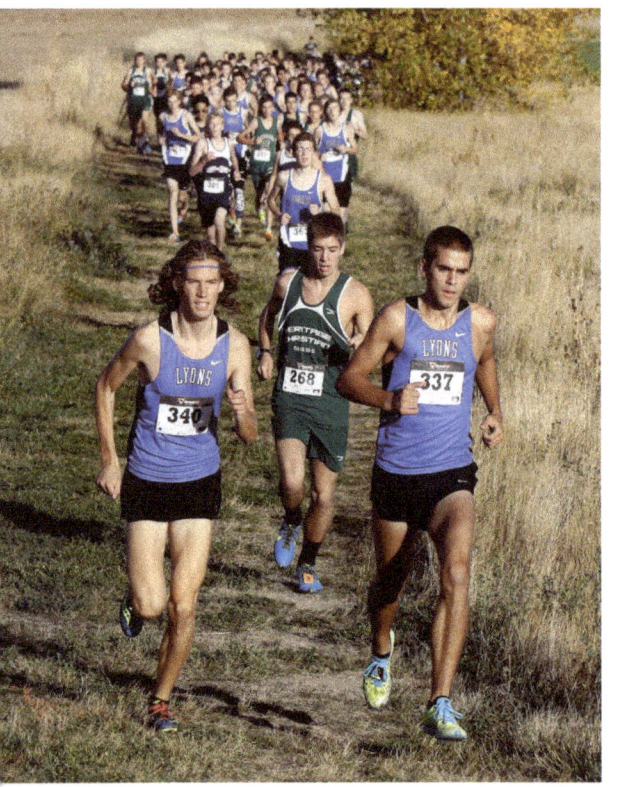

With the top four runners returning from the previous season's team, Paul's sophomore campaign proved to be a special one for him and the team. The Lions were the favorite going into the state championship and would put a stamp on that expectation. Behind Paul's second individual title, brothers Marcel and Joel Such completed a 1-2-3 finish, securing a second team title.

Paul's junior cross country season would not see the same dominating team victory as the previous year. But the team was still able to take the top honor behind Paul's third individual title and strong support from his teammates. While the scholastic accomplishments were exciting, Paul was able to venture onto the international cross country scene by virtue of his 6th place finish at the US Cross Country National Championships - appropriately held in Boulder. He would be the only high school junior to make the US team for the IAAF world championships held in Guiyang, China.

Later that spring on the track, Paul had a notable performance in the 3200 meter run. Under the lights of the Stuttler Bowl at Cherry Creek high school, he ran 9:13 for the distance. This was the sixth fastest time on Colorado soil by a high school boy. He took that fitness all the way to the state meet, winning the 3200, 1600 and anchoring the victorious 4x800 team. These contributions helped the track and field team to their fourth championship in five years.

Entering his senior cross country season, Paul was facing a unique opportunity.

**With a victory at the state meet, he could become the first boy to win four individual titles. While that held a certain allure, Paul knew that if the team performed well, they could also capture their 4th consecutive title.**

As the season progressed, Paul and the team's standing looked good, but the race still needed to be run. And run they did! Paul turned in the fastest time of the day to capture his 4th individual crown. Following in second was his training partner and friend, Joel Such. Led by the strength of the 1-2 finish, the team also secured their 4th title.

In his first 17 years of life (15 or so of them spent running), Paul Roberts has had a marked early career. From chasing his brother and sisters down to the local park and eventually up and over hills in China, much of Paul's development as a runner has come from trying to help friends and family run to their full potential.

Culture of Run

# Trucker Hats

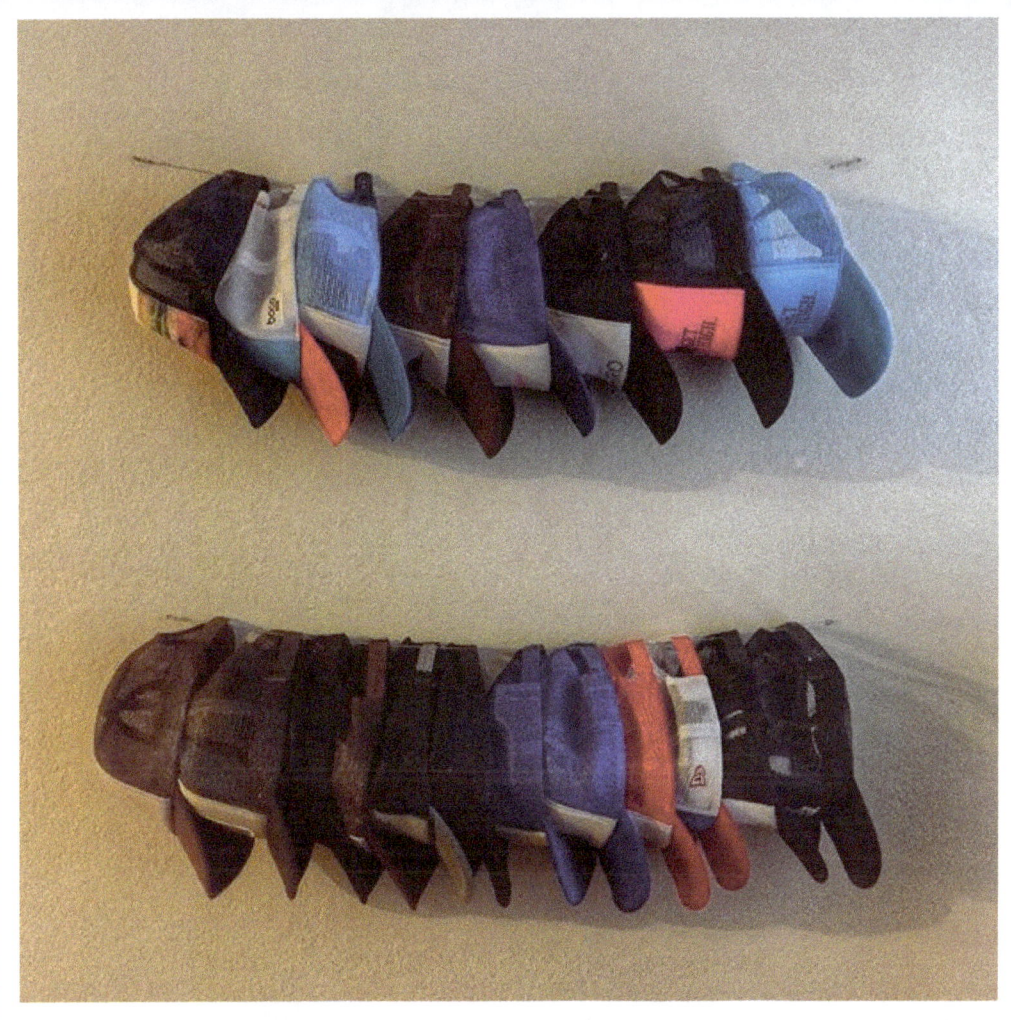

#TruckerHat collection as aesthetic functional wall decor.
@ginalucrezi

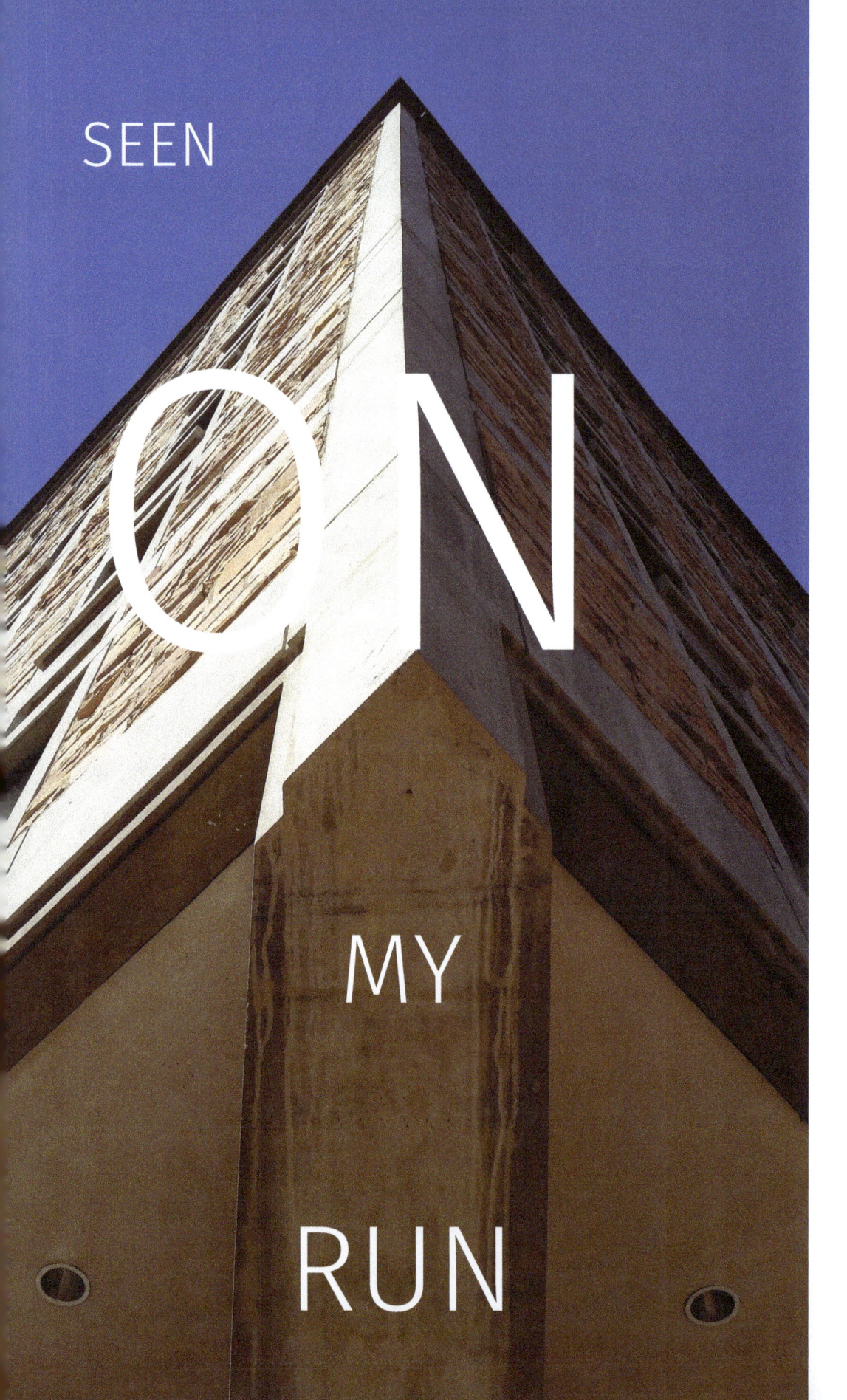

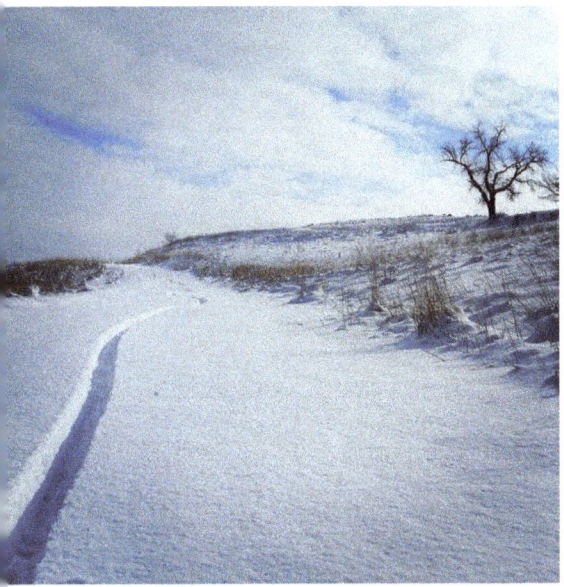
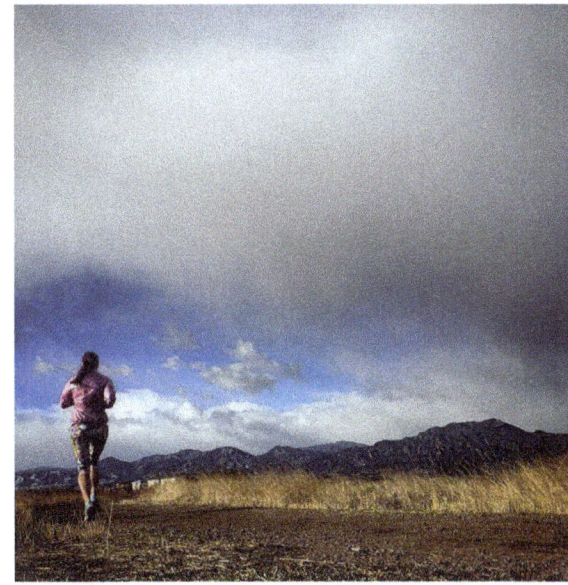
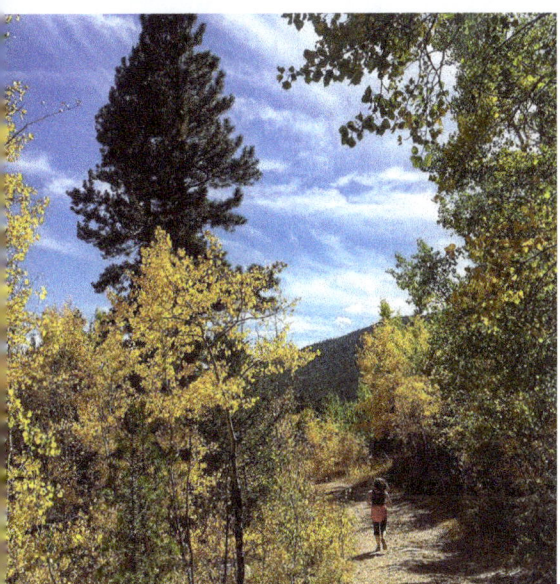
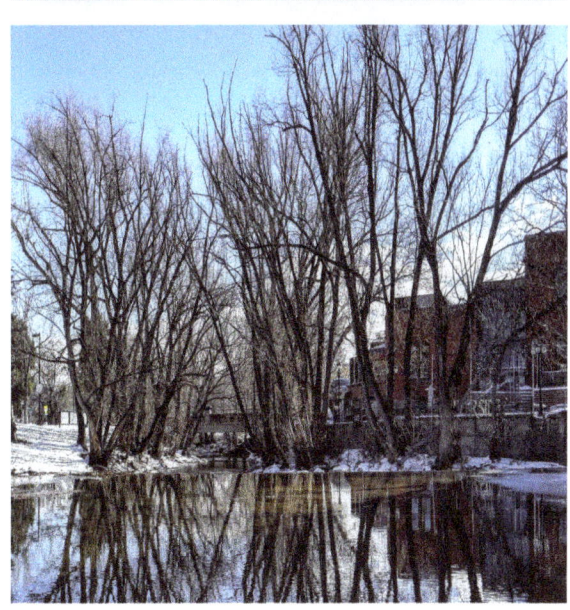

Being out on a run allows you to take in the scenery in a whole new way. Many of us carry our smart phone cameras, a GoPro, or even a sleek DLR. No matter your capturing tool of choice sharing what we see when we run is just another way for us to connect as a community. Here is a small collection of recent favorites from the feed.

If you would like to contribute, make sure you tag in **#SeenOnMyRun** and **#BoCo_Trails**.

@Becca_Prichard - @Mary_runs_Colorado
@mkibiloski - @BoulderRunner

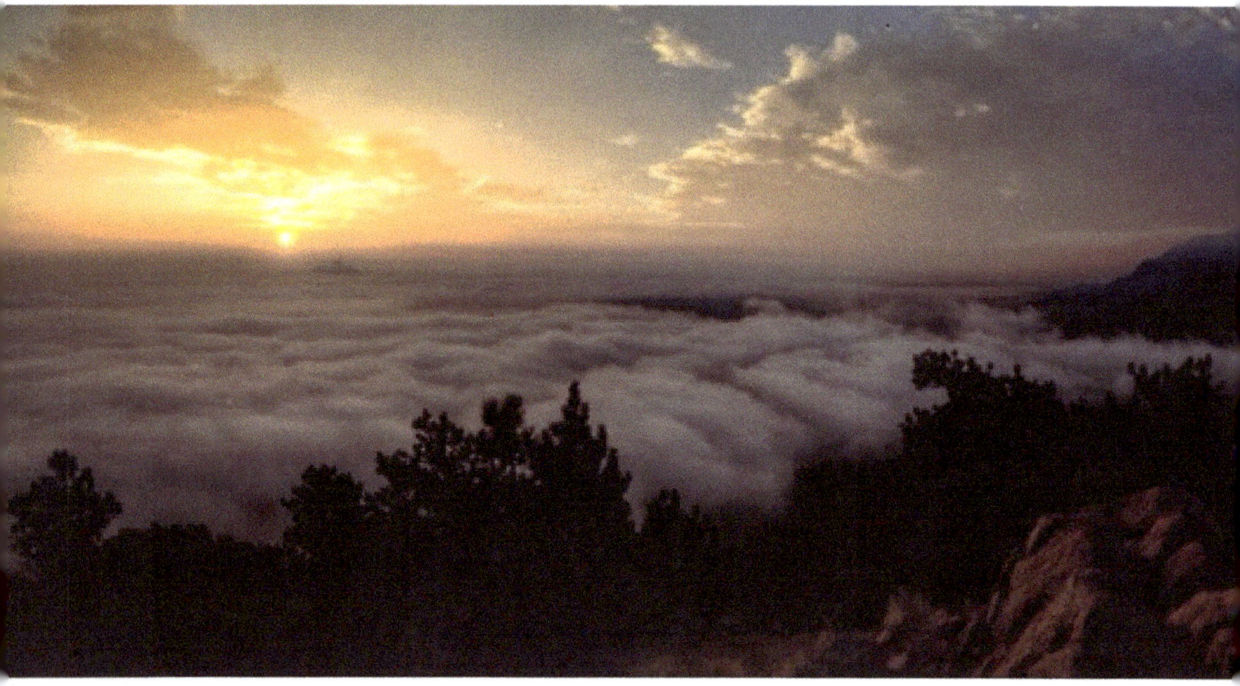

#SeenOnMyRun

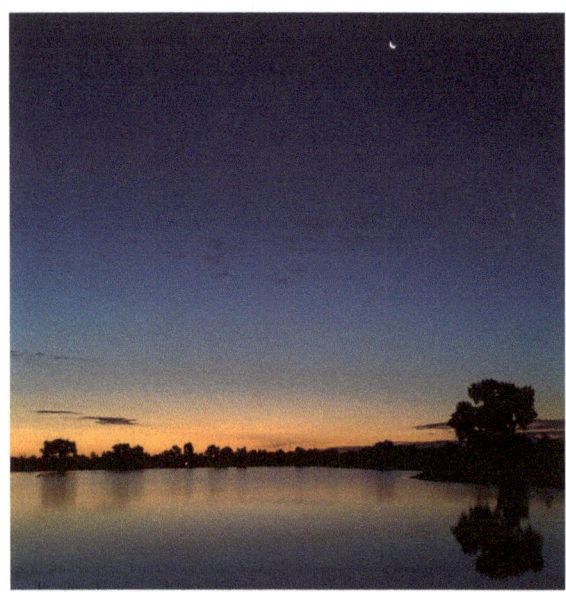
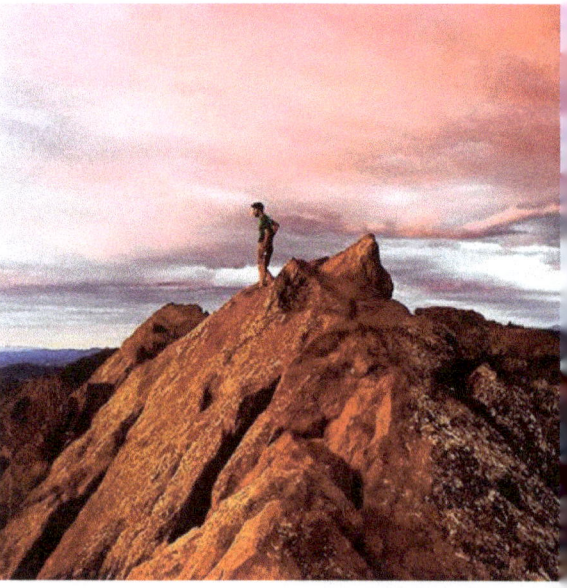

@skamm11
@Bud_T - @JacksonLong

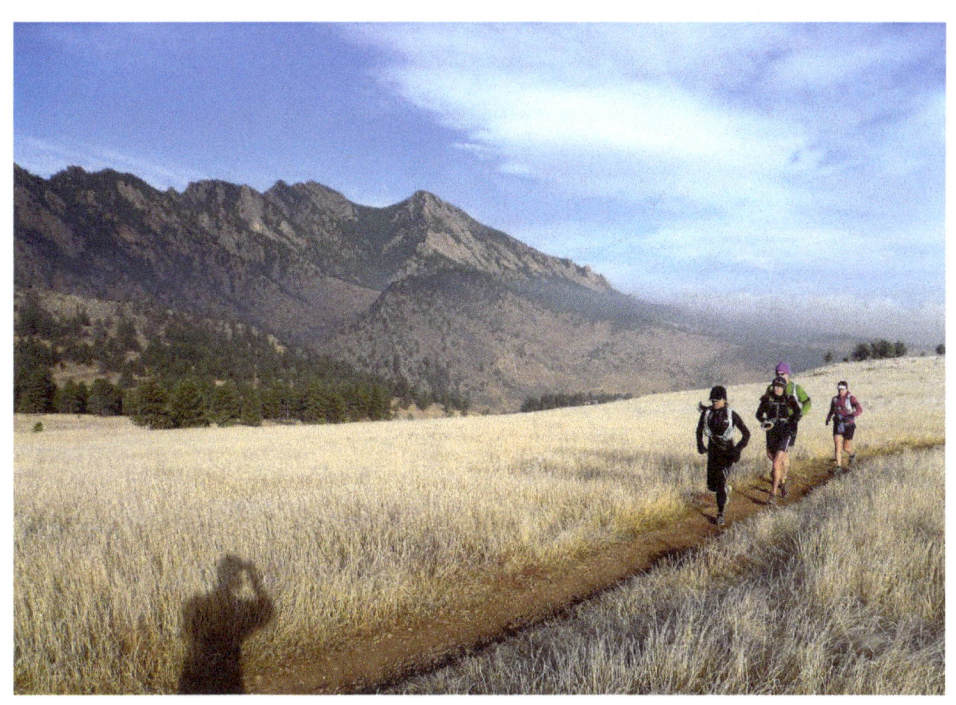

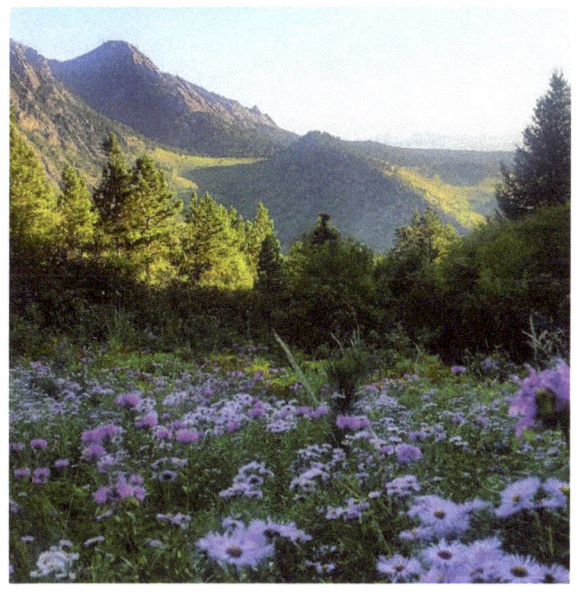

@mtnrunner_elee
@Becca_Prichard

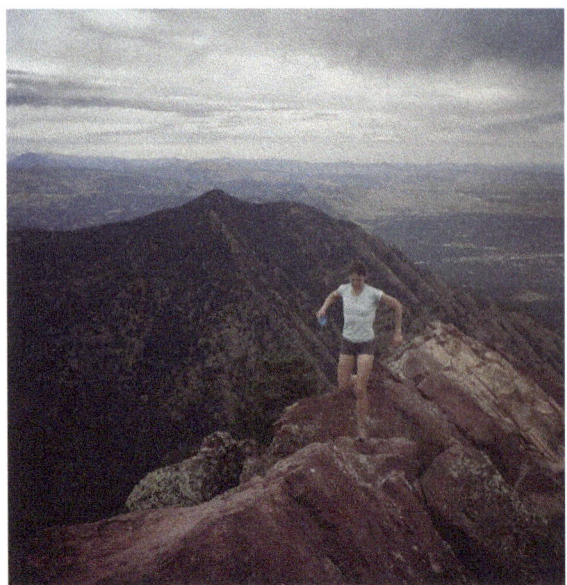
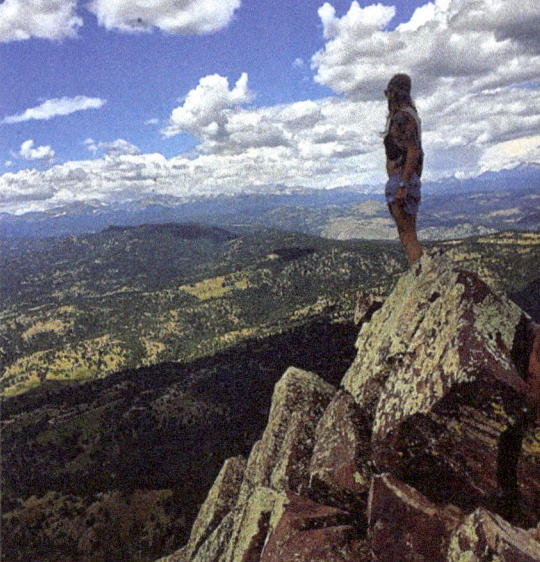
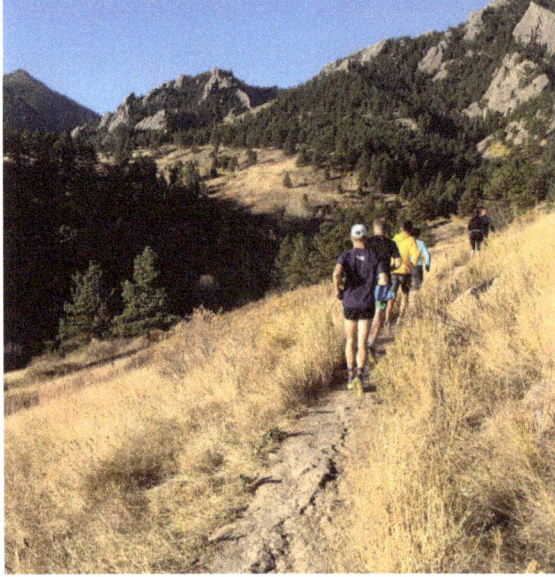
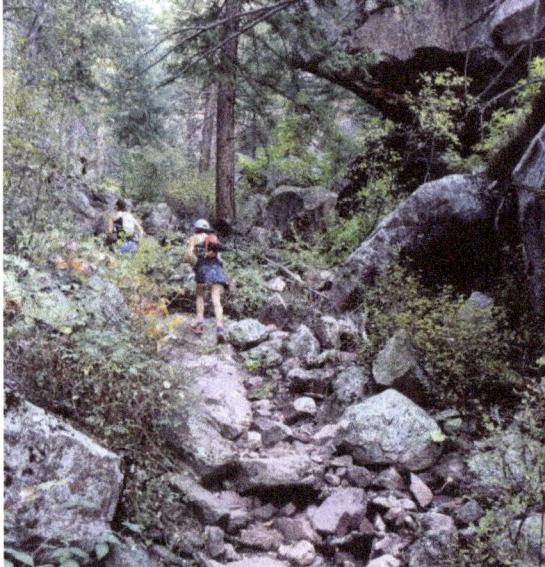

@Rlassen - @timothyallenolson
@lisawrites - @amachael
@amachael

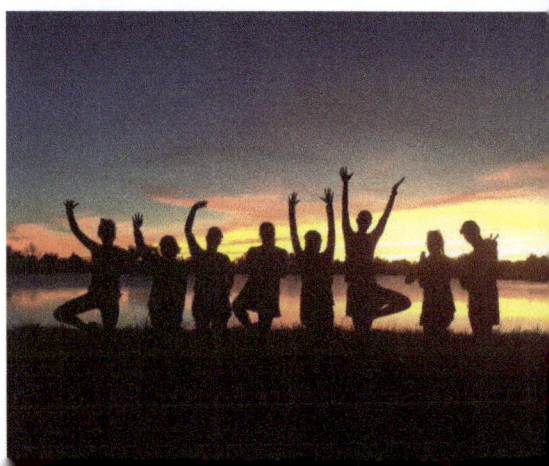

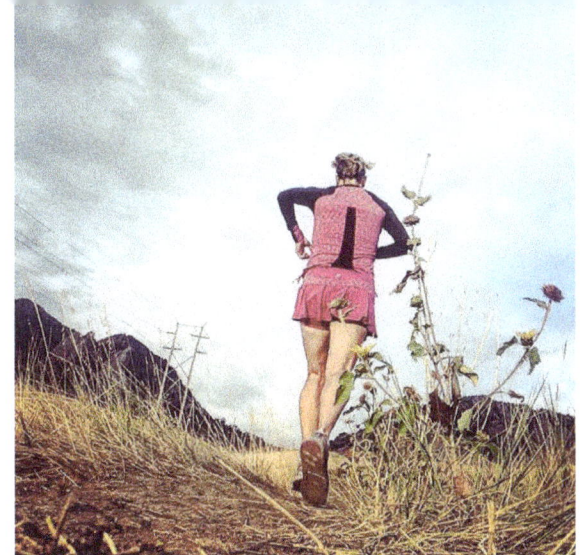
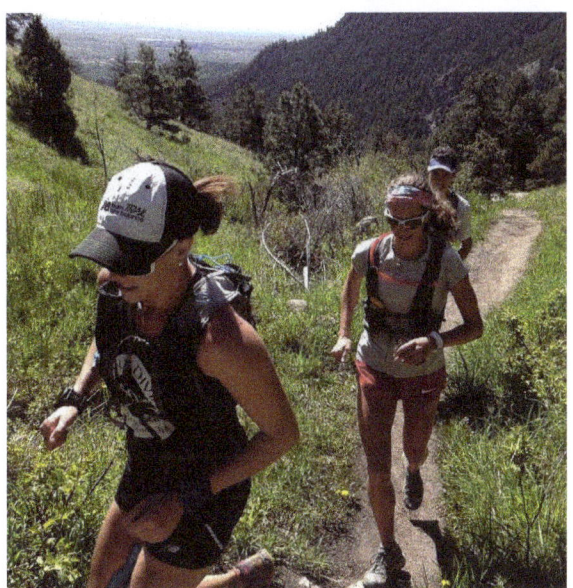
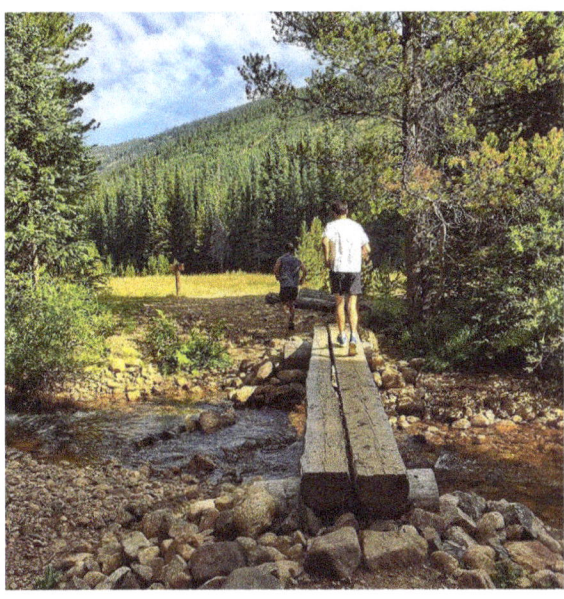

@nicoledeboom
@ginalucrezi
@mkibiloski

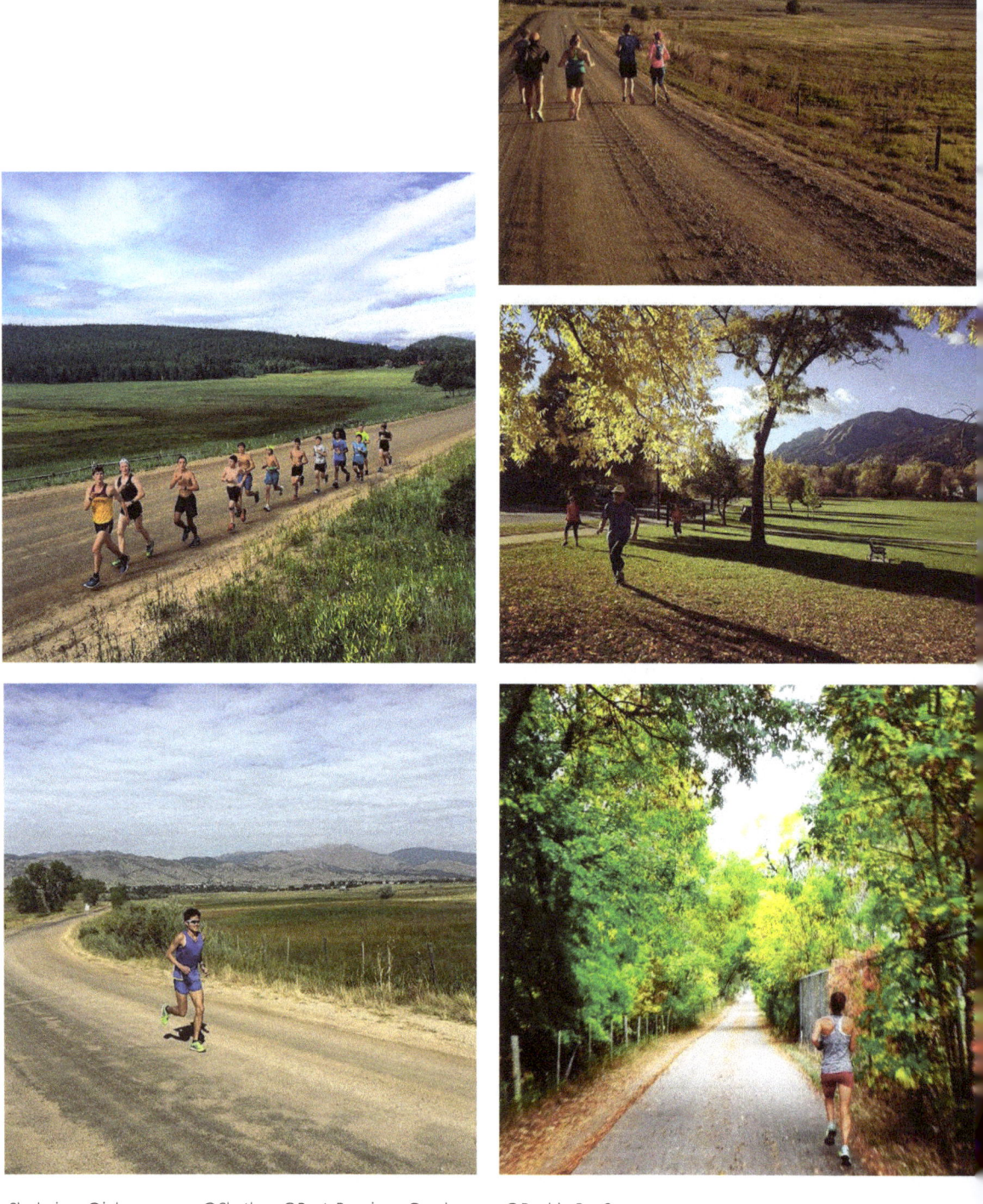

Clockwise: @johannavoss - @Chutler - @RootsRunning - @mokygren - @BoulderRunCamps

# BEFORE THE MESA TRAIL

Words by Mike Sandrock - Courtesy of the Daily Camera

Some decades past, when I first began running, attitudes toward runners were quite different than today. Not many people ran on the streets, and those that did were considered a bit off. And we rebels and iconoclasts probably were a bit off – to quote Frederick Henry in Ernest Hemingway's "A Farewell to Arms," pre-running boom runners were "just a little crazy."

During the ensuing years, the rest of society caught up to us. We did not change; society did.

Boulder native Roger Briggs began running in 1966 as a sophomore at Boulder High School. After finishing "laps" at the front of the pack one day in gym class, his teacher encouraged Briggs to join the Panthers' cross country team.

> Running was absolutely unheard of then. Running was completely out of the mainstream and off the radar.

Running was called by some "doing road work," a term often used to describe a boxer's training. Not interested in football or basketball, Briggs instead followed what appealed to him, which was climbing and running. He recalls running from Chautauqua Park to Eldorado Springs as a prep, tagging along with Craig Runyan, a top collegian at the University of Colorado, which even then had top runners.

There was no Mesa Trail all the way to Eldorado; the trail petered out somewhere around Bear Canyon. Said Briggs, "Nobody ran, and certainly not on the trails. There were scarcely any trails in the Boulder area. I rarely saw another runner. It was a very different world."

Indeed it was. Now, go out on the Boulder streets and the many trails any day of the week, and from dawn to dusk, and sometimes well into the night, and you will find people working out. There has been "just an explosion" in running, climbing, cycling, triathlon.

> I think climbing and running are very primal activities that connect us with our deep evolutionary roots.
> - Roger Briggs

# Rediscovering the Run

Words and image by Stefanie Kamm

Boulder once was a city I knew nothing about.... In my mind it was some place in Colorado that was probably full of a bunch of rocks. After being transplanted to this mystery city for work, I soon came to find out that it's actually a remarkable playground, serving as the home to outdoor enthusiasts, professional athletes, and activity addicts all who just want to play outside and live in the perfect place to do that.

Before Boulder, I was a former mid-westerner whose running world consisted of fast miles on flat ground. Trails were a foreign surface to me, unless you consider the bike path near my apartment a "paved trail system." I didn't appreciate my surroundings, but instead focused my attention on the mile count and split times displayed on my watch. At that time, these things were what I needed running to be. I used it as a way to escape life's stress, achieve a goal, and push myself to be the best I could be. While those are definitely all positive results of the sport, they can also cause added stress and anxiety when you don't perform as intended. I hadn't yet realized that running could provide a greater appreciation for some things in life that are more important than fast times.

Boulder came into my life and quickly taught me that race medals and PR's were just a small piece of the running puzzle. After panting my way through the altitude adjustment and conditioning my legs to get up this new "hill" concept, I finally fell into the same routine from back home of wanting each and every run to be longer and faster than the last. These long runs and fast times were not providing me with what I really needed here... friends.

I decided to join a trail running group to combine my love for the sport with a need to explore my new home and connect with others. This group introduced me to the unbelievable scenery that Boulder has to offer. It taught me that slow running with people you love can provide much more happiness than fast running by yourself. The most important lesson that I learned from this experience was how to appreciate the non-competitive aspect of running and that slowing down to enjoy the view can be just as rewarding as winning a spot on the podium.

Nowadays, I wake up with excitement to see where my run will take me. Will it be an epic sunrise or a quiet foggy morning? How many animals will I run into or have to run away from? What new hidden trail will I discover to take me to a place I've never been? Uncovering the answers to those questions on each morning adventure provides me much more excitement then a PR. Although I am now running slower than ever, (mostly because stopping to snap 100 pictures of the perfect cloud really decreases your mile time) I have never enjoyed running as much. I feel very fortunate to have discovered Boulder's unending trails and friendly faces as without them, I would have never realized that I run because it makes me love the feeling of living and not because I love the feeling of running.

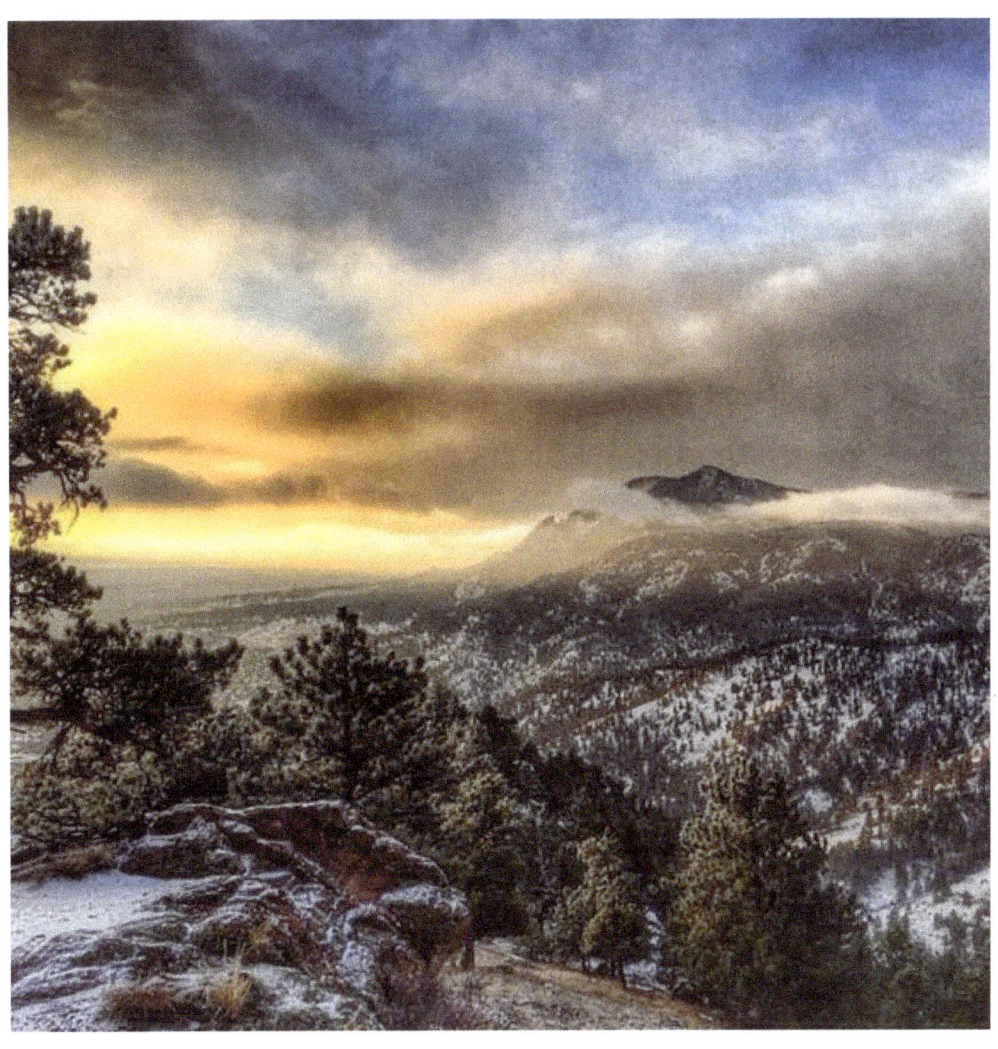

Nowadays, I wake up with excitement to see where my run will take me. Will it be an epic sunrise or a quiet foggy morning? How many animals will I run into or have to run away from? What new hidden trail will I discover to take me to a place I've never been?

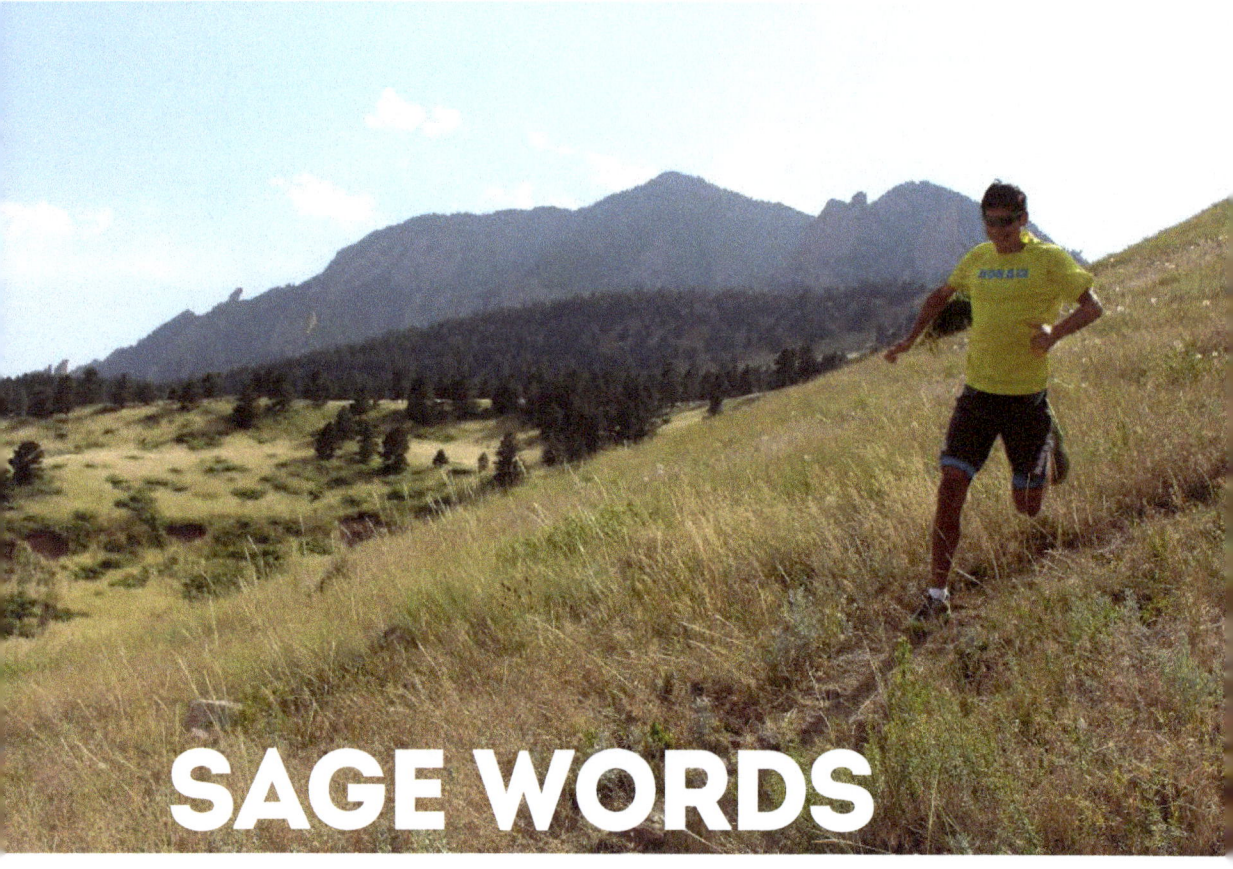

# SAGE WORDS

Words by Peter N. Jones - Photo courtesy of Sandi Nypaver

### Why Boulder

After finishing college at Cornell University and running for the Hansons-Brooks Distance Project team for three years, Sage Canaday had to make some serious decisions. He was fast – running PR times of 29:47 for the 10K and 2:16:52 for the marathon – but deep down he also wanted to expand his racing beyond the roads and onto the trails and into the mountains. After moving back home to Oregon briefly, he decided to pursue his dream of becoming one of the all-time greatest mountain, ultra, trail runners and packed up his bags and moved to Boulder. "I had to make a choice, and I chose to move to Boulder. I had heard about the trails, the culture, the food, the beer, and of course the people. I also wanted to train at altitude and my parents had gone to the CU, so I decided to make the move."

That was three years ago, and since then Sage has made a name for himself nationally and internationally within the mountain, ultra, and trail running world. "Boulder's running community is the perfect training environment. There are so many amazing athletes here – Olympians, World Champions, regular guys who get out on the trails every day, not to mention all of the various running groups and fun runs."

> "I love it here. My motto is 'any surface, any distance' and Boulder is the perfect place for that."

### Hoka One One

Not only does Sage love Boulder, but running and training in Boulder has allowed him to pursue his dreams, and that includes working with Hoka One One and being one of their elite athletes. "Hoka has been very supportive – I got in at the right time. It was really exciting to be helping to build the brand, to get in one the ground floor." When Sage first joined Hoka, they made high-platform extra cushy shoes primarily aimed at the ultrarunning market. Since, the brand has grown, and Sage has been a big part of that. "When they told me they were going to develop lighter weight road shoes that was a huge draw. I may have my aspirations focused on the MUT world, but I still do a lot of training on the roads and track, and seeing the growth Hoka was going through was really exciting."

With a B.S. in Human Factors and Ergonomics, Sage has been providing a ton of feedback to the Hoka design and engineer team. "I love getting involved in all aspects of running, not just racing and training, but on the design side too. Hoka has been really appreciative about my feedback, and that has been a positive aspect of our relationship."

### Living the Dream

"I'm living the dream, and I don't think it could happen anywhere other than Boulder. It's a place where you can realize your potential with a supportive community behind you." For Sage Canaday, that dream fits perfectly into the Boulder aura. It's not simply to win races and be sponsored – he's already done that. No, it's to create a streak, to "be the best mountain, ultra, trail runner in the world. I want to win Western States, Ultra-Trail du Mont-Blanc, Comrades, and other highly competitive international races."

If there is one place that allows someone to pursue such a dream, it is Boulder. Not only is there the legacy and history of other athletes achieving similarly grandiose dreams – in Boulder it's not grandiose, it's possible, it's real. That is what Boulder is all about, chasing your dream with the entire town behind you.

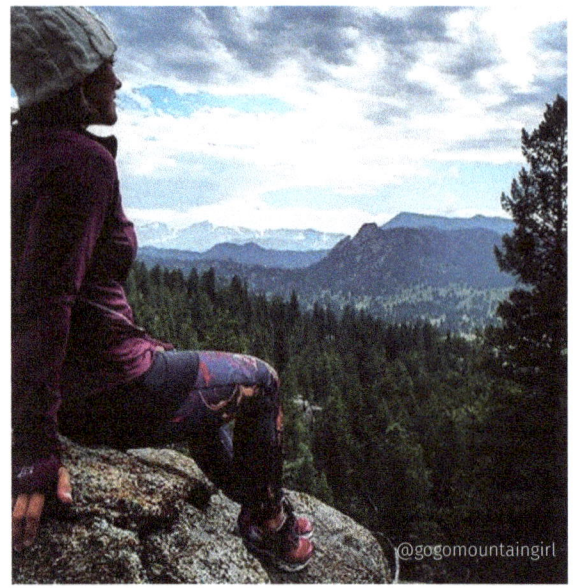

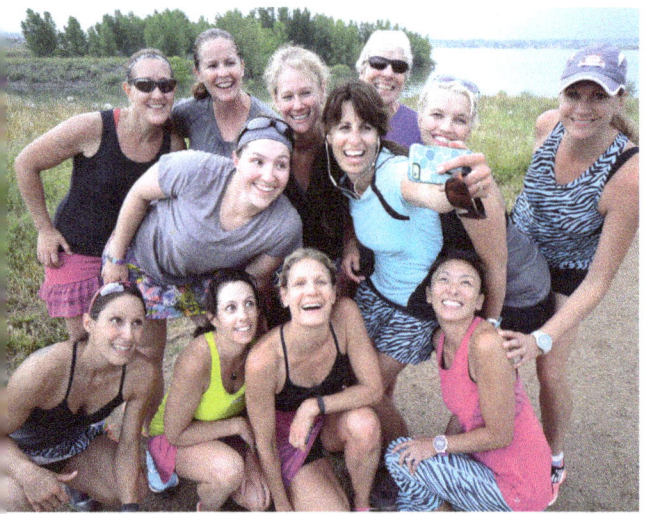

# #REALwomenmove

Triathlon champion Nicole DeBoom realized a dream with the founding of Skirt Sports, created from her own desire to wear sports apparel that is both feminine and bad-ass. In 2015, the company announced the launch of #REALwomenmove, a social media movement aiming to take that inspiration even further with the idea that fitness is for everyone – no matter their shape, size, ability, age or lifestyle. Women will be able to share stories and post real, everyday photos and videos of their active lifestyle using the hashtag #REALwomenmove.

"We are surrounded by messages of intimidation and exclusiveness in the world of fitness," says DeBoom.

"My goal with #REALwomenmove is to stop the madness and show women that being fit is something we can all do, regardless of our size, shape or activity level."

Thanks to Skirt Sports, they'll all be beautiful doing it, too.

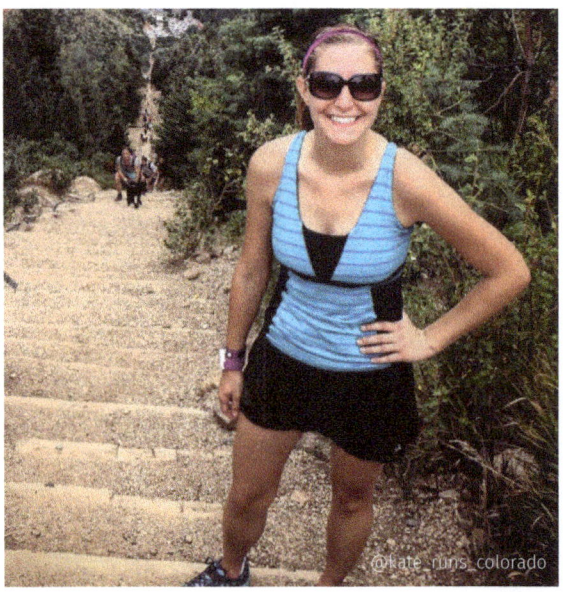

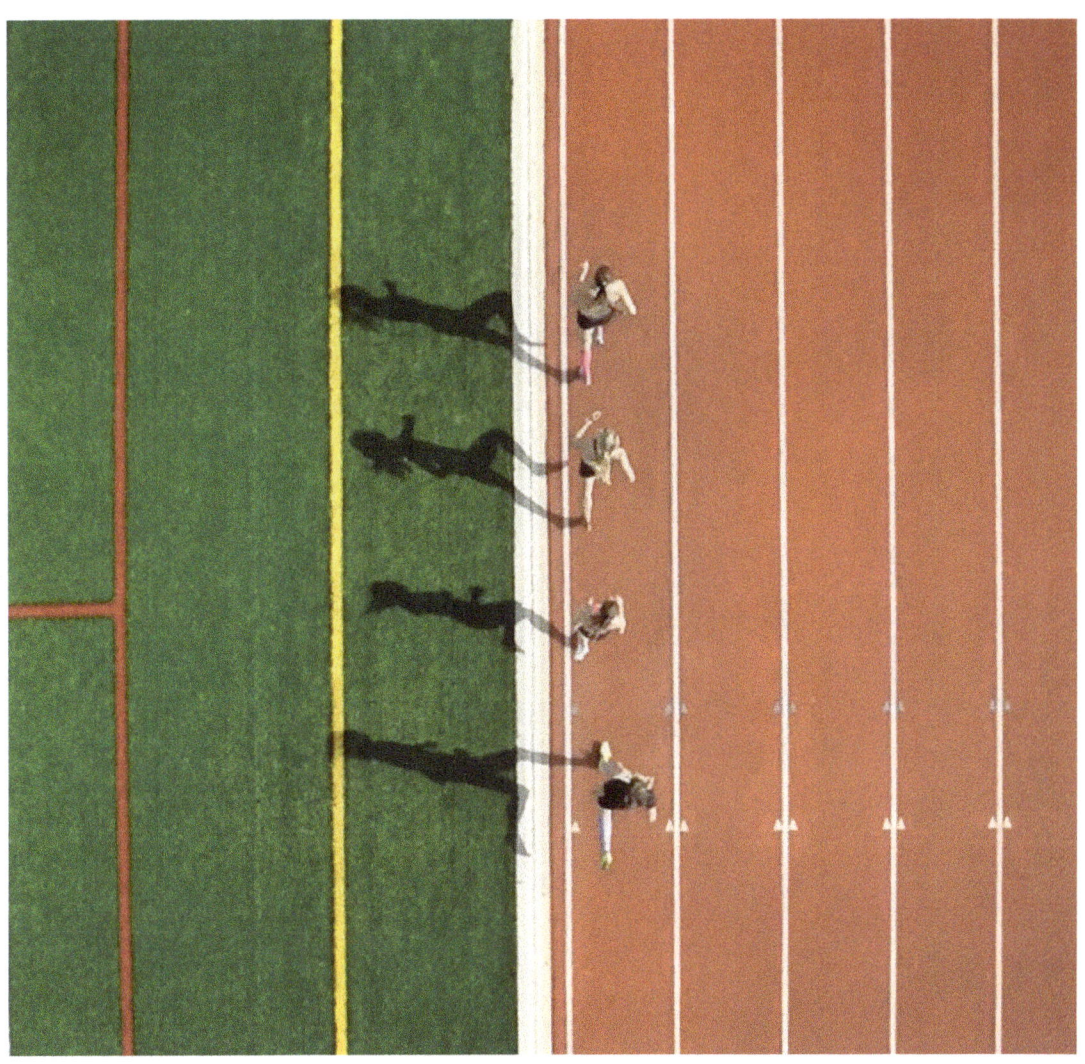

Hudson Elite women take it to the track in preparing for spring racing.
Photo by Seagul Photography

# Running Royalty

Words by Todd Straka
Photos courtesy of Monika King

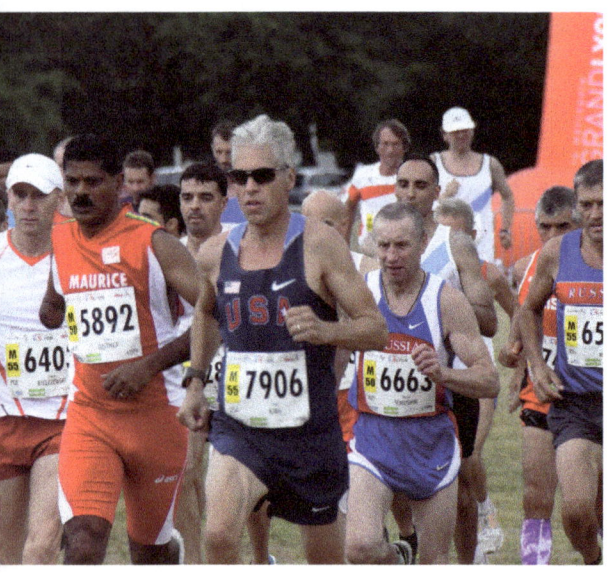
Dan King took 5th in XC at the World Masters Athletics Championships in Lyon, France.

"Dan King" rang out in both English and in Spanish over the loud speaker at the 1500 meter finals in the main stadium in Lyon, France. He took a step forward and gave a one handed wave to the crowd before stepping back to the line while the others were introduced. The field for the final, part of the World Masters Athletics Track and Field Championships, had been winnowed down from 85 men; more than 8,000 masters runners from around the world were there for all events. The day of King's race, athletes and fans packed the stadium and the roar of the crowd on top of the constant music added electricity to the air. "I was 5 times more nervous stepping up to the line that day," Dan noted as most of the events take place in venues with little attendance. "It was a very cool experience".

Previous to this race Dan took 5th place in the 8k cross country race and won the Bronze medal in the 5000m, despite the 100 degree temperatures, both in the 55-59 age group. And he ran a half marathon. Between the previous races, the heat and getting through the qualifiers he was spent but still ran a strong 4:37 in the 1500 meter final.

Dan can trace his lineage back to his father who was a strong middle distance runner training for the Olympic trials while teaching and coaching XC at the local high school. Even as he grew up he remembered that his dad would never miss a day of training. "Our entire life, it was part of his training routine. He loved to be fit and to compete."

Dan went to CU to run cross country as did his brother and sister. His other sister Laura didn't take to it then but is still a competitive masters runner with her husband Rick Bruess, also a Masters elite. The extended King clan often dominated the Family Competition in the Bolder Boulder while they still contested it.

Now the tradition has been passed down to his daughter Sarah who is competing in her third season at Fairview H.S.

To wife Monika and Dan's extreme delight, Sarah has fully embraced running and is good at it (she just finished 4th in the 5A XC Regionals where the Fairview girls dominated as a team and took first place). All summer, whether it was in the California Sierras, the German forests, all over Lyon, the hills of the French Provence or the Boulder Foothills with her Fairview team mates, Sarah diligently got her training/base building runs in.

And so did Dan, although since his is prone to nasty bouts of plantar fasciitis he had to approach it completely differently. It flared up again after running the mile on the track this summer just before heading over to France. So he got to the starting line through disciplined cross-training, putting in relatively few miles of running but doing lots of cycling, pool running, swimming, and hard sessions on the elliptical.

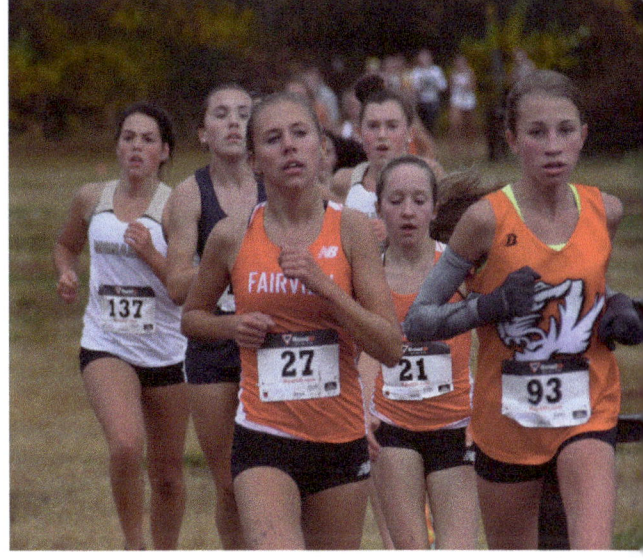

Sarah runs for Fairview and finished 4th in the 5A XC regionals.

> "I like watching the two of them experience so much joy, excitement, success and passion with their own AND each other's running"
>
> - Monika King

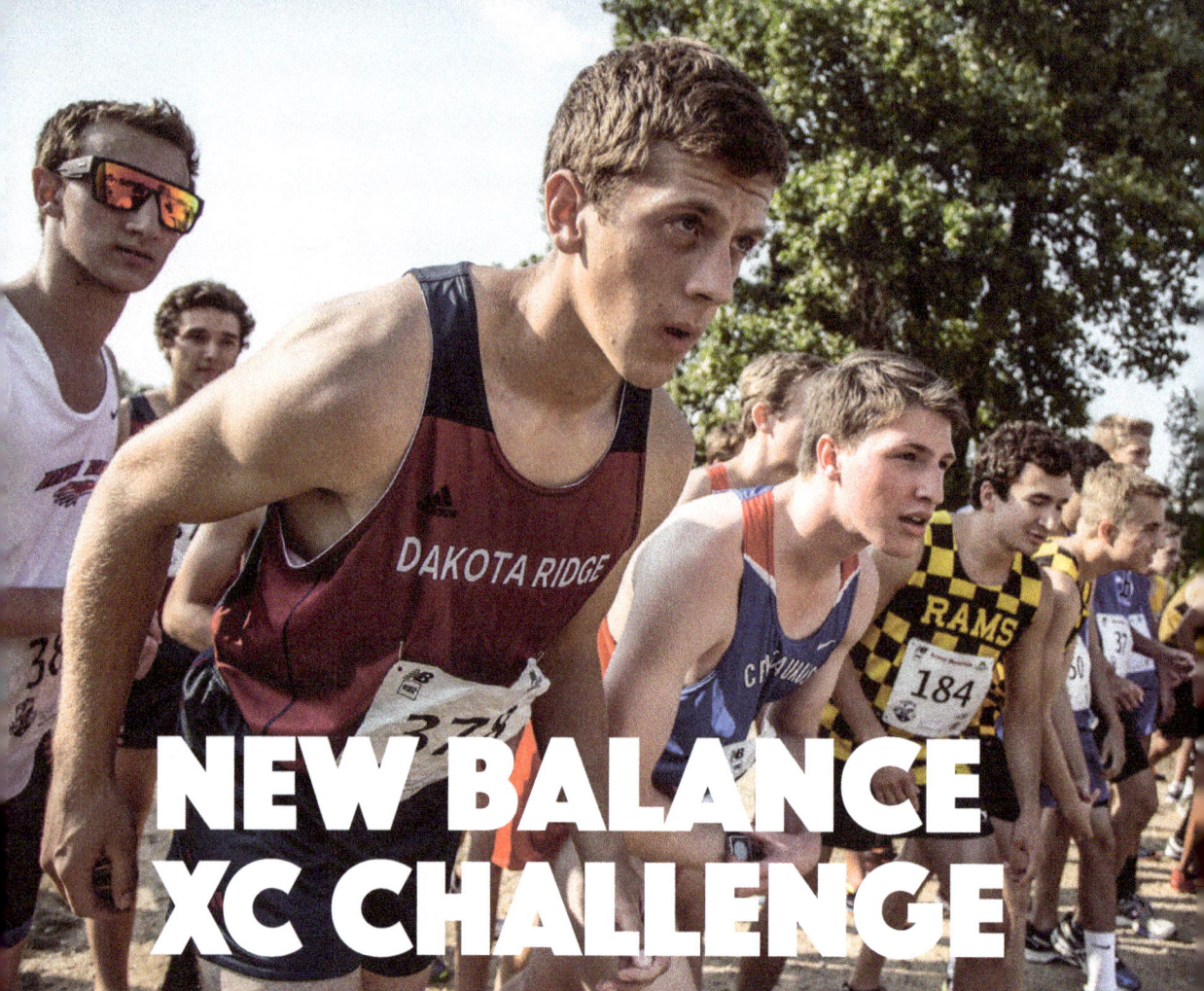

# NEW BALANCE XC CHALLENGE

Words by Todd Straka - Photos by Glen Delman and Todd Straka

## "Lets go! Time to get tough. Dig, it's racing time!"

George Zack yells at runners from Broomfield High School as they pass by him on the third and final lap of the 4.5 kilometer course at Valmont Bike Park. Ten area high schools came out on a Friday afternoon in early September to compete in this season opening race, the Valmont XC Challenge sponsored by New Balance and Flatirons Running. Zack was out there to cheer on his two kids, a freshman and a senior, who run for Broomfield High School.

This race is unique in that the course is too small for a large field, so the teams are split among seven fields, boys race with the girls, and teams compete within each race, so there is a bit of strategy to where you place your runners. High schools that were represented were Broomfield, Centaurus, Dakota Ridge, Green Mountain, Horizon, Longmont, Lyons, Mountain Range, Nederland, and Thompson Valley.

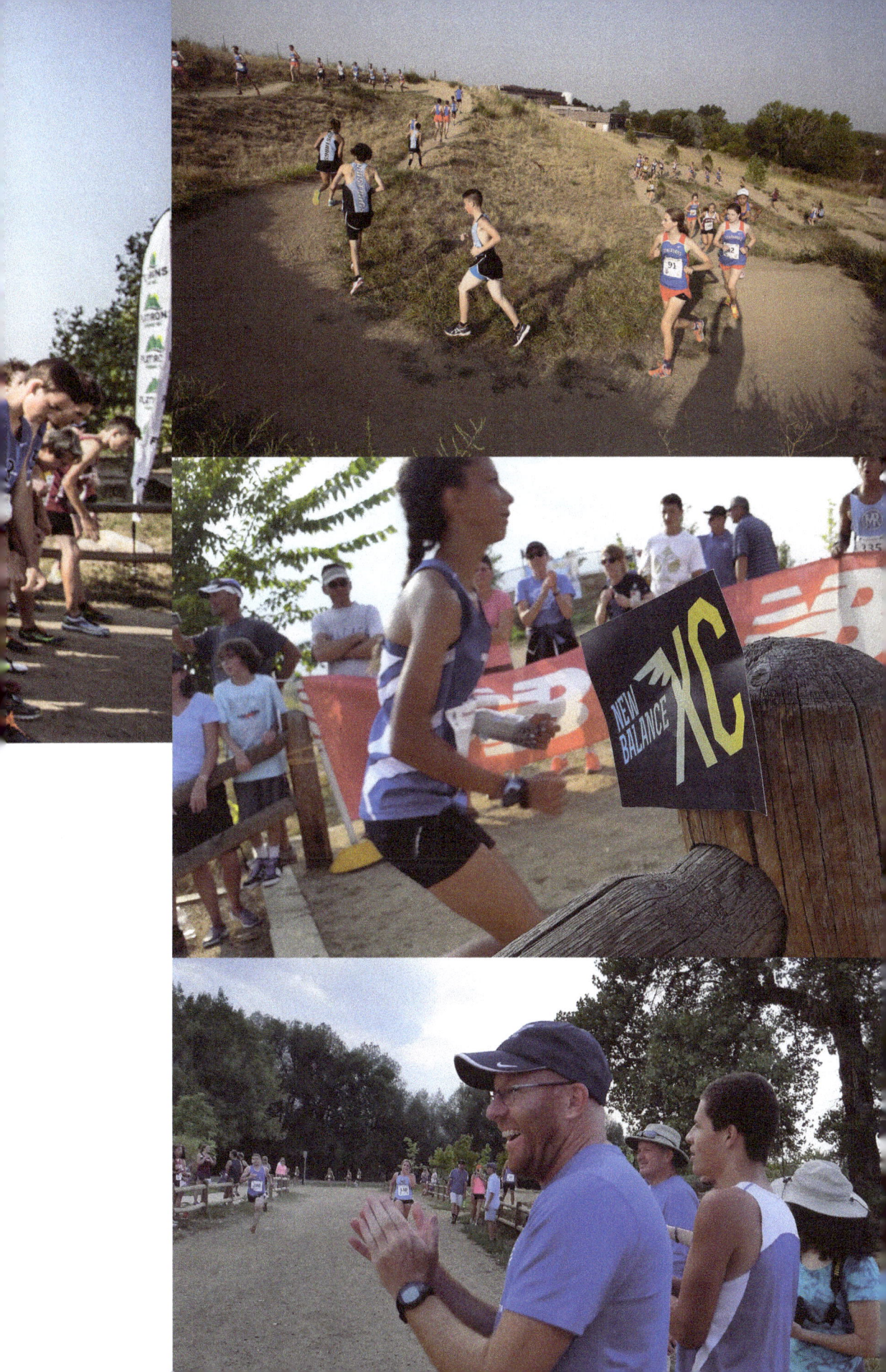

# Top Results
## July - September

On July 1, mountain runner **Eric Lee** of Boulder completed the first known Yosemite Valley Rim Circumnavigation. He ran the 64.5 mile loop solo and unsupported in a time of 17 hours and 55 minutes. Eric is the first known person to run this loop in a single push, and has opened up a new, exciting FKT.

**Neely Spence Gracey** had an amazing day on the Fourth of July. Just two hours after winning the Superior Downhill Mile in a time of 4:39.8 she also won the Avery Brewing Co's Four on the Fourth 4K in a time of 13:56. For the men's race at the Four on the Fourth 4K, Lyons' **Alex Monroe** came away with the win in a time of 11:52, while **Joe Bosshard** of Boulder came in third in a time of 11:59. In the women's race, **Emma Keenan** came in second after Neely Spence Gracey with a time of 14:08 while **Rachel Gioscia-Ryan** came in third with a time of 14:19.

The weekend of July 11-12 was a big one for Colorado ultrarunners. Down in the San Juan Mountains of southern Colorado, a little race known as the Hardrock Hundred Endurance Run was held. **Darcy Piceu** of Boulder ran a very strong race, battling with **Anna Frost** nearly to the finish line; Darcy finished in second place with a time of 28:57:07.

On July 19th at the Humana Rock 'n' Roll Chicago Half-Marathon **Jeffrey Eggleston** ran away with the win, finishing in a time of 1:05:05 and over one minute ahead of second place.

Also on July 19th, Louisville's **Justin Young** ran a strong race at the Napa-to-Sonoma Wine Country Half-Marathon with a time of 1:06:24, good enough or second place overall.

Finally in Aspen at the Audio Power of Four 50K **Josh Arthur** came in second with a time of 5:15:45 on the tough course that had over 11,000' of climbing. **Ashley Erba** of Louisville came away with the win in dominating fashion in a time of 5:53:25.

On August 1st at the inaugural Pikes Peak Ultra 50 miler **Ryan Smith** came away with the win in a time of 8:09:56. **Kerrie Bruxvoort** of Broomfield and **Silke Koester** tied for first and second place in a time of 10:16:19.

On a hot and humid Wednesday night in downtown Boulder, the annual Pearl Street Mile was held. Superior's **Stephen Pifer** ran a 4:09 mile for second place, while **Mara Olson** of Boulder ran a winning time of 4:47 for the mile.

At the highly competitive Pikes Peak Ascent, held on August 15th, **Andy Wacker** continued his outstanding season with a second place finish in a time of 2:18:37.

The following day, Sunday August 16th, the 43rd running of the New Balance Falmouth Road Race was held in Massachusetts. Superior's **Neely Spence Gracey** completed the 7 mile course in a time of 37:32, placing 4th overall among a strong field.

Early on the morning of August 22nd, the "Race Across the Sky" began. The Leadville 100 is a traditional rite of passage for many trail and ultrarunners, and numerous Boulder runners were there ready to give it their all. **Kara Henry** ran with abandon from the gun, clocking a time of 19:54:08 for the extremely hard course, which resulted in a second place finish overall in the women's field.

On the same day, up north in Squamish, British

Columbia, **Cassie Scallon** dominated the women's field (and much of the men's field), running a time of 8:37:31 for 1st place (and 7th overall).

In beautiful, sunny California on August 23rd, **Leigh Gilmore** ran a solid time of 2:47:40 to finish second in the women's field at the Santa Rosa Marathon.

At the Humana Rock 'n' Roll Virginia Beach Half Marathon, **Jeffrey Eggleston** ran a time of 1:06:01 for 2nd place, while **Matt Hensley** ran a time of 1:10:09 for 4th place. However, the performance of the day went to **Laura Thweatt** who not only won the women's race, but came in 8th overall and seven minutes ahead of the next woman. Her time of 1:12:59 was just two minutes off of the course record for the race.

On the same day, way out in the Pacific Ocean on the beautiful island of Kauai, **Tyler McCandless** easily won the Kauai Half Marathon in a time of 1:12:35.

**Andy Wacker** raced his heart out and became the 2015 USATF 50K Trail Champion on August 29th at the Headlands 50K in Tamalpa, California. Andy covered the course in 3:37:20, averaging an amazing 6:52 mile pace over the hilly course with 7,500' of elevation change.

On September 5th, Durango runner **Brendan Trimboli** won the Grand Traverse Mountain Run between Crested Butte and Aspen. **Kerrie Bruxvoort** won the women's race in a time of 7:43:48.5.

Up in Montana, at the Run the Rut 50K race on September 6th, **Matthias Messner** just missed getting on the podium by 9 minutes, finishing the hard run race in 4th place in a time of 5:38:42.

On September 7th, at the Faxon Law New Haven Road Race – which served as the USA Men's and Women's 20K championship race – **Brianne Nelson** of Golden ran to a 3rd place finish in a time of 1:07:28, while **Neely Spence Gracey** came in right behind her for 4th place with a time of 1:08:02.

On September 12th just outside of Empire, the second annual Devil on the Divide 50K was held. **Frank Pipp** of Longmont won the event in a fast time of 5:12:12, while **Matt Peharda** came in third with a time of 5:41:45. **Gina Ellis** was the first female in a time of 6:24:55.

In Steamboat Springs on September 18th at the Run Rabbit Run 100 mile race, **Andrew Skurka** had a spectacular race, coming home with 3rd place overall in a time of 20:12:50. **Kerrie Bruxvoort** of Broomfield finished 2nd for the women in a time of 22:54:45. In the 50 mile race, held on the same day, **Gabriel Small** ran to second place in a time of 7:54:12.

In Akron, Ohio on September 26, **Tyler McCandless** raced in the Akron Half-Marathon, finishing 4th in a time of 1:08:21. **Nicole Camp** of Longmont raced to 5th place in the women's race with a time of 1:21:42.

Also on Saturday the 26th out in Auburn, California at the Ultra Race of Champions 100K, **Kerrie Wlad** ran a very strong race over the challenging course, finishing 4th in a time of 11 hours, 22 minutes, and 17 seconds.

The following day, in sunny San Jose, California at the Rock 'n' Roll San Jose Half-Marathon, **Maor Tiyouri** ran a spectacular half-marathon debut race, finishing 5th in a time of 1:15:24.

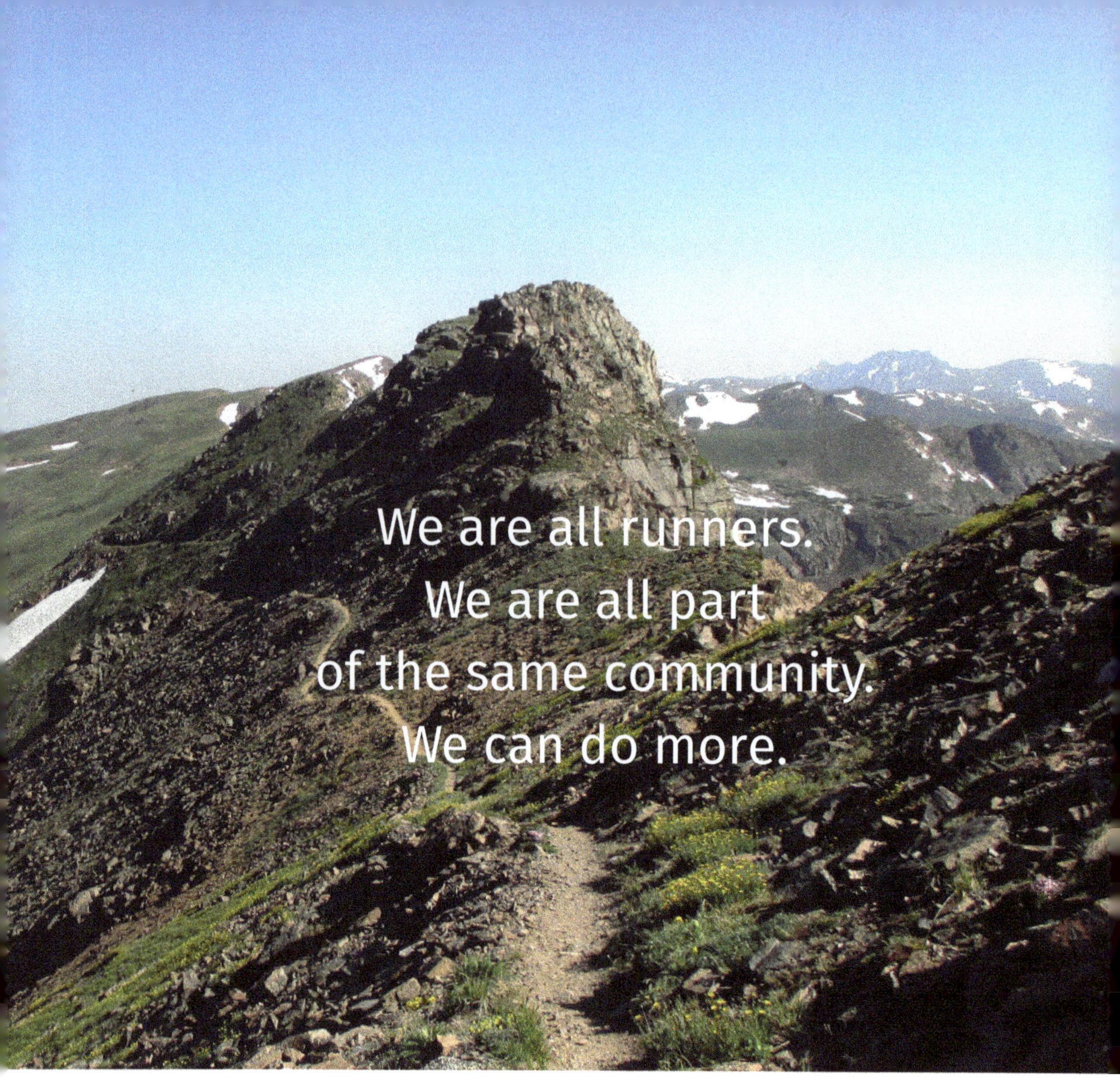

We are all runners.
We are all part
of the same community.
We can do more.

As runners, we have a personal stake in the health and integrity of our outdoor landscapes — the roads, the tracks, the urban paths, and the singletrack trails. Without them, we would have no place to run (except perhaps a treadmill). However, just loving our running routes, our secret trails, our personal loops through the neighborhood, our local track is no longer enough. As our sport continues to grow in popularity, overcrowding is stressing many areas, and other user groups continue to demand a share of the road, the trail, and even the track. This not only threatens access, but it can degrade the landscapes that we hold so dear.

There is a solution.

As runners, we are the natural stewards of our tracks, our trails, our roads. But we must be willing to stand up and care for them. The future of our sport depends on it. This is why the American Trail Runners Association is so vital to our sport.

The ATRA works hard, often behind the scenes, to educate the public, create alliances with organizations, facilitate stewardship of the environment, and to ensure that the sport continues to grow and is inclusive of all participants.

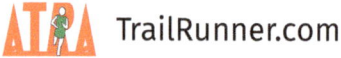

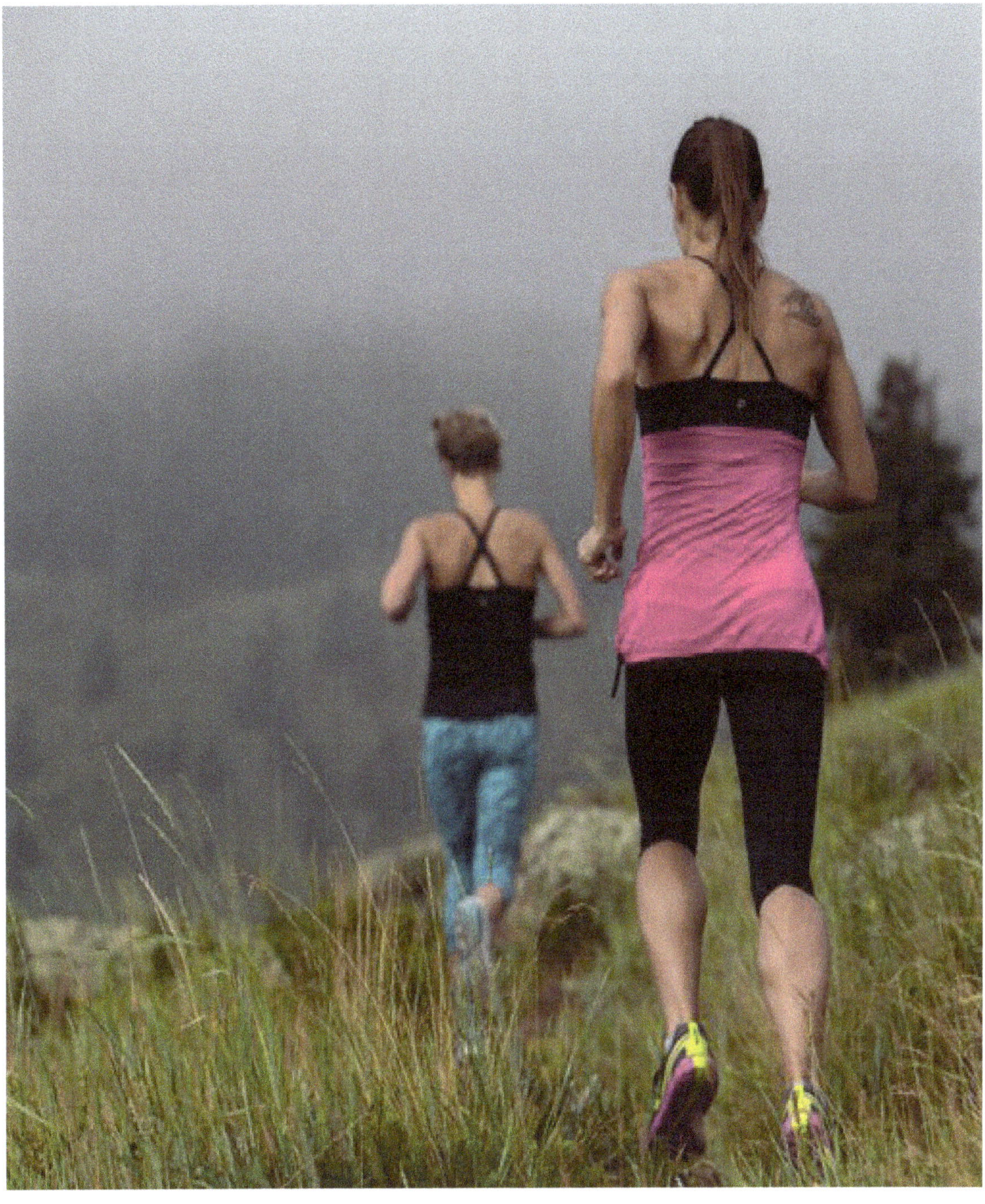

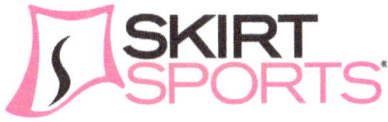

SkirtSports.com

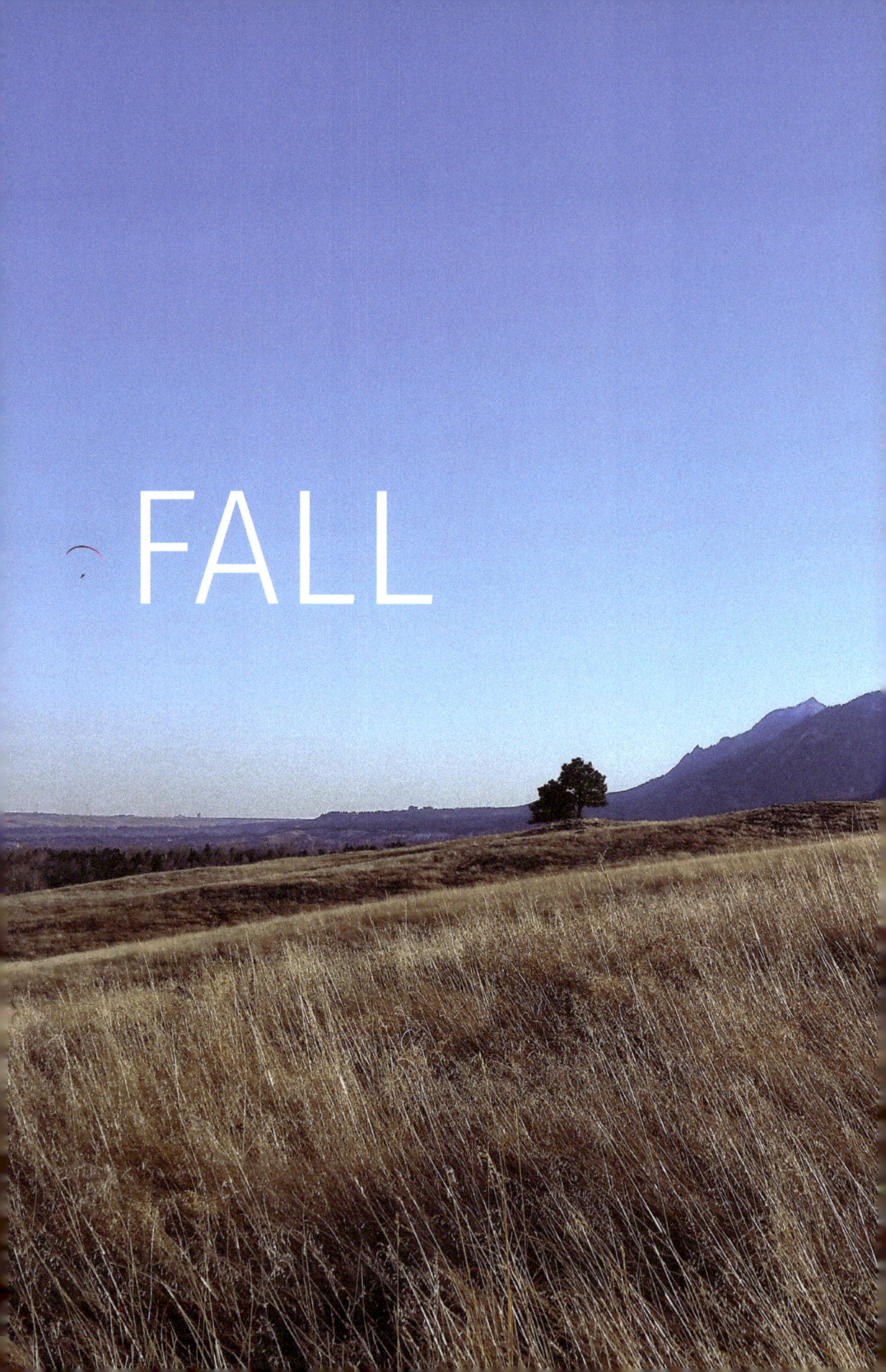

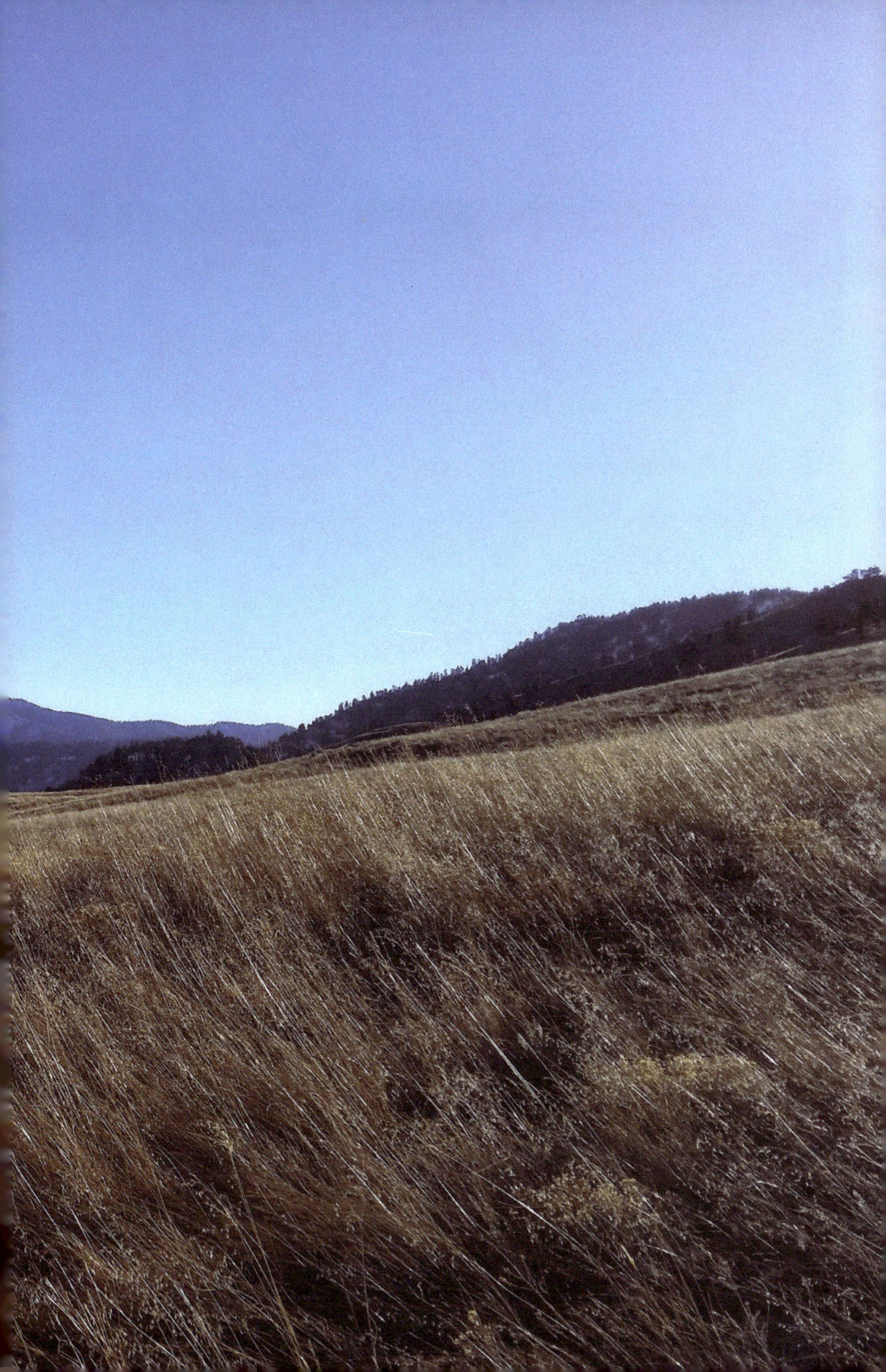

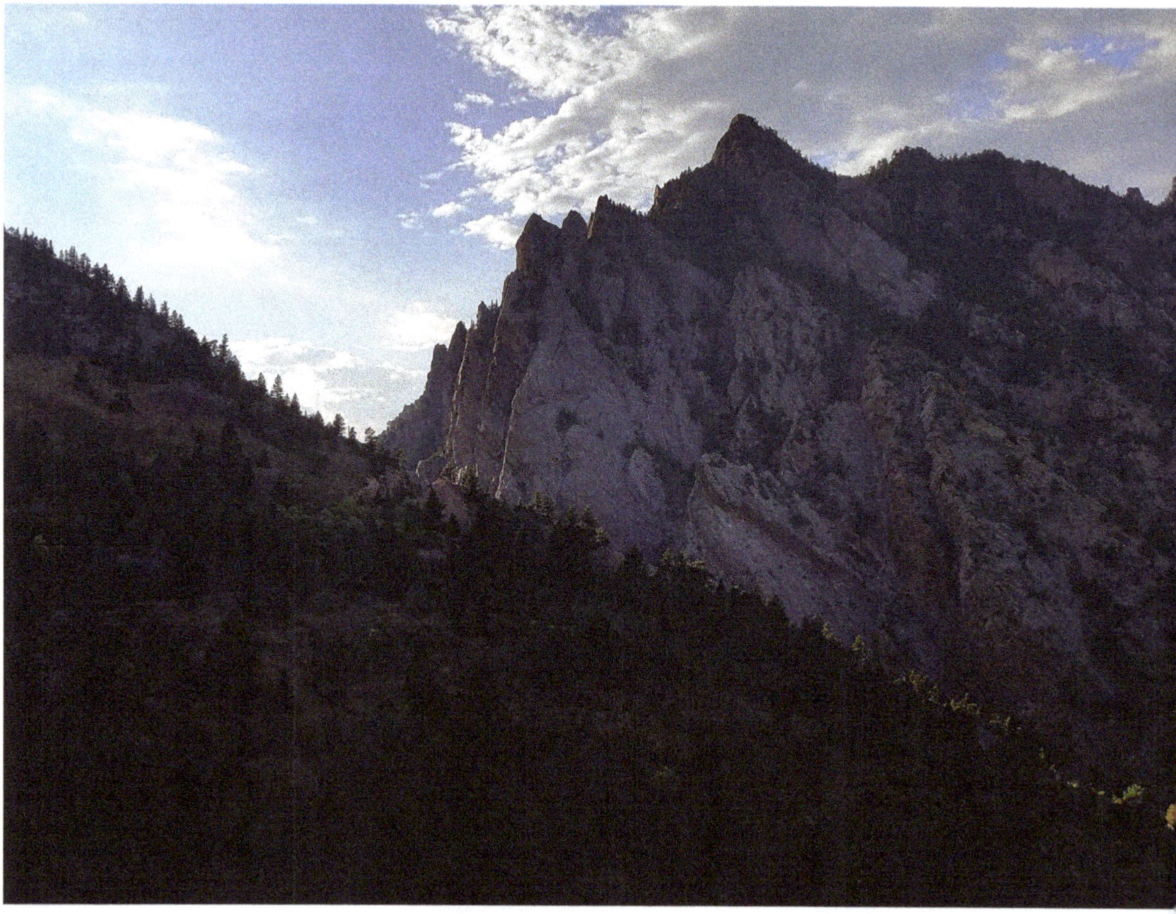

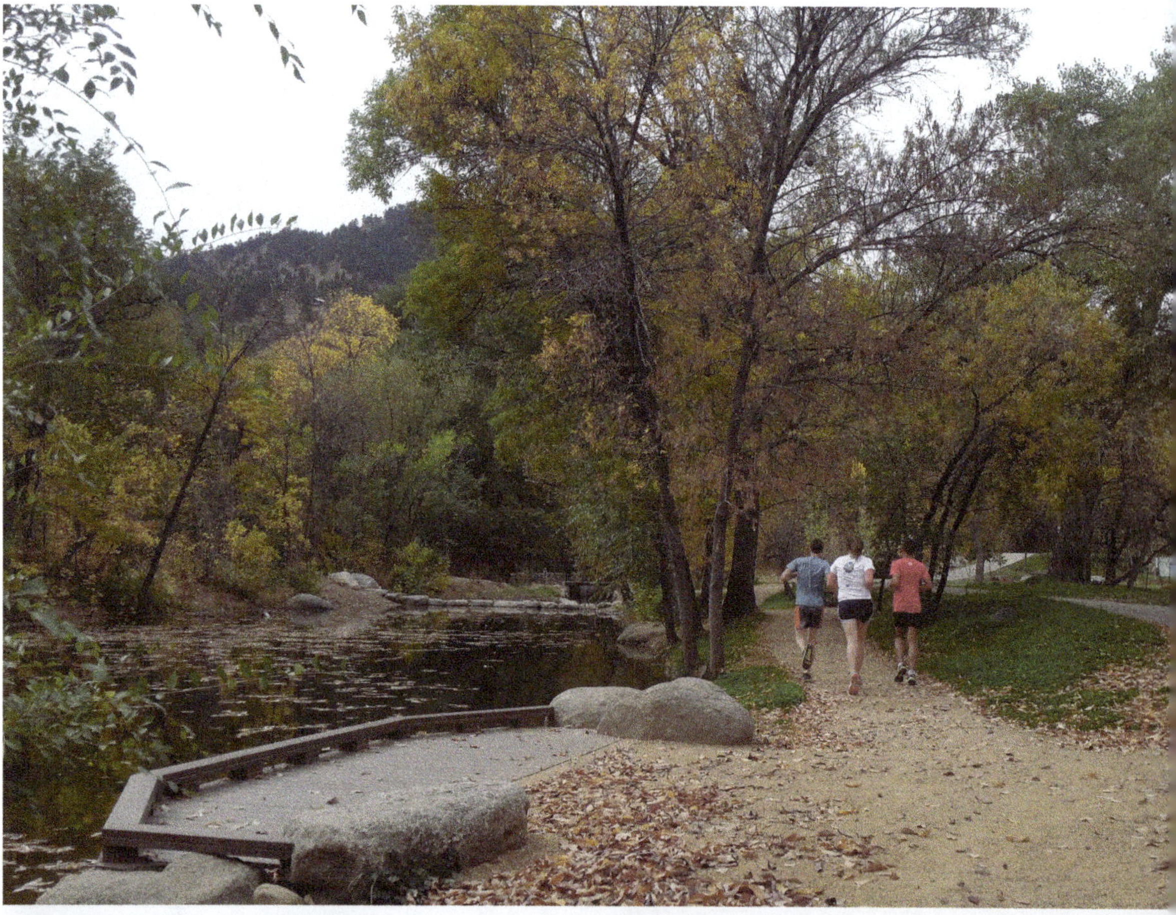

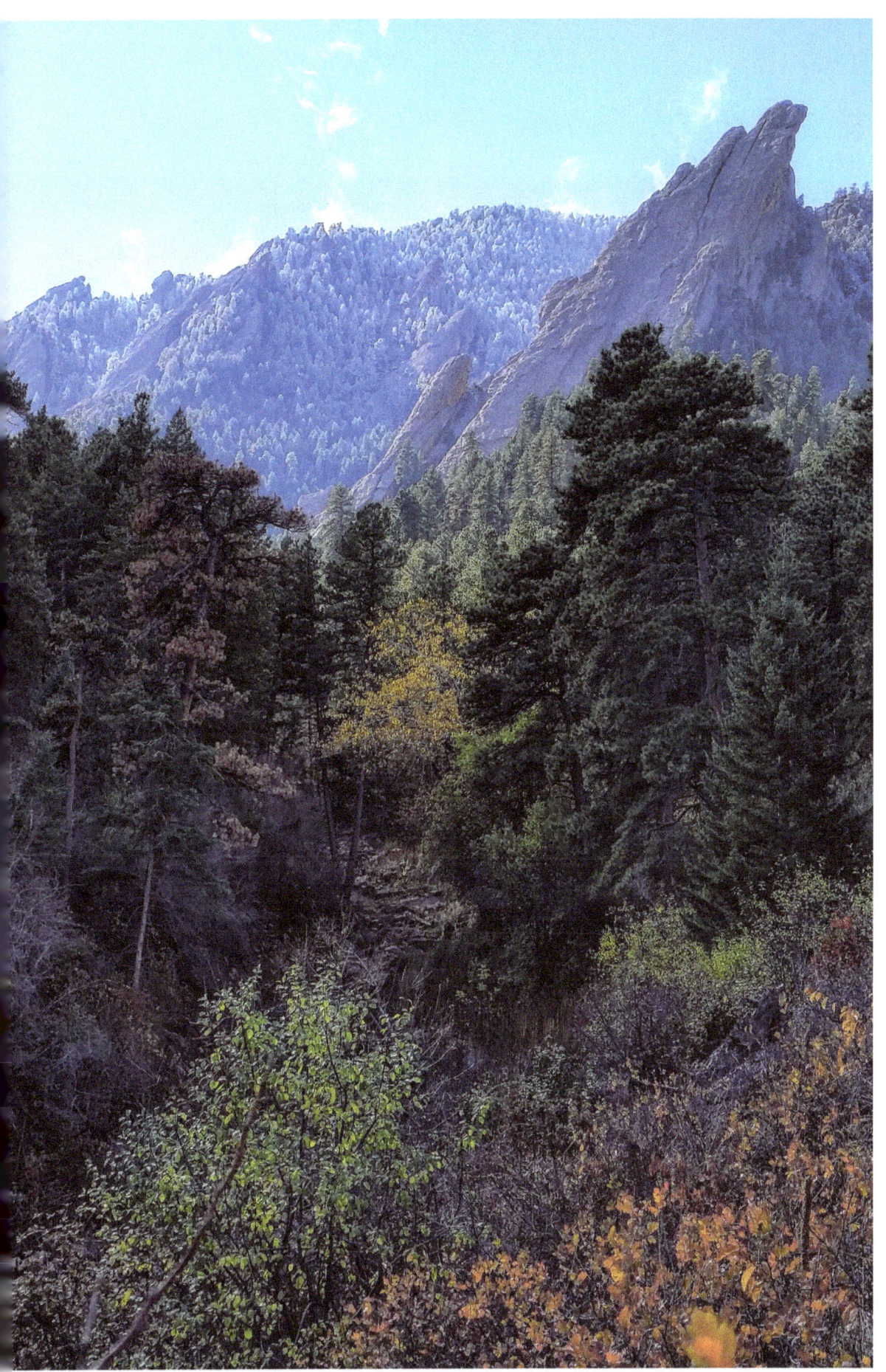

# JAMESTOWN JUGGERNAUT

On October 3, the Boulder Track Club organized a half marathon trail race, 2.5-mile hill climb and a family-friendly one mile. 100% of all proceeds benefited the mountain town of Jamestown which is still rebuilding after the floods of 2013.

Photo by Glen Delman

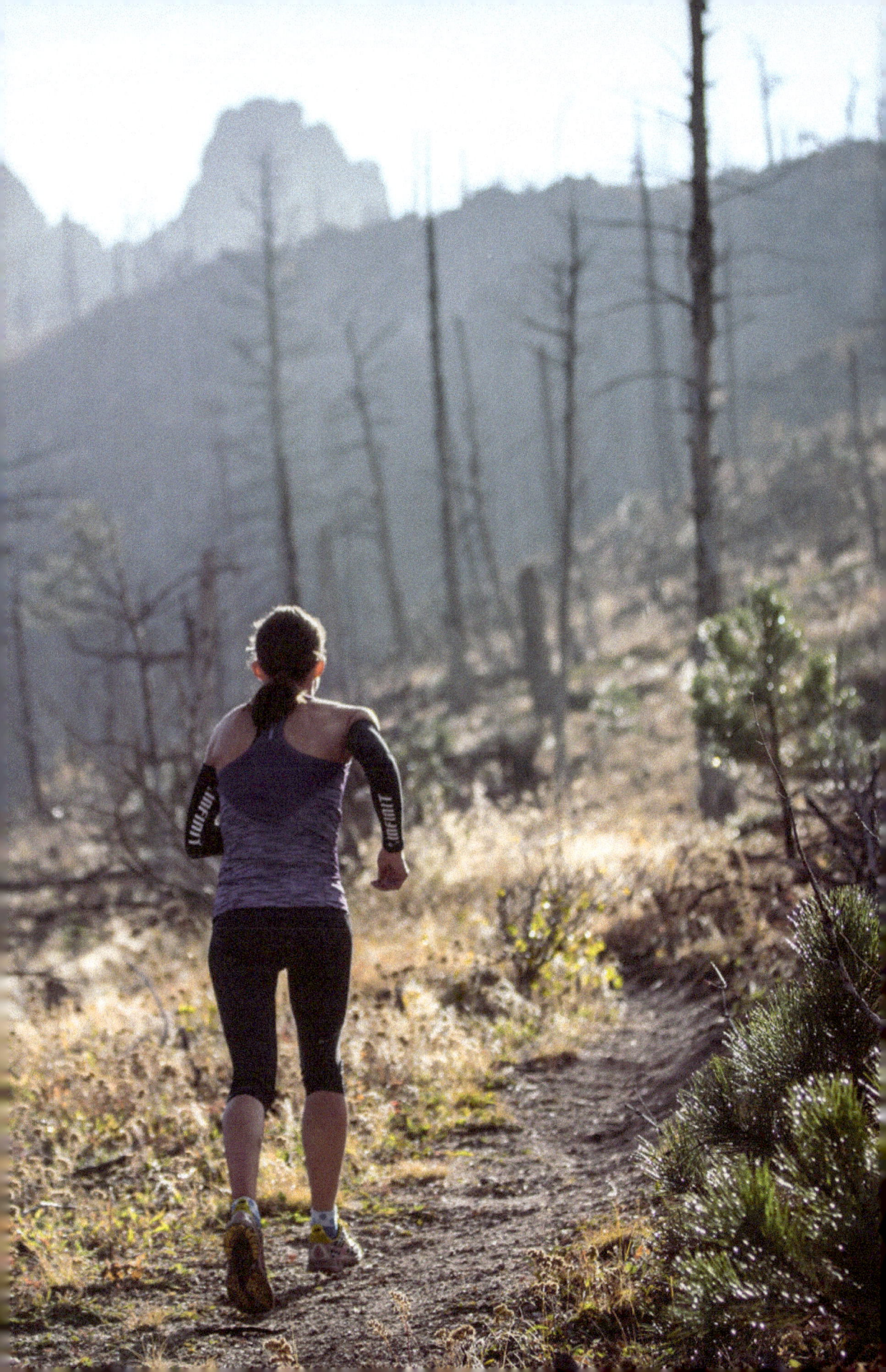

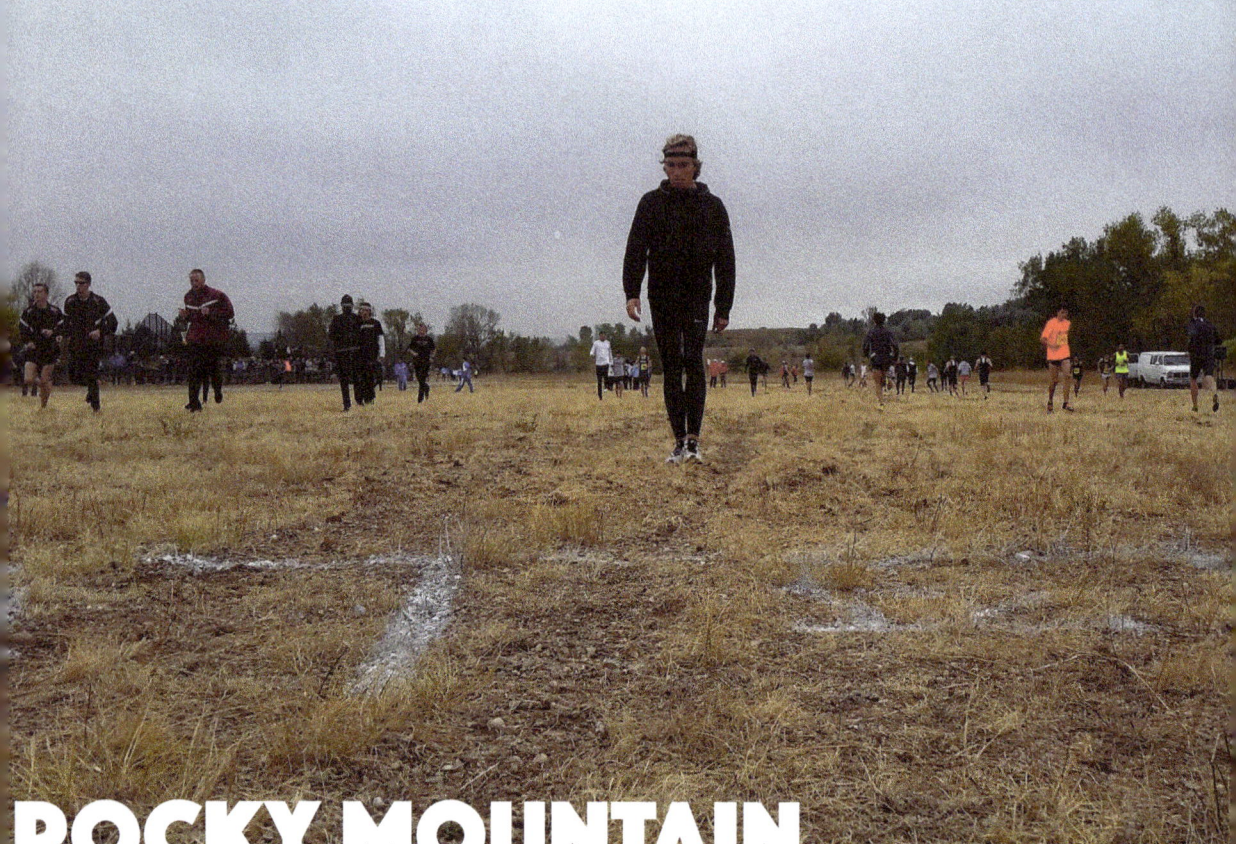

# ROCKY MOUNTAIN SHOOT

Photos by Todd Straka and Dave Albo

As two-time defending NCAA champions, the top-ranked CU men's cross country team knew they had a target on their backs. Returning to their home course at the 30th Annual Rocky Mountain Shootout, their focus was not just on the day but the next seven weeks in front of them leading to Nationals. Senior Pierce Murphy and junior Erin Clark took home top honors for the day leading both squads to Division I team victories.

"We talk about it sometimes but it's not something that affects us negatively," Murphy said. "If anything it makes us train harder. It's nice that we're not really hiding anything. Everyone knows we're good and they expect us to run fast so we just have to train hard and stay focused. In any race, any one of us could come first. Every race we have a different CU runner come in first so I feel like it's the same thing this year. Our top five, top six are pretty fit and it just depends on the race."

"Both teams are where we wanted them to be, maybe a tiny bit ahead," Coach Mark Wetmore said. "Now we have to manage the next seven weeks carefully."

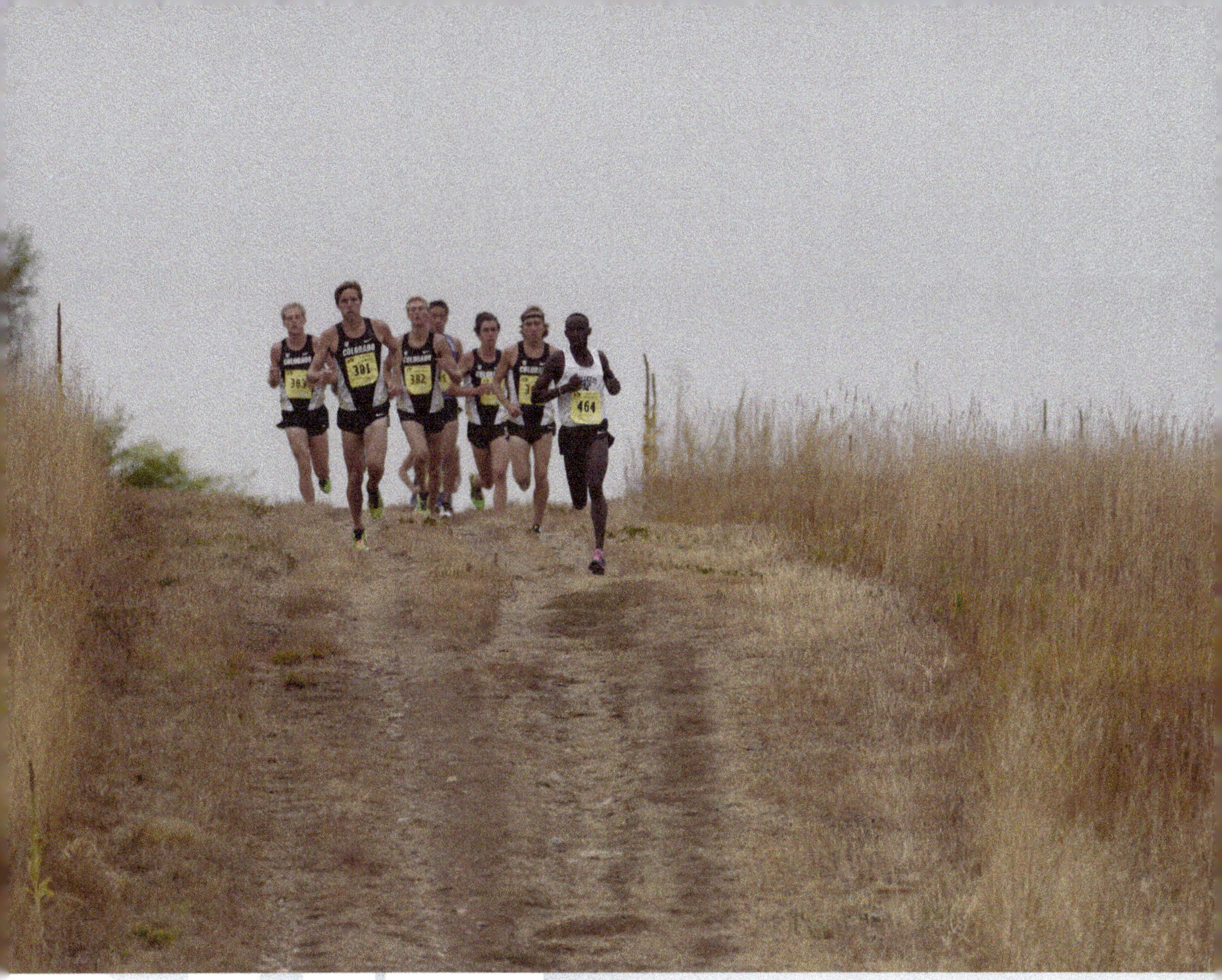

OUT

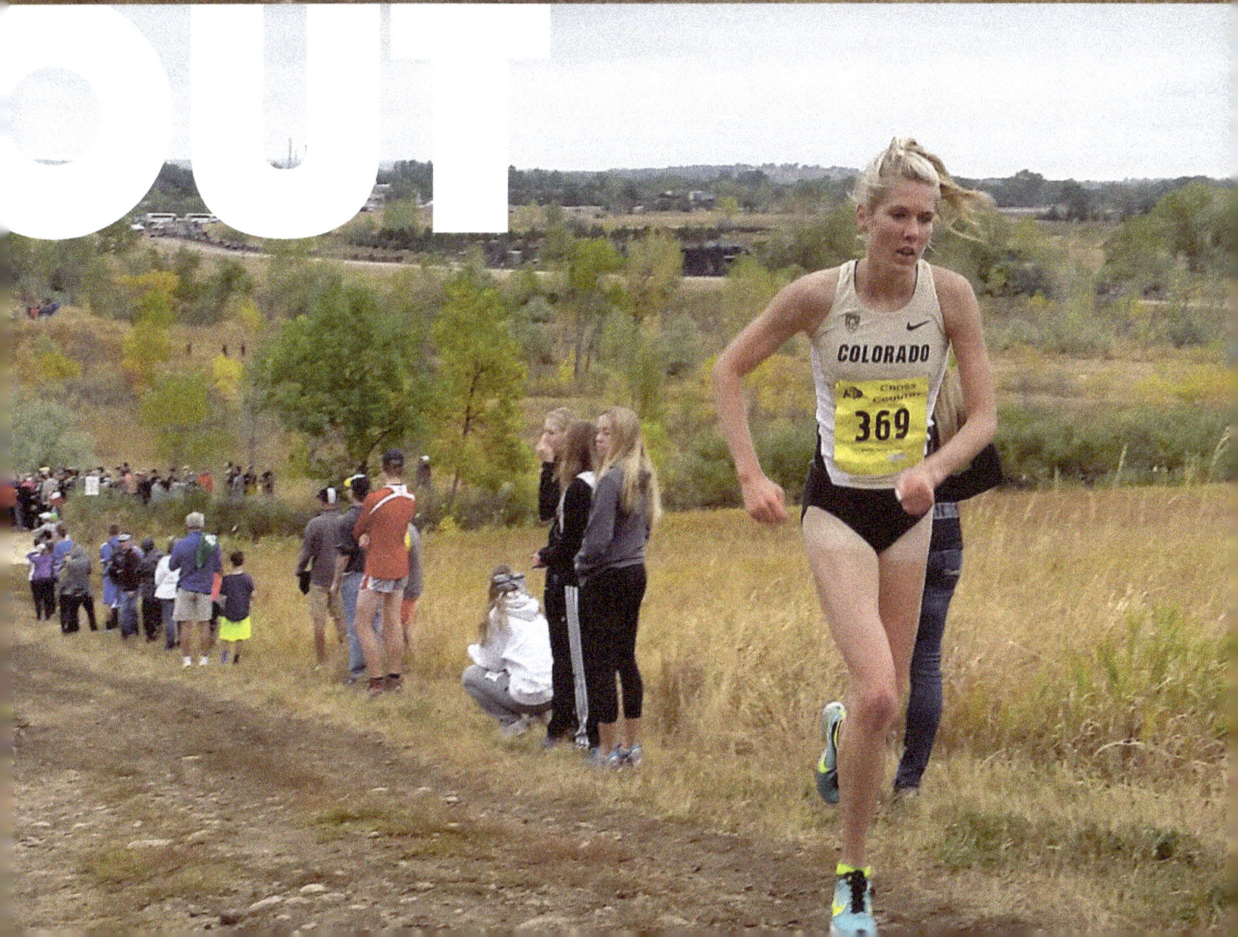

Laura Thweatt finished as the first American and 7th overall in the 2015 TCS New York City Marathon in a time of 2:28:23.

"It was definitely a very extended cross country race for me today," said Thweatt, a national champion in cross country. "I mean, the hills, just trying to stay attached to the lead group, I definitely had to call on my strengths... I definitely had to give it everything I had those last couple miles. It was brutal."

Though she qualified, Thweatt will not race at the 2016 U.S. Olympic Trials Marathon in February. Her coach, Lee Troop, told RRW that it was not good for her career [long term]. Instead they are aiming for the 10,000m on the track.

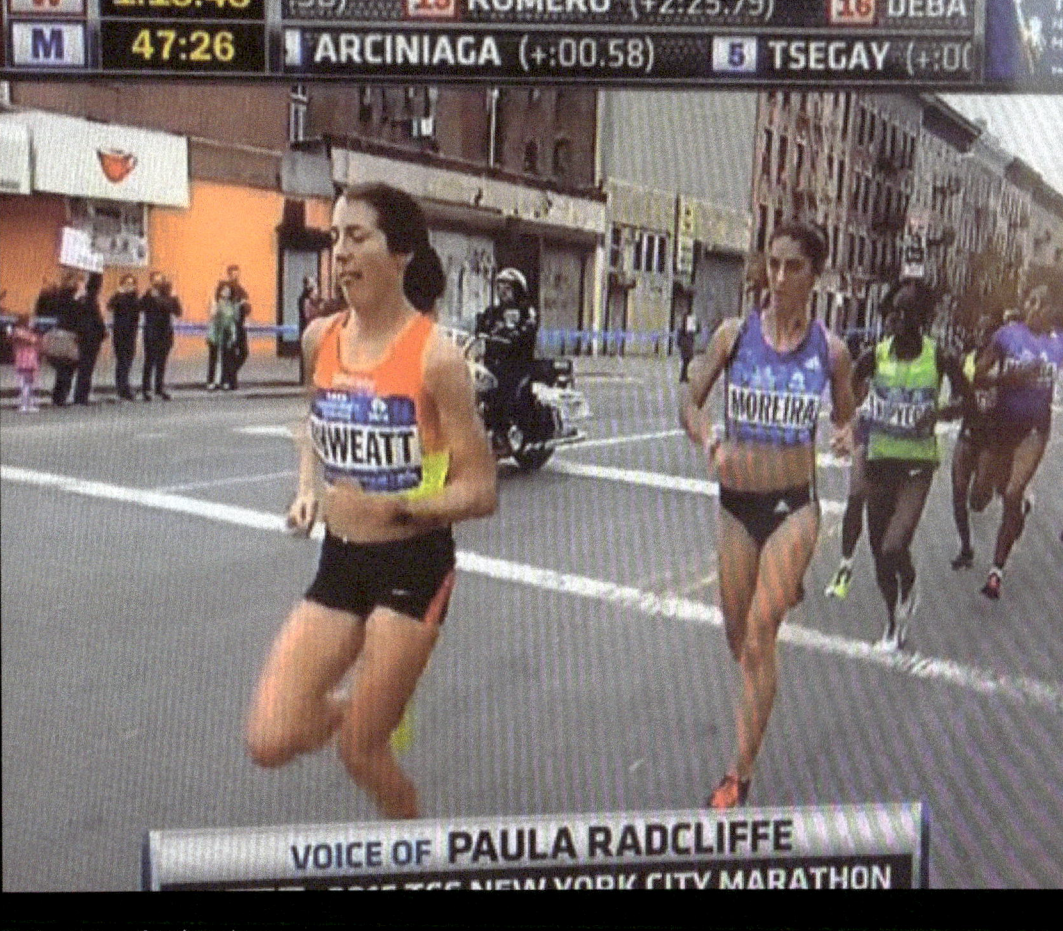

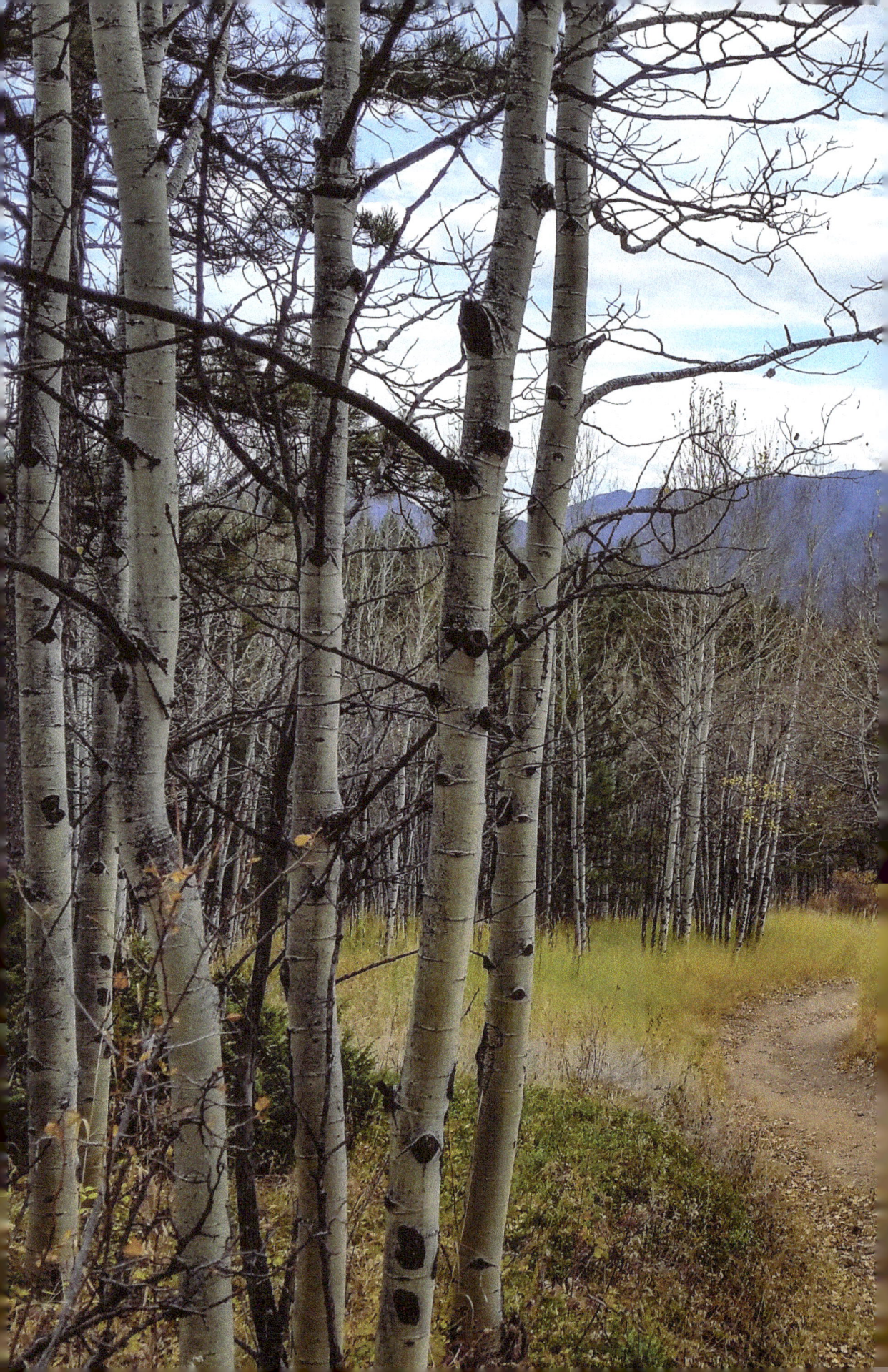

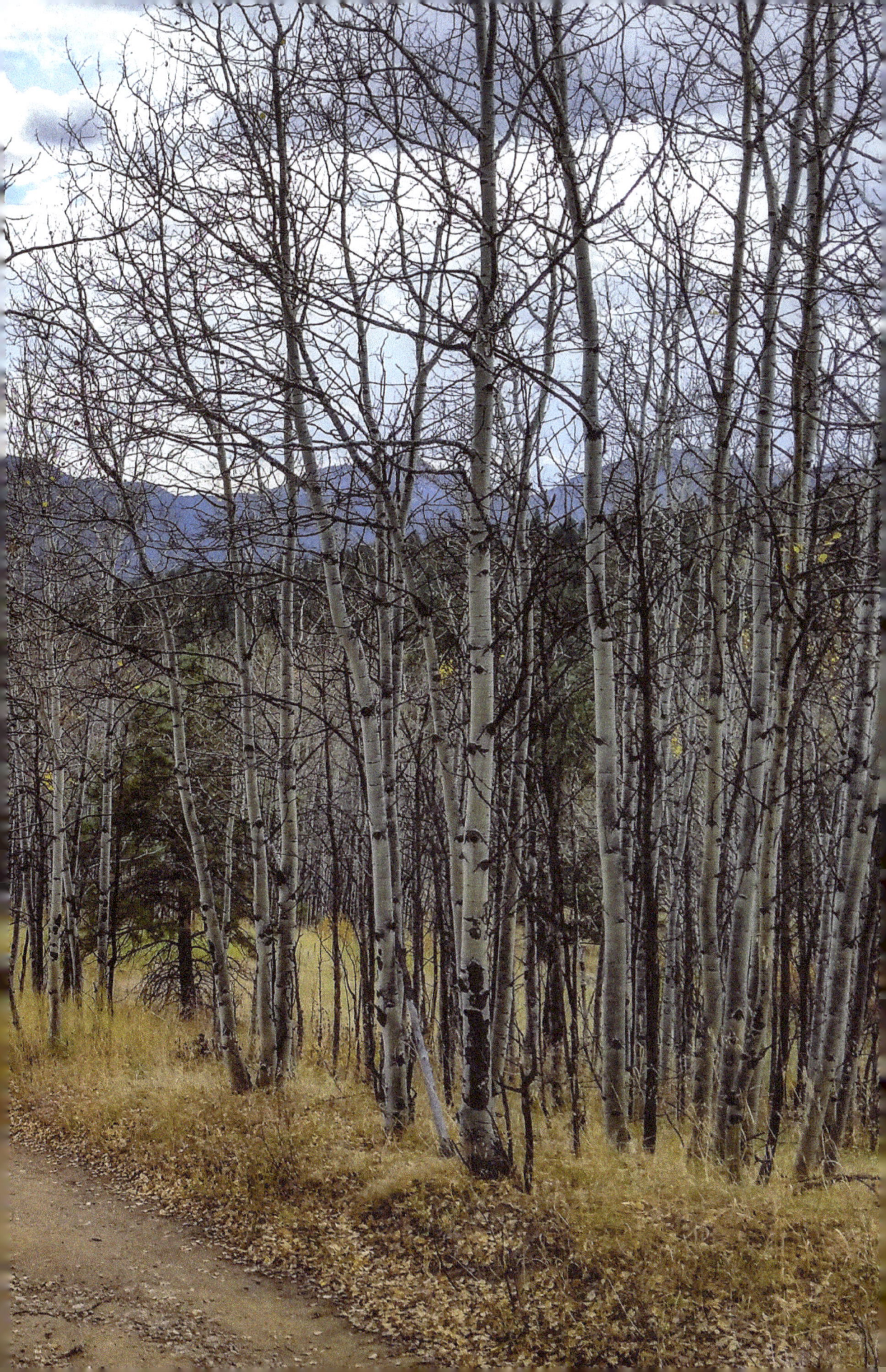

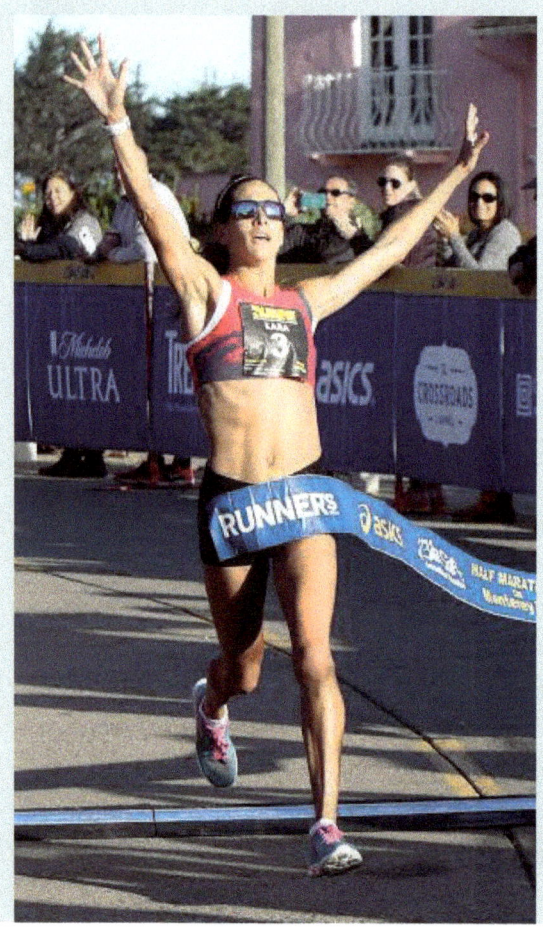

Kara Goucher of Boulder wins the Monterey Bay Half Marathon in 1:11:14 in her preparations for the U.S. Olympic Trials in February. Photo courtesy of Vern Fisher

I thought this course was going to be easier than it was, but I love a challenging course. This is the starting place for me leading up to the (Olympic) Trials. It's a good place to start; it's the fastest I've started in years."

# The Feed.
### Food for Athletes

# FUEL FOR YOUR NEXT RUN, DELIVERED TO YOUR DOOR.

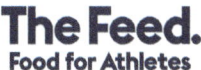

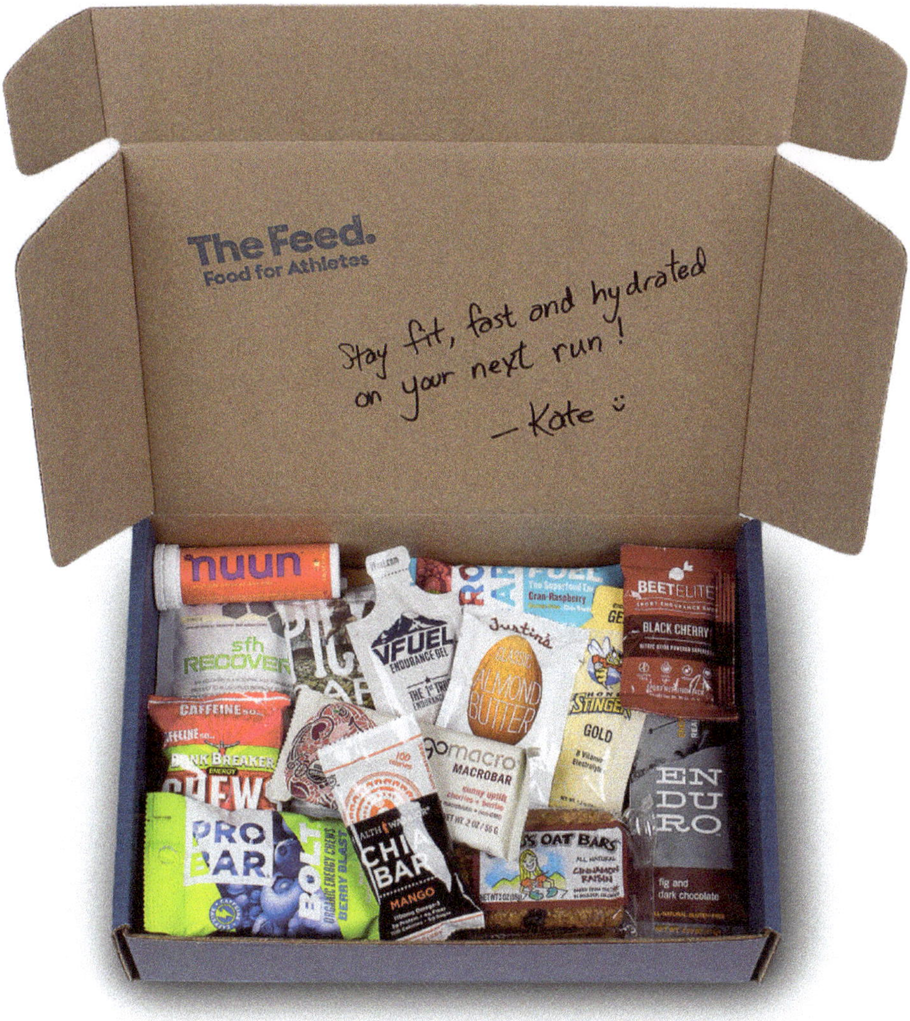

*Stay fit, fast and hydrated on your next run!*
*— Kate :)*

With over 100+ brands and 500+ products, The Feed offers the widest selection of sports nutrition and healthy snacks. Customize your order or choose one of our pre-built boxes.

Visit **TheFeed.com**

# CU TEAMS GO 2-2

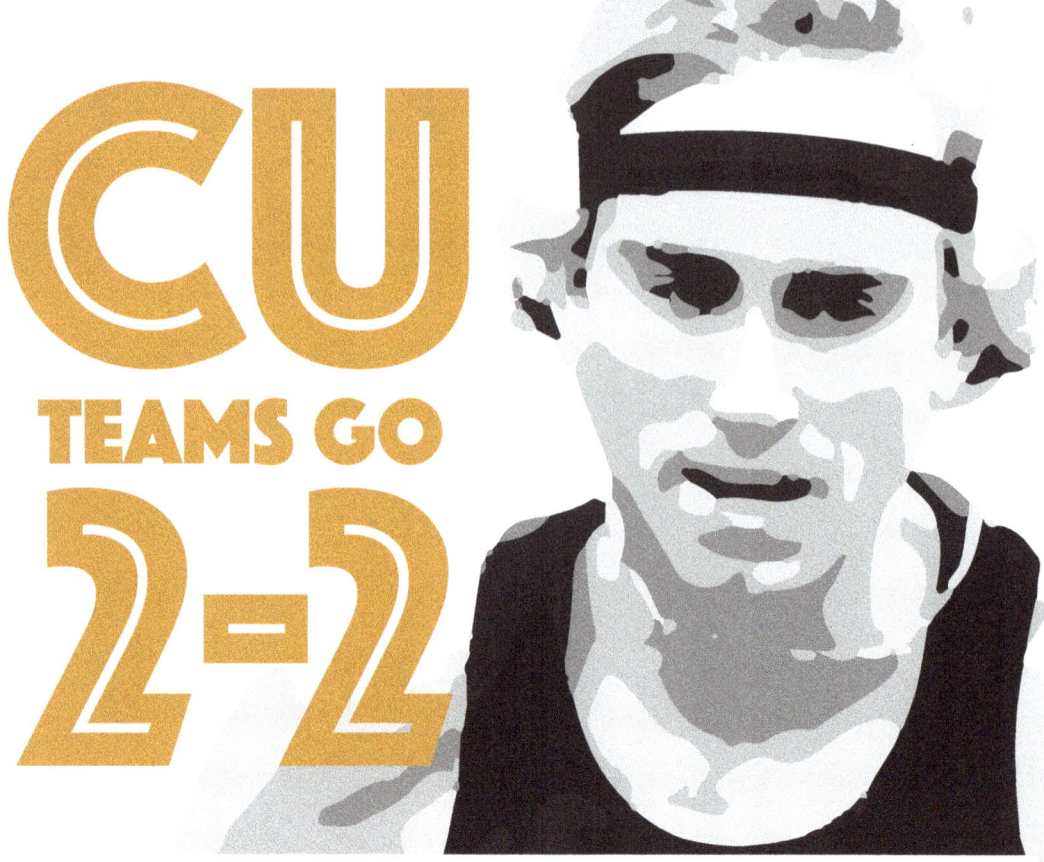

The University of Colorado took home a pair of second-place trophies Saturday, November 21, with the men and women both earning runner-up finishes at the 2015 NCAA Cross Country Championships.

"I'm proud of the women," head coach Mark Wetmore said. "I'm proud of the men. I wish we had 10 less points on the men's side but I know they ran their hearts out. I'm happy."

The Buffs had the best combined finish of any program in the nation, edging out Oregon for that honor. The Ducks finished third in the women's race and fourth in the men's competition.

Senior Pierce Murphy was the top individual finisher for Colorado, crossing the line in third place. Junior Erin Clark was the top woman for the Buffs, finishing 11th.

CU's men came in as the favorite and lost by just nine points to No. 2 ranked Syracuse (82-91).

"A tinge of disappointment is a good way to describe it," Wetmore said. "Second place by nine points in this deep of a field with all of the All-American recruits, I feel proud of them."

The women's team entered the meet ranked second overall and earned their ranking after their race with 129 points. Top-ranked New Mexico won with 49 points, while fifth-ranked Oregon placed third with 215 points. The runner-up finish is the highest placing for the Buffs since 2006, when they also placed second.

"They were seventh a year ago, but way, way back," Wetmore said. "New Mexico was a head taller than everyone else but our team did fine. They did everything we asked of them and they're all back but one so we'll be ready to do it again next year." The women were also excited about their finish.

"I think it's an awesome step forward for us," Clark said. "We worked really hard and well as a group for this all season. There's more to come."

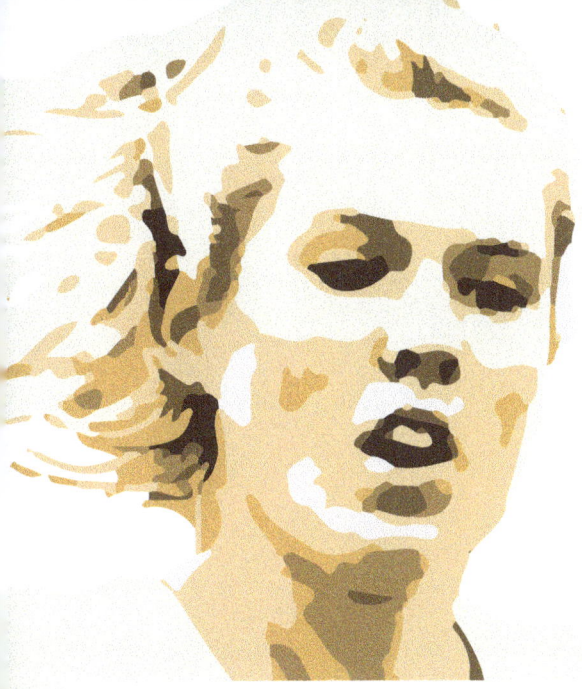

Sophomore Kaitlyn Benner, who finished 16th, said, "We definitely wanted to get second, maybe sneak away with the win if we could, but we're very happy with second.

Clark clocked in at 20:05.4 over the 6K course for her second straight All-American honor. Just behind her was Benner in 20:07.7. Benner's performance also garnered her All-American status.

"It's an incredible experience," Benner said. "I wasn't expecting to be able to be this high at the beginning of the season. I just wanted to be an All-American. But to be far up there, especially alongside my teammate, was an awesome experience."

Senior Maddie Alm was CU's third woman across the finish line, coming in at 47th overall (20:31.2). Freshman Dani Jones was two places from Alm at 49th (20:31.8). Redshirt sophomore Melanie Nun was the final scorer to finish for CU, taking 65th overall (20:37.9).

Redshirt freshman Val Constien and junior Carrie Verdon also raced at the meet. Constien finished 136th, (21:04.4) while Verdon was 146th overall (21:11.2).

CU has been rebuilding for the last few seasons and Alm has been a part of the process, running in the last two NCAA meets for the Buffs.

"It's amazing," she said about the team finish. "These girls are awesome and so fun to run with. They push me every day and I'm so happy to be a part of this awesome program. I'm definitely going to miss it."

In the men's 10K race, Murphy's finish was the best by a Buff since Dathan Ritzenhein won in 2003. Murphy, who has led the team all year, finished in 29:37, earning his third All-American honor.

"Pierce was 38th or 39th a year ago so that's a wonderful run for him," Wetmore said. "He's been a really patient, hardworking guy for us, better every year. He's a totally unheralded high school guy so Kauai is out there celebrating right now."

"I'm disappointed (about the team finish) but at the same time, I know we trained as well as we could have and ran as hard as we could have," Murphy said. "There was nothing else we could have done. We left everything on the course."

The Buffs placed all five of their runners in the top 35, but Syracuse had too many finish before CU's herd came through. Syracuse went 4-8-9-39-47 overall to edge out Colorado.

Senior Morgan Pearson was second across the line for CU, finishing 25th overall (30:16.1). True freshman John Dressel was 26th in 30:16.4. Just behind those two were junior Ben Saarel (31st, 30:19.8) and senior Connor Winter (33rd, 30:19.8). All five of CU's racers were tabbed All-Americans for their performances.

Senior Ammar Moussa just missed All-American honors with a 42nd place finish (30:29.9). Sophomore Zach Perrin also ran and placed 195th (31:57.0).

Courtesy of CUBuffs

# Colorado Club XC Championships

A fresh coat of white snow on the course, crisp blue skies, and just enough blustery wind to make it interesting.

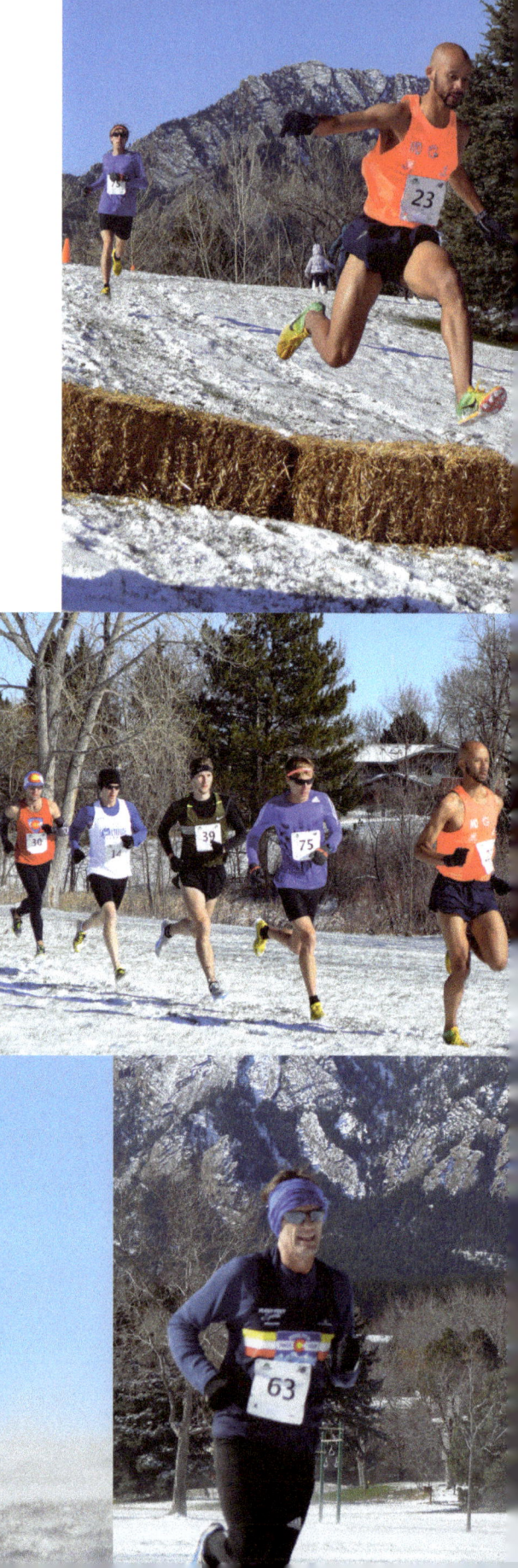

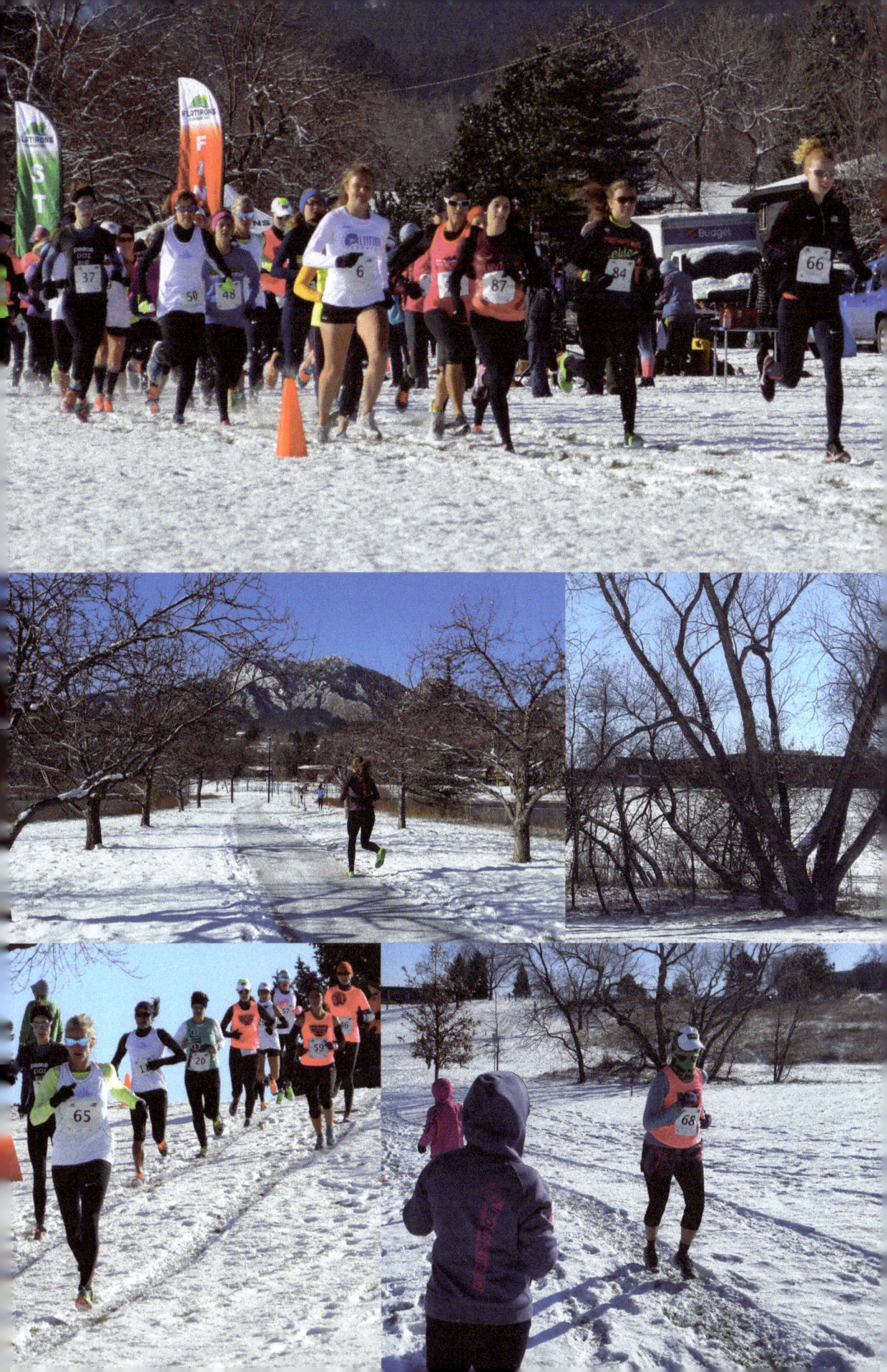

# Top Results
## October - November

In Flagstaff, Arizona the US Skyrunning Championships were held on October 2nd-3rd. Boulder's **Josh Arthur** ran to a third place finish overall on the tough 55K course that had over 10,000' of climbing in 6:00:20. Arthur also won the overall US Skyrunning series for 2015. **Ashley Erba** won the women's race in a time of 6:47:52.

On October 4th at the Medtronic Twin Cities Marathon, **Clint Wells** ran an outstanding race, finishing 8th overall and winning the Master's Division in a time of 2:24:00.

At the USA 10 Mile Championships, also part of the Medtronic Twin Cities event, **Jonathan Grey** ran a time of 47:12, a personal best and good enough for 5th place overall. In the women's race, **Neely Spence Gracey** continued her amazing streak and ran a time of 53:03, also a personal best and good enough for 2nd place overall. **Laura Thweatt** of Superior was 4th in a time of 53:14, also a personal best.

In Hartford, CT at the Eversource Hartford Half-Marathon, Boulder runner **Sarah Hutchings** came away with the win, running the 13.1 mile course in 1:17:09. In the men's field, **Christopher Guerrero** also had a strong race, placing 4th in a time of 1:08:31. At the 5K event, **Maggie Callahan** ran a 17:26 for the win.

On Sunday, October 18th at the Nationwide Children's Hospital Columbus Half Marathon in Columbus, Ohio, **Tyler McCandless** ran a time of 1:05:12 for third place. **Nicole Camp** of Longmont came in 7th for the women in a time of 1:21:44.

On the same day, down in Denver at the last Rock 'n' Roll Denver Half Marathon, **Andy Wacker** of Boulder ran a time of 1:09:56 for 5th place while **Guy Alton**, also of Boulder, ran a time of 1:10:52. **Leigh Gilmore** of Boulder came in second for the women in a time of 1:23:23.

Andy Wacker may have been a bit tired at the Rock 'n' Roll Half Marathon, since the day before, October 17th, he ran the Lake Padden Trail Run, which served as the USA Trail Half Marathon Championships, in Bellingham, Washington. His time of 1:22:12 was good enough for second place overall, just beating out Max King of Bend, Oregon. Boulder's **Lizi Bolanos-Nauth** won the masters race and title with a time of 1:49:03.

**Wacker** wasn't finished, and on the following weekend at the Oasis Rock 'n' Roll Vancouver Half-Marathon he ran a time of 1:08:50 for 4th place overall.

Halloween was not all tricks for Boulder runners this year; in fact, there were quite a few treats. At the Philadelphia Rock 'n' Roll Half-Marathon many Boulder runners finished in the top 20 for the men, but it was **Neely Spence Gracey** of Louisville who had the best race of the day, finishing 2nd overall with a time of 1:09:59, a personal best at the distance.

On a beautiful fall day in New York City, **Laura Thweatt** made her marathon debut in the 45th running of the New York City Marathon. Thweatt, who briefly held the lead, would have a superb debut run at the marathon distance, finishing 7th overall in a time of 2:28:33.

In Wichita, Kansas on November 8th, the Kansas Road Mile Championships were held. **Macklin Chaffee** ran a great race as he works himself back into form. With a time of 4:15.05, Chaffee came away with second place in the elite field.

Boulder's **Jeffrey Eggleston** came away with the win at the Geico Rock 'n' Roll Las Vegas Half Marathon on November 15th. Eggleston just edged out Paul Katam of Oregon with a time of 1:04:40 on the flat, fast course.

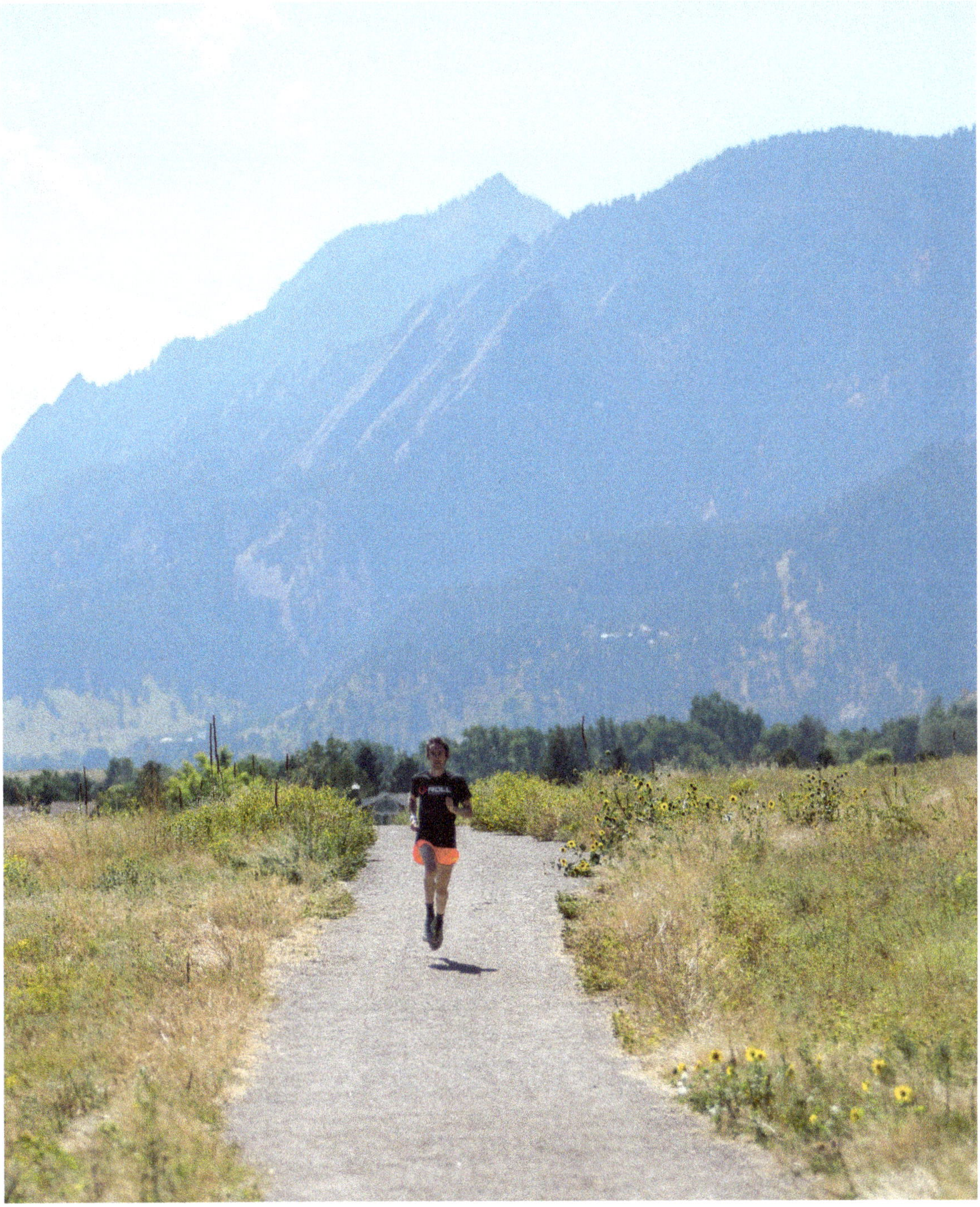

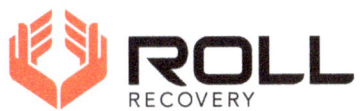

RollRecovery.com

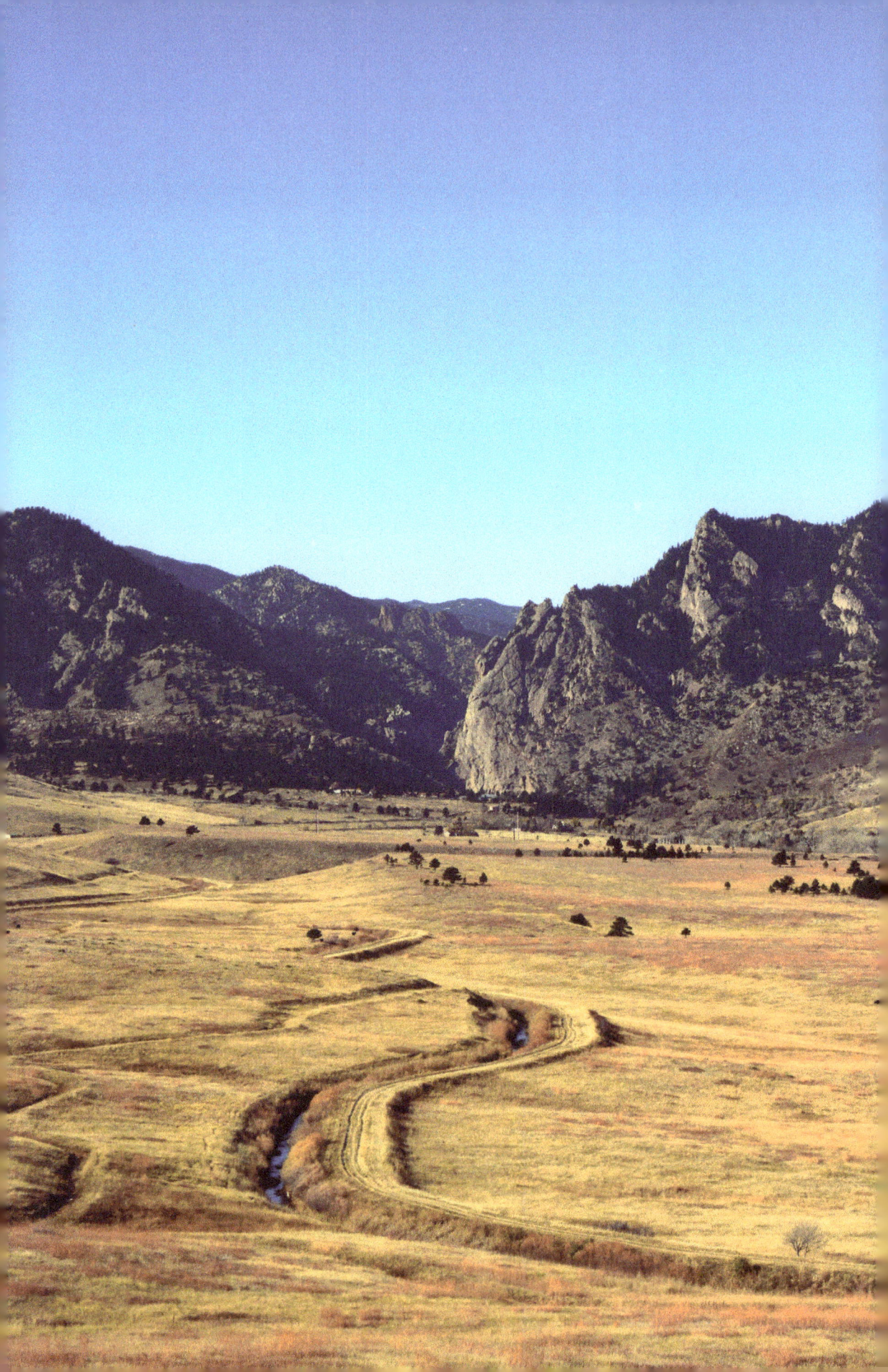

# GREAT RUNNERS EAT GREAT FOOD

Every RUNNER knows that the body is an engine and performs best with the proper fuel... fuel up at Alfalfa's.

- Largest selection of ORGANIC produce in Colorado.
- The finest hormone and anti-biotic free LOCAL meats.
- Plenty of energy bars and supplements to keep you going.
- We have the BEST organic juice bar and salad bar in Boulder.

## ALFALFA'S MARKET

BOULDER
BROADWAY & ARAPAHOE

ALFALFAS.COM

LOUISVILLE
SOUTH BOULDER ROAD & CENTENNIAL

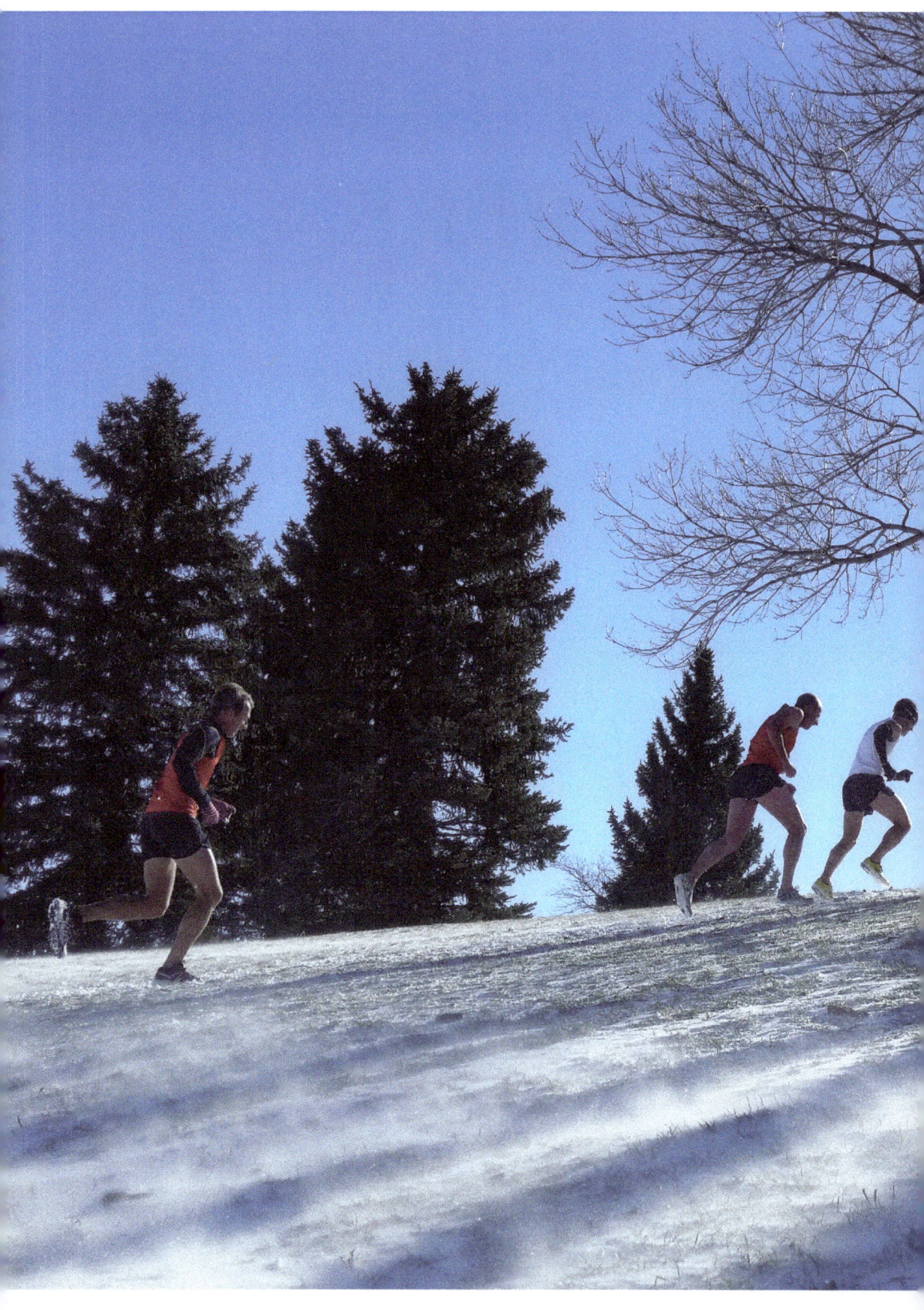

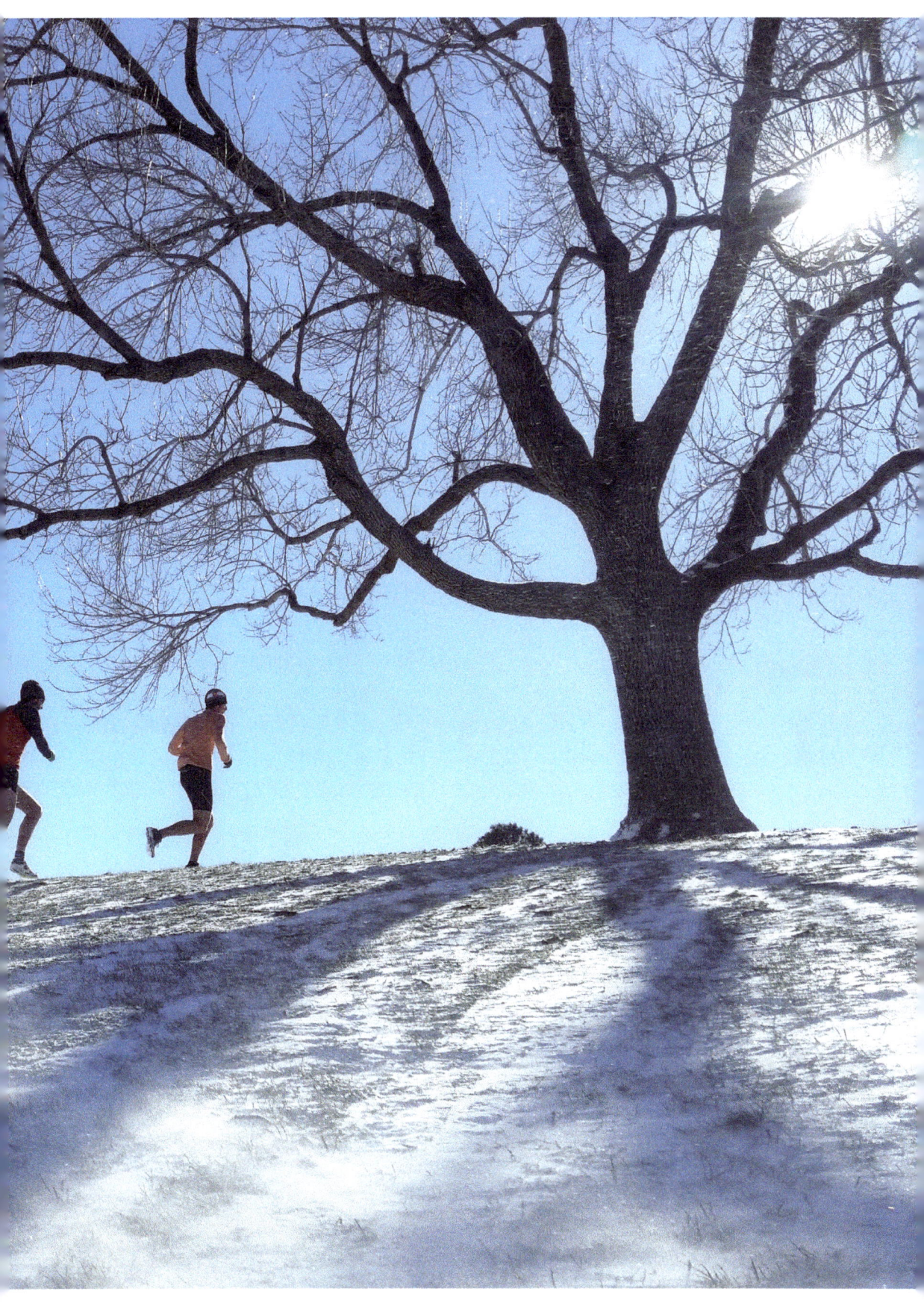

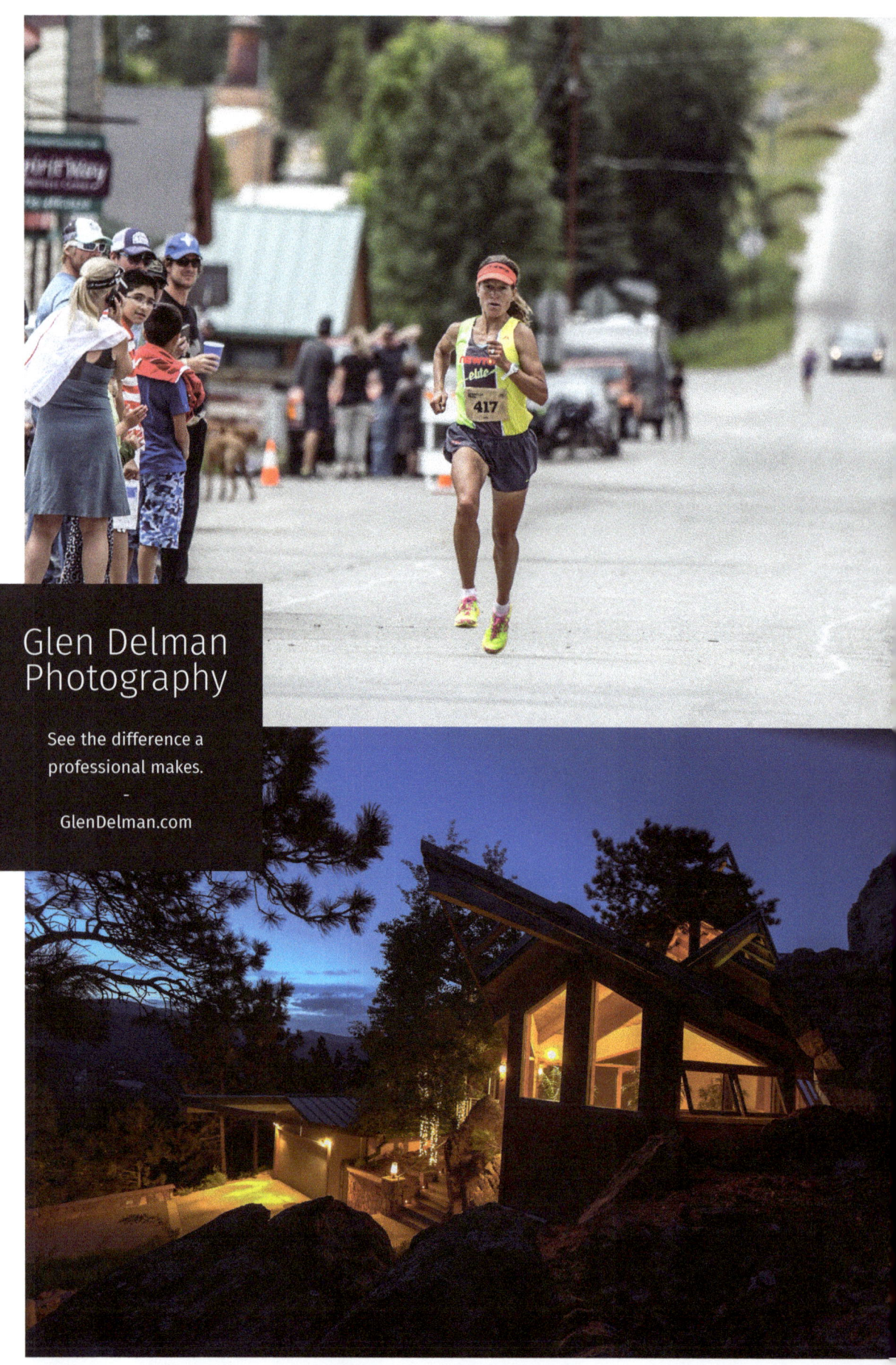

# Glen Delman Photography

See the difference a professional makes.
-
GlenDelman.com

2015

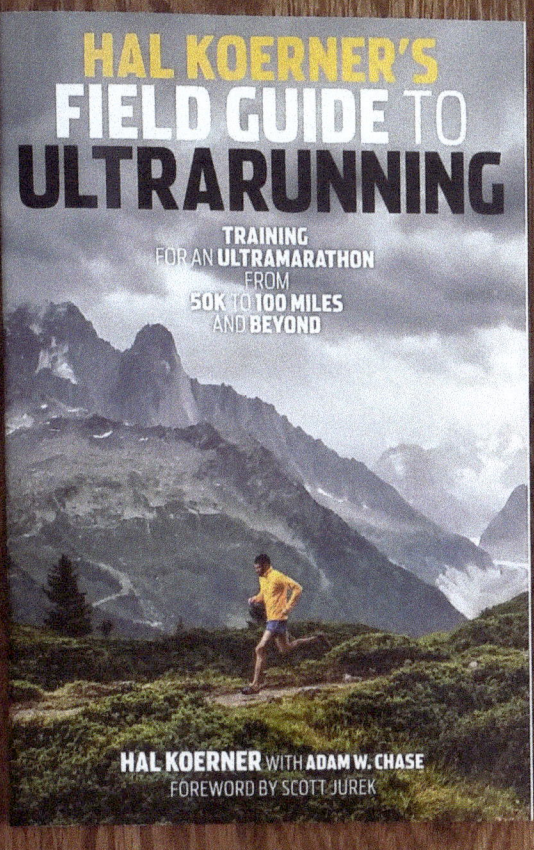

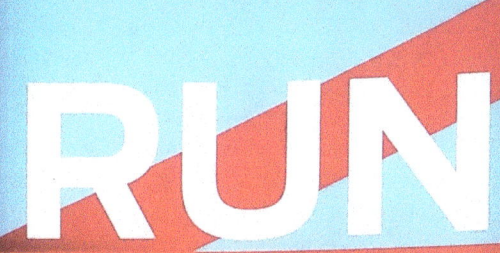

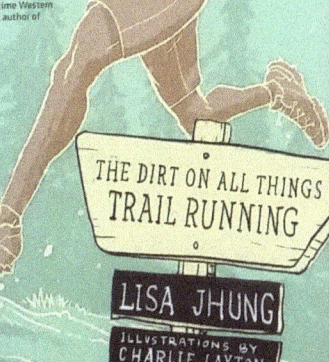

## MAKING FAST PEOPLE EVEN FASTER.

velopress®

velopress.com

# Editor's Note

From chaos emerges order; from ashes rises the phoenix. Those have been the two pervading thoughts in our heads as we attempted to pull off what some called "insane," "silly," and just plain "crazy." In late August over perhaps a bit too much coffee at the Trident in downtown Boulder, Mike Sandrock leaned over and in a hushed tone said, "you know what we need to do? We need to do a Boulder Year in Review." At the time the idea sounded grand – an adventure of sorts – and soon we were talking about it off and on: during a run, over a too salty burrito, via email and social media. Pretty soon, we had committed without committing. It was almost like signing up for a race six months out. Sure we were both in decent shape and had some great training plans in our head, but getting out the door and doing the workouts was tough. But what did it matter, the race was six months away, we could get after it next weekend.

Fast forward to mid-October and all of a sudden our lack of commitment to our training plan was starting to show our weaknesses. Putting together a new publication – one that had never existed before and that was going to cross all of the standard genres – started to freak us out. Could we really pull it off, or were we as people had said, "crazy"? It was time to do some crash course prep in hopes that a bit of leg speed might come back before the big dance. We are both long-time runners and over the years we have seen some people pull off amazing races on little or no training. Maybe, somehow, we could tap into that unknown and run like the wind.

The race is over, now the finish line has been crossed. What you are holding in your hand is the result of that daring leap into the unknown. We tapped into all of our networks, begged and pleaded, and worked our butts off. We toed the line – perhaps not in the best shape, but still with our heads held high and a determination to go all out. We will let you be the judge of our performance.

Coming from where we did, with our backgrounds and general life commitments, we are pretty happy with how it played out. Was it an Olympic Standard? No, but it was honest, and we left everything we had out on the course.

We hope that you enjoy the first Boulder Running Journal.

Todd Straka
Peter N. Jones

# Thank You

We could not have pulled this off without the help and encouragement of numerous people. A big shout out goes to Mike Sandrock for putting the idea in our heads and letting us believe that it was possible. Glen Delman was gracious enough to believe in us and allow us to use some of his amazing photos. Dave Trendler of VeloPress lit a fire under us, Brian Metzler of Competitor made us take a long, hard look at what we were doing, Terzah Becker gave a scrutinous eye to the words and our wives blindly gave us encouragement when we most needed it, as did so many in the community who cheered us on — too many to name here.

We take full credit for all errors, incorrect bylines, messed up facts, and exaggerated tales. If we misspelled someone's name, we are really sorry. If we got a race time wrong, it is our fault. If we included a photo that makes you look funny, good. This was a labor of love and we tried our best with what we had in the time we had. Hopefully this venture inspires you to get outside, go for a run, push past your internal comfort zones. We know that by working on this project, we have gotten closer to the Boulder running community and all that makes it so amazing. So thank you for letting us be a part of it all. We are honored.

Now to lace up our shoes and go for a run,
we think we deserve it.

Until the next issue...

Without the generous support of these contributors we would not be able to do what we did. So thank you for coming along for the run.

Glen Delman
Glendelman.com

Dave Albo
Lane1photos.com

Ryan Lawrence
RyanLawrencePhoto.com

Amanda McCracken
AmandaMcCracken.webs.com

Tevis Morrow

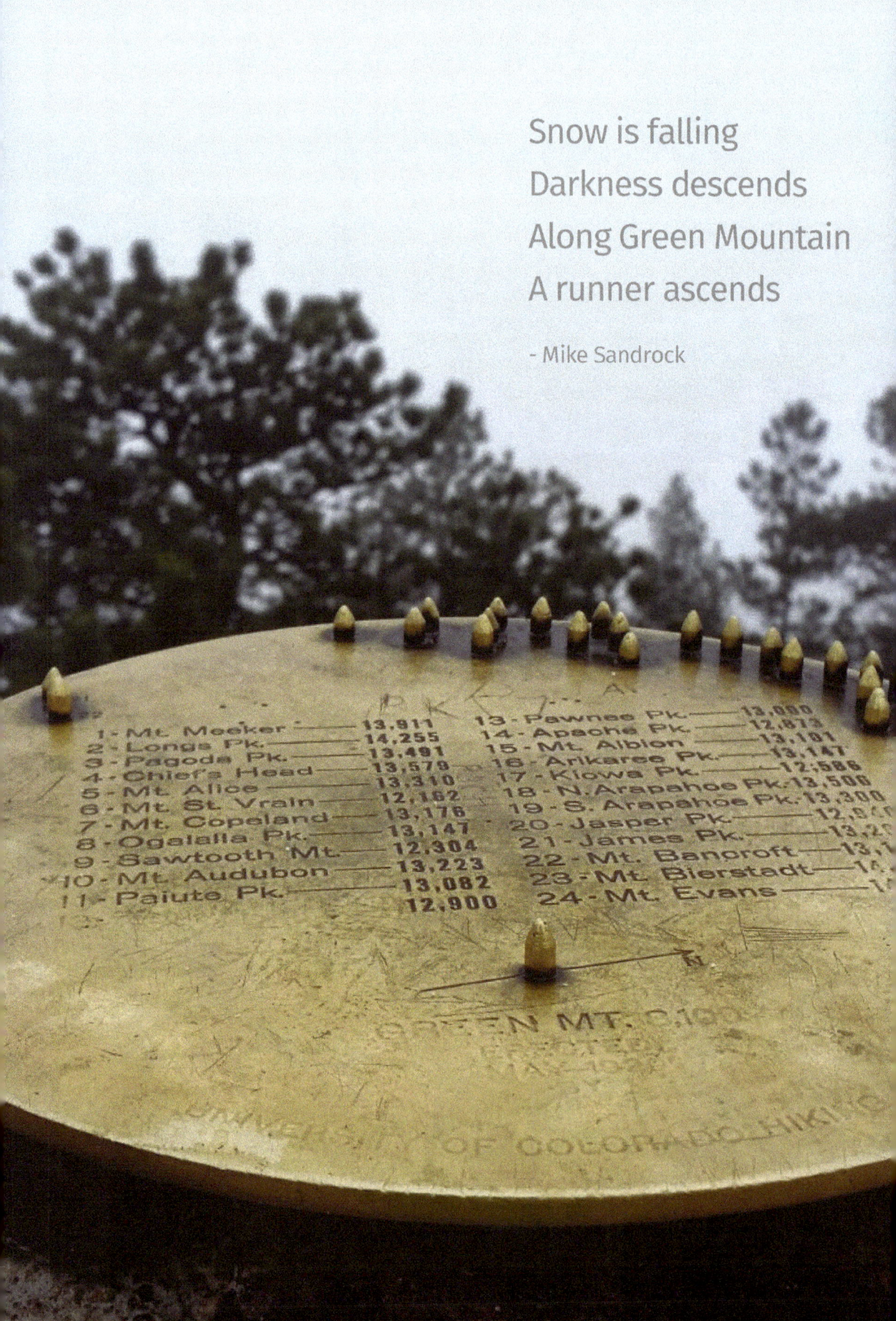

Snow is falling
Darkness descends
Along Green Mountain
A runner ascends

- Mike Sandrock

Without limiting the rights under copyright, no part of this publication may be reproduced, stored in or introduced into a retrieval system, or transmitted, in any form or by any means (electronic, mechanical, photocopying, recording, or otherwise), without the prior written permission of both the copyright owner and the publisher of this book
Copyright © 2015

Library of Congress Cataloging-in-Publication Data

Straka, Todd; Jones, Peter N.; Sandrock, Michael
**Boulder Running Journal 2015**
**Volume 1, Issue 1**

p.cm

1. Sports, Running. 2. Boulder, Colorado. 3. Outdoors, Sports

ISBN 13: 978-1-936955-16-9

All Rights Reserved. All copyrights remain with original owner. Photographs and articles used with permission.

**Boulder Running**
250 Mohawk Drive, Boulder, CO 80303
www.boulderrunning.com